The Kaiser's Army

THE KAISER'S ARMY

THE POLITICS OF MILITARY TECHNOLOGY

IN GERMANY DURING THE MACHINE AGE,

1870–1918

Eric Dorn Brose

OXFORD
UNIVERSITY PRESS

2001

OXFORD
UNIVERSITY PRESS

Oxford   New York
Athens   Auckland   Bangkok   Bogotá   Buenos Aires   Cape Town
Chennai   Dar es Salaam   Delhi   Florence   Hong Kong   Istanbul   Karachi
Kolkata   Kuala Lumpur   Madrid   Melbourne   Mexico City   Mumbai
Nairobi   Paris   São Paulo   Shanghai   Singapore   Taipei   Tokyo   Toronto   Warsaw

and associated companies in
Berlin   Ibadan

Library of Congress Cataloging-in-Publication Data

Brose, Eric Dorn, 1948–
The Kaiser's army : the politics of military technology in
Germany during the Machine Age, 1870–1918 / Eric Dorn Brose.
      p.   cm.
Includes bibliographical references and index.
ISBN 0–19–514335–3
1. Germany. Heer—History—19th century.   2. Germany. Heer—History—20th century.
3. Military art and science—Technological innovations.   I. Title.
UA712 .B76 2000
355'.00943'0934—dc21   00-061121

1 3 5 7 9 8 6 4 2
Printed in the United States of America
on acid-free paper

For Christine

ACKNOWLEDGMENTS

A SIX-YEAR PROJECT has generated more debts to helpful persons and institutions than can be named here. Thanks are due to the German Academic Exchange Service, which funded a large portion of the early research; Deans Thomas Canavan, Sam Bose, and Cecilie Goodrich at Drexel University, who facilitated a series of faculty development grants; and Provost Richard Astro of Drexel for his tolerance of a deparment head who still does research and writing. I have also received valuable assistance from the staffs of many repositories. Special thanks go to Drs. Tröger and Fuchs of the Kriegsarchiv in Munich; Dr. Trischler of the Deutsches Museum in Munich; Herr Dietze of the Military Historical Research Office in Potsdam; Dr. Fleischer of the Federal Military Archive in Freiburg; Fernando Acosta of the New York Public Library; and especially Deidre Harper and Peter Groesbeck of the Interlibrary Loan and Graphics departments, respectively, at Drexel. Three colleagues at Drexel, Walter High, Vivien Thweat, and Sidney Diggles, were always there when I needed them. For letters of recommendation and comments on the project, I am further indebted to Volker Berghahn, Dennis Showalter, and Williamson Murray. My final product was greatly strengthened, moreover, by the sound advice of Susan Ferber at Oxford University Press, as well as the numerous suggestions for revisions made by the external readers. Those who have helped me improve the manuscript are not responsible, of course, for the flaws that no doubt remain. Finally, I want to thank my wife, Christine, for her inexhaustible patience during too many research trips to Germany. This book is dedicated to her.

CONTENTS

The Kaiser's Army

INTRODUCTION

*T*HIS IS A book about human and institutional responses to technological change. It deals with times of peace and times of war. The institution in question is the German Army. The peacetime in question is 1871 to 1914. The people in question are the German officers who faced a dizzying succession of new technologies that challenged their notions of how men should fight. The wars in question are those that created the German Kaiserreich before 1871 and the Great War that finally destroyed it in 1918.

The German Army was so successful by 1871 that other powers feared it. It was still highly respected in 1914, but the planning legacy of Alfred von Schlieffen, chief of the Prussian-German General Staff from 1891 to 1906, did not produce another victory. Contemporaries, followed by historians, have debated the reasons for this ever since. A favorite explanation of Schlieffen's disciples was that his successor, Helmuth von Moltke (the younger), botched the master's work by weakening the armies that were to sweep through Belgium and surround French forces.[1] They did not mention the violation of Belgian neutrality or the provocation of both Belgium and Britain or the dubious diplomacy that landed Germany in a two-front war. Another scholarly hypothesis assumes recklessness and failed diplomacy but focuses on the unreadiness of a German Army allegedly too weighted down with aristocratic traditions to adopt expeditiously mechanical devices of destruction.[2] This thesis, associated mainly with Bernd Schulte, has come under the fire of other historians like Dieter Storz, who reject the idea that the German Army was an aristocratic, antimodern relic of a backward-looking era.[3] This school sees the German Army as not only less conservative than other European armies of the time but also, in some respects, very progressive.

I became interested in this debate after writing a book that deals with similar controversies in the Prussian Army before 1848.[4] From the perspective of my research, as well as that of others who had written about the earlier nineteenth century,[5] it seemed odd that soldiers who had come to accept modern industrial technology on the battlefield would give way to a generation of warriors that disdained its use. Suspecting, however, that the Imperial German Army may have relapsed and fought another great controversy over technology, I became determined to sort things out. Six years—and nine archives—later, the findings can now be presented.

The key lies in the decades between 1871 and 1900—years less intensely considered by other historians. Drawn more and more to this period as my research progressed, I found that feuding factions in the infantry, cavalry, and artillery had fought over the tactical and technological lessons of the Wars of Unification (1866–1870). Those who emphasized the superiority of man and morale over machine and firepower prevailed by the late 1870s—to the army's detriment. Regulations and majority prejudices called for tight infantry formations and shock attack tactics, large-unit cavalry charges featuring waves of massed horsemen, and offensive field artillery tactics that maximized mobility and valor while neglecting firepower and marksmanship. Heavy artillery was relegated to fortresses and all but ignored. It is not that the horrendous casualties of recent wars were forgotten by the dominant groups; rather, the offensive combat experience of 1866–1870 was interpreted from the heady, arrogant perspective of overconfident victors. These proud soldiers spawned a persistent tactical-technological tradition.

Russia's disastrous offensive tactics in the Russo-Turkish War of 1877–1878 aided the gradual ascent of more prudent and pragmatic factions in every branch of the German Army. The advent of magazine repeating rifles, smokeless powder, nitrogen-based high explosives, and modern heavy artillery in the 1880s and 1890s accelerated this trend, as seen by new regulations that called for dispersed infantry formations and small-unit cavalry tactics. The process of overcoming nineteenth-century traditions, however, was controversial, hard fought, and painfully slow. After 1900, a second wave of new technologies—including the machine gun; rapid-firing, shielded cannons; heavy-caliber mortar; rigid and nonrigid airships; and the airplane—exacerbated and intensified these factional debates and feuds as advocates and opponents of the new devices confronted each other and argued over the related tactical, operational, and organizational changes made necessary by their adoption. Although an accurate picture of the German Army in 1914 is probably closer to Storz than to Schulte, the former's image of calm, professional assessment of technology and steady progress toward change and reform does little justice to the historical reality.[6]

This became clear during the high summer of 1914 as the German Army strove for victory on the western frontiers. The campaign that Schlieffen had planned—and the younger Moltke executed in somewhat modified form—had a reasonable chance of success despite the risky provocation of Belgium and England. It failed, however, largely because of the residual effects of four decades of pride and stubborn adherence to the old ways.[7] The legacy of tactical and technological breakdown in 1914 was a bloody 4-year stalemate and a vain search for the new tactics and techniques that would end it.

It is important to examine these military-technological controversies in a wider sociopolitical context. As we shall see in the early chapters, these struggles were definitely influenced by the politics of social class. Thus, the army's conservative drift after 1871 fits nicely with those academic models that posit a Prussian-German state controlled by noblemen who resisted change. But there are problems with this model. The aristocratic state had been breaking down for decades as members of the middle class pushed upward into the citadels of status and power. The army reflected these trends, especially in the meteoric rise of its artillery branches. Whereas there was definite assimilation of bourgeois soldiers by the nobility, a process known as "feudalization," there was also a certain degree of "embourgeoisement," or middle-class encroachment on noble turf. Both processes, however, worked against the army factions favoring modernization. Later, both classes recoiled defensively as the working class protested its plight. The rise of the workers affected the tactical-technological debate, too, for some very highly placed soldiers argued that maintaining older shock tactics was necessary for fighting in the streets if revolution were to break out.

It is also important to realize that the Prussian-German Army was a state within a state—and a fragmented one at that. It was split among its infantry, cavalry, and artillery branches and, along another plane, among its political-functional units: the War Ministry, the General Staff, the Military Cabinet, and after 1888 the Imperial Headquarters. Departmentalism worsened during the reign of a psychologically unstable William II (1888–1918) because different branches and divisions found no firm, consistent, or effective guidance from the top. Internal struggles over technologies that were rapidly changing and evolving must be placed in the context of this rampant departmentalism and weak leadership. Thus, there were feuds over weaponry and technology-related tactics, strategy, and organization that pitted cavalry against infantry, field artillery against heavy artillery, and the General Staff against the War Ministry—all made worse by the last kaiser. This feuding was highly significant because it reduced Germany's military preparedness, especially in the decade before 1914, when bitter disagreements erupted over machine guns, airships, artillery, and levels of ammunition.

These disputes spilled over into society when a "right-wing" opposition centered in the Pan-German League and the Defense League charged that the army was not prepared.[8] These accusations of military unreadiness went beyond troop strength to modern weaponry—rightists cried out that army leadership had not procured enough machine guns and airplanes. Not surprisingly, they had very close friends and allies among army dissidents. These relationships, bridging army and society, point to a serious "legitimacy crisis" in the Kaiserreich. Rightly or wrongly, the New Right associated the last kaiser with the side of the army that was fighting change and resisting the seeming inevitability of modern weaponry. William II's relegation to the background during the ugly years of machine warfare from 1915 to 1918 seemed only fitting to technological enthusiasts in and out of the army.

This introduction skims the surface of a vast literature on the kaiser's army. Readers will find more complete citations in the chapters that follow. For now, I believe, the stage is adequately set. It is time to turn back the clock and open the curtains on a bygone era that was struggling, much as our own, to brace for the future by learning from the past.

CHAPTER I

OLD SOLDIERS

*T*HE COUNTRYSIDE AROUND Konitz simmered in the warm September sun. The fields were not planted. There were no rivers and few trees. An occasional, gentle rise in the landscape was all that interrupted the drab flatness of the area. Located in the Baltic province of West Prussia, far from the burgeoning cities and metropolises of industrializing Imperial Germany, Konitz offered the added attraction of its isolation. This was probably what appealed most to Prince Friedrich Karl, nephew of the old emperor and the empire's first inspector general of the cavalry. Indeed, the prince, turning more irascible and peculiar with every year since the great Wars of Unification, did not like outsiders to observe his annual cavalry exercises.[1]

Friedrich Karl stood atop a tall observation platform. Next to him were veteran cavalry generals just as enthusiastic as he was about the great impact that mounted warriors would have in a future war. For a week, two cavalry divisions had maneuvered against each other, roaming widely through the countryside around Konitz. Now, to hold down costs, just one division remained. The generals' binoculars focused on a spot about a mile away, where 3000 Teutonic horsemen were drawn up for battle.

That day's exercise was a tactical drill. The attackers would hit the enemy's flank, engaging his squadrons and beating them back. Assigned the task of breaking through were the Third East Prussian and the Fifth West Prussian Cuirassiers, their breastplates gleaming gloriously in the late summer sunlight. A second strike wave of lesser strength, about 100 meters behind the first, consisted mainly of lighter cavalry, including the famous "Blücher" Hussars of the Fifth Pomeranian Regiment. Their job was to protect the flank and rear of the first wave or to hurl themselves forward if a rout of the enemy was imminent—or if the Cuirassiers failed. Two regiments of Uhlan lancers stood in reserve about 400 meters behind the Cuirassiers. Barely visible from the platform was a regiment not assigned to this attack.

When the order was given, the Cuirassiers moved forward at a trot. After a few hundred meters the pace quickened to a slow gallop as the squadrons performed a diagonal echelon maneuver and prepared for the final charge into the enemy line. At this point Friedrich Karl swung his binoculars back to the left to observe the dispositions of the Hussars, the Uhlans, and the flanking regiment. Indeed, one of the main goals of the exercise was to coordinate the movements of the three waves with nearby units to maximize the advantages of attacking in great strength. The frown on the prince's face was indication enough that these formations were not showing proper initiative in supporting the attack. Further irritation followed when he noticed that the charging heavy cavalry had pulled up short, thinking, apparently, that it was just a drill.

Friedrich Karl's final report attempted to derive lessons that would be useful in the next maneuvers—and in the next war. "Three-wave tactics" would be effective in battle," he wrote, but the battlefield itself was no place to improvise them. These tactics had to be practiced in peacetime exercises that simulated actual battle conditions—including charges of cheering Cuirassiers ridden through to the end—until the commands and their execution became routine. Unfortunately, the German cavalry had little wartime experience with massed attacks. The result was that supporting and neighboring units were unclear and confused about their roles. The main goal of a successful charge was for the charging division to attract all nearby cavalry into the fray "like iron drawn to a magnet." Only a "well-schooled" cavalry division with good leaders would be "the cutting edge that decides a battle."

The Rebirth of the German Cavalry

The great cavalry exercises at Konitz in September 1881 were the high-water mark of a remarkable revival in the fortunes of the

German cavalry. The golden era of mounted warfare that Friedrich Karl and his professional entourage revered had lapsed into legend more than a century earlier. At Rossbach (1757), Leuthen (1757), and Zorndorf (1758), Prussian cavalry generals had led successive strike waves of Cuirassiers and Hussars that justified the confidence and faith of their great warrior monarch, Frederick II. This tradition crashed to the ground, however, during the Napoleonic wars, nor was the succeeding generation kind to Prussia's horsemen. Industrialism brought not only rifled steel cannons with greater range and accuracy but also mass-produced infantry rifles; the Prussian "needle gun"; and the French *chassepot*, which fired much more rapidly than the old muskets. Consequently, the cavalry was assigned no major role in Prussia's wars against Denmark (1864) and Austria (1866). The three Prussian armies that descended on Bohemia in the latter campaign deployed their cavalry in the rear. These units saw only limited action in the last hours of the great battle at Königgrätz.[2]

The turnaround began during the Franco-Prussian War of 1870. Indeed, a new cavalry legend was born as Germany's three armies marched west into Lorraine to engage Marshal François Bazaine's Army of the Rhine near Metz. Bazaine seized the initiative on 16 August against the German Second Army of Friedrich Karl, attacking him at Mars-la-Tour before the German First and Third Armies

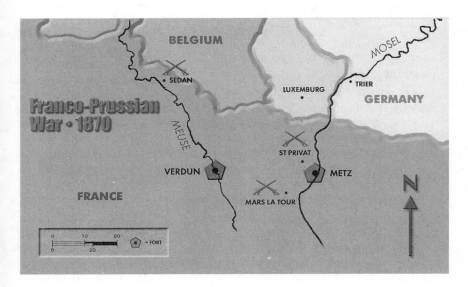

Figure 1.

could offer support. Outnumbered and pounded by superior French artillery, the Second Army was in a precarious position. Orders for an attack were therefore issued to General Bredow's cavalry brigade, consisting of one regiment of Cuirassiers and one regiment of Uhlans. Charging in one unsupported wave, the roughly 800 riders overran enemy infantry and artillery positions, penetrating some 3,000 meters before they were forced to retreat. The "Death Ride of Mars-la-Tour" had cost Bredow 379 men and 400 horses, but he had purchased valuable time for the Second Army. There were altogether eight cavalry charges during the battle, pitting cavalry against infantry, artillery, and opposing cavalry. Deciding the day, in fact, was a great clash of about 6,000 German and French riders.[3] Although Mars-la-Tour was a bloody draw, Bazaine fell back to defensive positions near Metz, where the Germans attacked with greater success 2 days later.

With the arrival of peace in 1871, Friedrich Karl and his closest colleagues began the work of reorganizing, rebuilding, and retraining the cavalry. Although the prince was clearly the driving force behind this reformation, he found support among many highly placed cavalry officers, above all Brigadier General Karl von Schmidt, a veteran of the decisive cavalry melée at Mars-la-Tour. All of them believed that the Franco-Prussian War had demonstrated the continuing effectiveness of cavalry in modern warfare, but they bemoaned the fact that mounted units had been mostly deployed for attacks in squadron, regiment, or brigade strength: "If, instead of Bredow's one brigade, an entire division had attacked with support," wrote the prince, "then this attack would have been decisive."[4] Preparation for such a glorious role in the next war should be the peacetime mission of the cavalry.[5]

The prince's men were ready with a preliminary report in 1873. Because contemporary cavalrymen had neither experience in commanding large bodies of horsemen nor any written instructions to guide them in this endeavor, one faction of reformers advised falling back on the three-wave tactics that had produced great victories in Frederician times. Foremost among them were the dynamic Schmidt, as well as Lieutenant Colonel Otto von Kaehler, commander of the Second Silesian Hussars and a devotee of cavalry tactics under Frederick the Great. The commission majority agreed, recommending guidelines for the deployment and mission of each strike wave—attack tactics to be used against infantry, artillery, and cavalry—and providing instructions for pursuing a routed enemy. As important as the tactical details, however, was the offensive spirit that should infuse all operations. "No leader, regardless of how weak or outnumbered, regardless of how unfavorable the battle situation facing him, may let himself be attacked by the enemy or wait for him with feet planted—he who allows himself to be charged is beaten!" The commissioners, observed Kaehler, wanted to "employ in present-day circumstances what Frederick the Great articulated in his [day]."[6] Devotion to the old tactics would produce new battlefield glories and surely lead parading Prussian cavalry back to the great king's statue on Unter den Linden, where, with banners lowered, they could proclaim: "Yes, Your Majesty, we are once again the best horsemen in the world."[7]

The draft regulations of 1873 soon led to factional disagreements in the application stage of the reform. Adherents of the "new" tactics envisioned a full range of offensive possibilities for the cavalry, including charges from the center or from either flank. Commanders had to be open-minded and flexible about deployment and the point of attack. Officers and men had to be trained, moreover, in the wider variety of complicated formations and battlefield maneuvers that the more eclectic tactics required. Thus, the Fredericians called for cavalry divisions made up of three smaller—and more easily controlled—brigades of two regiments each. The chief opponent of the backward-looking reformers was Major General Karl Friedrich von Witzendorff, head of the army's riding institute and a veteran of Mars-la-Tour. Although he warmed to the idea of a cavalry rebirth in modern times and especially liked the image of masses of horses, charging for shock effect, this seemed to warrant divisions of two big brigades of three regiments. Accordingly, Witzendorff was less insistent on three-wave tactics and also more skeptical about the practicality of intricate changes of direction under fire in difficult terrain. Preferring the "traditional" practices of the 1850s and 1860s, he wanted to position their regiments on the flank and limit the seemingly artificial, drill-like battlefield maneuvering. There was also a greater appreciation here for the cavalry's reconnaissance mission. Backing Witzendorff was Major Heinrich von Rosenberg, an equestrian competitor, promoter of improved horseflesh, and commander of the "Zieten" Hussars. Prince Friedrich Karl seems initially to have favored this camp.[8]

Large-scale exercises between 1873 and 1875—featuring six divisions in the later year—decided the debate in favor of Schmidt and the Fredericians, including a more enthusiastic Prince Friedrich Karl. Their victory was consummated with the publication in 1876 of the final version of the regulations. Further work and practice was still required for troops to learn the new tactics and come up to battlefield expectations. Thus, exercises in subsequent years concentrated on extending attacks from 800 to 1,500 meters, drilling officers and men in the various formations, executing shifts between battle formations, and—as at Konitz—coordinating the movements of the three strike waves. Most important was for German horsemen to remain worthy of past victors and "never again decline into a barely tolerated auxiliary branch," concluded Kaehler. Far from it; the cavalry must "maintain its rank as an equal comrade-in-arms—a status it has regained thanks to the tireless efforts of its leaders, and its own achievements in the face of enemy fire."[9]

This reacquired pride of position was not accomplished without generating considerable controversy. Already mentioned was the disgruntlement over brigade strength and what seemed to some a rigid, doctrinaire adherence to outmoded three-wave tactics. Others had the temerity to suggest that cavalrymen would not play an important battle role unless they utilized their mobility to reach threatened defensive lines, dismounted, and fought on foot alongside the infantry. Russian Major General Gourko's punishing raid behind Turkish lines in the Russo-Turkish War of 1877 offered some credence to this point of view, for he had made devasting use of mounted infantry, sappers, Gatling guns, and artillery. There was also grumbling in the ranks over maintenance of the cuirass, for the men knew from 1870 that steel breastplates provided protection against the swords of enemy cavalrymen but not against modern bullets. Although the matter was discussed upon Schmidt's commission, only one member actually proposed discarding the heavy cavalry's badge of honor.[10]

These disagreements and controversies spilled out of the cavalry corps in the months after the great Konitz maneuvers. An anonymous tract appeared that year, asserting with brutal cynicism that the era of mounted warfare had passed. So why not save millions by doing away with cavalry officers who "set greatest store in pretty horses and beautiful clothes" and tried "to conceal the real worth of their branch from those who know better"?[11] After Kaehler responded in understandably bitter fashion, Major Albert von Boguslawski, one of the infantry's most prolific writers on modern tactics and strategy, attempted to put out the fire in the Military Weekly, a journal edited by the Prussian General Staff. His article merely heaped insult onto injury, however, for after chastising the first writer, he turned on Kaehler, asserting that the cavalry's role should not be exaggerated. The cavalry and the artillery existed merely as auxiliaries to the infantry.[12]

Making matters worse for the cavalry was the deteriorating relationship between Prince Friedrich Karl and Arnold von Kameke, the Prussian war minister. Perhaps because of his background in the army engineers, Kameke exhibited a definite "lack of fancy"[13] for grandiose, impractical extravaganzas like Konitz. Although such uncavalier sentiments were fairly widespread in leading army circles,[14] the verdict was far from unanimous. Thus, some older infantry tacticians sympathized with the notion of heroic charges carried through to victory by man and beast, not by inanimate, unfeeling machines. Moreover two of the officer corps' most innovative publicists, Wilhelm von Scherff and Baron Colmar von der Goltz, wrote positively about the cavalry's revival, and another reforming voice in the infantry, Sigismund von Schlichting, supported at least part of the cavalry agenda. Despite the skepticism of the Boguslawskis and Kamekes, in other words, there was no guarantee that horse charges of divisional or corps strength would remain harmlessly isolated on the exercise fields. That two-thirds of Prussia's corps commanders in the mid-1880s were cavalry generals seemed, in fact, to guarantee just the opposite.[15] "If a war comes, as I fear it will," wrote Count Alfred von Waldersee of the General Staff, "the cavalry will be quickly torn up." This reality made it difficult for him to understand, therefore, why "the significance of the cavalry is now rising."[16]

Indeed, there was an irrational, even technophobic aspect to the rebirth of the cavalry. "No technology comes to our aid," boasted one proud officer. "We have only that which our ancestors had a thousand years ago: a man, a steed, and iron—everything else we have to create out of ourselves."[17] Such attitudes carried over into practice. Although Germany's Cuirassiers were equipped with pistols and other mounted warriors had rapid-firing carbines, for instance, the regulations of 1876 strictly forbade firing them during a charge. Attacks were to be carried out with cold, hard steel. To heighten the morale of the men, swords were drawn dramatically just before the charge. "The irresistible storming of horses packed in tight formation at full gallop is the main and fundamental strength of the cavalry."[18] Cavalry leaders also turned a deaf ear to arguments of the horse artillery that their guns be wheeled into forward positions to lend maximum support. In Friedrich Karl's words, the horse artillery "is not to be seen as a strengthening of the [cavalry's] offensive element."[19]

This type of bracing for the future by escaping into the past is hard to explain. It resulted partially from several peacetime phenomena. As the years that separate soldiers from combat experience lengthen into decades, memory serves less as a guide for wartime realism on the practice field. Prudent preparation for war is especially difficult for victors when the pride that comes from victory distorts sound judgment. Thus it was natural, in a way, that German cavalrymen seized on Bredow's glorious but deadly ride at Mars-la-Tour rather than focusing on the decimation 2 hours earlier of hundreds of French Cuirassiers. Blurring vision still more is the compounded effect over time of practice conditions: Soldiers are not actually shot and killed, dead horses do not really form a wall of flesh that blocks much of the second wave, and morale is never crushed in an instant by massed cannon fire—thus charges seem easier to accomplish than they are in reality. It was also tempting to choose locations for exercises with flat terrain and with no rivers to ford or dangerous sunken roads to negotiate. The horse artillery played a decreasing role at maneuvers as the 1870s unfolded, moreover, until finally only one lone battery rode. "[There were] many who felt that even one was already too much," recalled one cannoneer. Even when the horse artillery was invited by the top cavalry command to participate in maneuvers, it was given little to do, perceiving itself, he remembered, as a hampering "lead weight."[20]

But there were more powerful factors at work. The cavalry was the first and only army branch forced to ward off accusations of obsolescence. With technology already relegating horsemen to peripheral roles before 1815—a verdict confirmed by the Wars of Unification—pride and the spirit of the corps mandated a desperate struggle for survival in the face of modernity's challenges. Warriors on horseback were also symbols of the military mission performed for millennia by upper-class men. The sociopolitical position of this privileged male class was waning, however, as the modern society of city councils, civil codes, parliaments, factories, and joint-stock banks arose. Every passing decade, in fact, saw the middle class undermining the aristocracy's monopoly of ownership of landed estates, entry to the officer corps, and even entry to the nobility itself. The bourgeoisie was also playing an increasingly prominent role in the bureaucracy. Political developments took a toll as parliaments swept away the remnants of serfdom, aristocratic tax exemption, and local police powers of the nobility.[21] Largely sealed against nonnobles, the cavalry was an inner citadel of the upper class—6% of Prussian regimental commanders were bourgeois in 1865, as were only 7% in 1885.[22] With the castle's last bastion threatened, we can appreciate the defenders' siege mentality.

Matters came to a head in January 1883 during the budget debates of the Reichstag (Parliament) in Berlin. Of all the progressive developments over the long generation since the defeat of Napoleon in 1815, the creation of a German empire with nationwide elections was undoubtedly the most significant. The powers of the Prussian king and German emperor, William I, remained vast, especially in the areas of foreign policy, declarations of war, and army affairs. As a result of hard-fought, controversial compromises in the 1860s, however, parliament had earned the right to approve or reject budgets. The generals had insisted on multiple-year appropriations for the army, thereby keeping prying parliamentary eyes as far away as possible. But in Europe's hostile atmosphere, requests for new funding had usually occurred before these years had elapsed— and so it was in the winter of 1883. War Minister Kameke's temperature rose as, one after the other, speakers from the leftist parties used the opportunity to attack the Guard Corps, and the cavalry in particular, as preserves of noble privilege and prejudice—unnecessary, expensive "parade troops" intolerable in a modern nation.

Then Eugen Richter mounted the podium. Enfant terrible of the Progressive Party, the Reichstag grouping most dissatisfied with the limits of parliamentary power in Germany, Richter was both hated and respected in the rightist parties, the ministries, the army, and the palaces of power. He began disarmingly by stating that he did not wish to say much about the cavalry, then proceeded to unleash the full force of his rhetoric. If the main roles of the cavalry these days were reconnaissance and screening, not pitched battle, then "I am of the opinion, I say just in passing, that we have much too much cavalry."

But Richter did not let it pass, producing an article from the *Military Weekly* that labeled the cavalry's fur hats, swords, scabbards, and breastplates obsolete. After Richter mocked the "suicide rides" of the Cuirassiers during the 1870 campaign, members of the right-wing Conservative Party—some of whom had served with the cavalry—rose in protest. But he continued the offensive. "[You] may rightly say that when it comes to the attack, [the Cuirassiers] hit hard, but that's just the point: before they even reach the infantry they're shot through with bullets, the regiment is scattered about, men and horses have sunk to the ground." Breastplates "no longer offer protection against bullets."[23]

Figure 2. Cavalry Guard Corps parade before the kaiser on the Potsdamer Lust-garten. Source: Ernst von Eisenhart-Rothe, *Ehrendenkmal der Deutschen Armee und Marine 1871–1918* (Berlin, 1928).

Kameke knew that he had to respond. That he basically agreed with Richter did not make the task a pleasant one. So he ignored the attacks on the cavalry and the Cuirassiers, deflecting the whole matter by saying that Richter was the better orator. Kameke chose, rather, to protest Richter's previous remarks that had smeared the Guard Corps as so many superfluous, luxurious parade soldiers.[24]

The honor of the cavalry had gone undefended by the army's official representative in parliament. This was a mistake, for, as we shall see, Germany's mounted warriors would fare far better in the long run than either Kameke or the office of the war minister.

Only the Infantry

Albert von Boguslawski's *Tactical Developments since the War of 1870–71* appeared in 1877.[25] His conclusions concerning the bleak future of mounted warfare were fairly typical of the skepticism that the cavalry was fighting hard to change. Boguslawski's book was also very controversial, however, among infantrymen. It is unlikely that his tactical observations would have caused a furor among foot soldiers in the autumn of 1870, when memories of that summer's battles were still fresh. That it stirred a hornet's nest 7 years later was an indication that the same combination of social and psychological forces leading to Konitz was also at work in the infantry.

The battles in eastern France, Boguslawski observed, challenged the notion that cavalry could still decide modern engagements. Mass attacks of horse against infantry had not occurred. Rather, the cavalry had charged in smaller units, generally against opposing cavalry or artillery. Boguslawski was more impressed with the contribution of Germany's artillery to victory, pointing to the effectiveness of massed cannons in close support of the advancing infantry. Consistent with this respect for the firepower of modern weaponry, he also condemned the older shock tactics of the infantry. Combat experience in 1870 had quickly demonstrated the wisdom of spreading out into dispersed formations and taking cover when it was available—the same wisdom that led some infantrymen to frown on cavalry regulations that prescribed an "irresistible storming of horses packed in tight formation at full gallop."

The German armies that crossed the Rhine in 1870 were trained to attack in either company columns or battalion columns. The basic drill-field formation still called for regiments of three battalions, one battalion in front of the other at close intervals, each drawn up tightly in nine ranks of 100 men. This regimental attack column was born in the French Army of the early 1790s after the complex linear tactics of earlier wars had broken down in combat. The purpose of the new formation was to shock defenders and sweep over them in successive waves. With the coming of industrialization and more deadly weapons by midcentury, shock tactics began to yield in some German states to a preference for the smaller half-battalion or still more maneuverable company formations. The battalion was split into its four company columns, each drawn up in three broad ranks. It was not uncommon in the 1850s to hear Prussian officers mock battalion phalanx formations as "parade tactics" but praise company columns as "shooting war tactics."[26]

The advent of Prussia's rapid-firing needle gun induced army leaders to experiment with new tactics at divisional exercises in 1861. Special instructions stipulated that infantry units should move out in column depth, shift to formations with a broader frontage, and shoot while attacking in order to fully exploit the needle gun's firepower. These tactics were similar to the eighteenth-century practice of attacking in two long lines, halting midfield for the first line to kneel, and then firing volleys without decimating friendly ranks. As the decade wore on, some officers continued to advocate the modified linear, or wing tactics first practiced in 1861. To reinforce their arguments, this faction pointed to Austria's suicidal attacks against the needle gun in the Austro-Prussian War of 1866. But the reformers were unable to effect a new consensus in Prussia. Official infantry regulations, unchanged since 1847, still mandated shock attacks in column formations.[27]

The old wisdom was thoroughly shaken, however, at St. Privat. After the battle of Mars-la-Tour on 16 August 1870, Marshal Bazaine's troops retired eastward toward Metz. Still 150,000 strong, they had the entire day of 17 August to prepare defenses along a 7-mile front. Bazaine's position stretched along the crest of a ridge, presiding over a deep, glacislike ravine that was shallower, and thus easier for attackers to traverse, on his right flank.[28] On 18 August, Moltke ordered the German First Army to hit Bazaine's impregnable left near Gravelotte, while Friedrich Karl's Second Army marched toward the weaker French flank at St. Privat. While the French were repelling the Germans at Gravelotte, nearly routing the shaken First Army, 30,000 soldiers of the Prussian Guard were attacking Bazaine's right. The French had dug several terraced rows of trenches that rose to the town. The houses of St. Privat, towering "castle-like" over the trenches, were also manned. "An overpowering hail of projectiles poured over the open ground in front,"[29] wrote Helmuth von Moltke, chief of the Prussian General Staff.

The dense formations of the Prussian Guard moved out of the woods into this driving metallic rain. A thin skirmish line preceded the company columns and half-battalions of each brigade's first wave. The second wave consisted of half-battalions, and the third wave of each brigade drew up in full battalion phalanxes.[30] They did not wait for artillery support. Exhibiting incredible bravery under withering fire, the "parade soldiers of the Potsdamer Lustgarden"[31] performed intricate maneuvers to get into their prescribed battle order; then, with "shoulders hunched and heads bowed,"[32] they began to march up the steep slope. The French *chassepot* rifle, quick-firing and accurate to 1,200 meters, and the awesome *mitrailleuse*, an early machine gun that fired 37 barrels simultaneously, hit over 5,000 of these human targets in just a few minutes.

The troops and their company commanders desperately improvised new tactics. Half-battalions and battalions from the rear waves mixed with company columns and skirmishers in front, spreading out into one longer and less exposed line. After a murderous half hour they reached the first row of trenches, shot the defenders, and took cover.[33] Over the next hour, the infantrymen overran the remaining earthworks, charging in short sprints, sometimes pausing to shoot, sometimes not. By dusk the Prussian Guard had come to within 300 meters of St. Privat. Twenty-six artillery batteries had turned the town into an inferno. The last charge carried the position and netted 2,000 prisoners.

The battle had taken 3 hours and cost 8,000 German casualties. The price was nearly as horrendous as Benedek's assault on the Chlum Heights at Königgrätz and worse than Pickett's charge at Gettysburg in 1863. Unlike those bloodlettings, however, the attackers had won at St. Privat. Bazaine decided to withdraw into the fortifications of Metz where he was besieged and later captured. Although elated, the Germans did not ignore the obvious tactical lesson of St. Privat. In a special order on 21 August 1870, King William of Prussia praised the courage displayed by the troops. He was careful to add, however, "that I expect from the intelligence of the officers that in future they will succeed in achieving the same results with less sacrifice by means of a smarter use of the terrain, a more thorough [artillery] preparation of the attack, and by using more appropriate formations."[34] Older and more of a traditionalist than his General Staff chief, William was probably yielding to the advice of Moltke.[35]

The bloody results of Gravelotte–St. Privat and the king's subsequent order reignited the tactical controversies that had raged before the war. Conservatives like General Paul Bronsart von Schellendorff, a veteran of Königgrätz and chief of operations at royal headquarters in 1870, and General Alexander von Pape, commander of the First Prussian Guard Division at St. Privat, frowned on the deterioration of battlefield order and control that resulted when junior officers took too much initiative, either in pursuing a disorganized foe, as in 1866, or when dispersing and seeking cover, as in 1870. On the other side were Young Turks like Julius von Verdy du Vernois, a military publicist and instructor at the War School in Berlin, and pragmatists like Moltke, who pushed for reform to reduce casualties.[36]

The clash of opinions continued through the first peacetime year. Army leaders finally agreed to experiment with new tactical formations that would strike a balance between saving soldiers and "organizing the disorder."[37] What the reformers presented on the Tempelhof Field in early 1872, however, made the conservatives shudder. The attackers were preceded by two lines of skirmishers to increase offensive firepower. The first and second following waves were drawn up in dispersed lines or line segments. The goal was to advance in short sprints, gradually consolidate the first waves, and feed soldiers forward to support the skirmishers. The third wave of reserves formed in company columns. The notion of tactical experimentation begun at Tempelhof received official sanction by royal decree in June 1872.[38]

The king and the traditionalists soon ran out of patience. Polemics in military journals were disrupting army unity. Most corps commanders, exploiting the freedoms they enjoyed, interpreted the king's order as license to render definitive judgments about proper tactics.[39] In another decree of March 1873, therefore, William terminated the experiment and announced new compromise infantry regulations. The company column was now the "normal" offensive formation. Lines and line segments were also permitted, but not in dispersed formations. Short sprints were allowed, but feeding soldiers forward to the front was dropped to prevent the "ruinous breaking up of the tactical units." Permeating the new regulations was a determination to keep all battalions firmly "in the hands of commanders who order the company columns, just as the regimental commanders order their battalions." William was confident that the new ruling did justice "to the demands of modern-day combat."[40]

The first decree had started something, however, that was not so easily stopped. Thus Sigismund von Schlichting, regimental commander at Spandau, was one who believed passionately that the regulations of 1873 did not correspond to "the new tactical imperatives."[41] As a battalion leader in 1870, he had observed the impact of modern weapons on attackers in tight formations. Promoted to colonel in 1874, Schlichting ignored the regulations—and the scowls of his superiors—and trained his companies to spread out. Captain Mieg of the Bavarian Shooting School was another officer who swam against the current. To overtake the *chassepot*, Germany had introduced first an improved needle gun, then the M-71 Mauser. Somewhat like his eighteenth-century predecessors, Mieg advocated new formations to maximize the new rifle's offensive capabilities. His school practiced firing from 1,500 meters in loose, random order. The practice of random-order salvos spread quickly from Bavarian to Prussian rifle ranges, becoming Germany's standard teaching method in 1877.[42] Hoping to counteract the confusion created by marksmanship guidelines that contradicted official infantry regulations and to silence unauthorized experimentation like Schlichting's, the army reprinted official regulations in 1876. But still the debate raged, witnessed by the appearance in 1877 of works by Wilhelm von Scherff, Verdy du Vernois, and Albert von Boguslawski. After Boguslawski discussed ongoing experiments at far greater length than official tactics, the *Military Weekly* quipped wryly that he should change his title to "Tactics of the Future."[43]

The point was well taken. Despite the attention they had clearly acquired, Schlichting, Mieg, and Boguslawski had not altered the tactics that Germany's generals would have employed had the tocsin sounded in the late 1870s. Most division and corps commanders agreed with Bronsart von Schellendorff and Alexander von Pape about the need to maximize control on the battlefield. As one company commander remembered, officers drilled and redrilled their troops "in all of the massed column formations, evolutions, wheeling maneuvers, and artificial movements on which a great part of . . . time was spent in those days." Autumn maneuvers emphasized the same "parade ground" tactics. Massed company and battalion columns with thin skirmish lines were the norm. There was little training in dispersed formation. "The second strike wave, packed tight, pushed right up behind the skirmish line—this was where a decision was expected, not from the firing of skirmishers."[44] It was no wonder that the top army command preferred to hold annual maneuvers in flat, open terrain that approximated drill fields, occasionally selecting a hill to re-create the Prussian Guard attack at St. Privat for the nostalgic pleasure of the aging Kaiser William.[45] "Infantry tacticians, for all intents and purposes, had learned little or nothing at all from the experiences of 1870/71."[46]

This state of affairs prompted Schlichting to appear before the prestigious Military Society of Berlin in March 1879. Chief of the General Staff of the Prussian Guard Corps since 1878, he was determined to exploit his newfound proximity to the center of military power to reform infantry tactics before a series of St. Privats led to debacle, disaster, and defeat in the next war. If more proof were needed of the murderous effect of breech-loaders and modern artillery on massed infantry columns, one merely had to examine the success of Turkish General Osman Pasha's defenses at Plevna during the summer of 1877. "Even in the untrained hands of Turks so much lead flies that the attacker is devasted—in the face of this firepower his titanic courage just sinks into the dust."[47] To Schlichting the lessons were obvious. Unless the terrain provided concealment, there should be no cavalry heroics, no frontal assaults with fixed bayonets, no intricate wheeling maneuvers and lateral shifts in full view of enemy gunners, and no deep infantry formations in the direct flight path of their bullets.[48]

Rather, an attack should proceed more cautiously and cleverly. The lead battalions, facing the enemy's entrenched center, had to advance in dispersed skirmish order supported by field artillery, find cover or dig in,[49] and then return fire almost as if they were defenders. Trailing battalions positioned themselves behind the outside flanks of the point units. Reserve battalions did not bring up the center rear, exposed there to the volleys of the enemy center; rather, they took up position behind the brigade's exposed left or right flank—whichever was unprotected by an adjacent attacking brigade. As the attack developed in this inverted "V," or wedge, formation, rear-echelon battalions advanced into the front line and extended it, making it possible to slip around the enemy's flank as reserve units joined the fray. For the most part, however, Schlichting did not believe that tactics were an antidote to the defensive firepower of modern technology. Rather, battles would be won by superior operations that moved whole armies around the flanks of the enemy. Thus battlefield tactics seemed to be more important as a way not to lose battles.[50]

Just as important as proper tactics was the need to delegate control of an attack to regiment, battalion, and company leaders. The fixation with centralized control, Schlichting believed, was the reason for the failure of Germany's bold tactical experiments of the early 1870s. No formation, however innovative, was a solution by itself to the unpredictable challenges of terrain and enemy surprise. Only the junior officer who was trained to be innovative and spontaneous could make proper tactical decisions. "Out of the incidentals of combat emerge a variety of local tasks—a country shed here, a farmstead there, or one wing of an [attacking] wave may have to swing over to the defensive."[51] Schlichting was careful to add that junior officers could never act arbitrarily, occupying a village or taking flight in a forest merely on a whim. They had to proceed within the framework of their superiors' general orders. "The battalion must be strictly drilled, therefore, in these lessons—the drill field takes on added significance!"[52] In this combination of general battle orders, delegation of authority, and disciplined refusal of company commanders to exhibit excessive freedom, Schlichting believed he had found the formula for "organizing the disorder" of modern battle.

This was a serious assault on the citadel of tactical orthodoxy and tradition. For one thing, a presentation before the army's in-

tellectual elite lent added authority to Schlichting's words. They also
gained wider circulation in a special volume of the *Military Weekly*.
The proselytizing colonel used his presence in Berlin, moreover, to
campaign for new battle tactics in the Prussian Guard, the General
Staff, and the War Ministry.[53] The intensity of this crusade helps to
explain the vitriolic reaction of his enemies.[54] Major Jacob Meckel,
a General Staff officer and teacher at the War School (who would
gain fame as the reorganizer of the Japanese Army in the mid-
1880s), avidly defended the advantages of charging with fixed bayonets in brigade or division masses. General Bernhard von Kessel,
a respected veteran of the Prussian Guard attack at St. Privat and
current commander of the Prussian Fifth Division, engaged in a
lengthy and bitter polemic with Schlichting, warning against the
dangers of discarding tactical rules and principles that had stood
the test of combat in three wars. Germany should not abandon close-
order wave attacks that promised battlefield order and smashing
breakthroughs for "mistaken" dispersal tactics designed with the dubious—because unrealizable—goal of reducing casualties. "Good
discipline holds more troops at battle-ready command than any formation designed for protection—so look for formations that uphold
discipline."[55] Schlichting's innovative assault methods were especially
annoying to Alexander von Pape, promoted to commander of the
Guard Corps during the controversy, for they could not be squared
with official infantry regulations. "Such attacks are forbidden!"[56] he
barked.

Army leaders finally stopped the feuding in 1880 with a note in
the *Military Weekly*. "It would be unwise to twist the meaning of rules
and regulations, or want to replace the given with newly conceived
reforms, for once this starts, there is no end." There had already
been "too much sinning" against regulations. "The given must now
be regarded as permanent."[57] With this announcement, the General
Staff left Schlichting in the lurch. Although he would continue politicking for change in private, he was now muzzled in public. Another warning in 1883 branded any campaigning against regulations
as a violation of an officer's "holy duty" to obey the kaiser.[58]

The resolution of these disagreements supports the conclusion
that most infantry commanders of the early 1880s harbored a technophobia similar to that which afflicted the cavalry. The Prussian
Guard assault at St. Privat, like Bredow's "Death Ride" at Mars-la-
Tour, had taken on increasingly legendary and mythic proportions
with every passing year of peacetime drill and exercise.[59] Even officers like Pape and Kessel, who had been there, soon forgot the basic

lesson that Moltke and the king had drawn three days later. As memories adjusted to more soothing explanations, emphases shifted away from the unnecessary losses to the bravery of the troops and the successful end result. In the process, the fact that technology had killed a sixth of the corps in a few minutes was suppressed by the fact that superior technology and high ground had not saved the French. "Victory does not depend on weapons," observed one colonel, "but rather on soldiers." It was not "the greater or lesser technological perfection of an impersonal tool that decides battles," he continued, but rather "the spirit, morale, and leadership" of the army. "Prussia would have won in 1866 without the needle gun, while the French, on the other hand, could not help themselves to victory in 1870/71 with the *chassepot*."[60] This unshakable belief in the human dimension of victory was clearly more palatable for male human beings who somehow had to mentally prepare for war in a rapidly unfolding machine age.

Together with the deleterious cumulative effect of peacetime maneuvers that were growing increasingly unrealistic, these factors help to explain many specific instances of technophobia among postwar infantry commanders. Many were convinced, for example, that digging foxholes was dangerous "because it damaged the offensive spirit of our infantry."[61] Similarly, most commanders frowned on the notion that distant volleys or firing from cover carried an attack to victory, preferring the brutal rush forward with fixed bayonets, the "triumph of the game,"[62] as Jacob Meckel put it. Suggestions that bayonet drill wasted time in the age of modern firepower triggered a flurry of protests and warnings from infantrymen worried about undermining the army's all-important offensive spirit.[63] For many years after the Turks used magazine rifles to deadly effect at Plevna, moreover, infantry traditionalists in Germany scoffed at the idea that repeaters offered any great advantage. On the contrary, they would undermine morale when soldiers shot up their ammunition too quickly and panicked. Thus a commission stacked with old veterans turned down magazine rifles in late 1880. It took the persistent efforts of two war ministers over the next 3 years to prevail over this entrenched opposition.[64] It was small wonder that the cavalry's rebirth was critized mainly by innovators like Boguslawski and not by conservatives, for the latter basically agreed with the cavaliers that spirit and flesh trumped technology every time.

Research on the changing social background of the officer corps facilitates additional comparison between these two branches of the army.[65] As we know, the cavalry remained a social bastion and a political symbol of the nobility in an increasingly bourgeois age. In Prussia, for example, the percentage of noblemen who were commanding cavalry regiments remained at 93% to 94% from 1865 to 1885. This undoubtedly strengthened the preference of its officers for attacking in traditional fashion. The infantry, on the other hand, did not escape a process of embourgeoisement as the Prussian army expansion of the 1860s, followed by the creation of the German empire, opened military gates to the sons of businessmen, professionals, and untitled bureaucrats. In Prussia, the middle-class share of regimental infantry commands rose from 5% in 1865 to 24% by 1885. The result, particularly during the first intense period of mixing and mingling among class elites in the 1870s, was a strong desire on the part of army newcomers to conform to older ways in order to gain acceptance. One historian argues that as the middle class in uniform strove for conformity and acceptability, it turned away from liberalism and technology, opting for conservatism and outmoded military tactics.[66] Although it is obviously impossible to formulate generalizations applicable to all bourgeois officers, it is probably safe to conclude that social pressures—a "feudalization" of middle-class officers—reinforced the effects of victors' pride, peacetime drill, and commanders' fixation with battlefield order and control to create a strong preference in Germany for massed infantry charges. It was a disaster waiting to happen.

CHAPTER 2

QUEEN OF THE BATTLEFIELD

*T*HERE WAS A clearing in the woods high above the Meuse that commanded a beautiful view. Far below, the river meandered through its valley. A few miles away on the opposite side, a bare hill ascended away from the glistening water, angling steeply upward until it reached a forest known as the Bois de la Garenne. This thick wood was itself nestled in a bowl below precipitous ridges that yielded in their turn to the darkness of the Ardennes farther up. The whole majestic landscape seemed to crown the town of Sedan hundreds of feet below on the valley floor.[1]

Moltke had selected this clearing for the headquarters of the German Army. The morning mist on 2 September 1870 limited King William, Bismarck, and the royal entourage to the mere sounds of escalating violence, but by noon nature's curtain had parted before the full panorama of battle. The hillside above Sedan was dotted and speckled with the bivouacs of the French Army and the brightly colored uniforms of tens of thousands of desperate soldiers. Two long lines of German cannon could be seen below on the closest bank of the Meuse, and high above the town friendly gun crews wheeled their engines of destruction into position and began to fire. Their distant roar echoed the louder shots from the guns in the valley. "Now we have them in a mousetrap,"[2] exclaimed Moltke the day before as he surveyed the ring of his armies, tightening around the French. But the mechanized terror that followed would mock these words, so incongruous were they with the high-tech killing of the Battle of Sedan.

By late morning the Germans had pushed the French from the highest forward outposts to the hillside between Sedan and the Bois de la Garenne. By early afternoon shots from 540 cannons saturated the enemy's exposed positions and penetrated the woods, where many units sought shelter from certain death. From Givonne on the ridge above the Bois de la Garenne, General Pape readied his Prussian Guard division for the assault but was dissuaded by General Hohenlohe, commander of the Guard Artillery, who knew Pape well enough to mix black humor with his warning. "I guess you want to lose as many men as you did two weeks ago—if you attack the forest before I completely break those guys over there, I'll shoot *at you!*"[3]

And so the carnage from above continued. The French made many attempts to break out of Moltke's "mousetrap," but two earned the victors' lasting respect. Around 1:00 P.M., 6,000 infantrymen tried to punch a hole in German lines. Needle guns and cannons blasted away at the tightly packed attackers, and when the smoke cleared, Hohenlohe's blood ran "literally ice cold" at the terrible sight below him. "The entire enemy column was destroyed,"[4] he recalled. A little later, the French cavalry made three wildly desperate charges. Like the infantry, they were mowed down. "Oh the brave gentlemen!"[5] exclaimed King William from the clearing above the Meuse.

The heads of all observers at headquarters jerked suddenly upward toward Givonne at 2:30 P.M., for at that moment all 90 cannons of the Prussian Guard let loose a "frightening detonation."[6] It was Hohenlohe's signal for Pape to begin his attack. The First Guard infantry descended slowly and carefully from their perch. No Frenchmen fired or counterattacked as the Prussians approached the outskirts of the Bois de la Garenne. Not wishing to join the 40,000 who already lay dead, dying, or wounded, the defenders raised their hands in surrender.

Elsewhere on the battlefield Frenchmen were also waving the white flag. Altogether 104,000 unwounded French soldiers were taken. It had been a glorious day for the German Army—but an especially important one for the field artillery. Following closely on the heels of other artillery heroics since war broke out, Sedan was a culminating breakthrough for the cannoneers. They had finally proved their worth.

Cavalier Cannoneers

The Prussian artillery that Hohenlohe joined as a young man in the 1840s was known for its technical expertise and stubborn independence. This army branch boasted its own academy, where cadets mastered a demanding curriculum of math, physics, chemistry, and liberal studies. The requirements went so far beyond those of the divisional schools, or even the elite War School in Berlin, that infantry and cavalry officers spoke skeptically about "the secret science of the black collar"[7] that seemed to lie behind artillery technology. "The gunner of those days," recalled Hohenlohe, "took pleasure in a mask of learning under a veil of mystery, which, though it estranged the other arms from the artillery, yet caused them to entertain a certain respect for it on account of its unknown erudition." So proud were artillerists of their expertise that they were strictly forbidden by regulations "to betray anything whatever of the secrets of the artillery beyond the regiment."[8] Artillery regulations also required that they protest orders by superior infantry and cavalry officers if the resulting gun deployment was considered incorrect. If he did not protest, an artillery officer was held personally responsible for setbacks.

Class and political tensions further distanced the artillery from the rest of the army at midcentury. Whereas it was next to impossible for bourgeois Prussians to become officers of the Guard Corps or cavalry, the artillery remained predominantly middle class.[9] Thus a strong social bond reinforced the technical pride of the cannoneers and, conversely, the near contempt felt for them by noblemen, who viewed war as an affair of caste honor best resolved by blue-bloods well versed in such niceties. And although aristocrats concealed a certain respect for the knowledge of the artilleryman and grudgingly admitted that cannon fire was necessary, they also believed that there was something derogating and dreadful about an officer who reeked of axle grease or loved work and machinery, which nobles widely assumed was the unwelcome fate of every artillerist. Reinforcing the prejudices and animosities on both sides were deep political divisions. Although broad generalizations are problematic, it is true that much of the middle class favored the liberal movement to establish parliamentary constraints on the monarch. Nor should it be surprising that the artillery was a hotbed of liberal politics in the army or that opposition to army liberalism was centered in the Guard Corps.[10] Thus class and politics deepened the rift between different branches of the service in Prussia.

All of these divisive factors contributed to the artillery's extreme embarrassment during the Königgrätz campaign of 1866. "Men are not machines," wrote Hohenlohe, "and those who know each other well, and live together on equal terms, work more harmoniously together in action, than they would if they were strangers to one another."[11] It was understandable, therefore, that the three Prussian armies that moved south through the Bohemian passes that summer placed their field artillery units in the rear with the cavalry. The marching order was not determined by the narrow defiles of Upper Bohemia, nor was it a coincidence, for some commanders were heard saying that "they needed no artillery and didn't concern themselves with it."[12] As Prussian infantrymen overran one Austrian position after another in the early battles, they often charged before the artillery could move up, relying mainly on the deadly needle gun for tactical victory. When the cannons were finally in place—as at Königgrätz, by late morning—they were usually outnumbered and outgunned by the Austrians and thus forced to change position frequently or to withdraw. In these instances, the independence of the artillery seemed like cowardice in the eyes of foot soldiers. Hohenlohe drew the conclusion from his experience that "if many infantry generals, after they had won victory in 1866 . . . felt a certain triumphant joy at the fact that the scientific arm was not needed, I for one cannot wonder at it."[13]

The tarnished image of the artillery let loose among its officers all of the emotions—denial, anger, embarrassment, self-pity, guilt, and envy—of men who felt they had neglected their duty. A collective soul-searching and inward reflection wracked the corps that had once been so proud and independent. One result was a complete turnaround in organizational independence as artillerymen requested to be placed under the orders of corps commanders in war and peace. Another was a series of tactical proposals approved by Moltke that called for the artillery to march near the front and swing quickly into battle. The immediate aftermath of Königgrätz was also the time of Prime Minister Otto von Bismarck's great political compromises. The long, bitter constitutional struggle came to an end, setting clear limits to the powers of both crown and parliament in Prussia and North Germany. With the aristocracy and bourgeoisie burying the political hatchet, with cannoneers less headstrong and secure about their secrets and separate status, and with the infantry itself beginning to experience an influx of middle-class officers, blue-bloods began to reach across branch divisions and socialize with artillery commoners much more frequently. The stage was set for different relationships and wartime experiences in 1870.[14]

Even before the first battles on the frontier, there was a new cooperative spirit. Thus, gun teams accommodated infantry units on the road by transporting provisions, a service that artillerymen considered beneath them in 1866.[15] Battle performance was an added cause for self-congratulations, despite the fact that there were also certain disappointments. About 150 guns, firing ceaselessly, were massed by midafternoon at Mars-la-Tour and advanced into forward positions with the infantry. The artillery even conducted its own separate engagements against French infantry. It was Bredow's brave cavalrymen who saved the day, however, before the cannons were ready. At St. Privat the artillery was reminded of how "unnecessary" it was when the Prussian Guard attacked without so much as requesting support. But the batteries moved rapidly and selflessly to the infantry's aid, pulling their pieces forward to the trapped defenders, setting the town on fire, and facilitating the final push up the hill with 230 guns. The ultimate gratification for the artillery came at Sedan, where the infantry waited for 540 cannons to soften up and break the French. "The heart of every gunner throbbed with joy when he found that all of our leaders had but one desire: to bring up their artillery."[16]

How long could the euphoria and camaraderie endure in peacetime, however, if it were true that the artillery was now "queen" of the battlefield? Indeed, infantrymen, sobered by St. Privat, were very sensitive about the role prescribed for them in war's next chess match, whereas cavalrymen were offended that they had been used like reserve pawns in the last one. Within a few years, officers whose "one desire" had been to bring up the guns now remembered that there had been too many for "an energetic waging of war."[17] As strong as their new bond was with their comrades-in-arms, moreover, artillerymen had neither forgotten the disgrace of 1866 nor overlooked their vast potential for an even greater performance in a future war. Interservice harmony seemed likely to deteriorate once again.

After 1871, in fact, the artillerists could present a strong case for investing heavily in them. In observing the Franco-Prussian War, the other Great Powers concluded that Prussia's rifled-steel, breech-loading field gun had pushed the smooth-bore muzzle-loader made from bronze into obsolescence. They began to convert, therefore, to newer, state-of-the-art models. Worn out from heavy firing in eastern France, Germany's arsenal of 4- and 6-pounders needed replacement in any event. It was obvious, therefore, that the new gun had to be a superior artillery piece. More than two years of debates and tests resulted in the so-called C-73 cannon. Its 88-mm caliber was just slightly less than that of the old 6-pounder (90 mm), but improved gunpowder and a reinforced barrel nearly doubled the maximum range to 7,000 meters. Because all of the old 4-pounders were replaced by C-73s, firepower was significantly increased. Newly designed iron cannonballs that exploded into twice as many fragments—70 or 80 versus 30—greatly magnified the killing effect. A few years later, C-76 ring grenades were issued that burst into about 150 sharp, jagged pieces. When it was introduced in 1874, System C-73 was the best in Europe. Increasing the long-range might of the German Army still more, each of the empire's 18 corps received an additional two field artillery batteries of six guns each.[18]

Despite the augmented range of the C-73, it is nevertheless understandable that German artillerists had no real desire to lob shells at the enemy from a distance of several kilometers. Who could forget the searing emotional lows of 1866, when the cannons had been too far back, or the exhilarating highs of 1870, when guns had blasted from 1,000 paces into the Bois de la Garene? The great artillery lesson from the Wars of Unification, it seemed, was to stay on the heels of the infantry—and to do that one needed mobility.

Figure 3. The C-73 cannon in the open field. Source: Max Köhler, *Der Aufstieg der Artillerie bis zum Grossen Krieg* (Munich, 1938).

One reflection of the desire to be even closer to the infantry in the next war was the appointment of Theophil von Podbielski as inspector general of the field artillery in 1872. An artillerist who had also commanded a cavalry brigade, he soon made his presence felt by successfully opposing the War Ministry's demand for heavier cannon with more destructive effect against enemy artillery and entrenchments. For all its improvements, the C-73 was still light enough to be wheeled into action by six—as opposed to eight—horses.[19] During his first year, moreover, Podbielski had separated the field artillery from the so-called foot artillery. By enabling officers to avoid long sedentary tours of duty behind fortress walls, this separation allowed artillerists with riding experience to specialize in moving their cannon into action more quickly. Two of the many results of this new concentration on horsemanship were a closer working relationship with the horse artillery and the adoption by the field artillery of the cavalry's exercise manual. Symbolizing the increasing emphasis on mobility, the field artillery also adopted the blue overcoats and bandoleers of the haughty horse artillerists.[20] "Largely because of its close ties to the horse artillery, today's field artillery is transformed when it comes to dash and mobility," proclaimed one proud officer, "and if Frederick the Great had possessed as mobile an artillery as the modern field artillery, he probably would not have formed the horse artillery in the first place."[21]

Drawing lessons from Sedan would prove just as difficult for the field artillery as Mars-la-Tour had been for the cavalry and St. Privat for the infantry. As the first decade of peacetime wore on, artillerymen's memories of actual combat were warped by self-adulation and an increasingly inflated sense of self-worth. Accordingly, the preoccupation with mobility and dashing forward became an obsession. Annual maneuvers became the crucible for these distortions and exaggerations. Shooting the cannons accurately from a reasonable distance played no role when blanks were fired, for this "bang, you're dead" logic was lost on umpires who were more impressed by bold action and movement. The judges were subject, moreover, to the pressures of infantrymen and cavalrymen who were highly excitable and sensitive about their own images. The norm during the C-73's first maneuvers in September 1874, long-distance firing had yielded by the following autumn to the practice of "pushing the artillery farther and farther up to the most effective distance from the enemy for a final decision."[22] The cannons were even rushed forward without caissons to increase speed, a few blank rounds stuffed into the gun limbers being enough for mock combat.[23]

The deleterious effects of maneuvers were compounded by Podbielski's decision to separate the two branches of the artillery. Aspiring officers were placed on two tracks. The mathematically and intellectually inclined received a challenging education in the Artillery School and then advanced to the fortress artillery, whereas the best equestrian talent, educated less rigorously, like candidates from the infantry and cavalry, went into the field artillery. Each artillery branch, moreover, had separate proving grounds. This resulted in field artillery tests and experiments that were riveted on the goal of lightness and speed to the exclusion of other concerns that did not interest them.[24] Mobility is a very important consideration for the artillery, of course, but "it should not be taken so far," warned one officer years later, "that the good rider counts for more than the good artilleryman, the horse more than the cannon, and moving quickly into position more than marksmanship."[25]

The bold, new offensive doctrine of the field artillery soon found articulate advocates in print. The first was Ernst Hoffbauer, a major in the Badenese field artillery, whose *Tactics of the Field Artillery* appeared simultaneously in 1876 with his multivolume history of the artillery during the Wars of Unification. Hoffbauer argued that the field artillery's mission was, first, to smash enemy cannon and then to advance to within 700 meters of his lines, firing hundreds of guns over the attacking infantry. "Massed rapid fire" was the order of the day. Adolf von Schell, commander of an artillery regiment in Westphalia until 1878, when he became chief of staff for Podbielski, took Hoffbauer's ideas to extremes. After winning the decisive artillery duel, he believed, gunners should charge shoulder-to-shoulder with the first wave, bringing their "powerful destructive force"[26] into the fray, just as they had at St. Privat. These aggressive concepts found the support of Heinrich von Löbell, editor of a military journal. Impatient with conceited infantrymen, cavalrymen, and engineers blind to new developments, Löbell claimed that the artillery was no longer a technical or specialized auxiliary wing of the service. It "had long ago cut itself off from technology as a special branch, shoved these technical specialties into the background, and turned with all of its energy to the great tactical tasks which it has to fulfill."[27] Cannoneers belonged in the thick of the battlefield, in other words, for victory was unattainable otherwise.

Such field artillery chauvinism sparked immediate controversy. Hohenlohe, commander of the Prussian Guard artillery, published his own paean to the heroic achievements of 1870 but mocked the notion implicit in much of this literature that artillerists were somehow superior. Rather, they were "one in every respect with the others, an arm of equal standing."[28] Count Herrmann Thürheim of the Bavarian Artillery rejected Hoffbauer's inflexible insistence on massed, close-range fire, hinting at the absurdity of cannons that could shoot accurately from a few thousand meters but always closing to a mere few hundred. He also charged that many field artillery officers were losing sight of the technical side of their weaponry. Many others pointed to the visibility, accuracy, and fire-control problems associated with massed rapid fire—simply put, there would be too much smoke. Infantry officers like Boguslawski and Scherff scoffed at the suggestion, meanwhile, that the artillery was anything more than an auxiliary branch, and the cavalry denied that cannons could make any contribution to the "offensive element" of their corps.[29]

These disagreements reached Moltke's desk in 1880. Taking over for Podbielski in 1879, General Hans von Bülow had requested and received an expansion of the field artillery from 300 to 340 batteries. With over 2,000 C-73 cannon in the army now, the top command needed to decide how best to use them. Moltke argued that a few batteries should move up with the troops but that the bulk of Germany's field pieces should fire from at least 2,000 meters. "The real effectiveness of the artillery lies in staying put."[30] Kaiser William agreed with his legendary General Staff chief, and the corps commanders were so ordered in July 1881.

This decision was unacceptable to Adolf von Schell. Unwisely, Bülow's chief of staff defended his gallant shoulder-to-shoulder approach in the *Military Weekly*. He charged that the new orders contradicted field artillery regulations of 1877 that were the result of a careful and in-depth study of combat conditions. The infantry would have a "bitter experience" if the artillery "in full consciousness of its worth" had to wait in the rear for a call forward. "We all want to be spared from seeing this."[31] Schell's insubordinate article cost him a demotion to regimental command, but army insiders worried about similar rash behavior in real battle. Moltke should have spoken out against drill and maneuver practices, wrote the Saxon military attaché, for "the rapid advance is now enormously exaggerated by the artillery, especially the unlimbering of guns at a gallop, the emphasis on forming long artillery lines, etc."[32] The Prussian war minister was also concerned. Arguing against another appropriation for the field artillery in 1882, Kameke complained that the guns "already assume too broad a front in the battle order—a further strengthening of this branch makes the other branches into a kind of covering service for the artillery."[33] In the last analysis, moreover, "artillery fire can never lead to a decision by throwing the enemy out of his dug-in positions." The former chief of the engineers had no more respect for the artillery than he did for the cavalry, especially after the Russian artillery's embarrassment at Plevna in 1877.

Class relations that were improving after 1866 entered a different, more complicated stage during the army in-fighting of the late 1870s and early 1880s. On one level, the hard-charging field artillery was indeed kowtowing to the nobility. The deemphasis on education and the stress on horsemanship, the adoption of cavalry regulations and horse artillery uniforms, the exaggerated call for frontal attacks—all of this was consistent with the prejudices of conservative Junker soldiers. The field artillery also shunned the fortress gunners; renewed its request for a dependent status under noble corps commanders; and intensified efforts to socialize with the other branches, especially the cavalry.[34] These trends appear to strengthen theses that emphasize the accommodating and assimilating behavior of bourgeois newcomers in the army. According to Volker Mollin, however, there was a deeper phenomenon at work. Just as the middle class had reduced the exclusive power of kings and noblemen, so now the artillery was successfully challenging the battlefield preeminence of the cavalry and infantry. Far from kowtowing to bluebloods when aping their ways, artillerists were proudly displaying trophies of class war and touting the arrival of a powerful new guard in the citadel. The social forces at work in the army were obviously highly complex.[35]

Dawn of the Big Guns

The afternoon before the attack at Plevna it began to rain. That night a succession of violent thunderstorms dropped an immense quantity of water, turning the ground into a pasty, black mud. To soldiers, these were not good omens.

As morning gave way to afternoon, the smoke of 500 cannons hung thick and pungently in the damp, foggy, motionless sky around Grivitza. For 3½ days, Russian gun crews had fired their rounds, most of them aimed at the redoubts and earthworks that enveloped the little Bulgarian town. The last stop on the road to Plevna, Grivitza formed the impregnable center of a line of Turkish fortifications that zigged and zagged for over 20 miles through the embattled countryside.

Eyes watering from the acrid air, Osman Pasha raised his field glasses and waited for something to come into focus through the drizzle and man-made ground fog around him. Somewhere on the other side, 60,000 Romanian and Russian infantrymen said their prayers. Had their leaders learned from July's debacles? Osman Pasha prayed they had not.

Plevna guarded northwestern Bulgaria against the right wing of the Russian army.[36] To pass through the Balkan Mountains farther south and advance toward Constantinople, the tsar's forces had first to seize Plevna. Osman Pasha and 25,000 soldiers had a few weeks to dig trenches before the first attacks in late July 1877. A 6-hour bombardment by light field artillery failed to soften up the Turks, whose Krupp cannons and Peabody-Martini rifles—the best breech-loader in the world—inflicted 11,000 casualties.

While the Russians marshaled a larger strike force, the Turks doubled their own numbers and prepared elaborate earthworks. By late summer, the center around Grivitza boasted six defensive firing lines flanked by two massive redoubts. When the bombardment began in early September, the Turks were burrowed deeply underground in dugouts that protected them from shots and shells. Shooting from long range, moreover, the Russian light artillery pieces were so highly elevated that their explosive shells dove almost vertically into the dirt, often failing to explode or, if they did, merely heaving up mud harmlessly.[37] When the seemingly endless Russian barrage finally stopped, the defenders sloshed above ground with their Peabody-Martinis.

Osman Pasha knew that the undimished strength of his defenses would surprise the enemy. But would overconfidence, reinforced by years of tradition and routine, induce his opponents to pack their troops into tight formations as they did in July? As the fog and smoke dissipated, permitting a clearer view, the Turk's taut face relaxed a little. In the distance, he could see the Romanians and Russians—60,000 strong in dense columns—approaching.

The third Russian assault against Plevna on 11 September 1877 failed miserably. By dusk the muddy field was strewn with 18,000 dead and dying soldiers. Osman Pasha would hold up the Russian advance for another 3 months before his troops, nearly out of ammunition, were finally defeated.

German field artillery experts wrote off the heavy artillery after 1870. The decisive battles of the Franco-Prussian War had proven the worth of mobile field guns whipped rapidly forward to bolster the infantry. Instances when the 4- and 6-pounders had wasted their ammunition against fortified positions—as at Toul and Montmédy—were considered of peripheral importance. Even the devastating performance of the big 210-mm siege guns outside Paris seemed anti-climactic in comparison to Sedan. When the Prussian War Ministry demanded more destructive power from the artillery in 1872, therefore, the defiant answer was the light C-73 cannon. And when Young Turks in the artillery advocated the short 120-mm cannon, a howitzer with higher trajectory, Podbielski's General Inspection squashed the idea in 1877, pushing instead for 40 new C-73 batteries.

Not surprisingly, the news from the Balkans that year made little impression on the German field artillery. Despite a 3-day bombardment of Osman Pasha's formidable redoubts at Plevna, hundreds of Russian guns failed to soften up the Turkish defenders. Consequently, the attacking infantry suffered terrible casualties. But the Russians, it was said in Germany, had been too timid about moving up their guns to more effective range. This mistake was compounded by halting the bombardment before the infantry assault, rather than pinning down the defenders until the infantry was within a few hundred meters. In short, the Battle of Plevna was no reason to doubt Germany's steep investment in field artillery.[38]

There had to be some response, on the other hand, to this new defensive challenge. One promising answer lay in a return to shrapnel, a hollow shot filled with iron balls that were scattered lethally in all directions by a bursting charge. If field guns could spray enemy fortifications with tens of thousands of these bullets, defenders would be forced to take cover while the infantry approached. There would be no need for huge siege guns to demolish the next Plevna. Forty years of tests had been abandoned in 1866, however, because of difficulty with timed fuses. Field artillery experiments in the early 1880s failed for many of the same reasons. The flat trajectory of the C-73 cannon, combined with unpredictable fuses, produced a very high percentage of shrapnel rounds that did not burst directly over the trenches.[39] Regular, black-powder C-76 grenades, moreover, had no effect at all on earthworks. Unless German experts were somehow right about the faulty artillery tactics employed at Plevna, their field cannons were going to be as useless as the Russian ones had been against strong fortifications. Fearing the worst, General Inspector Bülow circulated a report to army commanders in late 1882, warning that the artillery "lacked adequate punch for the tasks placed before it in a future war."[40]

The failure of the German field artillery to rise to the challenge of Plevna looms larger in significance when placed in the wider context of French and European developments. General Revières, drawing immediate lessons from his nation's successful defense of Toul and Montmédy in 1870, proposed construction of a system of impregnable fortresses in the eastern provinces. Stretching from Dunkirk to Belfort, the first line of defense was reinforced by secondary complexes around Laon and Dijon. An imposing double line of forts around Paris served as the last line of defense. The strongest forts on the frontier at Verdun, Toul-Nancy, Epinal, and Belfort had vaulted underground magazines beneath protective earthworks. Aboveground were formidable escarpments, ramparts, and gun towers.[41] "Hohenlohe's image of lines of guns standing in the open blasting away," writes historian Dennis Showalter, "seemed to promise the approximate results of flinging handfuls of dried peas against a wall."[42] Revières's fortification system was nearing completion, in fact, just as German shrapnel tests ran their negative course.

Moltke was worried. The Russo-Turkish War and the subsequent Congress of Berlin had already disrupted Bismarck's alliance system. The Three Emperors' League, uniting the monarchical powers of Russia, Austria-Hungary, and Germany against France, yielded in 1879 to a Dual Alliance that linked only Berlin and Vienna. As Paris smiled, Russia signaled its likely belligerence vis-à-vis Central Europe by stationing large bodies of troops in its western provinces. The resulting tensions were not entirely erased by the resuscitation of the Three Emperors' League in 1881. In conjunction with France's new wall of fortresses—and Germany's seeming inability to break through it—these diplomatic developments convinced Moltke to revise the empire's mobilization plans. In memoranda, he substituted defensive alignments for earlier offensive operations in the west. His plans for an eastern offensive were complicated in the early 1880s, however, by Russian investment in a series of strong fortifications throughout Poland and Lithuania.[43] The anxious victors of 1870 were faced with an ominous strategic dilemma.

Much to the chagrin of the field artillery, Germany's salvation appeared to lie with the lowly fortress artillery. The "stepchild of the entire army"[44] had been cut off from the privileged field artillery in 1872, banished from maneuvers, and saddled with older staff officers considered unfit for service in the field. "Bad treatment, however, frequently cultivates and raises up an inner strength of sorts,"[45] recalled one old artillerist. Indeed with its own testing commission and proving ground, as well as access to the most demanding classes of the Artillery School, the heavy artillery began to "cultivate and raise up" a new cadre of officers proud of their bourgeois heritage; eager to perpetuate middle class beliefs in education, science, and progress; and determined to call on these traditions if given a chance to prove themselves.[46]

The opportunity came in the aftermath of Plevna, for around 1880 Moltke's staff began to press for a heavy artillery solution to the fortress dilemma. The eager foot artillerymen responded in 1882 with a new 150-mm mortar to support infantry attacks from ranges of 1,200 to 2,000 meters.[47] Although tests showed that neither the new 150- nor the older (1872) 210-mm rifled mortar could demolish elaborate forts like Verdun with conventional, black-powder rounds, experiments with nitrogen-based high explosives in the Bavarian heavy artillery during the early 1880s contributed to a dramatic breakthrough during Prussian test firing in 1883. A 210-mm C-83 grenade filled with gun cotton and planted a few meters deep into the earthworks of a mock fort obliterated everything from the magazine to the gun towers. "The world held its breath," remembered one Prussian General Staff officer, for "it seemed like hundreds of millions had simply been thrown away [on useless fortresses]. Engineers on both sides of the border wrung their hands."[48]

It was far too soon, however, for the heavy artillerymen to gloat.[49] For one thing, gun cotton was a highly volatile and unstable substance, not well suited for rugged battlefield conditions. There remained the additional steep challenge of making the huge siege guns as mobile as the rest of Germany's quick-moving army. Panicky fortress engineers on both sides of the border also determined quickly that earthen layers of 2- to 5 meters provided adequate protection against C-83 grenades. Cheap and easy to install, appropriate additions were carried out by France during 1885–1886. Gun cotton tests at the Kummersdorf proving grounds (outside Berlin) showed, moreover, that 96.9% of mortar rounds fired at forts strengthened with armored turrets and reinforced concrete failed to penetrate. Present at a demonstration in 1885, the Saxon military attaché concluded that defenders would have been able to continue fighting, just as they had at Plevna. "To be sure," he added, "the effect of [some direct hits] was frightful," hurling 1000-pound chunks of the fortress into the air "like toy balls."[50] French forts between Verdun and Belfort had steel towers in place by 1887–1888. More elaborate renovations with thick, 2.5-meter reinforced concrete began in 1888. Taken together with gun cotton's other problems, it seemed clear that Germany had still not solved its fortress dilemma.

The narrower technological problem of the artillery was rever-
berating, meanwhile, in the wider world of army politics and intrigue. Beginning in January 1882, an aging, overtaxed Moltke gave
the bulk of his General Staff duties to a new quartermaster, Count
Alfred von Waldersee, commander of the Tenth Hanoverian Corps.
With a lengthy background in the artillery and cavalry, the new man
soon emerged as an avid champion of the need to pack more mobile
offensive punch with howitzers and heavy artillery. Waldersee was
seconded in this campaign by one of his aides, ex-cavalryman Alfred
von Schlieffen.[51]

Standing squarely in their path, however, was War Minister Arnold von Kameke, the army's political chief and spokesman in parliament. General Staff officers eager to promote their agendas bristled at Kameke's seemingly liberal respect for the parsimonious
wishes of the leftist Reichstag parties. In fact, the minister believed
in the necessity of maintaining good relations with parliament,
which included giving the deputies a share in military affairs.[52] Tensions with the General Staff mounted in late 1882, when Kameke
squashed Inspector General Hans von Bülow's attempt to
strengthen both artillery branches, belittling the general's warning
that foreign cannon were superior. This might be so, wrote Kameke,
"but the experience of war has taught us that such a material superiority, even if it were great as in this case, is only very seldom of
influence because it is outweighed in significance by other more
important factors."[53] Generally reluctant to alienate the Reichstag,
the war minister would be doubly resistant to do so over an apparently umimportant issue like artillery improvements. But when Kameke next tried to gloss over the artillery crisis by claiming, quite
contradictorily, that Germany's cannons were now the world's best,
Waldersee found this "inconceivable," for "every artillery officer
knows that the German artillery is on the contrary the worst in the
world except for the English."[54] Waldersee's comments were exaggerated but reflected his knowledge that C-73 cannons were inadequate in the post-Plevna era.

Waldersee seethed with anger and plotted his revenge. The controversial exchange in the Reichstag between Kameke and Eugen
Richter in January 1883 gave the General Staff's dynamic second-
in-command his chance, for Kameke's unwillingness to defend the
cavalry's honor was "most unsatisfactory"[55] to Waldersee. Compatri-
ots for the intrigue were found quickly and easily. The chief of the
king's Privy Military Cabinet, Emil von Albedyll, had worked persis-
tently since assuming office in 1871 to remove army affairs from

public, parliamentary scrutiny. He joined the conspiracy to further this end and expand his agency's influence at the expense of the rival War Ministry. Always willing to undermine a friend of parliament, moreover, Chancellor Bismarck also turned on the hapless political soldier. Kameke was gone by spring.[56]

With him went much of the power of his ministry. The personnel department—and thus all decisions over appointments and promotions—was transferred to the Military Cabinet. To the General Staff chief (or his deputy) went the privilege of direct access to the king and kaiser. Now all three chiefs had the ear of Kaiser William. Finally, Kameke's successor, the conservative Paul Bronsart von Schellendorff, agreed to a much more uncooperative role in the Reichstag: "In the political realm I will oppose with severity and determination any attempt to endanger the rights of the crown, as well as any pretension on the part of the political parties to win any influence whatsoever over the power of command."[57] The long-term significance of these changes did not lie in the further reduction of parliament's already circumscribed powers, for the Reichstag knew how to guard its constitutional rights and continued to play a major budgetary role. More important was the breakup of the administrative unity of the army as the War Ministry's predominance yielded to a three-way struggle among jealous, mutually independent power bases with overlapping and unclearly delineated competences. After 1883, feuds between the War Ministry, Military Cabinet, and General Staff "were frequent, acrimonious, and damaging to the efficiency of the army," observes historian Gordon Craig.[58] In later chapters we shall see how very true this was.

The picture we have of the German Army in the mid-1880s is not a flattering one. At the apex was a gerontocracy headed by Kaiser William, Helmuth von Moltke, and 18 aging corps commanders whom the sentimental head of state refused to retire despite Albedyll's repeated urgings. Most of these elderly generals frowned on the prospect of wartime field duty—an obvious and embarrassing failing that emboldened French revanchists.[59] Army administrative leadership was increasingly divided, moreover, after the forced resignation of Kameke. These counterproductive divisions exacerbated already existing rivalries among the three main branches of the service.

Cavalry, infantry, and artillery squabbles over military technology and appropriate tactical responses further divided the army against itself. It is significant that in all three branches, conservative factions managed to write their technophobic doctrines into regulations.

Looking to St. Privat, infantry leaders opted for massed company and battalion columns that may have been easy for commanders to control but offered tempting targets to defenders equipped with repeaters. Hoping to draw lessons from Mars-la-Tour, the men around Friedrich Karl resuscitated eighteenth-century three-wave tactics. The artillery was also split between a dominant wing and a shunned stepchild. And similarly, it was the privileged field artillery that glorified Sedan and seized most of the resources for itself. Pointing to Plevna after 1877, the promising but underfunded heavy artillery began to struggle against great odds to redeem itself.

Foreign military developments made Germany's drift toward antimodernism even more alarming. As we shall see, it was the French and (to a lesser extent) the Russians, not the Germans, who blazed the trail of modern military technology in the 1880s and 1890s. It was also the French and the Russians, not the Germans, who correctly stressed the advantages that contemporary technology lent to well-fortified defenders. But none of this mattered to the worshipers of Mars: Germany's rich neighbors may have superior equipment, weapons, technical education, and "an armor of fortresses," noted one German military writer, but their officer corps could not match Germany's in "warlike intelligence, independence, initiative, and moral strength."[60]

These developments meant that Germany's casualties were likely to be disastrously high in wartime. Observing the French maneuvers of 1878 for the German General Staff, Colmar von der Goltz was very impressed with France's determination to reverse the verdict of 1870 by modernizing. The German tendency to stick to outmoded ways worried him. It was all too easy "after great successes," he concluded, "to view ideas and means which have once led to victory as necessarily correct for all time."[61] French observers at German maneuvers in Alsace-Lorraine came to the same conclusion in 1886. The real lesson of St. Privat had been forgotten in Germany. There was "an inclination to return to antiquated battle formations."[62] Waldersee was troubled by the same attitudes. "The more distance there is between us and [our last] war, the more backward our judgment has become." He had raised his voice against these trends, "but to no avail." Yet Waldersee, the one man who should have appreciated Germany's military disadvantages in a two-front war, began to press for a "great war"[63] in the mid-1880s as the only solution to the strengthening Franco-Russian rapprochement. Had it come to blows, however, only the intervention of Mars could have prevented a terrible German defeat.

CHAPTER 3

BETWEEN PERSISTENCE AND CHANGE

*T*HE NATURAL AROMA of moist turf still hung in the air. A midday downpour had laid the dust on the Longchamp, but the martial enthusiasm of the anxious throng that packed the viewing stands had not been dampened in the least. By 3 o'clock, over 100,000 patriots had made the short journey through the Bois de Boulogne from Paris to the parade grounds. For 6 years the Republic had celebrated Bastille Day with a great military review. Because no Frenchman wanted to remember a time when it had not been so, a new tradition had been born.

No one was disappointed by 14 July 1886. The main attraction was the dashing new minister of war, General Georges Boulanger.[1] Since January, his flurry of reforms had energized the army and turned the heads of a bored populace. Military education was modernized and reorganized. Many of the exemptions and loopholes were removed from France's compulsory military service. He improved food in the mess halls, painted sentry boxes with red, white, and blue stripes; and permitted the soldiers to be men again by allowing them to grow beards. Boulanger's energy and machismo told patriots that there would be surprises for the Hun if war broke out.

Indeed France was in the midst of a remarkable military revival. From the shambles of an army left after the debacle of 1870, its generals and politicians had reconstructed an impressive force.

There would be more infantry battalions and artillery batteries in the field than the German Army could muster after mobilization, and the number of cavalry squadrons was drawing closer—385 to 465.[2] If the Germans were forced to fight on two fronts—an eventuality that the diplomatic genius of Bismarck had thus far prevented—the quantitative advantage would swing more decisively in France's favor.

Many qualitative indicators also pointed west. Whereas cavalry and artillery tacticians aped the recklessness of their German counterparts, and thus offered nothing new or better, French infantrymen had developed the most progressive tactics of the day. They broke from the company column into smaller formations that assumed a broader front in order to survive defenders' fire. In 1886, moreover, the French began to rearm with a Lebel magazine rifle that shot nearly twice as rapidly as Germany's M-71/84 Mauser. About 60,000 Gras-Kropatchek repeaters equal to the Mauser were also available for an emergency.[3] And there were other impressive technological improvements, such as state-of-the-art observation balloons and tricycles for "velocipedists" in the messenger corps. The French also replaced gun cotton with cordite, a smokeless explosive, and melinite, a stable nitrogen compound. Although the speed of mobilization remained slower than in the legendary German system, the gap was narrowing as rail capacity between Paris and fortresses on the eastern frontier tripled in less than a decade. While reserve units manned the ramparts, the nation's regular army would flank the forts in a clever defensive strategy designed to parry German offensive blows, then counterattack.[4]

Boulanger, a general of the cavalry, rode onto Longchamp atop Tunis, arguably the finest horse in France. The white plumes, gold epaulettes, turquoise blouse, purple shoulder strap, and pink breeches of his parade uniform contrasted stylishly with the jet-black muscular frame of his regimental chief drummer's mount. While everyone waited for the review to commence, Boulanger leaned slightly backward in his saddle and guided Tunis with an easy rein through a series of difficult equestrian maneuvers. Shouts of "Vive Boulanger! Vive l'armée!" mounted as the tall steed performed all commands effortlessly, halting after the last few delicate steps with one foreleg crooked circuslike in the air. After a second's pause, 20 brass bands burst into the rousing *Marche indienne*. As if on cue, Boulanger wheeled round and gave the order for his bearded warriors to march past.

The crowd worked itself up into a nationalistic frenzy. Women and men cheered and wept. After the final mock charge of the red-pantalooned troops, the people rushed past police lines onto the field. Only grudgingly allowing the general on his black horse to leave, they lingered on the Longchamp for hours. Then they jammed the Bois de Boulogne and headed into Paris for an evening of celebration.[5]

War Scares

Lieutenant Colonel Karl von Villaume, German military attaché in Paris, observed the remarkable events of Bastille Day 1886. His dispatches to the German Foreign Office had already sounded the alarm about Boulanger's political ambitions. As the moderate center crumbled, giving rise to extremes of royalism and radicalism, a military seizure of power could not be ruled out. Villaume noted with considerable suspicion that many of the soldiers passing the reviewing stand gave an "eyes right" to Boulanger, ignoring the president and premier on the left. The general's popularity shot up in the weeks after July 14 as local rifle, gymnastic, and patriotic societies adopted him as the nation's savior. In the autumn, Villaume warned that posters were depicting Boulanger at the head of French columns, marching east against Germany, and that he was actually plotting such vengeful action.[6]

Although it was deeply troubling in Berlin, "Boulangerism" was just one of many inextricably interrelated developments that were weakening German security. France's militant resurgence necessarily directed Berlin's attention to the great Russian colossus—for here, at Germany's back, the situation was also threatening. The Russo-Turkish War and subsequent Congress of Berlin (1877–1878) had foiled Russia's aggressive designs in the Balkans. The nationalists' dream of a great Russian-controlled Bulgaria, largely frustrated at Berlin, was further undermined in 1886 when upstart Bulgarian leaders ended Moscow's manipulative influence in Sofia. The unacceptable outcome moved Pan-Slav publicists like Mikhail Katkov to advocate an end to the constraining influences of the Three Emperors' League. Russian hawks pointed angrily to Vienna and Berlin, where parliaments deliberated increases in armaments. For the belligerent supporters of Katkov's "free hand" policy, there was only one viable alternative: They established contacts with Georges Boulanger and urged a French alliance on Tsar Alexander III.[7]

The dispatches from Paris and St. Petersburg alarmed Otto von Bismarck. By 1886 the septuagenarian had ruled Prussia and Germany for nearly a quarter century. The defeat of Austria and France, the creation of a mighty Second Reich, the compromise settlement with parliament, and an ingenious web of treaties and alliances that anchored Germany's security were well behind him now. Confident in early 1885 that the peace of Europe would hold, Bismarck was expressing his first doubts when Boulanger took office a year later: "The stronger the chauvinistic element becomes among all parties in France, the more important it is for us to ascertain Austria's position . . . [should we] become involved in a war with the French Republic."[8] Ascertaining the Russian position was equally important, but this grew increasingly unpredictable as the autumn of 1886 approached. By November, Bismarck seemed to know that control over events in Europe was slipping out of his aging hands. Waldersee, who spoke with Bismarck frequently, was usually skeptical when the great statesman showed any feeling or emotion, perceiving some ruse or subterfuge to manipulate the army. But three times that fall the deputy chief of the General Staff noticed genuine worry: "The more time I find to think quietly about things, the clearer it is to me that the chancellor has become uncertain about his policies." There were signs that Bismarck was "concerned that his [life's] work could collapse."[9]

On New Year's Day 1887, Waldersee wrote in his diary that everyone around him believed a war between Germany and France was "unavoidable." With Russia joining France and Austria backing Germany, "it must become a world war."[10] For over a year he had pondered these possibilities, concluding with increasing conviction and resolve that this was Germany's bright moment. Although France and Russia were preparing for action, Waldersee was confident that neither country would be ready to attack for a year or so. In his anxious, troubled mind it was only logical that Germany should launch a preemptive strike without delay. Waldersee wanted to shift Germany's strategic emphasis from east to west. Only 6 German corps would assist the Austrian Army in a decisive winter offensive into Poland. Then, when the French attempted to exploit the eastern campaign with an invasion of the Rhineland, Germany's remaining 12 corps would repel the enemy's 18 corps and crush them with a brutal counteroffensive. Moltke accepted this revised plan in February 1887.[11]

Waldersee had calculated that Germany would win because of its unmatched combination of high intelligence and superior technology. The heavy artillery possessed high explosive rounds that could destroy all field fortifications, as well as permanent forts not reinforced with steel and concrete. In 1884, moreover, the infantry had decided to procure a magazine repeating rifle. The M-71/84 Mauser went into production in 1885, and by early 1887 the work of rearming had passed the halfway point. The new guns were held secretly in army arsenals to enhance the element of surprise.[12] But his calculations were far too sanguine. In the east, Russia had re-armed its infantry with the best single-shot, breech-loading rifle in Europe—and the Austrians had no magazine rifle to trump it. Learning from Gorko's raid of 1877, moreover, the Russian cavalry now possessed a long-distance strike capability that would either up-set enemy operations or at the very least tie down large bodies of German cavalry in Poland or Galicia. Similarly, the sheer size of the Russian Army—its standing forces were greater than the combined Austrian and Germany armies—should have given Waldersee pause.[13]

There were also huge problems on a hypothetical western front. Germany had a technological lead with the M-71/84 rifle, but the advantage was quickly swinging back to France as it equipped its corps with Lebels. The French rearmament process would run its course by 1889, about 18 months after Germany completed all 780,000 of its M-71/84s.[14] There were three other considerations that Waldersee ignored: The French field artillery outnumbered the German, its cannons were fitted with new breech and chamber mechanisms that facilitated a more rapid fire than the C-73s, and the field capabilities of the German heavy artillery were purely the-oretical.[15] Detracting still more from Germany's chances were its outmoded field tactics. Thus one corps commander warned the dep-uty chief that German infantrymen "will all be shot down like a nation of partridges."[16]

But Waldersee saw only brilliant opportunities. This martial blindness is not easy to interpret, for he was aware of many of the facts discussed above. One explanation lies in the general's notori-ous pugnaciousness. His world was full of enemies. At home were liberals, socialists, Jews, and Freemasons; abroad was a Europe full of jealous, grasping foes. Waldersee suspected them all of something sinister—a near-paranoid mind-set that clouded his vision and found ultimate expression in a belligerent desire to strike out in many directions at once. For all of the respect he professed for modern technology, moreover, Moltke's quartermaster was more a product of the army prejudices of his day than he liked to admit. Waldersee thought that technology was necessary, yes but no real soldier would postpone the day of reckoning because of alleged technical deficiencies. For someone who saw the world in this way, the caution of others was equated with an unmanly timidity he could not respect. Speaking with assembled corps commanders in January 1887, for instance, Waldersee complained that he found only two "whom I trust are eager to go to war." Crown Prince Frederick had also expressed "something like fear about a war against France." Even worse was the fact that the heir to the throne "did not speak very highly about our army." Faced with such alleged unsoldierly bearing at the top, Waldersee bided his time, negotiating in the Military Cabinet and War Ministry to replace aging corps commanders with fresh talent at the outbreak of war.[17]

In the following months, the danger of war subsided but did not pass. For one thing, Boulanger's cabinet colleagues maneuvered him out of office, forcing "General Revenge" to take his message to the French people. In June 1887, moreover, Bismarck offered Russia a "reinsurance" treaty to replace the Three Emperors' League. Each nation pledged benevolent neutrality if the other waged war—nullified, however, if Germany attacked France or Russia attacked Austria. In addition, Germany promised moral and diplomatic support to Russia in the Balkans. As Bismarck's son, Herbert, observed, however, the treaty did not guarantee peace. "It puts some pressure on the Tsar and should, if matters become serious, keep the Russians off our necks six to eight weeks longer than otherwise would be the case." And that, he added soberly, "is worth something."[18] Indeed Russo-German tensions soon flared up again over Bulgaria. Alexander III's visit to Berlin in November 1887 barely papered over the widening rift between the two empires.[19]

Waldersee was now determined to push for preventive war. In an impressive round of politicking—especially impressive given army divisiveness at top levels—he was able to convince the heads of the General Staff, Military Cabinet, and War Ministry—Moltke, Albedyll, and Bronsart von Schellendorff, respectively—of the wisdom of a winter campaign in the east. Such a powerful coalition of army leaders usually had its way in Prussia. On 17 December 1887, the four generals held a "council of war" with Kaiser William. The decrepit old monarch had recently nodded off in the midst of an important military briefing. Then during the tsar's visit he had demonstrated what struck Waldersee as pathetic weakness before the enemy. "If you want to wage war against us in alliance with France, then you will be stronger and can destroy us," he told Alexander, "but believe me, Europe will not stand for it." With the crown prince dying slowly of cancer in Italy, Waldersee thought it advisable to bring along his warmongering protégé, Prince William, as a representative of the future of the monarchy. To his credit, the kaiser made it clear that he preferred peace. However, he agreed with all of Moltke's recommendations for troop dispositions in the event of a two-front war, including negotiations with Austria to coordinate the two armies.[20]

Bismarck believed less and less during the winter of 1887–1888 that peace would hold. But he refused to succumb to the seemingly inevitable, seeing no more wisdom in preventive war than suicide for fear of dying. And he absolutely refused to tolerate military interference in responsible civilian affairs. In a confrontational meeting with Moltke, Waldersee, and Albedyll on 20 December 1887, Herbert Bismarck, acting for his father, succeeded in backing Moltke away from the brink. The kaiser professed his peaceful intentions the following day. Having split the unity of the generals, Bismarck proceeded to lambaste the "war party" in the government-controlled press.[21]

To prevent what could have been a disastrous war, moreover, Bismarck intensified a strategy that he had begun to use during earlier crises. The veteran politician who brooked no interference in civilian affairs was not above meddling in army business if he deemed it necessary. Well informed about military matters—and fully convinced that discretion was the better part of valor—his approach was to point out embarrassing army weaknesses in order to dampen martial enthusiasm. Early in the Boulanger crisis, for instance, Bismarck inquired in the War Ministry about the old age and cavalry background of Germany's generals, implying that the French factored this into their victory calculations. The whole affair incensed Waldersee, but his own efforts to bring up young blood proved that Bismarck was right. The chancellor resorted to this successful tactic shortly after the infamous "council of war" by raising the crucial issue of infantry rifles. Seemingly better informed than the General Staff, he argued for a two-year postponement of war until Germany could replace the M-71/84 with an 8-mm rifle equal to France's Lebel repeater. Germany's inadequate rifle factories and powder works necessitated this lengthy delay.

This revelation placed the army in an extremely awkward position. Government arsenals had just finished producing 780,000 magazine rifles, each capable of shooting 26 bullets per minute. For over a year, however, rumors had abounded that a new French rifle was superior. Tests at Spandau during the winter of 1887–1888 proved the wisdom of the chancellor's counsel, for the new small-caliber design was indeed quicker, firing 43 bullets per minute. Conservatives such as War Minister Bronsart von Schellendorff reminded critics that better rifle technology had not produced victory for France in 1870, but prudent voices in the army urged restraint and delay.[22]

The spring of 1888 brought new challenges. In March, old Emperor William finally breathed his last. Frederick III followed his father to the grave in May, bringing 29-year-old William II to the throne. Moltke, having desired retirement for many years, now yielded office to Waldersee, the spiritus rector of preventive war. The young kaiser had been close to his new General Staff chief for many years, tending to see the same world full of enemies when he surveyed the domestic and international scene. Bismarck saw black, foreboding events. "The young man wants a war with Russia and would like to draw his sword right away if possible," complained the tiring chancellor. "Woe to my grandchildren," he added prophetically.[23]

From the beginning of his reign, the headstrong emperor demonstrated an independent streak that soon began to worry Waldersee. Without consulting the generals, for instance, William undertook a purge of many corps and division commanders, replacing them with loyal favorites. Eventually, Waldersee and the new chief of the Military Cabinet, Wilhelm von Hahnke, regained control of the process, but there were soon other causes of worry. The General Staff chief noticed a tendency on the kaiser's part to play at soldiering, which manifested itself in a superficial, useless preoccupation with uniforms and an exaggerated reliance on massed cavalry charges. By the late summer of 1888, we find a far less sanguine Waldersee, confessing to his diary that it was military nonsense for the cavalry's star to be rising, the artillery's sinking, and infantry firepower ignored. Amid feverish efforts that autumn to retool state arsenals for a new magazine rifle, increase cannon production, and improve heavy artillery capability against reinforced fortifications, he lectured the impetuous kaiser on the undeniable technological progress of the French army.[24]

Bismarck now pressed his advantage. During a briefing by Waldersee in November 1888, he acted very annoyed about the prospect of going before the Reichstag with demands for more cannons. Waldersee noted that the chancellor appeared to be much more anxious about France's smokeless melinite artillery grenade and "great progress in the technological area." Later, after Germany's high-explosive capability improved, Bismarck professed to have sleepless nights over France's alleged 500-cannon advantage. The infuriating implication was that the army's artillery requests had been too low! No less exasperating was his continued manipulation of the rifle issue. When Waldersee told him of plans to accelerate the stockpiling of the infantry's new 8-mm M-88 by subcontracting with American rifle factories, Bismarck expressed grave misgivings that the French might attack if they learned about Germany's act of desperation.[25] By April 1889, the bellicose General Staff chief came surprisingly close to an admission of political defeat. "We must use the great talent and worldwide reputation of the chancellor to maintain peace for a while longer [until] our armaments are ready."[26]

From 1886 until 1889, war scares brought Germany and Europe to the brink of war. For much of this time, two factors worked to avert a cataclysm. First was the desire of old Kaiser William to live out his remaining years in peace. Second was Bismarck's belief that Germany's interests were better served by peace than by war. Affecting the pacific stance of both men, however, was genuine anxiety that Germany, so recently victorious in one war, could conceivably be crushed in the next. Crown Prince Frederick, surrounded by some of Germany's most progressive generals, expressed similar fears, and with good reason—in addition to its many qualitative advantages, France could field an army of 2,633,000 soldiers in 1886, a 483,000-man edge over Germany. If Russia joined France, Germany's quantitative deficit would stretch to 1,168,000, even with Austria at its side. Moreover, Russia had started to narrow the technological gap with Germany in 1889 by rearming its infantry with Lebel magazine rifles and introducing 210- and 230-mm mortars to the field artillery. The French introduced heavy field howitzers a few years later.[27]

Aged Field Marshal Helmuth von Moltke was not as pessimistic about a German defeat, but he had abandoned hopes for repeating the quick victories of 1866 and 1870. If it came to blows, he told Herbert von Bismarck, "it could easily become a Thirty Years War." Waldersee boasted that the war he was preparing would "be the most furious that has ever been waged."[28] The postponed day of reckoning, he thought, would come in 1890.

Blessed were the peacemakers who prevented him from seeing the results. As we shall now see, the infantry did not really solve its rifle problems until 1899. Adding to army difficulties was the fact that outmoded conservative tactics continued to haunt the infantry,

as well as the cavalry. Even more alarming, the field artillery continued to sink in effectiveness and preparedness throughout the 1890s.
Neither the field artillery nor the heavy artillery, moreover, had
solved the problem of France's now-modernized fortress wall. When
the new century dawned, Germany was still not ready to wage war
successfully.

New Bottles, Old Wine

The heyday of Frederician horse tactics waned not long after the
great Konitz maneuvers of 1881. Prince Friedrich Karl's optimistic
final report led to repeated summer exercises to restore eighteenth-
century glory to German riders. With every passing season, however,
the prince harbored more doubts about the feasibility and advisa-
bility of successive charges of large bodies of cavalry. Indeed, his
confidence may have been undermined by the Reichstag's embarrassing attacks. In June 1884, insiders reported that little significance was attached in cavalry circles to the once highly touted lessons of Konitz. Friedrich Karl's death in June 1885, followed months
later by the fatal illness of Frederician enthusiast Otto von Kaehler,
signaled the end of a bold experiment.[29]

Their passing opened the door wider to the enemies of three-
wave tactics. One was General Gottlieb von Haeseler, former adjutant of Friedrich Karl and now commander of the Thirty-first Cavalry
Brigade in Strassburg. Having served at Mars-la-Tour, where all available horses had been thrown immediately into the fray, Haeseler
opposed what he considered to be an overly cautious tactic of holding back regiments for a second and third charge. Once the enemy
was located, there could be just one order for German cavalrymen:
"Amass the entire detachment!"[30] Another was Karl Ludwig von
Schlotheim, commander of the Eleventh Corps in Kassel. A "traditionalist" like Haeseler, he favored crushing charges of mounted
warriors but frowned on the anachronistic intricacies and complex-
ities of Frederician battlefield methods. Schlotheim simplified tactics
at the Buxtehude maneuvers in 1885, massing the bulk of his regiments into one great shock wave. To the horror of three-wave pur-
ists, the second and third lines were downgraded to minor support
and reserve functions.[31]

These simpler tactics found the backing in April 1886 of a special commission that had been assigned the task of revising cavalry
regulations. It was headed, not surprisingly, by Schlotheim and in-

cluded Brigadier General von Rosenberg, one of the chief opponents of Frederician tactics from the 1870s; Gebhard von Krosigk, head of the army's Riding Institute; and Haeseler. The new regulations varied Schlotheim's "three unequal wave" methods for use in different battlefield situations. The shock tactics introduced at Buxtehude would be employed against infantry and cavalry, for instance, whereas a thin first line, trailed by waves of massed squadrons, was recommended against artillery. In the same spirit of simplification, the commission also abolished many of the intricate echelon formations, difficult right-angle and diagonal maneuvers, and the complicated battlefield command signals of the older system. Haeseler put the new regulations to the test during cavalry exercises at Hagenau in August 1886, then later that summer at imperial army maneuvers near Strassburg.[32]

These reforms angered the now-leaderless Fredericians.[33] Claiming to speak for all top officers who had accumulated large-unit cavalry experience in the maneuvers of the 1870s, General Walther von Löe, commander of Eighth Corps in Koblenz, bemoaned the violation of Karl von Schmidt's principle of three equal brigade-strength waves of attacking horse. Too much had been made of Schlotheim's charges at Buxtehude, which in Löe's opinion had not succeeded. Given the negative effects that he attributed to the 1886 regulations, it is remarkable that Löe still considered Germany's cavalry "the most advanced branch" of the army. The Rhenish corps commander believed that the cavalry's development in recent decades had been based on actual combat lessons from 1870—all of this in stark contrast to the "suffering"[34] infantry and artillery.

While the older generation of generals quibbled over the best path to certain glory, younger cavalrymen shook their heads. Reflecting what was certainly an increasing sentiment among junior officers, Friedrich von Bernhardi, a brash squadron leader in Düsseldorf, remembered the 1886 regulations as "contradicting all modern views" because they assumed "that cavalry had to fight on horseback, and mostly against other mounted horsemen, completely ignoring the fact that weapons in the meantime had developed extraordinary capabilities—and that the enemy cavalry was free to use them."[35] Like many of his kind, Bernhardi was swayed by the awesome firepower and willingness to fight on foot displayed by the Russian cavalry in 1877. He made sure that the 100 horsemen under him would be ready for the modern war that appeared increasingly likely as 1886 yielded to 1887.

Waldersee, an ex-cavalryman himself, shared these concerns. Indeed, the letters of his old friend Löe must have raised his eyebrows more than once. The deputy chief of the General Staff was incredulous that the cavalry had managed to revive itself after accomplishing very little during the Wars of Unification. He rated Friedrich Karl's abilities as a cavalry general very low and considered Schmidt and Kaehler one-sided and unimpressive. He was astonished, moreover, that the cavalry had adopted such unrealistic and impractical regulations in 1876 while the sobering wartime experience of 1870 was still so fresh. "[The regulations] can only have been invented by small people and parade ground heroes."[36]

Waldersee's assessment of the 1886 regulations was apparently no higher, for in early 1887 he convinced the War Ministry to issue special "field service orders" for the cavalry. Should war break out, each infantry division was allotted one cavalry regiment for reconnaissance, screening, and flank protection duties. Even Young Turk cavalry reformers resented the "scattering" of 54 "division-cavalry" regiments—nearly half of the army's horse—for "internal infantry service."[37] The army also planned to mobilize 8 free-standing cavalry divisions—the remaining 62 regiments—but the special orders disparaged the cavalry's chances in an age of rapid-firing rifles and smokeless-powder cannons. Without the cover of gunsmoke to conceal them, squadrons should use the protection offered by terrain whenever possible, accelerate to a gallop when in open country, and never charge an unweakened infantry position. Despite the obvious wisdom of the orders, Waldersee had no faith in the prudence of the Schlotheims and the Löes. Thus, he wrote in the autumn of 1888 that the war, which was evidently approaching, would destroy Germany's cavalry.[38]

As explained above, however, the clouds of war blew over before unloading their deadly rain. The prolongation of peacetime afforded pragmatic elements in the mounted corps an opportunity to assert themselves. One was Major Georg Friedrich von Kleist, a cavalryman who valued the strategic role of patrols above the seemingly suicidal tactical mission of the past. His writings prompted large-scale reconnaissance exercises in 1890 and 1891. The enthusiasm of junior officers like Bernhardi for dismounted fighting techniques soon exposed the need for shooting practice and marksmanship guidelines. With cavalry officers beginning to frequent infantry ranges to shoot their M-88 carbines, the mounted corps saw the need to write three successive shooting manuals in 1888, 1890, and 1894. Others remembered Gourko's devastating raid of 1877, arguing that cavalrymen could do far more destructive work in the age of nitrogen-based explosives. Accordingly, new demolition guidelines were issued in 1888, then revised in 1893.[39] All of these innovations and novelties were reflected in provisional cavalry regulations published in 1893.

Over the next two years, however, old-school cavalrymen fought back. Their rising influence was felt at autumn maneuvers. Almost without exception, the cavalrymen of the opposing units ignored their reconnaissance missions and rushed into battle against one another, leaving the infantry on both sides exposed and uninformed about enemy troop movements and artillery dispositions. Then there were the rousing cavalry charges. In September 1893, for instance, Gebhard von Krosigk amassed 12 regiments of horse for a glorious attack; then the emperor, not to be outdone, attempted to repeat the feat.[40] In 1894, similarly, General Hans von Plessen, head of the kaiser's Imperial Headquarters, led his cavalry division over 1,000 meters of open ground in a frontal attack against fresh infantry units. Belying his underlying approval, William criticized Plessen for issuing the order but praised him "for the way it was executed."[41]

Reactionary tendencies were even more in evidence by 1895. Early that year the Military Society heard Major General Moritz von Bissing, commander of the Fourth Guard Cavalry Brigade—and very close personally to Kaiser William II—advocate crushing attacks of 25 regiments. Not since the Battle of Nations in 1813 had 10,000 German horsemen arrayed themselves for one mighty charge. The same spirit reigned at cavalry maneuvers in August when Bredow's "Death Ride of Mars-la-Tour" was reenacted for the emperor.[42] These trends culminated in September with the issuance of a finalized version of cavalry regulations.[43] There was less emphasis now on reconnaissance and dismounted fighting, but an entire section missing in the 1893 draft had been added on the cavalry's tactical battle role. Moreover, traditionalists of the older generation pointed with great pride, to the inclusion of Schlotheim's "three unequal wave" shock tactics.[44]

Knowing that performance tends to reflect rehearsal, insiders worried that the cavalry—as indeed the entire army—was not served well by tactics that were so out of touch with the times.[45] Indeed, there seemed to be a lot of "old wine in new bottles" in the mid-1890s.[46] Had anything really changed since Konitz and Buxtehude?

Sigismund von Schlichting received command of the First Guard Infantry Division in June 1885. He had served as chief of staff of the Prussian Guard Corps until March of the previous year, then a brief stint with the Fifteenth Division in Cologne before returning to the Guards Corps. Although it is true that divisional command was a coveted position, his abrupt goings and comings in peacetime have all the earmarks of high-level intrigue. Indeed, Schlichting's reforming zeal had made impressive friends, not just enemies; one friend was General von Winterfeld, commander of the First Guard Cavalry Division and personal adjutant to Crown Prince Frederick.[47] These were important allies during the twilight years of William I, as official Berlin, even crusty political veterans like Otto von Bismarck, maneuvered themselves into positions of favor with the emperor-to-be.[48] Schlichting was in print again soon after arriving back in Berlin, urging the army to bring its offensive tactics into line with the lethal weapons available to defenders. Aging Guard Corps Commander Alexander von Pape was "too broken down" to stand in the way of his innovating subordinates.[49]

Schlichting demonstrated new methods of attacking fortified defenders after the conclusion of Guard Corps maneuvers in October 1885. Set against the backdrop of Plevna, the completion of the French forts, and the growth of infantry firepower, the planning staff simulation, known as a "staff ride," was an attempt to build on and revise those tactics that Schlichting had first unveiled in 1879. It pitted a Red Army moving west from Berlin against Blue Army, which was using Spandau Fortress to shield its positions farther west and south of the city. The attackers slowly and systematically closed the ring by exploiting the cover of darkness, digging trenches and foxholes, and drawing on powerful artillery support. Troops moved forward position by position, dispersed in wedge and echelon formation, never in massed waves. Schlichting drew officers for his exercise from the different army branches, further enhancing the educational value by inviting scores of observers. Afterward he published a pamphlet that drew the salient lesson: "A planned defense must be confronted by a planned attack."[50] The autumn Guard Corps maneuvers of 1886 were followed by another brochure that pounded out the same basic message—that infantry attacks like those at St. Privat and Plevna were suicidal in the technological age. He reinforced the point in the fall of 1887 with a 5-day exercise devoted specifically to the lessons of Plevna.[51]

If war reared its head during the Boulanger crisis, Schlichting, Winterfeld, and fellow travelers in the Guard Corps wanted German infantrymen to be prepared for modern combat. But the new ideas were just beginning to spread through the top echelons of the command structure. Thus, the General Staff issued special instructions to all corps and division commanders in 1885; the instructions drew a distinction for the first time between company column shock tactics, to be employed when opposing armies stumbled on one another, and the dispersed order of battle required when assaulting entrenched positions. Despite the fact that massed waves of attackers were "forbidden" in the latter situation, staff officers sympathetic to the new ruling complained about corps commanders who ignored it lest they violate official infantry regulations, unchanged since 1873. Even when division and corps leadership observed the instructions, high officer transfers at lower levels ensured a steady flow of the old ideas, and thus constantly undermined the work of reform.[52]

As Europe's crisis worsened, Walther von Löe expressed his deep concerns about the army to General Staff Quartermaster Alfred von Waldersee. After the two observed Wilhelm von Heuduck's Fifteenth Corps during maneuvers in 1886, Löe predicted that if the German infantry attacked in this outmoded way, "then it [will be] torn apart by the opposing artillery" before it reached enemy lines. "This is no slap at Fifteenth Corps," he added, "for it is no better anywhere else, at least not in my [corps], despite the fact that every officer has worked in this direction."[53] A year later he was sure that Germany's footsoldiers "will all be shot down like a nation of partridges." Löe was contemptuous of colleagues who believed that past glories would translate into future victories and found little solace in the fact that foreigners continued to be impressed. "Nowadays everyone is still much more afraid of us than we really deserve."[54] It is small wonder that Löe used every opportunity to counsel his Hotspur friend—as tactfully as possible—to keep swords sheathed.[55]

Differences of opinion over tactics turned polemical in late 1887, just as the Bulgarian crisis and a Russian arms buildup brought Europe to the brink. Jacob Meckel had observed Schlichting's return to favor while serving as a military adviser in Japan. Upset by what struck him as a deterioration of Prussia's long, glorious attacking tradition, he published *A Midsummer Night's Dream* shortly before assuming regimental command in Wesel. Meckel's tract indicted the new tactical theories and praised the realism of advancing in one powerful wave. Picking up the challenge, Schlichting's camp lambasted in the *Military Weekly* the "crude reality" of this approach. The editors of this prestigious army journal kept the final word for themselves when, in February 1888, they doubted whether dispersed squads of 15 to 20 men would have enough punch for a breakthrough or adequate strength to resist counterattacks. The authors favored shifting back into massed company columns for the final charge into enemy lines.[56]

Surrounded by critics of the status quo like Winterfeld and Schlichting, Crown Prince Frederick also worried about Germany's chances in a war.[57] It was no surprise, therefore, that the ascension of Frederick to the throne in March 1888 led to immediate efforts to revamp infantry regulations. Frederick allowed Winterfeld to appoint the reform commission, with the result that Schlichting became its dominant voice. Finalized in June, the new regulations restricted the old shock formations to those rare instances when defenders had no time for preparations. Normally, company columns would shift into skirmish lines at about 1,500 to 1,600 meters, then into randomly dispersed battle groups at 600 to 800 meters, firing at will rather than in volleys. Assaulting units relied on intense artillery support, foxholes, and the cover of darkness, if necessary taking two or three days to close the distance to a few hundred meters. Only after the dispersed battle groups had established superior firepower over a weakened defender would the final charge occur. Significantly enough, all tactical decisions—even the formation chosen for the last rush forward—were delegated to squad, file, company, battalion, and regimental leaders on the battlefield. Thus, the final attack might feature some units in tight traditional order with trumpets blaring and drums beating as others chose to remain dispersed. The so-called delegated tactics of the 1888 regulations were their hallmark—as well as their most controversial element.[58]

The ascension of William II to the throne that spring did not undermine Schlichting's reform. Although the emperor later favored traditional infantry tactics, the appointment of his old brigade commander in the Guards Corps, Wilhelm von Hahnke, as head of the Military Cabinet ensured that for now innovators would be favored as corps commanders were retired and replaced. Hahnke was loyal to the reformist ideas of his Guard Corps commander, Schlichting, who received the Fourteenth Corps in Karlsruhe. Hahnke's advice to the emperor was seconded by Waldersee in 1888–1889 as five additional corps, including the prestigious Guard and Third Brandenburgian commands, went to members of the Winterfeld-Schlichting clique, and two more went to sympathizers.[59]

When the warmongering Waldersee expressed frustration that the sad state of infantry tactics had not been more quickly reversed by all of the new men, Löe attempted to explain why the turnaround required more time.[60] The vast majority of the army's division, brigade, and regimental commanders were at best captains with 200 men in 1870. Then came two decades of peacetime drills, "which [were] absolutely worthless for combat." As the captains moved up through the ranks, they received "the highest praise" for deploying correctly and advancing in three waves. Realistic maneuvers in the countryside took a backseat to "virtuosity on the parade ground." So where was the army to find the kind of "leadership potential" it needed for today's top-level commanders? The "sinning" would continue indefinitely until the regulations sunk into "the flesh and blood of the troops."[61]

But the infantry's problems went beyond the understandable difficulty of breaking with old routines. Scattered throughout all levels of command were officers who simply opposed the regulations of 1888 and "in no way fell silent" with their beliefs. Indeed "a movement went through the army"[62] against new-fangled ways of fighting that were seen as a step backward. Given the official sanction that Schlichting's methods had won, this opposition was limited at first to private correspondence and dinner table politics. But the level of dissent was significant enough to warrant defensive brochures in 1891 by Schlichting and Bronsart von Schellendorff. The old traditionalist and former minister of war, now commander of First Corps (East Prussia), had finally broken with fellow old-timers who could not divorce themselves from the misinterpreted lessons of 1870. The so-called regulation attack of former days "is actually nothing more than a huge interference by top command into the detailed work of lower-level leaders." Such assaults were only possible on level drill fields; would not succeed in combat, even on flat terrain; and were therefore "totally useless and harmful on the vast majority of battlefields."[63]

These semiofficial publications had no noticeable effect on the diehard opposition, as seen by the ongoing struggle between persistence and change at Imperial Army maneuvers. Bavarian observers noted in 1891, for instance, that Prussian brigade commanders were so intent on coordinating the attack themselves that they marched into battle with the first wave. Although the assault succeeded, the brigadiers shunned the wisdom of regulations by undermining the initiative of lower-level officers. In the process of staying close, they also lost sight of the whole tactical situation. Two years later, however, Schlichting shone after his division counterattacked, brilliantly employing dispersed formations and delegated tactics. His regiments were so spread out that they occupied a front normally broad enough for a division.

Although he was singled out for praise by the kaiser in 1893, Schlichting was only a temporary hero. Thus, *Löbell's Annual Report* noted in 1894 that opponents of the 1888 regulations were beginning to gain the upper hand, forcing Schlichting's adherents to admit privately, later openly on the maneuver grounds, that compact battlefield formations had their place. Thus in 1895 William led two entire corps tightly massed into battle. Because the bullets were not real—and he was, after all, the emperor—William and his men miraculously avoided being "shot down like a nation of partridges." In 1896, moreover, Baron von Hodenberg, commander of Twelfth Corps (Saxony), led his men in densely packed formation against dug-in artillery on high ground. This time the referees declared one of his two divisions knocked out of action. Only the kaiser, it seemed, was allowed to perform miracles. But again in 1897, *Löbell's Annual Report* observed an even stronger tendency of infantry units—entire divisions—to advance en masse.[64]

The effectiveness and preparedness of the infantry were further weakened by defects in the M-88 magazine rifle. The new weapon had been designed hurriedly, in the anxiety of successive war scares, then rushed into production in June 1889. The state's three gun factories turned out nearly 1 million pieces by the end of 1890. A private firm, Ludwig Löwe & Company, produced additional hundreds of thousands in a bid to meet Waldersee's deadlines for putting Germany on a war footing.[65] After the infantry was fully reequipped in 1891, however, technical difficulties surfaced with the M-88. The magazine and firing mechanisms possessed "childhood diseases"[66] that prevented soldiers from taking full advantage of the weapon's semiautomatic features. Continued tinkering throughout the decade could not obviate the necessity of starting over with a new design, the M-98, which went into production in 1899.

Factional politics also stood in the way of enhanced infantry firepower. Although the 1888 regulations prescribed firing back during the advance, a number of highly placed officers opposed this tactic in the belief that valuable time would be lost.[67] This view eventually prevailed, as shown by the preponderance of commanders at maneuvers in 1895 who ordered their men not to return fire lest the pace of the advance be slowed.[68] Similar concerns moved the Prussian War Ministry to reduce the daily allotment of bullets in wartime to 1870 levels. The rationale was to reduce marching weight and increase mobility, but incredulous insiders wondered "what good it does the infantry to perfect weapons if it is not issued enough ammunition to make corresponding use of them."[69] Although logic was on their side, the Prussian General Staff and the Prussian and Bavarian shooting schools were unable to reverse this ruling. The schools also waged a systematic campaign throughout the 1890s to train cadre after cadre of officers in the best shooting techniques, as well as the most appropriate tactical formations to employ in the age of semiautomatic rifle fire. It did not augur well for the infantry, however, that as late as 1898 instructors still had to preach against company columns as "the most disadvantageous formation for frontal attacks over flat terrain."[70]

Indeed, by this time the controversy over infantry tactics was growing more public and polemical. Pointed articles first appeared in the *Military Weekly* in 1893–1894,[71] but it was the forced retirement of Schlichting in 1896 that intensified matters. The astonished general believed that he had been ousted by "mechanical three-wave tacticians" with influence in high places.[72] He had "swept before his own door," trusting in the collective effort of 18 corps commanders "to clean the whole common sidewalk." Training Fourteenth Corps according to the new regulations was not enough, however, for "things looked different up and down the army's street."[73] His comments were testimony to a situation that the literature on the German Army has largely passed over—the remarkable autonomy of corps commanders to practice the tactics they preferred.[74] Unless the kaiser imposed uniformity, as William I had done with infantry assault tactics in 1873 and 1883, corps commanders were free, for all intents and purposes, to interpret or even ignore official regulations when training their regiments. As we shall see in chapter 6, the function of imperial maneuvers as a proving ground for rival tactical schools based on the corps commands, and the emperor's relationship to these struggles, was growing more controversial as the twentieth century drew near.

With time to write, the bitter pensioner published an elaboration and defense of the new tactics. His opponents wrote three counterattacks in 1897, inducing Schlichting to reply the following year. He was also at work on a detailed tome, drawing on the exercise and maneuver experience of his eight years in Karlsruhe. In print by 1899, Schlichting's three-volume *Tactical and Strategic Principles of the Present* became the bible of progressive tactics for commanders who saw the folly of concentrating forces in front of the enemy's rapid-firing guns. His detractors now redoubled their polemical efforts, criticizing the alleged chaos of delegated tactics and pleading for more battlefield control and more offensive punch over the final few hundred meters. The real folly, they argued, was Schlichting's casualty-shy attempt to avoid the unavoidable losses of war.

Largely unnoticed by either side, the army introduced machine guns at maneuvers in September 1899.[75] One month later, the Boer War broke out in South Africa. The feud over tactics would soon worsen.

The war scares of 1886–1888 caught Germany's cannoneers in an alarming state of disarray. As tension mounted in Europe over Boulanger and Bulgaria, reports reached Julius von Voigts-Rhetz, inspector general of artillery in Berlin, that the French had hundreds more cannons. The prospect of losing the edge that had produced victory at Sedan moved Voigts-Rhetz to petition army command for a significant artillery expansion.[76] Included in the request was a bid to modernize, as well as to expand. Tests of the early 1880s with shrapnel shot out of C-73 cannons failed because shell trajectory was too flat to ensure proximity detonation with faulty time fuses. Consequently, many field artillerists wanted to replace the C-73 with a 120-mm howitzer light enough to be wheeled into action by regular six-horse teams.[77] Its higher trajectory would increase the likelihood that shrapnel rounds would explode directly over the enemy. Therefore, Voigts-Rhetz requested this new gun as the standard field piece of the artillery.

The petition generated tremendous controversy. Hotspurs like Prince William, son of the crown prince, were appalled that Germany lacked the numerical advantage required for the enveloping offensive tactics boasted of by artillery chauvinists. Eager for quick breakthroughs, Waldersee and his aide, Alfred von Schlieffen, also lined up behind Voigts-Rhetz. On the other side were field artillerists who had pushed aside the traditionalists and their bronze smooth-bore anachronisms in the 1860s, then marched to Paris in 1870 with the revolutionary rifled cannons. They simply could not imagine a weapon superior to the C-73. Voigts-Rhetz, they felt, should recall the wisdom of his predecessor, Podbielski, who had successfully resisted howitzers in 1877.[78]

Deserted by the general inspector, C-73 champions found allies in the Artillery Department of the Prussian War Ministry; they were backed, in turn, by infantryman Bronsart von Schellendorff. Indeed the war minister looked on more cannons as "unnecessary."[79] Battles were won by attacking infantry battalions in close-range fire fights. Magazine rifles were a very important element of victory, but even this technology—not to mention artillery—paled in comparison to talented battlefield command, innovative tactics, and the morale of the troops who pressed forward. "One can also have *too much* artillery,"[80] Bronsart liked to say. That the General Staff backed Voigts-Rhetz was another good reason for Bronsart to oppose him, for the minister was increasingly wary about protecting his own turf. Thus, in 1887 the War Ministry rejected the request for more cannons and only grudgingly agreed to the idea of testing 120-mm howitzers.[81]

Voigts-Rhetz repeated his demands for expansion in May 1888. The ascension of William II a month later enhanced prospects for approval because both the emperor and his new General Staff chief regarded a big artillery buildup as an indispensable element of success in the next war. Indeed, Waldersee was struggling on many fronts to overcome backwardness, eliminate deficiencies, and prepare the army for battle. The cavalry tried to adjust to his special field instructions to avoid being "torn up" in modern combat. The infantry rushed the M-88 rifle into production and attempted to accelerate implementation of the new, innovative assault tactics. The heavy artillery began hurried experiments, moreover, on field mobility. When Bronsart von Schellendorff continued his opposition to an artillery increase, he was replaced in early 1887 by Julius von Verdy du Vernois, a protégé of Waldersee who pledged his full cooperation in preparing for "the most furious war that has ever been waged."[82]

Contrary to these grandiose plans, however, the battle readiness of the field artillery continued to decline. For one thing, the 120-mm piece allegedly failed its tests.[83] Howitzer advocates complained that unsympathetic gunners unfamiliar with high-trajectory weapons aimed for airborn detonation 75 to 100 meters in front of the trenchworks, a technique that was logical for the flat-trajectory C-73 but guaranteed failure with howitzers. The fact that Bronsart had invited few 120-mm howitzer enthusiasts to the test created more bad blood. Then, after subsequent firings proved more successful, a final exercise in November 1888 reversed the positive results. An infantry battalion was given more than 10 hours to build defenses. When shrapnel from above failed to break up 50 inches of earth and wood, field artillery experts rendered a negative verdict.[84] Contributing to their decision was the fact that C-73 cannons that fired high-explosive grenades seemed to achieve better results in December. When subsequent routine firing of C-73s determined that iron grenades loaded with picric acid shattered into too many pieces—

and steel grenades into too few—to be effective over trenches, the reports were ignored. The traditionalists won a hollow victory, for they had sacrificed firepower for familiarity—and gained precious little mobility.[85]

The resolution of these issues in mid-1889 was followed immediately by another dispute. At imperial maneuvers in September, Kaiser William II urged the field artillery to move into their positions and unlimber out of plain view. His words prompted artillery experts from the firing ranges to advocate defilade, or indirect fire—shooting from completely hidden positions, usually at long range—as a more realistic battlefield practice. The more complicated procedure had been practiced at the ranges but not in the field with large bodies of artillery. The suggestion triggered bitter opposition from advocates of massed, close-range artillery support like Ernst Hoffbauer, commander of the Fifth Artillery Brigade and, after 1891, general inspector of the field artillery. He used his influence to redraft field artillery regulations in 1892 and defeat the advocates of defilade fire. Open field positions were favored over hidden positions. Hoffbauer also plotted with the kaiser to bring back schrapnel shells after the disappointing tests of iron and steel high-explosive grenades. Schrapnel use, particularly at ranges closer than 1,500 meters, was an important part of the revised 1892 regulations. Hoffbauer's victories were additional indications of the increasingly conservative drift of the field artillery—and indeed of the German Army.[86]

An even nastier controversy was raging, meanwhile, over cannon barrels. Some artillery officers favored a return to the lighter bronze material of older days, but the War Ministry rejected this proposal because bronze was too soft to withstand high explosives. The same held true, however, for existing C-73 material dating from the black-powder era. Verdy du Vernois expressed concern that Krupp's steel barrels would wear out quickly and could not survive if a round exploded disastrously in the barrel. A decision became imperative in the spring of 1890 when parliament approved the minister's request for 70 additional C-73 batteries. That summer he proposed a cheaper, lighter bronze replacement barrel with a reinforcing steel interior. Much to the furor of Verdy and his artillery team, Krupp managed to convince the kaiser that a new nickel-steel alloy was superior. William succumbed to War Ministry counterarguments in August, then reversed himself again, deciding for Krupp steel in September.[87] An order for 70 new batteries was filled in Essen that autumn, but Germany's existing 364 batteries never saw the im-

proved material. The ministry would later claim that it had overcome "serious doubts" about maintaining the outdated steel because
the old barrels were "in such unobjectionable condition."[88] Given
Verdy's previous argument that the antiquated barrels represented
a danger to the lives and morale of artillery crews, however, it appears that spite and revenge against Krupp's civilian interference
and his alleged selfishness and greed were the real motives.

Without new gun material the position of the field artillery worsened as routine firing with high explosives burned out barrels, weakened gas seals, and shook apart gun carriages.[89] In 1892 all of the
badly worn barrels of batteries that had participated in peacetime
firing were exchanged with the less used barrels of rear-area and
reserve batteries. The Army Bill of 1893 expanded the number of
field artillery batteries from 434 to 494, but this figure was mislead-
ing. The Prussian war minister reported in 1896 that only 294 batteries actually had usable barrels, and a mere 85 had barrels still
capable of firing high-explosive rounds. It was nothing but a dangerous illusion, therefore, when the cavalier spirit of the gunners
enabled them to reach new heights of bravery at annual maneuvers,
charging forward with the infantry as at St. Privat.[90] In reality, the
once awesome field artillery was far from ready—and German national security had sunk to a very low point. Waldersee's visions had
turned into nightmares.

And it got worse before it got better. In 1897 the field artillery
began to equip its batteries with a new 77-mm cannon.[91] The so-
called C-96 was in some respects an improvement. Its nickel-steel
barrel rose to the metallurgical challenge of the latest nitroglycerin
explosives, and a braking device reduced recoil and permitted good
crews to fire five to nine rounds per minute—two to three times the
speed of the C-73. The new piece (including the loaded caisson)
was also impressively mobile, weighing about 600 pounds less than
its predecessor.[92] But problems with the new gun were detected during testing. It bucked powerfully with every shot, necessitating constant reaiming and thus hurried and inaccurate firing in the anxiety
of combat. Even worse, if inclined below the crest of a hill for cover,
the C-96 tended to flip over backward. If one did not intend to hide
or shoot from long distances, of course, these were not real defects,
and thus they were ignored.

Errors of omission were even more egregious than errors of
commission. In 1894, the field artillery tested a patented semirecoilless cannon. Not yet perfected, the odd-looking weapon was
quickly rejected: "Away with the monstrosity,"[93] barked the com-

Figure 4. The proud crew of a C-96 cannon. Source: Max Köhler, *Der Aufstieg der Artillerie bis zum Grossen Krieg* (Munich, 1938).

manding officer. Less concerned with artillery aesthetics, French experts patiently developed the patent's potential, introducing their famous 75-mm cannon in 1898. Because only the barrel recoiled, not the entire gun, crews could fire up to 20 shells per minute without reaiming. As the century turned, England, the United States, Russia, and Austria followed the French lead—even Norway did not want to be left behind. But the German field artillery, still more concerned with mobility than firepower—the C-96 was over 500 pounds lighter than the French 75—stubbornly refused to rearm.[94]

It required intervention by the General Staff to begin to restore the field artillery's competitive position. After tests in 1896 confirmed the ineffectiveness of flat-trajectory cannons against field entrenchments, Alfred von Schlieffen, Waldersee's successor as chief of the General Staff, prodded artillery experts in the War Ministry and the General Inspection of the Field Artillery to reinvestigate the potential of field howitzers.[95] The forced result was the 105-mm, rapid-firing l.FH-98, a lightweight, mobile, versatile weapon capable of shooting seven types of shells, including grenades and shrapnel. The opponents of the stubby-barreled howitzers offered some co-

gent criticisms, pointing out, for instance, that the cumbersome ammunition train would impede rapid engagement. The advocates of
l.FH-98 added unnecessary controversy by raising the old specter of
completely replacing C-96s with howitzers as the field artillery's standard cannon. This fear elicited responses from the other side that
reflected a deeper and more basic reason for resisting the new device. The howitzer's "mortar-mouth existence was only to be explained by the fact that [it] was constructed under the banner of
those who argue that shovels will play a much greater role in future
wars."[96]

To those who believed that victory belonged to the audacious,
the mere discussion of defensive strategies—or, in this extreme case,
even the offensive weapons to counter them—was intolerable because this smacked somehow of weakness and unmanliness. Schlieffen's most influential opponent in this struggle was Ernst Hoffbauer,
general inspector of the field artillery from 1891 to 1899 and, not
coincidentally, an outspoken advocate since the 1870s of field artillery mobility and close-range support of the troops. "Given this general resistance," said Schlieffen in 1897, "I don't know if we're on

Figure 5. The "mortar mouth" 105-mm. howitzer (l.FH-98). Source: Köhler, *Der
Aufstieg.*

the right path." He resisted the temptation to yield, however, and in 1900 the l.FH-98 finally exited the factories to join the C-96 in the field artillery's arsenal.[97]

The German Army was torn between advocates of change and champions of the old ways. The former mounted a serious challenge in the late 1880s, as shown by the adoption of the M-88 and new infantry regulations that reflected the reforming principles of Sigismund von Schlichting. By the mid-1890s, however, his enemies regained the ascendancy, forced his retirement, and brought the old company and battalion columns back into vogue. A similar dynamic was at work in the cavalry. Progressives around Bernhardi and Kleist provoked more emphasis on reconnaissance and firepower, only to see their gains undermined by conservatives. The cavalry's tactical dream of deciding battles with muscle and cold, hard steel was still quite potent at mid-decade. Similarly, champions of new field artillery models made proposals in the late 1880s but were frustrated by C-73 and C-96 enthusiasts who staunchly opposed rival designs. The General Staff's backing for field howitzers finally began to modify this situation in the late 1890s.

Institutional factors exacerbated these divisions. Thus, feuding factions in the field artillery, Prussian War Ministry, and General Staff exploited mutual animosities to advance technological agendas. As we shall now see, champions of the fledgling heavy artillery sought out the same General Staff allies in a parallel, largely unsuccessful struggle with field artillery traditionalists in the Artillery Department of the Prussian War Ministry. At the very apex of the command structure, moreover, stood a psychologically unstable and extremely contradictory Kaiser William II. As we have observed with nickle-steel cannon barrels, the army's overlord found it very difficult to make up his mind. In chapter 6. we will investigate the role this baffling monarch played in exacerbating army tensions related to technology and tactics. Ominously, the kaiser's waffling and vacillating called seriously into question his ability to lead.

CHAPTER 4

THE PLANS OF SCHLIEFFEN

A UNIFORMED MAN was ushered into the room. It was an exclusive gathering of turn-of-the-century, Berlin high society. The feathered ladies, wives of top officials from the Foreign Ministry and Reich Chancellery, were dressed as if they expected the kaiser to appear. The men were attired formally and stiffly, as befitted their station in life and the state. As civilians, however, they lacked the status, the rank, and the eye-opening excitement of the elder man who walked in. It was not the emperor, but everyone knew that when Europe exploded, when mounting tensions forced a new martial resettling of European relations, when war brought the reordering of the continent that would finally give Germany its due, Alfred von Schlieffen, chief of the Great General Staff, would again guide Germany's men to victory. It was unquestioned.

Schlieffen's receding hair, elongated ears, and chiseled features marked him as an old and serious man. His subordinates would later talk about his legendary intensity. When one pointed out the beauty of a valley during a staff ride, he would say coldly that it was only a minor obstacle for his army. When juniors received an operational problem on Christmas Eve, answers were due on Christmas Day. Schlieffen was a dogmatist, a doctrinaire, and a theoretist. His dogma was the offensive; his doctrine was envelopment; and his operational theories, tested by loyal professionals, were developed to reproduce glories as great as Waterloo, Königgrätz, and Sedan.[1]

The eyes of the former cavalryman narrowed as he entered, seeking out the German ambassador to England, Hermann von Eckardstein, on a brief leave from London. There would be time for the general's questions after dinner when the men repaired to smoke and discuss serious matters alone. When that time came, Schlieffen queried Eckardstein about unsettling news he had received of England's growing estrangement from Germany. "If you are correct in terms of our relationship with England, I will have to change my entire campaign plan." Surely Eckardstein was too pessimistic? But when the ambassador persisted in his belief, remarking further that if Germany marched through Belgium "we would have England on our necks immediately," Schlieffen fell silent. Soon the conversation ended and the general, his aging brow furrowed, slipped away to process this new information.[2]

The howitzer disputes of 1886–1888 and 1896–1898 were part of a much larger disagreement in the German Army over the relative advantages of offense and defense. This wider controversy had grown more intense with the disastrous Russian attacks at Plevna; the completion of France's fortification system; and the advent of repeating rifles, smokeless powder, high explosives, and rapid-firing cannon. A new tactical wisdom was strikingly apparent to an influential minority of cautious observers who studied these unfolding trends. To these officers, it now appeared suicidal to expose long lines of field cannons and attacking waves of tightly packed cavalry and infantry to bullets and shells that seemingly could not miss. This faction argued that it made more sense to build fortifications, defend river lines and hilly terrain, and exploit the offensive folly of the enemy.[3] Helmuth von Moltke paid some homage to the new technical realities after 1879–1880 by shifting offensive plans to the east and adopting more prudent defensive arrangements in the west. The wily hero of German unification was prepared to punish the French as they advanced across the west-bank Rhineland, then stop them at the Rhine.[4]

For many other army officers—probably the majority at all ranks—the notion of altering or diluting attack traditions, let alone abandoning the offensive, was heresy. They railed against those who wanted to substitute outflanking maneuvers for frontal assaults; entrenching exercises for bayonet drill; dismounted cavalry tactics for mounted charges; and distant, concealed artillery fire for point-blank support of the first-wave troops. Conservatives castigated all of these changes as harmful to the "old Prussian tradition of the offensive."[5] Tactical formations designed to reduce casualties were also resisted as weak-kneed sops to the wrong-headed idea that war could somehow be made less costly. In short, such theories were dangerously and unforgivably naive because men not steeled against the reality of massive bloodshed would quickly break and run.[6]

The army's reactionary champions of the offensive also harbored deep resentments against modern weaponry. The long, persistent opposition in the infantry to magazine rifles, for instance, went well beyond ammunition-related discipline problems. Beneath the bravado about hardened men who would overcome all obstacles was a nagging anxiety that repeaters would simply make it impossible to attack. All agreed that taking the offensive was the only solution. But one had to ask: "How will we manage to execute tactical offensives in the lead-filled atmosphere of the new weapon?" Many infantrymen concluded that it would be better to fall back on "our tried old-Prussian principles" and reject "the quest for innovation."[7] Similarly, one field artillerist bemoaned the likely passing of the old ways in one of those rare honest moments that soldiers who must somehow prepare psychologically for combat permit themselves: "The proud moments when our batteries, accompanied by the cheers of the sister branches, galloped briskly into position and answered the enemy with quick, sharp cannon fire seem today as if they will never return."[8] Such wistfulness was easily turned against the technological culprit, however, as shown by the field artillery's campaign against the "mortar-mouth" howitzer, that intolerable concession to the coming of long-range defensive warfare. One lead article in the *Military Weekly* was even franker about the vexing problems technology created:

> We live in an age of inventions. In weapons technology, just as in other areas, one discovery chases after the next. Now every military establishment would be very pleased indeed to see a slower tempo of improvements to the tools of war. They would not have to come before the peoples' representatives so frequently with new weapons appropriations, the impact of every single improvement on the waging of war could be examined more thoroughly, and the training of troops would be less hectic.

Added to this was the regrettable fact that today's military technologies "alter the way wars are fought" because each change "tends to be seen as a strengthening of the defense."[9] In sum, then, technology was responsible for rapidly complicating and undermining the manly art of war.

Modern times contributed in other ways to the demise of aggressive warfare.[10] If attacks were to break through, it was clear that extremely well-disciplined frontline soldiers would have to perform at nearly superhuman levels. Army leaders were shocked to observe, however, that a process of human degeneration was apparently underway that undercut the prospect of battlefield success by reducing the number of salvageable recruits. This deterioration of the human condition was caused by the "softening societal influences"[11] of rapidly accelerating population growth, rising numbers of people in crowded cities, the ever faster and more hectic pace of urban life, and the dehumanizing conditions of factory labor. Medical experts pointed with alarm to allegedly degenerative symptoms like the rise in smoking, alcoholism, suicide, venereal disease, masturbation, homosexuality, male hysteria, and nervous breakdowns. "The fast manner of living at the present undermines the nervous system," declared one military expert. "The physical powers of the human being," he added, "are on the wane."[12] How could the army make soldiers out of such miserable "human material"?[13]

Strikes, socialism, atheism, and republicanism were related modern phenomena that were allegedly ruining Germany's male stock. All were blamed on the rapidly rising Social Democratic Party (SPD) of Germany. From meager beginnings in the 1860s and 1870s, the Social Democrats grew larger and more resilient in the 1880s, despite Bismarck's carrot-and-stick campaign of social insurance and discriminatory, antisocialist legislation. The elections of 1890 gave the SPD nearly 1.5 million votes and the largest share (19.6%) of votes cast. During the early 1890s, their trade unions succeeded in recruiting hundreds of thousands of blue-collar workers. These trends caused "deep dread"[14] among army commanders, who had failed to prevent socialist recruits from entering the ranks. The subversive, antiestablishment bias of the Social Democrats was compounded, it was alleged, by a cowardly, unmanly antimilitarism expressed in mocking, insulting, antiarmy language that was more threatening than the criticism of Eugen Richter and the Progressives.[15] If the SPD succeeded in driving a wedge between officers and men, would common soldiers refuse to take orders in battle, especially if ordered to undertake a frontal charge?[16] It was the army's worst nightmare.

How should the army combat all of these forces that were eroding the masculinity of potential recruits? Answers were forthcoming. Regimental commanders such as Lieutenant Colonel Paul von Hindenburg were no doubt fairly representative when they gave officers problems in maneuvers and insisted on offensive solutions because, as the later legendary figure liked to say, "defense is womanly, offense manly."[17] Through harsh training programs, moreover, officers and noncommissioned officers (NCOs) could build discipline, cultivate "manly breeding," and promote the "soldierly upbringing of men."[18] Nevertheless, given all of the dangers associated with urban life, it seemed prudent to recruit soldiers disproportionately from rural districts, which still produced healthy men,[19] and to admit privately that the others would probably not hold up for long in combat. On the other hand, nothing was more "corrupting"[20] than to argue publicly, that it was impossible to withstand modern rifle and artillery fire during attacks—which is why champions of the offense found their opponents' publications so unforgivable.

During the late 1880s and 1890s, a synthesis of sorts emerged from the antithetical arguments of the advocates of defense and of offense. Sigismund von Schlichting was one of the first to combine elements from both feuding sides in a new tactical approach. He doubted the basic wisdom of exaggerated defensive strategies, pointing to the fact that Osman Pasha was trapped at Plevna and eventually defeated.[21] As we have seen, however, Schlichting's offensive innovations incorporated the defender's advantages of systematic planning, cover, and carefully directed firepower. His views were adopted as official infantry regulations in 1888.

Others built on Schlichting's belief that careful, prudent attackers could turn the advantages of defense against defenders.[22] Thus General Staff Quartermaster Alfred von Waldersee was usually very critical of traditional tacticians in the cavalry, infantry, and artillery but, somewhat like Schlichting, could not bring himself to abandon the offensive. Convinced by the mid-1880s that Germany should shift the bulk of its corps westward to block a French offensive—leaving six corps and the Austrians to cope with the Russians—Waldersee progressed as chief (1888–1891) to more offensive western strategies. Given the rapid development of nitrogen-based high explosives, could the heavy artillery blast through the French fortresses? Advised by his deputy, Alfred von Schlieffen, who had assembled an impressive team of artillery experts, Waldersee proposed borrowing defensive technologies such as stationary fortress guns and siege cannons and converting them into mobile offensive weapons. Once the field trenches and permanent forts were destroyed and the enemy was retreating in open country, repeating rifles, hard-charging field artillery, and swooping cavalry units would give the opposition no time to dig more earthworks. Once again, attackers, not defenders, would reap the advantages of technology. The corrosive effects of socialism and urban life were no less alarming to Waldersee than to the most reactionary technophobes. Unlike the antimodernists, however, the new General Staff chief planned to exploit the machines of war. Germany's modern man would have a technological shield to keep morale artificially high and prevent panic, whereas the "nervous"[23] citizen soldiers of France would be subjected to "the most brutal war ever waged." It would soon be over, for humans, especially the "decadent"[24] French, could not long endure such slaughter.

These ideas remained purely hypothetical until well after the war scares of the 1880s had passed. Although heavy artillerists had test-fired 210-mm gun-cotton mortar rounds against mock French-style forts as early as 1883, the results were only marginally encouraging. The first generation of nitrogen explosives decimated earthworks but only rarely damaged the iron and concrete reinforcing layers that fortress engineers were already adding to their designs. Gun cotton was extremely volatile and difficult to transport, moreover, and no one had shown how traditional siege trains of more than 200 guns would keep pace with an army expected to move rapidly into enemy territory. Added to these impediments was the opposition of a cost-shy War Ministry that was jealous of the rival General Staff. Finally, Inspector General of the Artillery Julius von Voigts-Rhetz had no intention of allowing the stepchild foot artillery to steal a march on the prestigious, status-conscious field artillery. His office was the only remaining link between the two branches after 1872, but this was enough to squelch all notions of a mobile heavy artillery. The faction around Voigts-Rhetz wanted the 120-mm howitzer to provide the field artillery with all necessary firepower.[25]

The heavy artillery began to free itself from these shackles in the winter of 1887–1888 when Johann Roerdantz, an ennobled career artillerist, received command of an independent General Inspection of the Foot Artillery. Three of his early demands relected the General Staff intrigue that lay behind his appointment. He wanted heavy artillery units to participate with the other branches in annual maneuvers; its officers should have tours of duty in the infantry and field artillery; and finally, the big guns should march with the field army. This program was furthered avidly by young Emperor William; indeed, the same man who warmed to the idea of 10,000 charging horses seemed to incorporate in his person all of the army's contradictory tendencies.[26]

William's backing, encouragement, and enthusiastic appearances at the Jüterbog firing range did little to accelerate the General Staff's ambitious plans for the heavy artillery. For many years after the young kaiser's ascension, in fact, the potential to advance quickly and blow holes in France's fortress wall eluded German military planners. Thus a special attack exercise on Fort Rheinhell near Koblenz in September 1888 attempted to enhance heavy artillery mobility by reducing the siege train to 8 batteries of 150- and 210-mm guns—36 howitzers and mortars in all. The cumbersome column of wagons bogged down in the narrow Lahn Valley as Waldersee and Schlieffen looked at their watches and shook their heads. It took 3 days to move from Diez to the Horchheimer Heights and another day to prepare gun emplacements for a mock bombardment. The infantry could not attack until the fifth day. Such delays would be extended in actual combat, reducing to near zero the chance of rapid western breakthroughs. Waldersee decided to jettison the notion of a minisiege train in favor of autonomous batteries, each with its own teams of horses.[27]

The experience of the horse-drawn heavy artillery was somewhat better. A succession of exercises between 1889 and 1892 overcame problems of mobility, but construction of gun positions and platforms still took from 2 to 12 hours, depending on conditions. This eliminated any element of surprise against permanent forts and gave enemy infantry in the field too much time to dig in. The General Staff insisted, therefore, that heavy mortar crews fire without installing wooden gun mounts—just like the field artillery. The technique was eventually mastered, but not without internal resistance from skeptical artillerists that necessitated years of tests.[28] The limited effectiveness of the 150- and 210-mm guns created additional worries. In short, destroying field fortifications proved easier at the firing range than in the field. Inadequate forward observation impaired accuracy, leading to a large expenditure of shells and a bombardment time longer than the 1-day limit set by the General Staff. Permanent forts were much harder to damage.[29]

Interservice friction and prejudice added to these difficulties and delays. Bavarian observers at annual maneuvers in 1891 noted that the two participating horse-drawn heavy artillery battalions were relatively quick and efficient but that troop leaders at all levels had no appreciation for the potential of the new branch "because outside of maneuvers they have nothing to do with it." The lack of contact between the services meant that the problem was likely to perpetuate itself.[30] The Reichstag decreased the chances of more effective interservice cooperation by cutting heavy artillery appropriations in 1893. The number of horse-drawn battalions was halved, from 16 to 8.[31] The appearance at exercises and maneuvers of rented horse teams with civilian teamsters—a condition necessitated by the Reichstag cuts—undermined still more the image of the mobile heavy artillery.[32]

Technical problems also postponed the day when German columns could confidently move west. Because the existing 150-mm cannons and 210-mm mortars were fitted with bronze barrels, picric acid explosives quickly ruined them. Both pieces were refitted with steel inner barrels in 1891–1892, but this was merely a stopgap measure because metallurgists had no means of durably adhering the two metals. The barrel problem was finally solved in 1893 with the introduction of a heavy field howitzer made of resistant nickel-steel. Although successive exercises and tests improved the effectiveness of the 150s and 210s against quickly constructed field fortifications, there remained the elusive problem of demolishing France's permanent forts, especially the fortresses between Verdun and Belfort, whose walls had been reinforced with steel and concrete during the late 1880s and early 1890s.[33] The Krupp Company offered a potential solution in 1893. The arms manufacturer constructed a huge 305-mm mortar transported by rail, which was designed to hurl massive, 725-pound, nonexploding shells a distance of 7 kilometers. Fortress walls would be so battered and weakened that high explosive rounds from the smaller mortars could complete the destruction. Proving exercises with prototypes of the new mortar got underway in 1894.[34]

Diplomatic and military developments in the early 1890s, meanwhile, made it doubly important for the General Staff to assess the real potential of mobile heavy artillery. Indeed the dismissal of Chancellor Otto von Bismarck by the capricious William II had cascading consequences for Germany and its chief military planners. The emperor listened to Bismarck's former protégé, Friedrich von Holstein, who distrusted the Russians and therefore advised that Germany abandon the ingenious Reinsurance Treaty. Tsar Alexander III, surprised to find his empire suddenly and unexpectedly in the apparent camp of Germany's enemies, approved military talks with the French that produced agreement in 1892 for a defensive alliance between the two states. Since the Congress of Berlin (1878) and subsequent cooling of Russo-German relations, the General Staff had been considering the possibility of hostilities with Russia.

Now war would make that a certainty. It was therefore small wonder that the dismissal of Bismarck strained the loyalty of the officer corps,[35] initiating a process of declining respect for the kaiser that would reach critical proportions after 1900.

In the autumn of 1892, Waldersee's successor, Schlieffen, began his intellectual struggle with the military conundrum of how to achieve eventual victory in a two-front war.[36] During the first years of staff work, Schlieffen's team had reason to be guardedly optimistic about the role that offensive military technology would play. A second, improved generation of high explosives (picric acid) was on hand, and metallurgists were modifying barrels and introducing new models to meet material demands. The problems of interservice coordination; the procurement of enough horse teams; the quick initiation of fire; and the effectiveness of fire, especially against fortresses, were not yet solved, but solutions appeared possible.

In his first response to Germany's strategic predicament in 1892, therefore, Schlieffen put greater emphasis on winning in the west. The strategy of Moltke, Schlieffen's greatest predecessor, was to attack Russian Poland with the Austrians while holding a defensive line in the Rhineland. The plans of Moltke's successor, Waldersee, included eastern, as well as western, offensive options. If war erupted during the good weather of the summer, he preferred to commit 5 to 7 corps to a joint Polish offensive. With 2 newly created commands, this left 13 to 15 corps to hold the Rhine and then counterattack, surrounding and annihilating the French in eastern Lorraine before the retreating columns could regain their fortress line.[37] If war broke out during the inclement autumn, Waldersee was tempted to defend the eastern border while attacking the French forts with 17 army corps and a full complement of horse-drawn heavy artillery.[38] Schlieffen, for his part, was skeptical about quick victories in Poland, for under the new arrangements with France, Russia had shifted the bulk of its strength from Galicia to Poland (i.e., from the Austrian to the German front). Moreover, the Russians had completed their own reinforced fortresses along the rivers of northern Poland. Even if the Germans broke through, the Russians would just withdraw farther east: "We would not achieve a decisive battle or the destruction of the Russian army," wrote Schlieffen, "but rather a series of frontal battles." A crushing victory required at least 11 corps, "much more than we could spare in the West."[39]

These considerations moved Schlieffen, the new General Staff chief, to revisit Moltke's original plans for breakthrough on the western front. Worried about a French thrust at Saarburg, his first operational concept of 1894 envisioned a preemptive strike:[40] "To win, we must endeavor to be the stronger of the two at the point of impact. Our only hope of this lies in making our own choice of operations, not in waiting passively for whatever the enemy chooses for us."[41] Schlieffen's first plan called for 16 corps supported by 16 battalions (56 batteries) of horse-drawn heavy artillery—the number that was halved by the Reichstag in 1893—on a front stretching from Luxemburg to upper Alsace. The bulk of the big guns—between 120 and 144, including a small number of 305-mm mortars—would penetrate defenses around Nancy. Seizure of the plateau west of Nancy would render the rest of the fortress line indefensible. The ensuing open-field retreat, panic, and human breakdown would be disastrous for the French Army.

Schlieffen's confidence in this plan had eroded by 1896–1897, largely because of technological failings on the German side. The heavy artillery's proving commission conducted tests with 210s, as well as prototype 305s, from 1894 to 1896. Target forts of the latest French and Russian designs had 2.5 to 3.0 meters of reinforced concrete covered by an equivalent layer of earth. Gun towers were protected with armored plate. These state-of-the-art turrets withstood the onslaught of the 210s and 305s. The forts also proved very difficult to damage with either 725-pound, nonexploding shells or 880-pound, high-explosive rounds. Direct hits from the 305s penetrated to the inner concrete layer but blew away chunks only 0.5- to 1.5-meters deep. The forts were finally destroyed after a succession of tests and hundreds of shots.[42]

Nine of the fearsome 305s were ordered in 1896, although the General Staff had placed no great trust in the allegedly satisfactory test results.[43] As early as August 1895, General Staff Quartermaster Friedrich Köpke advised Schlieffen to forget about "rapid and decisive victories." The advances in French fortress technology meant that "even with the most offensive spirit . . . nothing more can be achieved than a tedious and bloody crawling forward step by step here and there by way of an ordinary attack in siege style."[44] Reinforcing Köpke's gloomy predictions was the fact that even the proving commission soon recommended raising heavy artillery calibers above 305 mm to create a "monster cannon."[45]

Further pessimism resulted from the dwindling number of horse-drawn 150s and 210s that were available on paper for the great assault against Nancy. Compounding Reichstag decisions in 1893, which had cut appropriations by 50%, the War Ministry halved again the monies earmarked for horse teams, giving it instead to allegedly more important cavalry messenger squads.[46] The ministry had never been enthusiastic about heavy artillery, sympathizing with General Inspector of the Field Artillery Ernst Hoffbauer and the Artillery Department's Colonel Reichenau, who believed the field artillery could accomplish the army's mission without the aid of heavy artillery.[47] Consequently, only 4 of the requisite 16 horse-drawn battalions were on hand by 1897.

That summer's reassessment prompted a series of new deployment options between 1898 and 1902. More serious consideration was given to attacking with the bulk of forces in the east and defending in the west, for instance, whereas other variations combined Austro-German thrusts into Poland with daring counterattacks from the Rhine. Yet another scenario sent powerful western armies into France in the event that Paris opted for a defensive fortress strategy.[48] It is significant, however, that all of the General Staff's western operational plans—whether attacking or counterattacking—sought to envelop France's seemingly impregnable fortifications by hurling the right wing into Belgium: "An offensive which seeks to wheel round Verdun," Schlieffen had already observed in 1897, "must not shrink from violating the neutrality of Belgium as well as Luxemburg."[49] The swing could not be so far north and west that German armies lost the possibility of fairly rapid eastward transport to Poland from home railheads. One plan of 1900, for example, envisioned a crossing of the Belgian Ardennes southwest of Liège by 10 or 11 corps. Their objective was the stretch between Rheims and Verdun. Center and left-wing armies would attack the fortresses, mainly to tie down French armies and allow time for the right wing to circle around from the north. Another exercise of 1901 ended in campaign victory just across the German-Belgian border.[50] A fateful die had been cast, nevertheless, for if Germany opted for any one of these western operations, the presence of German troops in Belgium would surely trigger British intervention.

There was a desperate quality to Schlieffen's western scenarios. Since Plevna 20 years earlier, uniformed Cassandras had warned that Prussia's glorious offensive tradition was an anachronism in the machine age. For 10 years Waldersee and Schlieffen had proudly, defiantly, and stubbornly insisted that the frightening aspects of modern war could by sheer will be turned against hapless defenders whose nerves would snap. Heavy artillerists had breathed deeply the air of confidence and emancipation that swirled through their ranks in the early 1890s, seeming to know that the future belonged to them.[51] Now there was an abrupt change of course. With an ironclad military logic, hoping desperately to avoid the nightmare scenario of a martial quagmire painted by Köpke, Schlieffen turned away from the concept of "smashing through" to the idea of "running around."[52]

These operational changes necessitated a shift to lighter, less awesome technologies. It was no coincidence, for instance, that Schlieffen fought with Ernst Hoffbauer about adding light, 105-mm howitzers to the field artillery in 1897. If the French were to be outflanked, the armies that would sweep through Belgium had to advance very quickly, blasting French infantry out of their foxholes and hastily constructed earthworks. Tests with the C-96 field cannon in 1896 had proven that it was not up to this task. The heavy artillery's 150-mm field howitzer was also assigned a critical role: "Fortresses which can't be completely circumvented are staring at us just one or two days' march across the border—they must be attacked."[53] Schlieffen did not overlook the importance for the move through Belgium of the nickel-steel 210-mm mortar introduced in 1899–1900. But with fewer modernized forts north of Verdun, it now received less emphasis.[54] Meanwhile, the 305s were quietly forgotten, and calls for "monster" mortars of even larger caliber were ignored.[55]

Instead, the General Staff fixed increasingly on the field mobility of Germany's 38 heavy artillery battalions. Thus, when Hoffbauer attempted not only to downplay his "alleged" howitzer setback against the heavy artillery but also, somewhat contradictorily, to exploit it, by arguing that his light 105s obviated the need for heavy 150s in the field, the General Staff took up the challenge. Comparative firing tests at Tenth Corps maneuvers in 1900 dealt a solid defeat to field artillery extremists. "It was not too long ago," proclaimed a jubilant emperor, "that the heavy artillery did not accomplish half as much in 24 hours as today in 80 minutes."[56] Schlieffen's preoccupation with mobility soon spread throughout the heavy artillery corps itself, alienating the remaining isolated advocates of large-scale fortress warfare. It seemed that their branch was succumbing to the same cavalier, antitechnological biases that had overtaken the field artillery in the 1870s.[57]

Indeed the shifting emphasis to lighter and quicker artillery pieces was also mixed with an element of escape or retreat into an antitechnological mind-set. Whereas the Army Bill of 1893 increased heavy artillery battalions from 31 to 37, for instance, the acts of 1896, 1899, and 1904 together produced only one new battalion. General Inspector of the Heavy Artillery Heinrich Edler von der

Planitz had pushed for 33 new battalions in 1900, but Schlieffen joined forces with Karl von Einem, chief of Military Operations under Prussian War Minister Heinrich von Gossler, to oppose the increase. The two convinced a skeptical Gossler to block these "futuristic plans" in favor of "far more necessary" infantry appropriations.[58] The army expanded from 20 to 23 active corps in 1899,[59] but Schlieffen's ambitious plans after 1898 called for 23 regular corps on the western front alone. At least 3 active corps had to be left to defend the east. For this reason he was pressing for 4 new corps plus a Guard Reserve Corps.[60] Although the increase to 27 regular corps was to be accomplished largely by reducing strength in existing units, costs would still be very high. Matériel considerations like the 150-mm field howitzers remained important to the success of Schlieffen's operational plans, but flesh and blood was clearly "far more necessary" than a doubling of the heavy artillery. Schlieffen could dispense with more of the big guns.

Problems with these plans became apparent shortly after 1900. The first involved the number of army corps on the western front. Unwilling to disclose the details of his top-secret thinking to Gossler—a man whose job necessitated negotiations and deals with unreliable parliamentarians—Schlieffen was unable to convince him of the urgent necessity of 27 active corps.[61] A stopgap compromise whereby 3 "wartime corps" would be thrown together during mobilization by stealing from units all over the empire[62] was no real solution in Schlieffen's eyes. The active army remained at 23 corps from 1899 to 1912—26 with the Kriegskorps. There would not be enough troops any time soon to execute Schlieffen's operations.

It seems the two men envisioned a different kind of future war. Recent research demonstrates that Schlieffen was not gambling on rapid annihilation of the French so much as quick frontier victories that would destroy up to nine enemy corps, thus freeing two German armies for the east. Remaining divisions would pursue the campaign into the French interior. The crucial initial battles of what perhaps would be a 6-to-9 month struggle on two fronts would be won by a beefed-up peacetime, regular army, fleshed out with reserves. The war minister, however, seems to have remembered Helmuth von Moltke's dire prediction of another Thirty Years' War.[63] To prepare for it, scarce resources should be invested in armaments and productive capacity. Army troop strength could be expanded entirely with reserves in wartime.[64] Thus, Gossler rejected four new regular corps, turned his back on the field artillery, and pushed in vain for substantially more heavy artillery—well after Schlieffen had abandoned the idea.[65] He also favored a network of defensive forts. "Gossler has really caught the fortress bug,"[66] lamented the ex-cavalryman. As we shall see, Gossler was not alone in stressing the need to prepare for Armageddon.[67]

The odds of achieving success lengthened for Schlieffen in 1902. The General Staff chief had informed Foreign Ministry officials confidentially of his intention to invade Belgium if the situation in Europe called for a western (not an eastern) campaign. Upon receipt of this information, his close friend Friedrich von Holstein fell into deep thought, then concluded that "if the Chief of the Great General Staff, and particularly a strategic authority like Schlieffen, [thinks] such a measure to be necessary, then it would be the duty of diplomacy to adjust itself to it and prepare for it in every possible way."[68] When Schlieffen heard in October 1902, however, that relations with Great Britain had deteriorated to an alarming degree, he approached Hermann von Eckardstein, Germany's ambassador to England. "If you are correct in terms of our relationship with England, I will have to change my entire campaign plan."[69] As we know from our opening scene, the ambassador's negative, alarming comments about a British expeditionary force "on our necks immediately" ruined Schlieffen's evening.

Now, in fact, the great planner did change course. Formulated that autumn, western deployment plans avoided Belgium entirely. Germany would attack between Epinal and Verdun with 40 divisions. The massive assault was designed to draw all French forces eastward—including an army Schlieffen suspected would be positioned above Verdun to block German armies from invading Belgium. In one exercise, the German First Army, stationed south of Aachen with 12 divisions, counterattacked in a southwesterly direction, outflanking this northern French army as it approached the German Mosel. In December 1902, moreover, Schlieffen proposed another alternative to the violation of Belgium: a strike into Poland with 36 divisions.[70] It is also significant that the western staff ride of July 1903 sent half of the German Army into Poland while the other half defended Metz.[71] Thus, Schlieffen was somewhat more attuned to the Belgian problem than previous historians have assumed.

In 1903 and 1904, however, crucial changes in German thinking returned Belgium to its tragic hypothetical fate. Critiques of eastern invasion scenarios highlighted the limitations of the railroad network in East Prussia and Posen, as well as the old dilemna of piercing formidable river fortifications in Poland.[72] There was also the troubling fact that Metz's defenses had not held in the 1903 staff ride. Expanding the fortress into a Verdun-style fortified zone was an option—Verdun was not one but 60 small, medium, and large forts. Schlieffen rejected this option because he had "no reason to hinder the French from taking this unfavorable route of attack [against Metz]"[73] while he outflanked them through Belgium. Indeed, Schlieffen was now downplaying the significance of violating Belgian neutrality, believing that both sides would abuse the little state to the surprise of no one, including the Belgians. It is safe to assume that his friend Holstein had strengthened Schlieffen in the comforting conclusion that the British would not be shocked by these violations—certainly not to the point of sending troops. In three western staff rides in 1904 and early 1905, there was no British Expeditionary Force (BEF) to contend with in Belgium when Germany and France ordered troops across the soil of this hapless country. In all three exercises Schlieffen directed two or three right-wing armies into Belgium, with Verdun-Lille as the intended pivot region of the great envelopment. In every case, however—even when Schlieffen personally commanded German armies during the third ride in 1905—the right wing wheeled southward almost immediately in order to outflank French armies that were attacking in Lorraine. Early victories near the frontier were preferable, given the necessity of shifting divisions by rail to the eastern front. Winning was not assured, however, for during the second staff ride of 1904 the Germans, not the French, were defeated.[74]

There were additional reasons for caution during these same years. England was not moving into Germany's camp as Holstein had predicted it would; rather, the great imperial power negotiated an alliance with Japan in 1902. An understanding between England and France in 1904 confirmed the correctness of Eckardstein's unsettling remarks—and Schlieffen's earlier instinct to change his "entire campaign plan." Although he reacted prudently at first, in the end Schlieffen did not discard his Belgian operational plans. Considering all of this, one is drawn back to Jack Snyder's observation that "the operational analyses of Schlieffen and his General Staff manifested a systematic bias in favor of prevailing doctrine and the preferred plan."[75] A technical factor that reinforced the narrowing fixation with invading this neutral nation was the existence of a dense railroad network on both sides of the border for the transport of large numbers of troops.[76]

Indeed, the magnitude and extent of Schlieffen's "preferred plan" was growing. During winter exercises in November and December 1905, the aging chief acted on his strengthening assumption of having to fight England by positing a BEF for the very first time.[77] In the now famous "Schlieffen Plan" memorandum, written shortly after these exercises, he called for a massive force of 45 divisions that would smash into Belgium and swing around Lille. Although it was probably a worst-case scenario, requiring a risky 8 or 9 weeks, the right wing should be prepared to march as far west as Paris if earlier victories proved elusive. Was not this memorandum perhaps his response to the likely appearance of the BEF on the French left, extending its defenses farther north and west? Was Schlieffen beginning to abandon the notion of wheeling directly behind Verdun to remain close to the frontier? As Schlieffen's plan became more grandiose, confidence mixed with worry and arrogance with anxiety about the likely outcome in a shooting war, for there were unnerving questions that cried out for answers. Would Germany have enough corps to defeat the Belgians, the French, and the British too? And how soon would the Cossacks attack in the east? This was the stuff of ulcers, wrinkles, and more gray hair.

CHAPTER 5

PAST AND PRESENT COLLIDE

JOHN ATKINS OF THE *Manchester Guardian* peered through a naval telescope at British entrenchments 3 miles away. From this distance the khaki uniforms of the 2,000 brave Englishmen who had seized the heights of Spion Kop during the night looked dirty brown. As he squinted to see the action, the whole ridge appeared to quiver in the hot glare of the midmorning sun. Suddenly, the brown wall of men rose to charge, heads and torsos bent instinctively forward into a curve. "They looked like a cornfield with a heavy wind sweeping over it from behind."[1] It was as if their bodies spoke to the superior force of Mauser and shrapnel fire, cutting into them like a scythe.

It was supposed to be different. By taking Spion Kop and digging trenches, the British were to jeopardize the Boer positions around Ladysmith, forcing the hardy burghers to break themselves in successive charges against an impregnable position. Indeed, 400 Boer attackers had scurried up the northern slope on the morning of 24 January 1900; but having reached the summit opposite their hated enemy, they, too, took cover. There was no final charge. Rather, the Boers' magazine rifles kept the British belly-down in their shallow trench, while rapid-firing, French-made, 75-mm cannons rained deadly shrapnel shells. With their position jeopardized, the British were forced to charge. Reinforcements were sent to the top, but the Boers could not be dislodged. With nearly 300 of their number dead and 900 wounded, the British finally withdrew under cover of darkness. "I shall always have it in my memory," wrote Atkins, "that acre of massacre, that complete shambles at the top."[2]

The Boers had employed similarly innovative offensive tactics 3 weeks earlier. Their nighttime assault on the Platrand Heights around Ladysmith took the British regiments there completely by surprise; since the war's outbreak in October 1899, the Boers had clung to defensive tactics, forcing "the khakis" to squander lives in costly charges. Now Boer volunteers moved quickly up the hill to within yards of the top and then poured a withering fire into British lines. Morning found the attackers concealed behind rocks and shrubs. The defenders mounted successive counterattacks and succeeded in pushing the Boers halfway down the slope by nightfall. But it was a remarkable battle. Attacking with vastly inferior numbers against an enemy on high ground, the Boers suffered a mere third as many casualties as the British.[3]

The Khakis were also learning. At Colenso in December 1899, they confronted defenders who had burrowed deep into the ground behind the Tugela River. Field artillery failed to dislodge them—as at Plevna—with the result that British regiments, attacking the Boers' right flank in conventional, tight order, were bloodied and pinned down. In the center, however, Major General Hildyard formed up his brigade in half-companies with 6 to 8 yards between each man and 50- to 80-yard intervals between each half-company. In this extremely open order, they managed to advance a full mile into rifle and artillery fire and take cover within 800 yards of the Boer trenches. Their losses were minimal.[4]

The Boer War—the first struggle between Europeans in the new century—offered military observers many glimpses of combat in the modern era. The spade, one of the Boer's best weapons, served them well along the Tugela. Slit trenches were inadequate, however, as the hapless British learned on Spion Kop. Moreover, rapid-firing rifles and cannons, rendered virtually invisible by smokeless powder, concealment, and long distances, created a new kind of warfare that demanded innovative tactical responses. If more proof were needed, after St. Privat and Plevna, that stubborn traditionalism cost lives, here it was.

Twilight of the Old Conservatism

The British did not cross the Tugela River line and relieve pressure on beleaguered Ladysmith until March 1900. For 5 months before this their attacks had been stymied in South Africa, supplying prudent observers in Europe with new arguments against taking the offensive in modern times. With close ties to the attack-minded Prussian General Staff, the editors of the *Military Weekly* had to be alarmed by such expressions of caution. Whereas some might be convinced, they wrote, that the Boer War had demonstrated the superiority of the defensive, Germany could draw only one lesson from the fighting: to redouble the nation's commitment to the offensive. Germany, surrounded by hostile powers, could not afford to dig in and wait for enemy strength to build: "Our only salvation is to strike down the nearest and most dangerous enemy before others can perhaps intervene in the fighting."[5] To accomplish this feat, German divisions had to move quickly, accompanied by mobile heavy artillery. The article clearly had Schlieffen's imprimatur.

Although operational questions had prompted some public discussion in the 1890s,[6] it was the welter of tactical options that divided military experts in Germany most sharply. Sigismund von Schlichting's *Tactical and Strategic Principles of the Present* which appeared in three volumes between 1897 and 1899, unleashed a nasty polemic that gained momentum as news from the Boer War became available. Schlichting's camp continued its struggle for delegated tactical decision making, open-order formations, and assaults that developed gradually and made full use of foxholes and cover. Conservatives countered that officers would lose control of the attack, that loose formations were vulnerable to massed counterattacks, and that the Boers' unorthodox methods of fighting would not be effective in Europe.[7]

The maneuvers of 1900 served as a trial for these opposing schools of thought. Leading the Guard Corps into battle was the kaiser himself. William's counterpart was General von Langenbeck, commander of Second Corps (Pomerania). After the two armies established contact, the Guard Corps massed its infantry for an assault. The Prussian elite charged without thoroughly reconnoitering Second Corps defenders entrenched on high ground with artillery. Reflecting the cavalier offensive-mindedness of the field artillery, Guard Corps cannoneers raced into the fray to take up forward positions right behind the infantry. The judges had the intestinal fortitude to declare the charge a miserable failure. But Langenbeck also experienced a setback with his Schlichtingesque tactics. Advancing against the Guard Corps in broad, open lines, his battalions did not have enough strength to break through. Intervals between lines were so great, moreover, that reinforcements from the rear did not arrive in time. The kaiser crushed Langenbeck's assault with a cavalry counterattack. In the end, although both corps were bruised, William's side was declared the winner.[8] That the emperor won, as we shall see in the next chapter, was not at all surprising.

Steady British advances forced the Boers to withdraw from large-scale engagements and adopt guerrilla tactics during the winter of 1900–1901. After evaluation in Germany of the war's final conventional campaigns—and renewed polemics[9]—a tactical experiment was held outside Berlin at the Döberitz parade ground in February 1902. The initiator of this special exercise was Lieutenant General Helmuth von Moltke, one of the kaiser's wing adjutants and commander of the prestigious First Guard Division. The purpose was to test new attacking techniques used in the Boer War and "to pay more attention than usual to the ravaging effect of modern weapons."[10] After a second drill and considerable publicity[11] that winter and spring, the division exercised before William II at Tempelhof in May 1902. Immediately converted—which was also not surprising—the emperor parroted Moltke and ordered every corps to familiarize its officers and men with the new methods. Imperial maneuvers in September was another trial for the so-called Boer attack.[12]

But these were not genuine Boer tactics. Moltke and his supporters, in fact, were just trying to breathe life into the dead letter of the 1888 infantry regulations. Fourteen years of traditionalist grumbling and sniping, conservative drill-field practices, and royal preference for massed company columns advancing with drums and bugles at maneuvers had altered Schlichting's creation beyond recognition. Foreign observers no longer witnessed skirmish lines that shifted into dispersed battle groups at 600 to 800 meters. Now German battalions remained in their skirmish lines. Thickened with successive reinforcements from the rear, these long, dense, Frederician formations were drilled by their taskmasters until they could sprint forward, often 100 meters or more, before falling to the ground to await the next command to race forward. Following close behind the "skirmishers" were the massed units of the old days. Schlichting's notion of small groups, ordered by lower-level commanders on the spot—digging foxholes, seeking cover behind rocks and trees, staying concealed overnight if the situation dictated it— had been practiced out of existence.[13] The generals behind the Döberitz initiative of 1902 were convinced that British losses in South Africa were the result of copying German drill field practices, not German regulations.[14] What the "innovators" demonstrated at Tem-

pelhof was the loose order of randomly dispersed, autonomous battle groups, which Schlichting had advocated since the 1870s. The
only sop to the Boers was the substitution of crawling forward—but
only at middle distance—for the short sprints prescribed by regulations.

The battle of words now began in earnest. Major Krug von
Nidda observed how typically Prussian things had looked at Tempelhof. The astute Saxon military attaché reported that the Guard
Corps buttressed its final attack by mixing one battalion phalanx
with other units deployed in loose formation. "[They will] probably
still make such casualty-generating concessions here twenty years
from now, regardless of how much is written and spoken in the
meantime about the modern art of war."[15] A Bavarian captain, Arnold Möhl, noted that this mixture of formations was the hallmark
of Schlichting's final assault but that a genuine Boer attack had no
last charge at all. Möhl believed that Germany should emulate the
Boers by taking cover a few hundred meters away, then shooting
the enemy soldiers out of their positions.[16] Others disagreed, ad-
mitting that dispersed skirmish lines reduced casualties but doubting whether there would be adequate punch to break through. One
writer expressed anger in the *Military Weekly* , charging that the reformers were oblivious to the awesome firepower of tightly packed
attackers: "Aren't *we* worth anything? Do our people have less courage and patriotism than our enemies? Isn't firepower a cover of
sorts?"[17] Similar sentiments were expressed by one of Schlichting's
most bitter polemical enemies, Wilhelm von Scherff, who published
his diehard ideas at book length.[18]

The Prussian General Staff took a middle position on the lessons
of the Boer War in various publications in 1903 and 1904.[19] Schlieffen's men favored denser skirmish line formations to achieve superiority of firepower over defenders. This meant that commanders
had to be willing to incur losses. Otherwise, the troops would quickly
sense that officers "no longer believe in the success of a frontal
charge against modern rifles," which would totally undermine "the
strong will to succeed no matter what the costs."[20] There were to be
no premature charges before defenders were sufficiently weakened,
however, and troop commanders should always strive to outflank an
enemy position before ordering a frontal assault. Patience and the
dictates of changing battlefield situations might necessitate attacks
like Hildyard's at Colenso, moreover, or even the use of spades.

The Boer, or open-field, attack became popular very quickly with
battalion commanders. Unaffected by the glories of history-book

wars they had not experienced, many younger officers saw the new technique as a means to certain victory in the age of magazine rifles and machine guns.[21] One corps commander who took the lessons displayed at Döberitz in 1902 to heart was Karl von Bülow, commander of Third Corps (Brandenburg) since early 1903. He was convinced that the attacking infantry had to stay in dispersed skirmish lines as long as possible. Every method of advance was fair in wartime: slithering, crawling, or short sprints to the next available cover. "Nothing will shake the nerves of the enemy as badly," he wrote in 1904, "as the steady and uninterrupted pushing forward of our firing lines." Bülow was not immune to the old fear of the traditionalists, expressed in countless polemics since the 1890s, that such an attack would be impossible for officers to control. He argued that repeated drill and the "fullest possible use of leaders in the ranks" would teach every man what he had to do. The key was close hand-and-eye contact among squad, platoon, and company officers and NCOs during the advance, practiced to the point of "meticulous order." The alternative—moving forward nearly shoulder to shoulder—was unacceptable to Bülow: "The best infantry in the world cannot bear this kind of casualties."[22]

Bülow's preference for frontal assaults placed him in the mainstream of corps commanders. Thus, Schlieffen shook his head in dismay that the General Staff's doctrine of the enfilade was so often ignored by generals who were fixated on the dangers of spreading their forces too thin.[23] But Bülow's skirmish attack formations also failed to resonate with many division and corps commanders. Indeed with no strict enforcement or authoritative interpretation of regulations and with polemics raging in print, most felt free to implement their own tactical preferences—a freedom that has been largely overlooked in the literature on the German Army.[24] As the Bavarian military representative in Berlin reported, all Prussian officers admitted freely that each corps had its own set of rules.[25] This variety in training methods on the drill fields of Germany's 23 army corps explains why some isolated observers believed that the Boer Attack was emerging as a new orthodoxy in 1903 and 1904, whereas others concluded, quite contradictorily, that it was nothing but a passing fad.[26]

Adding to the confusion were reactionary trends that emanated from the top. At its spring exercises in May 1903, for instance, the commander of the Guard Corps, Lieutenant General von Kessel, reverted to assaults with massed battalion and company columns. The "useless" nature of an exercise that "served only parade purposes" was frankly and sharply criticized by Kessel's chief of staff, Major General Sixt von Armin, as well as such other Guard Corps commanders as Moltke. The anger among reform-minded officers was also "very widespread" when an aged Count Waldersee praised the spirit of this attack before the emperor, for they felt that a soldier of Waldersee's stature should have criticized practices "which do harm to the army."[27] The Guard Corps also knew how quickly William fell into intrigues. In this case, however, the kaiser was merely drifting back into familiar patterns and habits. His preference for shock tactics was revealed in all its absurdity at September 1903 maneuvers when "modern imperatives" were ignored "to paint a pretty picture."[28] In September 1904, incredulous observers "shrieked to high heavens"[29] as they watched an even more appalling demonstration. With William riding into the tightly packed front ranks of the Guard Corps, frenetically trying to hurry the attack, regiments with no artillery support were allowed to overrun superior numbers of entrenched defenders without firing a shot: "Why do you Guardists bother to carry weapons if you don't even need them?" complained a major from the losing Ninth Corps.[30] His sarcasm accentuated the idiocy of the situation.

Ernst Rudolf Maximilian Edler von der Planitz[31] was a hard-charging horseman of the old school. His appointment as a new general inspector of the cavalry in April 1898 was a fairly good sign that the glorious age of mounted warfare had not passed. So was the meteoric advancement of the kaiser's friend Baron Moritz Ferdinand von Bissing, of the Fourth Guard Cavalry Brigade, to commander of Tenth Corps (Hanover). Imperial maneuvers that year pitted the Tenth Corps against the Seventh (Westphalia), with the cavalry playing their feature role under Planitz, Bissing, and—as usual—the kaiser himself.[32] The reason the cavalry took center stage in 1898 was the rumored plan of the Russians to flood East Prussia with Cossacks if war broke out. If Germany's mobilization plans were to proceed smoothly, the dreaded Russian riders would have to be met head-on. Pounding his fist, William insisted that the Reichstag approve creation of 16 new cavalry regiments.[33]

The frontal-assault mentality of Germany's three-wave tacticians, however, did not go unchallenged. One of the brashest advocates of change was Friedrich von Bernhardi, by early 1899 chief of staff of Sixteenth Corps (Alsace). That year he published *Our Cavalry in the Next War*, a call for expanded numbers of cavalrymen, heavily armed with magazine rifles, machine guns, and artillery. This "mounted infantry" would embark on raids and commando missions against enemy communications and transport; fight dismounted if the situation warranted it; or stay on horseback to punish routed, demoralized infantry with devastating, quick strikes. The cavalry's contribution to victory would come before and after the main battle—Mars-la-Tour was relegated to the history books.[34] That same year another reformer, Major Brixen-Hahn, contributed a chapter on the cavalry to a special twenty-fifth-anniversary edition of *Löbell's Annual Report* . His inquiry, in a sometimes irreverent tone, doubted the correctness of prevailing doctrine. Brixen-Hahn concluded that cavalrymen should accustom themselves to a more strategic mission, keeping an open mind about new communications and scouting technologies like telephones, bicycles, and airships.[35] Georg Friedrich von Kleist also emphasized the cavalry's reconnaissance role. Influential enough to implement the first reconnoitering exercises in 1890–1891, Kleist's voice receded when a reaction set in by the mid-1890s. He acquired new allies in the Prussian General Staff, however, as the decade unfolded.[36]

The result was a new mission for cavalry units at the first imperial maneuvers of the new century. The exercises were held, the reader will recall, under mounting impressions of the Boer War. At Talana, Colenso, and Magersfontein, the British cavalry had failed miserably in its reconnaissance mission.[37] Determined to avoid such disasters and enhance warlike realism, Schlieffen ordered the cavalry to scout, rather than parade, before maneuvers. The General Staff frowned on the spectacular public display that opened every autumn campaign because it brought both participating corps together in one location and contributed to the practice of being too close to one another at the beginning of the fighting. This popular routine also reinforced conservative prejudices in the cavalry by eliminating the need for long-distance reconnaissance and facilitating the much more exciting crush of horseflesh. Because the armies were ordered to bivouac far afield, the Guard Cavalry reconnoitered a distance of 120 kilometers before spotting Langenbeck's Second Corps. Exhibiting his contradictoriness—and underlying malleability—William praised the Guard Cavalry for covering the ground in 24 hours.[38]

Neither the reformers nor their allies in the General Staff, however, had any impact on Planitz. After Bernhardi wrote an article against Bissing that had "the whole world talking," Planitz ordered the reformer from Sixteenth Corps to attend special cavalry maneuvers at Altengrabow. It was the old order of massed thundering hoofs that was displayed there in August 1900, not surprisingly, but

Planitz was not satisfied with mere demonstration, subjecting Bern-hardi's views to "continuous attack" before the other officers. The public rebuke of the rebellious colonel had no apparent effect on the Young Turks: "It was a pleasure for me to see," recalled Bern-hardi, "that the great majority of cavalry officers stood on my side."[39]

Writing from the warped vantage point of the 1920s, a proud Bernhardi may have exaggerated the numbers. There can be no doubt, for instance, that older officers were certainly not in Bern-hardi's "great majority." In fact, whatever reforming impulses the Boer War generated on high, they dissipated during the first years of the new century—the same pattern we have observed in the in-fantry. Reflecting in early 1903 on the cavalry tactics preferred by Bissing and many other corps commanders, Alfred von Waldersee bemoaned the tendency to amass horse regiments in front of the advancing infantry, then rush them "head over heels into cavalry battles where they will be wasted prematurely." He preferred to see the French needlessly sacrifice their best horse in such attacks "while we keep ours in reserve in order to make full use of them later."[40] The Bavarian military attaché in Berlin also scoffed at "the custom-ary practice" of consolidating up to four divisions in giant cavalry corps. Had anyone thought through the logistics of feeding all of the horses? How could they fit onto one road?[41] Seeming to confirm the need for alarm, an article in the *Military Weekly* advocated the resuscitation of genuine Frederician three-equal-wave tactics against enemy cavalry in modern times. Lines had been "too thin"[42] in re-cent maneuvers, complained the author, leaving German cavalry vul-nerable to counterattacks.

Such sentimentalism, of course, was not universal, and a second edition of Bernhardi's *Our Cavalry in the Next War* appeared in early 1903. Some generals, like Karl von Bülow, commander of Third Corps (Brandenburg), implemented the younger man's recommen-dations, training their cavalry squadrons to dismount and fight like infantrymen.[43] Moreover, the large-unit attacks that were the kaiser's grand finale every September left many cold. Writing after the 1904 exercises, for instance, an old-timer lambasted "those who have only a pitiful shoulder shrug for massed horse assaults at maneuvers." Such indifference besmirched the memory of Mars-la-Tour and was "an egregious injustice to the cavalry and the entire army."[44]

The cavalry and the rest of the army reacted with a shrug of the shoulders, meanwhile, to one of the most novel, awesome, and con-troversial military technologies of the early twentieth century—the machine gun. Invented in 1884 by an American, Hiram Maxim, the ingenious device shot more than 600 bullets per minute. British soldiers used it with shocking effect against the Matabeles in 1893 and 1896 and again to defeat the Sudanese in 1898.[45] Neither side used many Maxim guns in the Boer War, but the 6,300 men of Britian's First Mounted Infantry Brigade used 20 of the killing machines in their punishing campaigns.

Machine guns were introduced in Germany in the early 1890s. For quite some time, German weapons testers had experimented with a workable bullet for Hiram Maxim's gun, only to balk at placing orders after problems were solved. "Large bodies move slow," was Maxim's way of describing the ingrained hesitancy of the army to accept novel devices. The kaiser intervened in 1894 on a whim. During a visit of British Prince Edward, conversation turned to arms. Edward suggested that William observe the Maxim machine gun, and a test firing was hurriedly arranged at Spandau Fortress. After the Maxim gun had fired 333 cartridges in fewer than 30 seconds, "the Emperor walked back, examined the gun, and, placing his finger on it, said: 'That is the gun—there is no other.' "[46] He ordered the War Ministry to resume tests.

The army purchased its first machine guns in 1895 from Maxim's licensee in Berlin, Ludwig Löwe & Company.[47] Prussian War Minister Walther Bronsart von Schellendorff was still unimpressed, however, complaining about all of the unnecessary expenditure that unofficial advisers—in this case William's uncle, Prince Edward—foisted on the impressionable monarch.[48] Bronsart appeared to be exacting a subtle revenge, therefore, when he gave the emperor's latest plaything to the field artillery for further experimentation "to determine a purposeful and successful use of such weapons."[49] The guns simply gathered dust until they were given to the Jäger battalions in 1898. The field artillery's indignant reaction to machine guns could not have surprised the minister of war. Prussia's proud gunners were wedded to the C-73 and C-96. By the 1890s, however, this familiarity had hardened into a masculine artillery aesthetic that rejected "mortar-mouth" howitzers and the "monstrous" French 75 mm. The field artillery had to shun a cannon whose odd-looking little barrel did not seem long enough for mounting between wheels.

It was now the infantry's turn. The Jäger battalions of First Corps (East Prussia) tested Maxims at corps maneuvers in 1898. Further experiments by the sharpshooters of the Guard, First, and Sixteenth (Alsace) Corps took place during the subsequent spring and summer in preparation for imperial maneuvers in September 1899. The

Figure 6. Meticulous order on the battlefield: Infantrymen practice short sprints and hit the ground. Source: Julius Hoppenstedt, *Das Volk in Waffen, Vol. 1: Das Heer* (Dachau, 1913).

Jäger were concerned with problems of overheating and jamming, battlefield tactics, and organizational deployment—that is, whether to allot a gun to each battalion or to group guns in six-gun batteries like the artillery. The testers recommended the latter form to guarantee that some guns kept firing when others broke down.[50] After a succession of negative experiences at imperial and corps maneuvers between 1899 and the early 1900s, however, the 16 Jäger battalions that had been allotted a machine gun detachment wanted little or nothing to do with the new weapon. Initial plans for integrating the guns into their battalions were jettisoned in favor of independent detachments stationed with the Jäger in peacetime but marching with the cavalry at maneuvers and during wartime.[51] The regular infantry had also turned thumbs down. When machine gun warfare raised its ugly head in the Far East in 1904, no infantry regiment in Germany had a machine gun detachment.

There were many reasons for the unsuccessful debut of machine guns in the infantry. For one thing, they weighed more than 60 pounds and were mounted awkwardly on sledgelike carriages that nearly tripled the total load. Attacking frontline troops simply could

not carry or drag them very easily.[52] The gun's immobility strengthened the quickly growing opposition of the artillery, stirred from its
indifference by the tactless boasting of machine gun enthusiasts who
claimed that Maxims could replace field cannons. Infantry officers
agreed with the artillery, stipulating in a 1901 draft of machine gun
regulations that detachments should remain behind the infantry,
advancing no closer than 800 meters from enemy lines and not
interrupting fire to change position. The Maxim could supplement
but never replace the field artillery "because it cannot maneuver
with horse on the battlefield."[53]

The resultant placement far to the rear, however, meant that
gun crews, laden with ammunition packs, were usually late in reaching forward positions. Critics also doubted whether enough ammunition could be moved up in actual combat or, if this problem were
overcome, whether mechanized shooting would be accurate. Firing
competitions between machine gunners and sharpshooters fell invariably to the Jäger. And woe to the attacking army that relied too
heavily on the firepower of machine guns, said the doubters, for a
jammed gun or one well-placed shot by a defender would reduce
the firepower of the assault by the equivalent of 30 to 70 men. The
best deployment of machine guns—assuming solutions were found
to many of the problems—was therefore to amass them in defensive
positions. But here was another reason to oppose the new weapon,
for if Maxim's gun aided only the defense, infantrymen preoccupied
with the offense wanted nothing to do with it.[54] Even the sometimes
very progressive Prussian General Staff showed no interest in
Maxim's invention, proclaiming that it was "completely unsuited for
offensive warfare."[55]

The kaiser, in the meantime, had noticed that British cavalry
and mounted infantry in South Africa were equipped with machine
guns. Always impressed by what the English were doing, William
decided immediately that his cavalry must have them too. This wish
was fulfilled during September 1900 maneuvers.[56] The reaction in
Germany's mounted corps was less than enthusiastic. Just one year
earlier, each cavalry division had been forced to accept two 6-gun
horse artillery batteries.[57] The transfer out of the artillery fulfilled a
decades-old wish of the horse gunners, but Planitz's men scowled at
the newcomers and their weighty cannons. The objection to machine guns was the same—they were simply a "new impediment."[58]
But this criticism was not limited to cavalry conservatives, as shown
by the controversy that Bernhardi's writings sparked among the reformers themselves. Whereas some rejected a technology that lim-

ited cavalry mobility, others feared that the new gun would delay efforts to train all cavalry units in dismounted fighting techniques. Indeed, with military experts estimating the gun's firepower as equal to 30 to 70 marksmen, a few Maxims could replace an entire dismounted squadron of 100 men.[59]

The maneuvers of 1903 marked the fourth year that cavalry divisions had dragged their "new impediment" into mock battle.[60] The guns were not allowed to rise much above the level of a nuisance. On the first day, the commander of Cavalry Division B let his machine gunners separate from the horses and advance with infantry skirmishers, where they were overrun by A's cavalry. On the second day, both participating cavalry divisions were placed under the emperor's command in a mighty corps that included 4 horse artillery batteries—24 cannons—and 4 machine gun detachments—24 Maxims. This awesome gathering of firepower was positioned with an infantry brigade on high ground in front of the massed horses. The enemy attacked across 2,000 meters of open ground with 1 infantry division, but the suicidal charge was ruled a success. The ridiculous decision played right into William's hands. He ordered a counterattack of the entire cavalry corps drawn up in three waves. The enemy infantry was routed by men on horseback, not machines. After a wild gallop of 6,000 meters, William's men also overran an artillery brigade, an infantry brigade, and an additional 18 artillery batteries. His machine guns and horse artillery provided unneeded support on the left flank. After the maneuvers, the guns went back to the Jäger garrisons, and the cavalry did not see them for another year— small wonder that a few years later the War Ministry considered reassigning Germany's machine gun detachments to fortress duty "because [they are] not being used by the cavalry divisions."[61]

On the eve of the Russo-Japanese War in 1904, therefore, machine guns had a lowly stepchild status in the German Army. Ten years after the emperor had said that Maxim's device was "*the* gun, there is no other," the artillery, the Jäger, and the regular infantry had all rejected it; William's pride and joy, the cavalry, had to tolerate it for a mere 5 days a year. Only the fortress commandants had the requisite humility to employ machine guns.[62]

The competition between field cannons and machine guns was very intense around 1900. Not only were advocates of the new weapon bragging that it offered better support for infantry attacks, but also machine guns appeared to be a genuine threat to artillery units that insisted on firing from exposed forward positions.[63] That the artillery

"fired back," lambasting the overzealousness of machine gun enthusiasts, was perfectly rational and understandable. We cannot appreciate the intensity of the artillery's new feud, however, without re-
calling how frayed the collective nerves of this army branch had
become after a succession of bitter defeats. Throughout 1897 and
1898, Ernst Hoffbauer, inspector general of the field artillery, waged
an unsuccessful counteroffensive against the light, 105-mm field
howitzers promoted by Schlieffen. Unable to block the new howitzer
batteries, he argued that their introduction into the field artillery
obviated the necessity of 150-mm field howitzers in the hated heavy
artillery. Hoffbauer and his followers also engaged in a rearguard
effort to have heavy artillery attack exercises canceled. But all attempts failed.

Field artillerists were in no mood to brook criticism of the new
C-96 cannon that began to replace worn-out C-73 batteries in 1897.
But hear it they did with the advent in 1898 of the rapid-firing
French 75. The idea of semirecoilless cannons soon found advocates
across the Rhine who wanted Germany to improve on France's design with a lighter, more mobile version. Foremost among them was
Lieutenant General Heinrich Rohne, a thoroughly practical field
artillerist who had never lost sight of the need—so obvious to cannoneers in wartime—for both mobility and firepower. Rohne pres-
sured the artillery proving commission to investigate new models,
even taking his campaign publicly into print.[64]

But the Young Turk could not budge his colleagues from their
rigid adherence to the light and mobile C-96. Soon they took the
offensive against the rapid-firing cannon, ridiculing its cumber-
someness; disbelieving its rate of fire under wartime conditions; and
doubting whether it would remain immobile while firing on sandy,
muddy, or frozen ground.[65] The controversy worsened in late 1900,
when France added shields to its gun and Prussia's proving commission refused to follow suit with the C-96. The added protection
that shields afforded gun crews against shrapnel, magazine rifle fire,
and machine guns fell victim to "serious concerns that the weight
of the field cannon will rise enormously, and that the mechanism
will have to be much more complicated than is presently the case."
Cannons with shields would be easier to spot and easier to hit, moreover, and direct hits would be more dangerous because of the need
to position caissons and ammunition wagons next to the quicker-
firing guns.[66]

By 1901 the beleaguered field artillery was apparently losing
again. War Ministry artillerists had long defended conservative gun-

ners around Hoffbauer from General Staff plans for guns that seemed militarily unnecessary, financially exorbitant, and therefore politically unwise. But now Schlieffen's men argued irrefutably that French cannons could unleash two to three times more shells per minute while shielding themselves from Germany's inferior return fire. The empire's proud field artillery would be "destroyed without a doubt before inflicting substantial harm [on the enemy]." Concurring with the General Staff that the situation was "extremely grave," War Minister Heinrich von Gossler ordered Rohne to terminate his polemics and consult the artillery proving commission on rapid-firing cannon designs. The new cannons would also have shields.[67]

But Schlieffen's victory was limited because Gossler was basically more interested in fortresses and heavy artillery than in the field artillery. Therefore he insisted on saving money with the new gun. To hold down costs, the gun would use existing C-96 barrels, even though they were shorter than French barrels and would sacrifice 1,000 meters of range. To keep the Reichstag Budget Committee at arm's length, moreover, the transition to the new cannons would be very gradual so that it would not provoke parliamentary criticism.[68] The insightful Bavarian military representative, Franz Karl Endres, sensed that there was more behind the delays than antiparliamentary strategy. Conservatives on the artillery proving commission were so angry at Rohne that the decision for rapid-firing cannon could be considered "provisional" at best,[69] and soon the kaiser was causing problems, too. Seemingly convinced in 1902 that shields were indispensable, a year later William wanted nothing to do with technical changes that endangered "the spirit of the attack."[70]

Circumstances were only marginally better in the heavy artillery. The plans of Inspector General Heinrich Edler von der Planitz[71] for a massive expansion of his corps were frustrated after 1900, when the General Staff worked out ambitious enveloping strategies that relied more on extra infantry corps and new field artillery capabilities like rapid-firing cannons and light howitzers. Eight of Germany's 23 army corps in 1903 had no heavy artillery batteries.[72] Prospects brightened somewhat that year with the introduction of a semirecoilless 150-mm howitzer (s.FH-02) mounted on wheels. The first 10 batteries were operational by 1904. Without more horse teams, however, the idea of putting heavy artillery units into the field remained theoretical. The number of horse-drawn detachments (combining 150- and 210-mm guns) increased slowly from 6 in 1897 to 10 in 1904. Schlieffen's earliest plans in the 1890s for breaking into France had called for 16.

The slowly expanding capabilities of the heavy artillery perpetuated harsh prejudices that were emanating from the field artillery, and this did further harm to Planitz's agendas. Unit commanders could not be expected to ignore the barbs of field artillerists and learn to appreciate the big howitzers and mortars if these guns remained immobile. Just as damaging was the subpar performance of the horse-drawn detachments. One commanding general complained after maneuvers that his onrushing regiments were forced to halt "in every village" so that heavy artillery teams could care for the horses: "I was told that their elephants have to be watered frequently, but obviously this really undercut my marching time."[73] These strong feelings may not have been unanimous, but they were widespread enough for Planitz to initiate special firing exhibitions in 1902 "so that generals of other branches can see the wartime effectiveness of the heavy artillery."[74] As late as 1904, however, Prussian War Minister Karl von Einem had to order commanding generals to maneuver more regularly with heavy field howitzers. "In this way all unit commanders and troops can be shown that the heavy field artillery is capable of being used like any other weapon in open battle, and must be brought in for the decision."[75] That he needed to issue the order in the first place spoke volumes.

The field artillery's rapid-firing cannon had still not debuted at the time of Einem's warning. Kaiser William finally assented to the new weapon in January 1903 but insisted it would not have protective shields lest they endanger Germany's attack mentality. It was only with considerable difficulty that Einem managed to persuade him otherwise. Production was not scheduled to begin until April 1904, however, and then only at the snail's pace of two corps per year.[76] These delays seemed to confirm the Bavarian military representative's prediction that artillery traditionalists would block adoption of the new design. Indeed, Rohne and other backers of the new field piece conducted a spirited defense of their ideas throughout 1903 and 1904. These were good indications that a battle still raged.[77]

The outbreak of war between Russia and Japan in February 1904 accelerated the tempo of artillery rearmament. Annual funding increased from 5 million to 12.5 million marks in June—enough to reequip five corps with field cannons by the end of 1905.[78] That 18 corps were still without the new gun did not worry cavalier friends

Figure 7. "Elephants" on the move: the rapid-firing 150-mm howitzer (s.FH-02). Source: Köhler, *Der Aufstieg.*

of the C-96, however, for spirit and mobility were considered much more important than firepower.

Technophobes and Technophiles

A "highly placed personage" in the army wrote Friedrich von Bernhardi in late 1901 with disturbing thoughts. An official trip to Bremerhaven had brought Bernhardi's "patriotically imbued" correspondent to the pier of one of Germany's great ships. He marveled at "the ingenious construction of its machines and the skill of our workers." Although it was definitely "a triumph of modern technology," there was still something about the awesome display that worried him: "The thought occurred to me that all of this [technology] should only serve the intellectual life of the nation, but not dominate it." High ideals and a sense of history underpinned the moral strength that had shaped modern Germany, but these qualities were rapidly disappearing: "It always seems to me as if we are standing on a small island, alone with the ideals that our fathers planted in us." Abject surrender was not an option, however, for an old soldier with strong convictions: "The materialistic-technological tendency of the times must be counterbalanced if it is not to be our ruin."[79]

As we have seen so far, this counterbalancing was exactly what many "highly placed" officers in the army had been doing for two decades. The notion that German warriors required apparatuses and devices to reproduce their great victories of 1866 and 1870 was contemptuously rejected and tenaciously resisted. There was a place for mechanized warfare, to be sure, but it was not a central one—as shown by the victories of soldierly spirit at Mars-la-Tour and St. Privat, as well as the inability of the French to save themselves with the *mitrailleuse* . The Russo-Turkish War and the Boer War did not substantially alter these widely held attitudes. Such antitechnological views lay behind internal army feuds over (and hesitant adoption of) magazine repeating rifles, machine guns, light and heavy howitzers, rapid-firing cannons, and artillery shields. In each of these hard-fought, usually incomplete victories, modernist factions attempted to follow up with corresponding tactical reforms but failed to fully implement them. Despite changes in the regulations, infantry and cavalry continued to amass their ranks in the face of what would be deadly fire. Artillery tactics remained unchanged, moreover, as traditionalists tended to ignore the opportunities that newer guns afforded for firing from hidden positions at longer range.[80] The operational response to modern military technology was arguably better—the entire rationale for Schlieffen's sweep through Belgium, after all, was to avoid the terribly destructive firepower of modern weapons, especially when combined with the defensive advantages of impregnable fortresses. There was a definite element of escapism here, however, as the Prussian General Staff deemphasized all technologies except those that seemed to promise rapid movement around the enemy. In other words, Schlieffen was by no means deaf to the Cassandras who were pointing alarmingly to the materialistic-technological tendency of the times.

The formidable position of army commanders who preferred to wage war in the old ways came under sharper attack as the century drew to a close. A turning point of sorts occurred in 1897, when the kaiser agreed to lift a decades-old, strictly enforced ban against published criticism of army policies and practices by officers on active duty. The War Ministry and General Staff had waged a campaign against these restrictions since 1889, uniting behind the argument that censorship and suppression inhibited the increasingly necessary

education of officers. Freer publication of opposing views would further the debate and discussion of modern military science. The
looser policy led to the founding of a spate of new journals—13
between 1897 and 1900—that spearheaded a wide variety of reformist causes within the army.[81]

One of the most significant new publications was the *Journal of
Technological Warfare*. Established in 1898 by Willibald Stavenhagen,
a retired captain of the fortress engineers, the enterprise gave vent
to a quarter century of pent-up, frustrated enthusiasm for military
technological development. Little is known about Stavenhagen, but
as a middle-class technician in the least glamorous branch of the
army, he would have possessed none of those upper-class, emotional,
ideological, or vested departmental attachments to outmoded, aging, or inappropriate technologies that burdened prouder corps like
the field artillery, cavalry, and infantry. In 1896, he proposed merg-
ing the weapons proving commissions, fortress engineers, sappers
(Pioniere), and all technical institutes into a special corps that would
report to a "Technological Department of the Prussian General
Staff."[82]

The *Journal of Technological Warfare* continued to advocate institutional reorganizations of this sort to guarantee a "successful response to the challenges of war" amid the "relentless advance of
technology."[83] Stavenhagen and the team of writers who worshipped
with him at the shrine of technology called for what a later American
generation dubbed the military-industrial complex: an intensified
civilian-industrial hunt for science and technology coordinated with
reorganized and rationalized army institutions that were capable of
transforming the torrent of ideas and inventions into practical battlefield weapons.[84] Not surprisingly, the pages of the *Journal of Technological Warfare* were also open to every army faction that was struggling against entrenched conservatism. Thus, Heinrich Rohne
published his defense of rapid-firing cannons here, and a steady
stream of articles presented the case for adoption of machine guns
before it was too late.[85] Stavenhagen wrote in the very first issue that
his journal would not kowtow to the feverish attack-mindedness of
the Prussian General Staff. No rigid believer in wars of movement
and quick victory within a year, the old fortifications engineer
wanted his writers to further the "appreciation of fortress warfare in
a strategical, tactical, and military-historical sense."[86]

To many readers, however, the new journal was too bizarre and
futuristic. What was one to make of its curious interest in the military
potential of X rays, ventilated bunkers, telephones, armored auto-

mobiles, and flying machines?[87] Even open-minded advocates of technology looked askance at the zealotry of Stavenhagen's editorial team. In November 1902, for example, a skeptical but very reasonable piece appeared in the *German Review* , a periodical that covered a wide range of issues. Written by General Rothe of the field artillery, the article analyzed the prerequisites of military effectiveness. Rothe included a lengthy assessment of technology's role, appreciating its growing destructive power, as well as its ability to accelerate transportation, improve communications, and facilitate a smoother functioning of mass armies. To benefit from technology, however, nations had to invest huge sums in research and development, education, and specialized training. Equally important, armies had to spend time and money in testing new devices for military practicality, then consider whether each new machine could be integrated easily into the existing army organization. Rothe concluded that it was imperative to reject innovations that were not simple or durable enough for battlefield use or that disrupted army efficiency in any way. "The progress of technology will perfect the art of warfare as long as proper limits are set to its adoption."[88] Adding to the article's unmistakable undertone of moderate conservatism were lengthy passages that emphasized the significance of nontechnical prerequisites of military effectiveness like physical and moral fitness, knowledge of military history, and courageous leadership. Rothe was clearly hinting that in a world of scarce resources and tradeoffs, these qualities and virtues were just as important.

The technophiles responded with a stinging rejoinder in early 1903. Rothe's opinions were so "widespread in the army" that anyone without prejudices about "the power of technology for an army and a people" had to be concerned. Was it really true that machines and inventions were peripheral to war's outcome or, as some would have it, even dangerous to an army? Those who looked objectively at the situation realized that the opposite was true: The real danger to Germany was the "backwardness" of its army in terms of "drawing on, and having on hand, the available [technological] means." Although it was obvious that each new device needed thorough testing and proving, "we can't wait forever for something better to come along." Such hesitation and reserve were at best a result of ignorance, but one suspected that constant refrains about preserving "simplicity" were just a cover for "a lack of interest [in] or even resistance [to technology]." Germany needed to unite its technical branches and ensconce their chiefs in top positions of authority. Only in this way would the nation be ready for the next war. Such measures were urgent, for "the more our warlike spirit decreases—despite efforts to preserve it from the *Zeitgeist*, today's soft living style, and the overpowering progress of culture—the more the importance of technology grows as a substitute."[89] If nerves were to break down in combat, in other words, it should be on the enemy's side.

It was a measure of the controversy that technological change was provoking in the German Army after 1900 that both technophobes like Bernhardi's correspondent and technophiles like Stavenhagen felt that they were losing ground. The journal's rebuttal of Rothe's article was exaggerated—it was more a reflection of the fact that nerves were frayed after years of frustration than a representation of any cogent criticism of his level-headed arguments. Germany had fallen behind its enemies in machine guns and rapid-firing cannons, and the potential equalizer—heavy field artillery—was still struggling to emerge. The reasons for the journal's overreaction probably went much deeper, however, for Stavenhagen's reorganizational and fortress-oriented agendas had also suffered recent setbacks.

Baron Colmar von der Goltz, head of the Army Corps of Engineers, as well as inspector general of the fortresses, had proposed the kinds of reforms that Stavenhagen and his followers believed were essential to Germany's military rebirth. An adherent of quick-strike offensive warfare as a young general staffer in the 1870s, Goltz became convinced by the lesson of Plevna that the next European war would be a bloody, see-sawing, mechanized slugfest.[90] The elder Moltke had come to the same conclusion, as had, more recently, General Staff Quartermaster Friedrich Köpke and War Minister Heinrich von Gossler.[91] To gird itself for a struggle of peoples that would not be over in a year, Germany needed to foster the kind of fighting spirit that had enabled the Boers to stand up for years to a far mightier empire—again, the agenda of nerves.[92] In addition, Germany needed more offensive firepower, ingenuity in the field, and the protection of state-of-the-art forts like Verdun. Goltz was aware that Heinrich Edler von der Planitz, inspector general of the heavy artillery, was trying to double his battalions; this would accomplish the first goal. In 1899 and 1900, Goltz approached the kaiser with a series of ambitious plans to fulfill the second goal, field ingenuity, and third, fortress protection.

The combat wing of the engineers, the Pioniere, would leave the Corps of Engineers to form an independent branch of assault sappers, specializing in the breach, demolition, and construction of all kinds of fortifications. Their strength would expand from 20 to 32 battalions—more than enough to cover every regular army corps. It was also necessary, Goltz argued, for the combat engineers' spirit of ingenuity to permeate the entire army. This could be accomplished if all regular infantry officers served tours of duty with the sappers.

The fortress engineers would also break out into an independent corps. Goltz wanted to move their classes from the Artillery and Engineering School to the elite War Academy, where they could study with the best students from the other branches. In this way, infantry, cavalry, and artillery officers might be tempted to join the engineering corps. Study at the academy meant, moreover, initiating engineers into the General Staff's operational mode of thinking. The new corps, in fact, would be called an Engineering General Staff. Goltz intended not only to upgrade the status and enhance the military significance of the fortress engineers but also to imbue the rest of the army with the engineers' technological mentality— the same purpose served by regular infantry officers that were having sapper duty. Altogether, these reforms would enhance the ingenuity of the field army and lay the groundwork for achieving the final goal of defensive protection. This last mission would be completed by constructing fortresses along the eastern and western borders. These new fortifications were to be integrated into the army's overall strategic planning—hence the importance of the upgraded Engineering General Staff.[93]

Goltz's proposals for state-of-the-art fortifications were presented to Kaiser William in March 1899. The eastern part of the concept was approved with little controversy in January 1900. The idea of building an impregnable line of forts from the Saar to the Swiss border, however, met resistance from Planitz, Schlieffen, and the kaiser's entourage. Planitz was driven by the artillerist's innate prejudice against engineers—cannons versus castles—but he also knew how the zero-sum budget game worked. Goltz's defeat would enhance Planitz's bid to double the number of battalions under his command. Schlieffen's objections were of a different sort. To facilitate a sweep through Belgium that would cripple France, he wanted the enemy to commit its forces in Lorraine, not to be deterred by fortress technology from attacking there.[94] To these criticisms were added those of Dietrich von Hülsen-Häseler, chief of the Military Cabinet, who declared that too many fortresses would undermine the army's offensive spirit. "We won't be able to push through our own barbed wire impediments."[95] William yielded despite the sup-

port of Gossler and his own "burning enthusiasm"[96] for Goltz's proposals. Western construction plans were shelved sometime in late
1901 or early 1902—about the same time, it is interesting to note,
that the emperor reversed himself and opposed shields for the field
artillery.

Goltz's plans for the sappers and fortress engineers were presented to the kaiser on 4 December 1900.[97] The emperor also heard
Planitz's artillery proposals at this time. Although William enthusi-
astically backed both men, his "decisions" were soon reversed. The
first setbacks occurred a week later, when Karl von Einem, the second man in the War Ministry, convinced both his skeptical chief
and Schlieffen to oppose these "futuristic plans." Expansion of the
infantry and cavalry was "far more necessary than an enormous increase in the specialized branches."[98] The kaiser yielded to this advice in March 1901. Neither the combat engineers (Pioniere) nor
the heavy artillery received the additional battalions that Goltz and
Planitz had requested.

It took a while longer for the rest of Goltz's plans to unravel.
Under the new arrangements approved by Emperor William, regular
infantry officers were supposed to include sapper duty in their service rotations. But complaints about "technical service" mounted
steadily in 1901 and 1902, until corps commanders finally terminated the unpopular practice in 1903.[99] The cooperation that Goltz
had wanted between fortress engineers and the regular army also
broke down. In May 1901, Gossler convinced the kaiser that engineering officers should study at a separate technical institute rather
than the War Academy. Realizing what was at stake, Goltz protested
that fortress engineers needed a thorough military education in tactics and strategy if they were to integrate their designs into army
planning. They had to go beyond engineering to master elements
of military theory like terrain, operations, transportation, and what
could be anticipated from the enemy. Gossler's proposals, in contrast, would "develop engineering officers even more exclusively into
technocrats and distance them even more from a lively contact with
the [regular] army."[100] Goltz's objections had no effect whatsoever.
Worse still, he was transferred as commander of First Corps in January 1902. Goltz believed—with good reason—that Hülsen-Häseler
had turned against him. The powerful Military Cabinet chief in
charge of army personnel matters not only feared the effect of fortress construction on army morale but also believed "that engineers
and sappers are basically superfluous."[101] It was better to have someone like Goltz in faraway East Prussia.

The banished general complained that the only product of his tireless efforts was the unwanted Military Technical Academy. Goltz predicted, however, that "soon enough no one will care about this institute—it will just completely ossify."[102] He was right. The snubbing began well before classes started in 1903. To compete with a War Academy that reported to the elite Prussian General Staff, the institute's new director, General Kersting of the heavy artillery, "practically begged" Einem, who had succeeded Gossler, to assume responsibility for the Military Technical Academy. "But no—he was too uncomfortable about concerning himself with such strange material."[103] So the school was given to the General Inspectorate of Military Education, which cared more about fencing and riding instruction than scientific "know-it-all-ism" that could "ruin discipline and produce disruptive spirits."[104] As a final indignity, Kersting had to accept the rank of brigadier (as opposed to division commander) and then swallow budget cutbacks that halved the inaugural class to a mere 50 students.[105] Widespread army prejudices against the "mechanics' academy" made it impossible to recruit this reduced number, however, just as the inability of Military Technical Academy graduates to get top assignments, even on the weapons proving commissions, further undermined its attractiveness in the eyes of potential officers.

The basic problem in the army that was drawing the best young men to the War Academy—and making them eschew its technological counterpart, the Military Technical Academy—was "a traditional worshipping of the deeds and fame of our great forefathers" instead of promoting the scientific knowledge necessary for "strategies that have to be executed with the technological products of modern culture." Students at the War Academy were too steeped in the consciousness that they were being groomed for the General Staff, an elite leadership position, "which since the day of Königgrätz, Schlieffen had said, was the proudest in the world."[106]

War in 1903–1904: A Scenario

Technophobes and technophiles both believed that their side was losing. On balance, however, the latter were closer to the truth. For a quarter century, proud, defiant conservatives had constructed myths about 1870. They worshipped man, muscle, and morale in the machine age. Although their victory was far from complete, its effects would have been disastrously evident had Germany faced

France alone in 1903 or 1904. Historians tend to shy away from counterfactual analysis, but this is exactly the type of thinking that military establishments undertake on a regular basis. By considering hypothetical situations, historians can gain a truer measure of the significance of the real and the actual. So here we ask: What might have happened?

The outcome would be determined in two theaters of action.[107] First, if France did not attack immediately, Germany planned to advance from Lorraine against the center of the French fortress line at Nancy. Schlieffen committed 28 active divisions (of 12 battalions each) and 3 reserve divisions to this assault.[108] The French anticipated a thrust south from Metz toward Nancy and planned to parry it with 3 armies. Echeloned to the west of Nancy, they totaled 28 regular shock divisions (of 16 battalions each). Two huge forces would lock horns between Metz and Nancy. The battle would be joined there first in the third week of mobilization. The French left 1 army of 8 divisions behind Epinal and another of 4 divisions to anchor the right wing west of Belfort.[109] Germany's weak left wing— 4 active and 6 reserve divisions—was deployed in Alsace opposite Epinal.

Meanwhile, Schlieffen sent 14 active divisions (of 12 battalions each) and 6 reserve divisions into Belgium. First Army marched across southern Holland, then southwest into Belgium between Antwerp and Liège. Second Army moved southwest of Liège into the Belgian Ardennes. The goal was to encircle the enemy somewhere behind Verdun and Nancy.[110] The French had rejected the possibility of a German thrust north of the Meuse and would have been greatly surprised to see one occur. To guard against it, they had only 4 reserve divisions (of 16 battalions each) at Rheims.[111] But French reinforcing units were not far away. The British took the threat seriously, moreover, and would have sent an expeditionary force. The BEF would head inland with 50 battalions, arriving in Belgium during the fourth or fifth week.[112]

The likely outcome in Lorraine was a German defeat. If there was no immediate French sortie from the fortresses, Schlieffen instructed his center armies to assemble around Metz and then advance toward Nancy. The German assault would attract enemy troops and set up a trap when the right wing completed its sweep.[113] But the French planned a trap of their own, waiting for the Germans to move south from Metz and then hitting their rear flank in the Saar with powerful forces. They had greater overall numbers—448 versus 372 battalions—plus the important element of surprise. Compounding and multiplying the overall effect was a vastly superior artillery. Because the 75-mm cannon was semirecoilless and the C-96 was not, the rapid-firing French field artillery had a 60% fire-power advantage, despite fewer cannons.[114] The 75's range was also 1,000 meters farther. Moreover, each of France's corps marched into Lorraine with 1 battery of 120-mm howitzers and 2 batteries of 155-mm howitzers—and the 155s were rapid-firing. The regular German corps had only 3 batteries of slower firing 105-mm howitzers, whereas the reserve divisions moved with nothing but a half contingent of light C-96s.[115] Finally, all French cannons and howitzers had shields, but the German weapons had none. In light of France's superior artillery, the preference of the German field artillery for massing in the open field and advancing with the infantry would be suicidal. The Germans would lose the artillery duel to 75s and heavier guns, firing half-hidden from behind the crests of hills.[116] The infantry and cavalry would pay a heavy price for this defeat, especially when they were thrown into the fray by panicky commanders who favored packed attack waves. The French cavalry had made a smoother transition in the past decade to a reconnaissance role, and infantrymen had somewhat fewer qualms about spreading out to avoid casualties.[117] Schlieffen would have been forced to retreat.

What of the German left? With only 10 divisions deployed in Alsace, Schlieffen must not have envisioned an attack; rather, these 120 battalions would simply guard the southern flank. After the debacle in Lorraine, however, he would have been forced to shift units from his left to stop the hemorrhage in the center. The likely French riposte would be to advance its Epinal army group of 128 battalions toward St. Dié and Strassburg to extend the right wing of the armies that were battling in Lorraine.

The news of fighting in Lorraine would have reached the German First and Second Armies midway through their traverse of Belgium. The right wing's 20 divisions (240 battalions) would have wheeled due south into the thickly wooded Ardennes and the deeply cleft Meuse Valley in the direction of Metz-Nancy. But the French were concentrating a sizable force north of Verdun. From Rheims came 4 reserve divisions (64 battalions). Transported from the area west of Toul, Epinal, and Belfort—quickly by rail over Paris—came the French Fifth Army (64 battalions) and 7 additional reserve divisions (112 battalions).[118] The French also had a powerful cavalry force of four divisions northeast of Verdun. From the far north, the French high command would most certainly have shifted the best of the 200,000 troops that were guarding the coast—at least 50 regular battalions.[119] The Paris garrison could have contributed another 16 battalions.[120] This northern army group would surely have delayed the Germans. Soon the British would be coming, and the right wing would be greatly outnumbered.

There would have been no German victory on the frontier, no crippling of the French to free two or three armies for the eastern front. More likely was a full-scale German retreat or, at best, a general stalemate—with the new dilemma, when Russia joined the fray, of stopping its hordes with 10 German divisions.

There was, of course, no continental war in 1903 or 1904. Rather, war broke out in Asia in 1904, destroying Russia's forces by 1905 and altering the balance of power in Germany's favor for many years to come. Nevertheless, an analysis of a hypothetical war is quite useful because in this case it highlights the potentially disastrous consequences of faulty German strategy and conservative tactics and technology.

The second German staff ride of 1904, held in June, drew some of the conclusions reached in our scenario, namely, that the right wing had to be strong enough to overwhelm all defenses. With only 20 German divisions pushing into Belgium, the French would eventually triumph on the western front.[121] In his last 18 months as chief, therefore, Schlieffen allocated troops from the center (as well as the eastern front) to the right, gambling even more on a massive sweep through Belgium to the rear of France's fortress line. When extra corps became available, Schlieffen's successor, Helmuth von Moltke, fine-tuned the plan by strengthening the center and left while keeping the right very strong. German internal debates after the Russo-Japanese War also led to tactics and technology more appropriate for "war in the present." Would it all be enough?

Another problem—much more sensitive and difficult to solve—involved the supreme warlord himself. What would have happened in 1903 or 1904 if William II had taken the field as commander of German forces? This was a hypothetical nightmare for the men who wanted to bloody France. But in this case, too, it was hoped that satisfactory solutions had been found.

CHAPTER 6

NO FREDERICK THE GREAT

*T*HE POWERFUL, rain-soaked wind was a rude greeting for the big white ship that bore the German kaiser. All night the storm screeched and howled, bending standards and ripping flags on the *Hamburg* as it steamed toward Morocco's shore. Superstitious old salts wondered whether anything good would come of this accursed mission.

On the stormy morning of 31 March 1905, a small sailboat ventured out to meet the imperial party. The captain of the *Hamburg* cut back his engines to allow the skiff to come alongside. The crew lowered a rope ladder for a German passenger dressed in full cavalry uniform. As the angry sea tossed the little craft up and down like a cork, he leaped for the ladder and grabbed on a split second before crashing into the hull. Slowly he muscled his way up, pausing seven or eight times to brace himself for repeated bangings against the white steel of the great ship. Finally the athletic feat was accomplished, and the horseless rider was pulled on board.

Moments later Baron Richard von Kühlmann, German chargé d'affaires in Tangier, was ushered into the emperor's stateroom. The uniform of the Bamberger Uhlans that the young man had donned on this foreboding, wind-swept day was soaked from the plume to the spurs. Squeaking and sloshing, oozing water from every seam, he finally halted at the prescribed distance and saluted.

Kühlmann looked into the face of William II. The waxed, upturned mustache and a martial stare could not hide the soft, dreamy quality of William's eyes. A withered left arm, damaged by forceps during a difficult birth, meant that he could never have accomplished what Kühlmann had just done, regardless of how strong the right arm had grown to compensate. The kaiser sought to deflect the awkward truth with a little humor. "I like your spirit, Kühlmann. If you fail as a diplomat there is a life-long position waiting for you at the army gymnastic school." "But," he continued quickly without taking a breath, "I shall not disembark for Tangier."[1] The absence of real harbor facilities at Tangier made a landing impossible.

William's boyish eyes reflected his anxieties and doubts. If somewhat calmer seas permitted the lowering of steps, would he make it to the boat? If he descended the steps safely, would the launch capsize when underway? If he reached shore alive, would he be able to mount and stay atop a strange horse that could throw him and break his neck or fall over on top of him? Would Spanish anarchists who used Tangier as a safe haven assassinate him? Or would the landing of the German kaiser in "French" Morocco trigger a war? "In Tangier the devil is already loose," he wired back to Berlin.[2]

The wind died down. Presently, the captain of a nearby French cruiser was admitted. Although he spoke the same truths the kaiser had heard from friends, such warnings were offensive when coming from the enemy. Consequently, the German warlord ordered Kühlmann and an adjutant ashore to investigate the possibilities. When they returned an hour later to report that the trip had proceeded smoothly and that thousands of Moroccans waited in feverish anticipation, the emperor seemed to waver. Kühlmann seized the moment. "Your Majesty should not forget that all of Africa looks to you."

Suddenly William's mind was made up. He ordered his field uniform and gun belt. "We are landing!"[3] he commanded.

The Royal Psyche

Kaiser William II was a bundle of psychological contradictions. He wanted to personify the image of a heroic, all-conquering warlord who would lead Germany to greatness and glory in modern times. Like his waxed mustache, however, William was artificially held in place. To be sure, there was a certain normality about the emotions he felt on that March day in 1905. The severe weather presented real challenges to a person with William's physical handicaps, and European anarchists had actually succeeded in killing other heads of state. It took real courage to leave the ship. Once on shore, the high-pitched shrieking of the Arab women and the traditional shooting into the air of Muslim militiamen twice spooked the emperor's horse, nearly fulfilling his nightmare of being crushed beneath hundreds of pounds of flesh. Like soldiers in combat, it was only normal to be afraid. The problem for Germany and the world, however, was that this rider in the streets of Morocco was not in a normal place in the rank. From the beginning, in fact, the glaring contrast between his abilities and the expectations of others had been the source of severe psychological problems.

William suffered from a narcissistic disorder that psychologists refer to as self-pathology. This inner emptiness and lack of cohesion at the center of the emperor's psyche is the subject of an analysis by Thomas Kohut.[4] According to his argument, William's imbalance stemmed from his relationship with his parents. British-born Victoria not only displayed obvious disappointment with the boy's physical shortcomings and intellectual mediocrity, but also overcompensated for this perceived personal failing of her own by infantalizing William—doting on him and refusing to allow him to grow up. Prussian-born Frederick was absent from the household most of the time. The image he projected was also very contradictory, for he was both a hero in the Wars of Unification and a weak and passive husband who was totally dominated by Victoria. As a result, the young prince was unable to bond normally with either his mother or his father. He did not internalize their calmness, self-confidence, and power because the hypercritical Victoria and the busy Frederick did not let William idealize or feel part of them. Moreover, he missed in his parents' faces that all-important pride in a boy's eager display of himself. In other words, they did not convey to him that they mirrored or were part of him, too.

Consequently, the boy who would be king grew into adolescence and adulthood insecure and psychically hollow, with an anxiety that something was wrong. "He never fully developed healthy self-esteem or internalized well-integrated aims and ambitions, and like a small child he continued to need other people as self-objects to supply externally what he lacked internally." Like all narcissistically disturbed adults, William "experienced himself as part of others and others as part of himself." He craved relationships with flatterers who would mirror or reflect his greatness, as well as strong fatherly figures whom he could idealize.

Mixed with this tendency was a strongly felt urge to prove his worth and abilities, especially to a mother who doubted them so much. By his early 20s, William was in an open love-hate rebellion against Victoria. Much of the young man's headstrong nature can be explained by this turbulent relationship, but deep down he was never strong and confident. A basic psychic weakness "was thinly covered by an agitated and anxious grandiosity, manifested by William's boastfulness, his love of public speaking and display, his tendency toward extreme exaggeration, and his belief in his own rightness, which at times appears to have verged upon the messianic." Kohut's analysis helps to explain why Emperor William's ambitions were so "unrealistic and inconstant," his behavior so "erratic and irresolute."[5]

Tactics, Technology, and Intrigue in the Military Entourage

We can use Kohut's model to speculate about the origins of William II's views on technology and tactics—the central focus of this study. Germany's last kaiser was an insufferable know-it-all who believed that he was always right. In reality, he tended to absorb the views of those around him with all the attendant contradictions and inconsistencies. One of the most influential was General Hans von Plessen, chief of Imperial Headquarters (1893–1918). He was a strong "Achilles" figure whom "Petrocles" could idealize. As a boy, William had received from his father terra-cotta statuettes of the famous Greek warriors. "I was never tired of looking at them,"[6] he recalled. The ancient duo's male bond modeled the emperor's complex relationship with men, for he yearned for "powerful men he could look up to," as well as "men who would look up to him as a powerful man."[7] That Plessen was adept at playing both the Achilles and Patrocles roles undoubtedly explains his long tenure in office.

The same can be said for Gustav von Senden-Bibran, chief of the Naval Cabinet (1889–1906), and Wilhelm von Hahnke, chief of the Military Cabinet (1888–1901). Senden was a career navy man who was determined to build Germany into a power on the high seas. The kaiser stood in awe of him and was "not embarrassed to ask or to allow himself to be taught." Hahnke, young William's commanding general in the First Guard Infantry Regiment, had a tall, soldierly bearing; a strict upright character; and a lighter, more humorous side, which—mixed with the good political sense to yield on occasion—made him "the perfect soldier" in the prince's eyes. Hahnke was "predestined"[8] to head the young man's Military Cabinet.

As the officers closest to a man who "experienced himself as part of others and others as part of himself," Plessen, Senden-Bibran, and Hahnke shaped many of their monarch's opinions about military technology and appropriate tactical responses. As we shall see, however, William was also led in other directions by other men. The result was not only more confusion and uncertainty at the top but also increased alienation between the monarch and factions that found their technological and tactical agendas in or out of favor as William absorbed this or that position, seemingly on a whim.

Thus we find Plessen, a "narrow-minded" general who spoke of "nothing but gunfire,"[9] ordering his cavalry to charge over 1,000 meters of open ground against entrenched infantry units during 1894 maneuvers.[10] The kaiser criticized Plessen's ridiculous decision but was obviously impressed, for such equestrian daring-do penetrated deeply into William's psyche. As a boy he had been forced to endure repeated falls from horseback before learning to ride with his one good arm. Hard-charging with sword waving would always exceed his capabilities, however, so the young man's consciousness of inadequacy and the urge to prove himself persisted.

After leaving the First Foot Guards in 1881, William received a regiment of Guard Hussars under Brigadier General Maximilian von Versen, another "perfect soldier" who quickly joined Hahnke in William's pantheon of heroes. Appointed one of the kaiser's personal adjutants in 1888, Versen joined a retinue filled with young wing adjutants from the Guard Corps cavalry whose function was to mirror the supposed greatness of their mounted warlord. The 29-year-old finally attempted to lead two divisions of charging horses in the autumn games of 1888.[11] Although the cavalry attacks were not unsuccessful, they did not impress Waldersee and the General Staff. Thus, the kaiser's feat would not be repeated until 1893—when he lost control and charged at his own men.[12]

Plessen's wild ride in 1894 was a turning point, for a seemingly more confident William followed his adjutant's lead that year and then led repeated charges in subsequent maneuvers, appearing to feel increasingly comfortable in the role of cavalry leader. Thus, when Schlieffen wanted to hold maneuvers in the lake country of theÜckermark in 1895, William vetoed the plan because his horses could not be massed there for the big charges he had come to love.[13] Having completed the evolution from Patrocles to Achilles—at least in his own mind—it was unlikely that this German emperor would ever forget his mounted warriors. "Woe to him who underestimates the cavalry," William declared in 1912, "for he can have a rude awakening."[14] The same man, however, could shock conservative cavalrymen by praising British mounted infantry and by insisting that his own cavalry must drag that ignoble impediment, the machine gun.

Hahnke's influence on the kaiser's tactical opinions was initially more progressive. Before his appointment to the Military Cabinet in 1888, the commander of the First Guard Infantry Brigade had committed himself to the dispersed battle order of his superiors, Schlichting and Winterfeld. With the help of Waldersee, who saw the emperor daily in the late 1880s, Hahnke convinced William to give the most prestigious commands to adherents of the new school. The heyday of "delegated tactics," as well as "three unequal wave" cavalry attacks—and controversies over both—the early 1890s produced many awkward situations for a young ruler with such chameleon-like qualities. Thus, in 1893 he took over Schlichting's Fourteenth Corps at maneuvers and presided over the general's victorious display of the new infantry regulations.[15] Afterward the real commander of the corps received his sovereign's praise. This was just a day after William had bungled a huge cavalry attack before the embarrassed eyes of Plessen.

However, different winds were blowing in the Military Cabinet by the mid-1890s. Informed military observers in 1894 placed Hahnke in the camp of those "mechanical tacticians" who were leading the counterattack against Schlichting.[16] Whether the conversion was genuine or opportunistic, it was undoubtedly related to the escalating controversy over public court martials.[17] One faction favored open proceedings along South German lines to improve the army's public relations, whereas opponents argued that it was a matter of class honor to protect trials between peers from the undeserving eyes of unequal civilians. If a soldier's dirty linen were aired in public, they said, army discipline would suffer irreparable damage. When Schlichting and other progressive tacticians such as Wilhelm von Blume, commander of fifteenth Corps (Metz), joined Prussian War Minister Walther Bronsart von Schellendorff in favor of public court martials, they were fired by Hahnke, who had the emperor's ear.[18] As we know, Schlichting attributed his "early retirement" to the intrigues of commanding generals who loathed 1888 infantry regulations—and he was probably right because his enemies' fear of deteriorating discipline and control under the new system was exactly what motivated Hahnke and Plessen to maintain Prussia's tradition of closed army courts. In both cases it was the antimodern spirit that conservatives conjured up to drive away evil.

The consistency of Hahnke's conservatism argues for the genuineness of his conversion to the old shock tactics. He had earned the assessment of others when he stepped down in 1901: "[Hahnke] belonged to the men of the old school who have difficulty adjusting themselves to new ideas and trends."[19]

Plessen's shaping of the kaiser would now combine with Hahnke's to twist William in yet another direction. Indeed, the general who "talked of nothing but gunfire" had extreme opinions on the most effective deployment of infantry. Class tensions between noble and bourgeois that had agitated politics earlier in the century had mellowed by the mid-1890s as fears of the upsurging proletariat and its popular political champion, the Social Democratic Party, became paramount. The upper classes argued about whether to solve "the social question" with ameliorating reforms or forceful suppression. Plessen headed an influential clique of courtiers and soldiers who adamantly favored the latter. Seconded by Hahnke, he encouraged the kaiser to introduce discriminatory legislation against the socialists, and if the parliamentarians refused, to call up the troops: "We must shoot," Plessen stated baldly in 1894. To be ready, regiments should be augmented with a fourth battalion; otherwise Berlin was "defenseless"[20] against the red terror. This was an added reason to adhere to close-order shock tactics that had proven their worth in foreign wars and would now ensure discipline and control in the battle for the streets.

Kaiser William was impressed, warning officers of a Guard Corps regiment not to shrink from using bayonets and grape shot against the people.[21] Maneuvers after mid-decade showed a marked tendency, moreover, toward glorious infantry and cavalry charges. In 1899, William himself led troops in a massive frontal assault, and in 1900 he took command of the Guard Corps in a "victorious" demonstration of the old tactics.[22] According to progressive army observers who struggled to find some rationality in all of this display, the maneuvers of these years were intended to showcase the emperor's leadership abilities, as well as impress and intimidate the larger public.[23] William's belief in frontal attacks and massed formations wavered briefly after British defeats in South Africa raised new doubts about the effectiveness of these measures, but the kaiser's preference for shock tactics remained basically consistent. Once he had internalized the opinions of a stronger person and then completed the transformation to "leader" in his own mind, William's pronouncements on an issue tended to be the same, sometimes for years—unless an even stronger personality made the emperor change his mind again, which happened all too frequently.

This abnormal need to absorb the stances and postures of others produced an odd and contradictory assortment of views. William's almost antiquated notions about cavalry and infantry, for example, were mixed with enthusiasm for both feuding branches of the artillery. His alter ego in this instance was almost certainly Alfred von Waldersee, of the General Staff. The warmongering general had formed a very close relationship with William in the 1880s, becoming a true Achilles to the loyal Patrocles.[24] When they first met, the prince was living the bawdy life of a Guard Hussar. Cannons, shrapnel, and ballistics were not part of his mental world. In what was probably their first official military business together, in December 1882, Waldersee briefed William on the General Staff's growing concern about penetrating the triple line of French fortresses.[25] As their friendship deepened after mid-decade, Waldersee's protégé developed a fanatical devotion to the artillery cause, replete with castigation of the "sins" of a frugal War Ministry and calls for a massive expansion of the field artillery. William was also an eager observer at heavy artillery firing ranges in 1887, just as the General Staff began its bid to develop the field capabilities of Germany's big guns. As the new emperor, moreover, he gave unquestioning support to Waldersee's artillery buildup, dismissing Prussian War Minister Paul Bronsart von Schellendorff for trying to stand in the way.[26] In 1890, the kaiser dismissed Bronsart's successor, Julius Verdy du Vernois, for opposing the purchase of nickel-steel cannon barrels from Krupp and, in 1893, Verdy's successor, Hans von Kaltenborn, for rejecting Krupp designs of the C-96 field cannon: "I've canned three War Ministers because of Krupp, and still they don't catch on!"[27] he bragged.

As shown by this statement, a more confident William had mastered the cannon-captain role first learned from Waldersee. The emperor had demoted his General Staff chief to corps commander in 1891 after hearing his own generalship criticized at autumn maneuvers. It was always a mistake to overplay the Achilles part. With the strong-willed man exiled from Berlin, the understudy—William—could step center stage and take over. And he played the role well, granting rights of personal access to jealous inspector generals of the field and heavy artillery, dazzling Krupp with special visits to Villa Hügel, personally presiding over the test firing of Germany's heavy field howitzers in 1900, and leading the heavy artillery in that

same year in a special attack exercise against French-style fortresses—all to the dismay of the field artillery, which was happier
when William denounced shields, preached the need to move up
close, or made other contradictory statements consistent with the
more sympathetic role of cavalier cannoneer.[28]

We can see the same psychological phenomenon at work in William's navy-building crusade.[29] His love of ships and enthusiasm for
nautical technologies—unheard of in the Hohenzollern family—
stemmed from Victoria's passion for the sea, rapturous childhood
memories of gawking at awesome men of war anchored in English
harbors, and pleasant hours of play with toy ships that evoked rare
nods of motherly approval. Torn between the need to prove his
Englishness to his mother and his Germanness to his father, William
grew into adolescence with a confused national identity. As a young
adult he groped for ways to reconcile this internal conflict, and as
emperor he sensed the need for policies that would impress both
the English and the Germans. The huge German naval bills of 1898
and 1900 were the result:

> The creation of a mighty German navy seemed the answer to [Wil-
> liam's] personal dilemma. On the one hand, the fleet would impress
> the British, for they, like his mother, only respected the formidable
> and powerful. On the other hand, the navy would simultaneously up-
> hold his honor and the honor of the Reich, for the increased power
> of the fleet was also an assertion of German armed might and repre-
> sented [William's] identification of himself with the military tradition
> of his father and grandfather. [William's] Germany would not be weak
> and dependent in relation to England as Friedrich had been in rela-
> tion to Victoria.[30]

Thus, William's insistence on naval construction, just like his preferences for certain cavalry, infantry, and artillery technologies or
tactics, was inextricably linked to his problematic relationships with
other people—in this case, his mother and the English.

It is interesting that this pattern of selfless absorption held consistently, even down to specific kinds of ships and naval technologies.
Normally the kaiser's naval preferences were shaped by Hahnke's
counterpart, Naval Cabinet Chief Gustav von Senden-Bibran. Because William "has only a superficial knowledge of the navy," observed one insider, "if he has a plan for the navy, or any desire or
thought, Senden has to put it in the correct form."[31] But other
strong personalities or combinations of influential persons in the
entourage could pull the monarch in other directions. In 1896, for

instance, the head of the Reich Naval Office, Friedrich Hollmann, advised against the large battleship fleet favored by Senden and prevailed when the chief of imperial headquarters, Hans von Plessen, supported Hollmann's idea of a cruiser fleet. "Now the great plan must be abandoned," pronounced William, "and spoken about no more."[32] Then, to the great surprise of Hollmann's replacement, Alfred von Tirpitz, the emperor changed his mind a year later and agreed with Tirpitz on battleships.[33] Although Tirpitz was strong-willed, he also had trouble with others who turned William's head: "If the emperor had spoken with some senior lieutenant or had seen something abroad, he was full of new demands, reproaching me with backwardness and even thinking to rouse me by means of warnings."[34] Tirpitz survived into the Great War by often threatening to resign.

The emergence of the kaiser in the role of admiral occurred simultaneously with his debuts as cavalier cannoneer, foot artilleryman, shock troop commander, and rough-riding cavalryman. Because his inner weakness drew him to anyone or any technology that exuded strength, awesomeness, and power, William II was compelled to play many roles regardless of the contradictions between them. As Tirpitz observed, the kaiser was easily won over by clever manipulators because of these weak traits. Bronsart von Schellendorff complained about the same phenomenon in 1895: "Irresponsible advisers always have some new invention on tap that catches the fancy of the Kaiser, especially in armament questions that involve the senseless expenditure of large sums."[35] The minister was referring, among other things, to William's successful campaign for adopting Hiram Maxim's machine gun[36] and his persistent backing of Krupp's artillery innovations.

Bronsart was also aluding to the emperor's passionate desire to ring Germany with state-of-the-art fortresses. This, in fact, was the ultimate contradiction; among the cavaliers eager to sweep into enemy territory, infantrymen and General Staff planners dreaming of taking the offensive, artillery officers confident that their technology would penetrate any defense, as well as naval commanders who longed for battle on the high seas, few had any use for fortresses. William's pet project was probably an idea planted by Fritz Krupp in the late 1880s: "The Kaiser regarded Krupp as his industrial counterpart," writes Isabel Hull, "a kind of bourgeois king whose meaning to Germany's strength, internal and external, was practically as important as his own."[37] As Waldersee noted with dismay in 1897, War Minister Gossler reinforced the message from Essen:

> Because [he] noticed that the Kaiser was interested in fortresses, and
> especially in technical constructions, [the war minister] became an
> overnight advocate of all defensive ideas and takes every opportunity
> to drive the monarch farther in this direction. Unfortunately, entirely
> dubious motives are also at work. Big Business, which makes prodi-
> gious sums on armored towers, turrets, gun implacements, steel plates,
> etc., exploits the inclinations of the Kaiser in order to make profits![38]

Indeed, with close ties to industry, Gossler "was not only 'the Kaiser's
General,' " continues Hull, "he was also Krupp's."[39] Given what we
know about Gossler's nightmarish vision of future war, however, it
seems likely that his motives for manipulating the monarch were
very complex. Others joined the plot in the late 1890s. Not at all
surprisingly, one was Baron Colmar von der Goltz, inspector general
of fortresses, head of the Army Corps of Engineers, reorganizer of
the Turkish Army, and another critic of short-war illusions. He
found a highly placed ally in cabinet chief Hahnke.[40]

With the encouragement of such friends and heroes, the kaiser
took up his new cause "with burning enthusiasm."[41] In 1900, he
approved massive new expenditures for fortress constructions and
extensions along the eastern frontier. When Goltz pushed for an
impregnable line of forts from the Saar to the Swiss border, however, the emperor's fortress-builder identity began to conflict with
other images he cherished, for Heinrich Edler von der Planitz, inspector general of the heavy artillery, advised against the plan.
Would the William who prided himself on backing the heavy artillery against its enemies in the War Ministry's Artillery Department
ignore Planitz? Schlieffen's rejection of Goltz's proposals intensified
the monarch's inner crisis.[42] The chief of the General Staff normally
avoided the kind of politics that had brought down Waldersee, saving his ammunition for really critical situations—and this was one
of them. How could William resist Planitz and Schlieffen or deny
Krupp, Gossler, Goltz, and Hahnke?

The resulting identity conflict, image contradiction, and role
confusion in the hollow center of William's psyche paralyzed his
ability to decide. Then Hahnke yielded office to Dietrich von
Hülsen-Häseler in 1901. A manly 6½-foot "Achilles" type, the new
man knew how to combine frankness and sarcasm in a way that
appealed to his sovereign. Hülsen declared that too many fortresses
would undermine the army's "spirit of the offensive": "We won't be
able to push through our own barbed wire impediments."[43] The
kaiser's indecision appeared to end in early 1902 when he banished
Goltz to First Corps (Königsberg).

Within a year, however, William was pushing again for fortresses in Lorraine. It was always difficult to give up a part once he had internalized the role. This created a predicament for Schlieffen. A war game in 1903 had proven the strategic inadvisability of relying too heavily on western fortresses. To William, however, "his" 1903 game proved that an extended line of forts offered the best chance of defeating France. Sensing royal determination, Schlieffen waffled and Hülsen fell opportunistically silent.[44]

Nevertheless, the fact remained that most commanding officers had a low opinion of the emperor as a soldier. It had been so almost from the beginning of William's reign. To be sure, veteran corps commanders learned to hold their positions by holding their tongues or, better still, by telling him "with tears in their eyes that every passing day he grew more like his illustrious forebearer, the Great King."[45] Private views of the kaiser were the opposite: "A Frederick the Great he will never be,"[46] said King Albert of Saxony after maneuvers in 1891. It was already widely suspected in the officer corps that these exercises were rigged by the General Staff to produce victories for the vainglorious kaiser.[47] Top-ranking generals laughed at the monarch behind his back—Schlieffen referring to him derogatorily as "Willi," and Plessen's predecessor at Imperial Headquarters, Adolf von Wittich, joking about "that nit-wit" and "stuck-up idiot."[48]

Waldersee's observations were equally devastating. William had a certain feel for the parade ground but lacked all combat experience and could not lead troops. He was usually out of control at maneuvers, racing back and forth, venturing too far forward into the first wave, interfering with his generals, issuing too many (and often contradictory) orders, and ignoring his staff. "He always wants to win and therefore is offended when field judges decide against him," Waldersee wrote. As his own star sank, Waldersee shuddered at the real possibility that the emperor wanted to be his own chief of the General Staff: "If he wanted to take command in war, not just nominally like his father or grandfather, there would be a disaster."[49] At a dinner of the commanding generals in 1895, the exiled reactionary was struck by their open criticism of the kaiser's weakness. It was particularly "shocking" to hear this from Hugo von Winterfeld, commander of the Guard Corps and an intimate friend of Hahnke. The cabinet chief was himself complaining of confusion, uncertainty, and the lack of "a firm hand" at the top.[50] As 1900 drew near, therefore, anxiety mounted in the army over the prospect of

marching to war behind "Willi." Adding to the army's resentment
of the kaiser was the certain knowledge that this would be a two-
front, likely much longer war—an unwelcome prospect caused by
the monarch's seemingly irresponsible dismissal of Bismarck and
subsequent diplomatic blunders.[51]

Criticism of William was widespread. On leave from Turkey in
1894, for instance, Colmar von der Goltz considered the kaiser's
charge at maneuvers with 60 cavalry squadrons useless theatricality.
Schlieffen should not tolerate such frivolity, he wrote, for "it is dangerous to practice something that must surely fail in war."[52] Participating in 1898 maneuvers, Karl von Einem, a moderately conservative official in the War Ministry, warned William that his corps was
in a vulnerable position and was appalled to hear that all was in
order simply because "Schlieffen will take care of everything." After
maneuvers the next year, Friedrich von Bernhardi, an innovative
cavalry officer, was embarrassed that foreign observers had seen William's suicidal frontal charge; and Waldersee, surveying the first reports from the Boer War, was concerned "that we can be shot down
just as easily as the English."[53]

These worries are better appreciated when viewed in the context
of worsening in-fighting over tactics and technology (see chapters.
3 and 5). Because corps commanders enjoyed wide-ranging autonomy in the German Army—and were rarely held accountable by
their peripatetic dilettante of a kaiser—they could drill their regiments in the manner they saw fit. If a commander's corps was selected to be among the two to four that participated in imperial
maneuvers in September, however, the commander was thrust into
a refereed arena where personal preferences were put to a competitive test. Increasingly in the 1890s and early 1900s, observers noticed that maneuvers were becoming a political battleground that
pitted one school against another. Sometimes Schlieffen chose two
rival corps for such a trial, as in 1900, when Second Corps and the
Guards Corps used contrasting infantry and cavalry assault tactics
that arose from the controversial Boer War. The General Staff's desire to exploit the corps-against-corps adversity of September maneuvers to produce useful lessons was growing around the turn of
the century as machine guns, light howitzers, heavy howitzers, and
other new technologies were introduced. Normally, however, there
was a more random nature to these corps confrontations, because
maneuvers rotated regionally in order to practice operations on the
eastern or western front and to distribute more evenly the propaganda benefits of these martial spectacles.

Although commanders were not generally traditional or progressive across the board—a cavalry background, for example, might lead to conservative horse and artillery tactics in combination with open-order infantry formations—the army's overall dialectic was moving tactics to the right. Thus Schlichting's infantry regulations fell victim to conservative counterattacks, progressive cavalry reforms yielded to traditional ways, and indirect or defilade firing techniques were smothered. William II exacerbated army feuding by flitting illogically and unpredictably between camps and poles. At maneuvers, this inconsistency made relations between factions even more adversarial, although here, more often than not, he showed a traditional side that alienated progressives. Worse still, the kaiser's insistence that his side win undermined the growing function of maneuvers as a level proving ground for competing tactical ideas. The constant meddling of the emperor—and the counterproductive, self-defeating tolerance of Schlieffen for such interference—imposed an arbitrariness, unfairness, and unprofessionalism that were deeply resented by all sides, not just by progressives, who were the bigger losers.

The army's mood darkened in the new century as these annual charades continued. Waldersee described spirits among the generals—including leading advisers like Hülsen and Schlieffen—as "gloomy" in 1902 and "downright depressed" in 1903. He predicted a "disaster" when William's desire to command armies "leads us to ruin." The war Waldersee was confident the army could win 10 years earlier would now be "a highly risky venture."[54] Waldersee was part of the problem in 1903, however; he flattered the emperor by praising an outmoded tactical exercise that William had arranged for the Guard Corps rather than showing courage and criticizing it. The elite commanders of the Guard Corps were incensed by the whole affair, "seeing in these things a playing at soldiering which does not correspond with the purpose of the army or seriousness of the internal situation, and which will lead to excessive mockery and criticism by [socialist] agitators."[55] The repetition of useless parade-ground antics at imperial exercises that autumn elicited a similar complaint from the Bavarian military attaché. The antiquated practices "do harm to the already endangered reputation of the army with the people."[56] In other words, the continuing legitimacy of the entire system was in jeopardy.

Count Robert von Zedlitz-Trützschler, royal chamberlain, left a detailed description of how far things had deteriorated by September 1903. Many officers in the General Staff and throughout the army were "depressed" by the ridiculous battlefield tactics imposed by the emperor and Hans von Plessen, who based the ground for engagements solely on its suitability for cavalry attacks. The reconnaissance mission was completely forgotten, and horse charges were ordered "as if it were still the era of flintlocks." The infantry charged in tightly massed columns with no artillery preparation, without firing back and having no regard for cover. Waves followed closely behind one another, officers in front pushing up past the skirmishers. The artillery galloped right behind the infantry, often pressing forward as far as the skirmish line. "Modern imperatives" were ignored "to paint a pretty picture." In short, "time and again one sees how not to do it."[57] His observations show how the kaiser's vacillating and contradictory opinions about military tactics and technology exacerbated the divisions in the army between conservatives like Plessen and others more attune to "modern imperatives."

The army's sensitivity about being led to slaughter by "Willi" was aggravated by many of his appointments to top positions. The promotion and assignment to the General Staff in November 1903 of Kuno von Moltke, a talented musician and wing adjutant who was "singularly ill-suited"[58] for the military, let alone for head of a department in the army's elite planning corps, raised soldiers' eyebrows. They dealt with it through humor, spreading the joke that Moltke would "found a new music department of the Great General Staff, then later, as its chief, direct the Concert of Europe."[59] In early 1904, rumors began to circulate that William was grooming Helmuth von Moltke, another personal favorite among his adjutants, as a replacement for the venerable Schlieffen.[60] Although Moltke was the nephew of one of Prussia's greatest generals, he had little operational experience and was chosen merely because the emperor felt comfortable around him.[61] Bernhardi, commanding a division in Münster at this time, took the unusual step of complaining to Hülsen about swapping Schlieffen for Moltke. When one observes "how deeply this affects confidence in supreme [command], and how widespread these feelings are, then one cannot help but look apprehensively into the future."[62]

War, Crisis, and Scandal

German officers had good reason to be anxious about unrealistic maneuvers and incompetent leadership. Japan's attack on Russia's Asian fleet at Port Arthur in February 1904 heightened tensions

throughout Europe. Then in April 1904, England announced a diplomatic understanding with France, the sworn enemy of Germany,
over Morocco. To anxious naval observers in Berlin, the meaning
was clear: England would transfer Mediterranean ships no longer
needed against France to the North Sea, a threat to Germany. Worse
still, diplomats warned that the Moroccan entente portended a triple alliance among England, France, and Russia that would be directed against Berlin. A chance to break apart Germany's encircling
enemies came that October, however, when Russia's Baltic fleet,
steaming to lift the Japanese blockade of Port Arthur, mistakenly
sunk English fishing boats in the North Sea. With England allied to
Russia's enemy, Japan, it was a perfect opportunity for Germany to
secure its position in Europe by allying with Russia. An offer was
made 3 days later.[63]

Dreams of fighting appeared to be coming true for German
soldiers, who had known only peace since 1871. Karl von Einem,
Gossler's successor in the War Ministry, was pleased when war broke
out in Asia. Now the world saw that "only weapons can arbitrate
serious disputes between nations."[64] He was hopeful that Germany
would finally enter a European war. Goltz, commander of First
Corps, welcomed the opportunity to break English supremacy. Like
Einem, he praised the Japanese for ending the "constant bawling
about peace"[65] and demonstrating what an honorable and heroic
nation could do. A war party in the kaiser's entourage, led no doubt
by Hans von Plessen, was also eager for combat. In similar circumstances during the Boer War, the chief of Royal Headquarters had
spoken of "throwing a division" over the channel to "finish off"[66]
the British or, if the Royal Navy blocked the way, marching with
Russia on India and Egypt.

War scenarios went through the active mind of Schlieffen, too.
A reckoning with England was one possibility; and if France sided
with England, he recommended sending German armies across the
Rhine. His temptation to seek victories across the frontier and perhaps "finish off" the French grew as it became apparent that Russia's
commitment in Manchuria had reduced its troops in eastern Europe
nearly to the point at which Austria-Hungary could deal with them
alone. Thus, Schlieffen estimated in early 1905 that only 7 of 26
army corps and 8 of 38 reserve divisions from this once mighty force
would be able to march west.[67] Tempering Schlieffen's bellicosity,
however, were worries stemming from the staff ride of June 1904:
The German Army had been defeated in a hypothetical one-on-one
fight along the western frontiers. Would a beefed-up right wing per-

form better—especially if England intervened—and would there be
enough divisions?[68] Reinforcing Schlieffen's predilection to play Fal-
staff instead of Hotspur was the knowledge that William still insisted
on assuming supreme field command of German armies despite his
"absolute military incompetence."[69] Only a year earlier William had
refused an aging Schlieffen's retirement feelers with the unnerving
words that "nothing would please me more than to solve problems
jointly with you in wartime [like those] that were presented to me
in war games, and, advised by you, [to] ride against the enemy."[70]

Matters came to a head amid ongoing international tensions in
January 1905. First the emperor was confronted with "what was spoken and whispered behind his back everywhere in officer circles."[71]
The brave informer was Helmuth von Moltke, the man William had
handpicked to succeed the chief of the General Staff. The meeting
had gone badly at first for the kaiser's adjutant. William interrupted
Moltke after a few sentences and then proceeded to explain that
war threatened, that Schlieffen was too old, and that together they
could rise to all challenges: "You do a little work in peacetime and
I'll help you in wartime." Later, when Moltke let the story out, some
were sure William had said: ". . . and in wartime I'll be my own chief
of staff."[72] Whatever the exact words, Moltke now screwed up his
courage to expose the kaiser's sham leadership. He criticized the
unrealistic war games that invariably allowed William to encircle half
a million soldiers in a few days. The generals that opposed him in
these games were tired of being served up with their hands tied:
"The confidence of the officers in the Supreme Warlord is deeply
shaken." Maneuvers were just as controversial because the emperor
constantly interfered with the initiatives of the commanding generals. "The maneuvers are discussed in the entire army, the whole
officer corps criticizes them—and the critique is growing sharper."
William was cowed by these revelations. He agreed not to participate
directly in games and maneuvers in the future. "Why didn't you tell
me about all of this a long time ago?" he asked meekly.

One week later came the deciding conference on William's pet
plan to buttress Lorraine with impregnable fortresses. Schlieffen,
Hülsen, and Plessen were present but opted for discretion over valor
before their imperfect sovereign. Not so Karl von Einem, who boldly
appealed to the Hohenzollerns' history of seizing the initiative
rather than "creeping into hiding." "And what will happen if the
French attack us?" queried a nervous kaiser. "Then we counterattack
and crush them!" trumpeted Einem. When William returned to the
alleged proofs of his fortress exercise of 1903, Einem lost his pa-

NO FREDERICK THE GREAT   129

tience—and risked his career: "The lessons which Your Majesty has been able to gather in these war games do not amount to a hill of beans."[73] Remarkably—but not surprisingly—Einem's forthrightness paid off. Although the kaiser was hurt and offended, he soon yielded and the grand fortress design was scaled back. If war came, the German Army would not "creep into hiding."

William's visit to Tangier in March 1905 was another indication of his growing inclination to yield to the agendas of stronger men. Friedrich von Holstein, senior counselor in the Foreign Office, was determined to regain the diplomatic upper hand that appeared lost when England and France recognized their respective spheres of influence in Egypt and Morocco. He believed Germany could break up the embryonic western entente by demanding an "open door" in Morocco. Holstein was prepared to risk war, but he thought the risk negligible if Germany remained firm. Not war, but a diplomatic victory was his aim.[74] By late 1904 he had convinced Chancellor Bernhard von Bülow of the correctness of this policy. After Bülow received emphatic assurances from Einem that the army was "ready for war,"[75] the chancellor in turn convinced the kaiser to dispatch a gunship to Morocco in mid-February 1905. When this diplomatic shot across the bow failed to unnerve the French, plans were hatched to turn the emperor's impending Mediterranean cruise into an international incident of the first order.[76]

William himself was disturbed by the course events were taking. He had said repeatedly since the 1890s that the construction of a powerful high-seas fleet would earn the respect and friendship of Great Britain.[77] To his surprise and disappointment, the opposite had occurred. Efforts to dislodge Russia from its alliance with France, seemingly so promising in the autumn of 1904, had also failed by early 1905. "The situation begins to look increasingly like that before the Seven Years War,"[78] William lamented to Bülow. Moreover, the message he was receiving from the generals was that they did not regard him as the next "Great King." As February gave way to March, the kaiser expressed his pessimism about a Moroccan venture that threatened to turn the world against Germany.[79] Then on 23 March in Bremen—just a few days before boarding the *Hamburg*—William declared that he wanted Germany's place in the world to be based on trust, not on the sword. The youths of the nation had to be "steady, peaceful, and patriotic" and should not want "to strive for the impossible." God surely had a great destiny in mind for the Germans, "but they have to be worthy of this."[80] And yet, barely 10 days later, William disembarked at Tangier. The kaiser was no coward, but he certainly lacked the courage of his vacillating convictions.

The diplomatic confrontation desired by Bülow and Holstein now occurred.[81] William's insistence in Tangier that Morocco was an independent state with sovereign rights to trade with all nations challenged France's claim to dominance there. As Europe waited anxiously to see if France's answer would be war, the German Army took steps to ensure that a "dilettante" who had "no really strict and authoritative military schooling"[82] would not produce battlefield disasters. "Things look different now," said Axel von Varnbüler in response to a general who predicted "hair-raising mistakes at the top" if war broke out. The especially well-informed Württembergian ambassador and intimate friend of William hinted that negotiations occurred during the Moroccan crisis, leading to an agreement that the emperor would not take personal charge of the armies.[83] Agreeing to relinquish de facto supreme command did not mean, however, that William would let his generals choose the moment for war. In meetings with Bülow, Schlieffen, and Einem in May 1905, he seized on the war minister's grudging admission that Germany's C-96 field cannon was inferior to France's rapid-firing 75mm. Now there could be no thought of preemptive war.[84]

Is it possible that the kaiser had gained a little strength, wisdom, and maturity from the trauma of the Russo-Japanese War and the adversity of several personal setbacks in recent months? Or was this the petty revenge of a childish man who was refusing to play if he was not allowed to control the game? Was the emperor subconsciously teaching the soldiers a lesson, in other words, by picking up a radical new role—that of pacifist? If so, there had been plenty of time for rehearsal, for William had had over 20 years of intimate contact with Philipp zu Eulenburg, a friendly, pacific courtier who abhorred the Plessens of the world. As titular head of the Evangelical Church, moreover, there had been numerous opportunities for William to absorb pacifism from those few clergymen who took the Sermon on the Mount seriously. That he was trying out a new role seems a likely explanation, given what we know about his porous personality. Or had he momemtarily stopped acting, allowing a true, inner peaceful nature to surface? Are we left in the final analysis with nothing more certain than his "baffling complexity and contradictoriness"?[85]

Whatever the case, the generals soon noticed their sovereign's aversion to war. When Schlieffen sent an article to William in June 1905 that hinted at the likelihood that Germany would wage a preventative war, the angry monarch scribbled in the margin: "No! I will never be capable of such an action!"[86] When the French dismissed their belligerent foreign minister, thereby defusing the spring crisis, William wanted to decorate the German ambassador in Paris "because he saved us from a war."[87] That same month the kaiser told the French military attaché that Germany had no intention of going to war over Morocco. Later in the year, he was even more frank with Einem: "I do not love war and would not like to wage one unless it is absolutely necessary." In January 1906, the emperor was still more emphatic, announcing to his corps commanders that there would be no war over Morocco. He "was thoroughly convinced that he was on the right track with his notion about loving peace," recalled Einem. "He was strengthened in his view of the frightfulness of war by the powerful and pervasive development of contemporary technology that was affecting warfare by creating more and more destructive weapons."[88] William seemed to have come a long way from the young Hussar who dreamed of thundering into battle. His narcissistic disorders were not cured, however, thus preserving the possibilty that Germany's leading actor might at any time don other costumes and recite other lines. In February 1906, for instance, his stance on Morocco toughened when the international conference at Algeciras, which had been called to adjudicate Franco-German differences, largely ignored German demands.[89]

War clouds finally dissipated after Britain and France agreed to a few minor concessions. That the crisis passed without hostilities was no consolation for German army leaders. Einem, for instance, was disgusted by the allegedly unwise and unmanly behavior of the "Peace Kaiser."[90] It is also said that Schlieffen pounded his fists privately, cursing the folly of not moving west while Russia was almost completely immobilized by war and revolution. In public he was allegedly barely able to contain his deep disappointment over Germany's missed opportunity to implement his evolving plans for taking down France.[91] This was probably surface bravado to impress loyal retainers, however, for it is simply impossible that all of Schlieffen's doubts about troop strength and deep incursions beyond the frontiers had been purged so suddenly. William's concession—to leave the wartime command of such risky western operations to the generals—eliminated one of Schieffen's, and the army's greatest anxieties, but this was soon undermined by the continued rise of Helmuth von Moltke. The emperor's favorite was given control of autumn maneuvers in 1905, a move that personally offended

Schlieffen. Then the older man retired in January 1906, much to the dismay of loyal followers in the General Staff who did not respect Moltke. Indeed, the mood throughout the army was depressed by the change of command.[92]

Germany's legitimacy crisis worsened in the spring of 1906 when newspapers printed revelations about the sexual deviancy of men in the emperor's civilian and military entourage. The alleged homosexuality of Philipp zu Eulenburg and Kuno von Moltke offered saber-rattlers a quick explanation for their sovereign's display of "cowardice." In the minds of members of William's closest military entourage such as Hahnke and Plessen, the effeminacy, weakness, and pacifism of the Eulenburgs was a boil that would have to be lanced.[93]

The ramifications of the Moroccan crisis were highly significant for the history of the German Army and Imperial Germany. For 16 years after the dismissal of Otto von Bismarck, most Germans suppressed whatever doubts they had about German diplomacy. Lured by the promises and pronouncements of greatness that would come in the wake of the kaiser's "new course," patriots in and out of government expected great accomplishments from William II and his entourage of loyal men. When, instead, the empire shrank from fighting during a war scare it alone had provoked and then found itself isolated at the conference table, receiving virtually nothing, the result was an alarming mixture of depression, disappointment, anxiety, and anger. "It has been said," reported a British diplomat from Berlin in 1908, "that 'fear was born when first man awoke in the dark.' "[94] Now Germany was shocked to discover that William and his retainers were not the masters of diplomacy they had seemed to be: "The extent to which the prestige of the Emperor and of the central authority has declined in the past year can hardly be exaggerated," said the diplomat. Germans had awoken in the dark to find themselves almost alone. "It is hardly too much to say that she is afraid, but Germany is undoubtedly strong, and the combination of fear and strength is dangerous."

The result was growing criticism of William II and an "almost pathological concern with weakness."[95] Leading the backlash was Maximilian Harden, editor of *The Future* and a longtime critic of the kaiser's absolutist tendencies. In a scathing article entitled "William the Peaceful," the courageous journalist reminded readers in 1907 that top-level blundering had galvanized English, French, and Russian opposition to Germany but that now the situation was more dangerous because foreign leaders had seen through William's militaristic facade. "Now it is said that Germany won't do anything to us; barks at the most, but won't bite; if we become nasty and pound on the table, she gives in."[96]

With an accuracy of sorts, Harden was convinced that the root of the problem lay with the men of the kaiser's civilian entourage, especially Count Philipp zu Eulenburg. The man who had the ear of the kaiser for 15 years had opted for inactive status in the diplomatic corps in 1902 but still saw William frequently thereafter, including a controversial visit of the emperor to Eulenburg's Liebenburg estate in the autumn of 1905. Because Eulenburg had also invited a leading French diplomat, Harden believed that pacifistic influences had been brought to bear on the kaiser that explained his "cowardly" behavior. Although the fearless muckraker was wrong about the specifics, he may have been right in a general sense, for Eulenburg was probably one source of William's "pacifism," a trait absorbed like so many other contradictory tendencies from years of close contact with persons whose personalities formed the shaky basis of the emperor's patchwork psyche. Harden's anger went much deeper, however, for his investigations of Eulenburg and other men of the "Liebenburg circle" had determined correctly that they were homosexuals. Succumbing to the prejudice and intolerance of his day, Harden, who winced at Germany's recent debacle felt compelled to expose the "mawkish, unmanly, sickly condition"[97] of William's entourage in the columns of his paper. Homosexuals "almost always have the unpleasant sides of femininity [and] where several of them are gathered together they can unconsciously do damage, particularly at courts, where complete men have a hard enough time."[98] William had to be rid of such unhealthy and insidious half-men who proudly claimed "to have formed a ring around the All Highest Person that no one can break through."[99]

But Harden broke through when his revelations forced Kuno von Moltke's resignation from the army in May 1907, then Eulenburg's from the diplomatic corps in June. It is significant that the kaiser's military entourage played a crucial role in the subsequent final stage of ending the allegedly weakening and enervating influence of homosexuals. Aware of the incriminating letters in Harden's possession, Military Cabinet Chief Dietrich von Hülsen-Haeseler convinced the emperor to insist that Eulenburg and Moltke sue Harden to clear their names. Hülsen knew full well that the resulting trials would ruin two men he had hated for years.

Former Military Cabinet Chief Wilhelm von Hahnke and head of Imperial Headquarters Hans von Plessen also tried to prevent William from yielding to his "growing yearning" for "poor Phili" and rehabilitating an old friend.[100] Kuno von Moltke did not reappear at court until 1911. Eulenburg was never received again. In Hahnke's characteristically crude phrasing, the "boil" had been "lanced."[101] "And who has influence now?" asked Court Chamberlain Robert von Zedlitz-Trützschler. "Primarily the military entourage,"[102] was his reply. Given the kaiser's susceptibility to the influence of those in his immediate surroundings, this was a highly important—and eventually tragic—turn of events. William, having already abandoned effective command of his armies, was now increasingly at the mercy of hawkish soldiers who wanted de facto control over the decision to use those armies in war.

The kaiser's hold on decision-making power was loosened even more after the *Daily Telegraph* published its gaffe-filled interview with him in late October 1908. In a succession of the most tactless, insensitive, and undiplomatic remarks ever made by a person in authority, William managed to insult the English, the French, the Russians, the Japanese, and—what was much worse—the Germans. He said, for example, that he had drawn up a battle plan for the British during the Boer War that had enabled Lord Roberts to proceed successfully against the enemy. In other words, the German emperor, not the proud British Army, which had really won the war, was responsible for a victory against a people of Dutch descent that had the full sympathy of the ethnically related Germans. William also claimed to be a friend of the English against the deepest wishes of his own people. As proof, he claimed to have rejected secret offers of the French and Russians for a continental alliance against Britain. "A dark foreboding ran through many Germans," recalled Chancellor Bernhard von Bülow, "that such clumsy, incautious, over-hasty—such stupid, even puerile speech and action on the part of the Supreme Head of State, could lead to only one thing—catastrophe."[103] "This publication," he continued, "as by some sudden slap in the face roused the whole nation."

True to their inner convictions, the Social Democrats called for a parliamentary regime. The other parties hesitated to make such demands but unleashed unprecedented attacks on William's irresponsible behavior and insisted that it be curbed in the future. Newspapers and journals undertook a merciless post mortem. Friedrich Naumann, a moderate Liberal, asked incredulously what good it did "to have the best army, if no state will negotiate with us secretly?

And what good is the fleet if it has a commander who spends his free time working up war plans for the English?"[104] Not surprisingly, Maximilian Harden was the most outspoken of all the bourgeois politicians and journalists. Before a packed audience in Berlin's Mozart Hall, he hinted at treason on high and declared that the embarrassing affair was "worse than a lost war because it means a loss of credit."[105] Privately he railed against a monarch who would never change. "To clear ourselves of shame and ridicule we will *have* to go to war, soon, or face the sad necessity of making a change of imperial personnel on our own account."[106] As he penned these words, Europe was slipping deeper into a Balkan crisis triggered by Austria's annexation of Bosnia-Herzegovina.

Harden noticed that many army generals attended his Mozart Hall speech in civilian clothes and applauded with the others. Indeed, the military was seething with embarrassment and discontent at this latest sign of their commander-in-chief's unstable and contradictory personality. Some officers quipped that the General Staff knew of no secret war plan for the British, so it probably stemmed from Friedrich Scholl, William's tall, handsome, and militarily clueless adjutant.[107] Hülsen's successor as chief of the Military Cabinet, Moritz von Lyncker, was more somber, charging that "everything that in the past twenty-one years has brought us down from our heights can be traced back in the last resort to the Emperor's influence."[108] Minister of War Karl von Einem let loose his frustration with a tirade before fellow Prussian ministers. There was "growing discontent in the army with the actions and attitude of His Majesty, with his abuse of personal prerogative and his temperamental outbursts and caprice." The soldiers would fight the next war as magnificently as earlier conflicts, "but the prestige of the Crown, the monarch's position with his officers, is less firmly established than it has been, and that is His Majesty's fault." The situation had grown so bad by early autumn 1908, Einem told another person privately "that a catastrophe [like the interview] was hardly feared anymore, rather almost wished for, because only such a [disaster] could bring an end [to such behavior]."[109] Colmar von der Goltz, commander of First Corps, agreed that changes were necessary. When feelers about the chancellorship were sent out to him, Goltz insisted that he be given the power to make declarations of war. When the fellow-traveling Pan German and long-time advocate of "the people in arms" also demanded a "far-reaching liberalization of the army," the military entourage balked and decided to keep Bülow.[110]

Goltz's first condition—the right to make war if the Kaiser "chickened out"—reflected the direction military politics was taking during the fall and winter of 1908–1909. At that time William seemed as susceptible as he would ever be to such a "silent dictatorship"[111] of the army. The monarch had showed some signs of cracking during the first weeks of the *Daily Telegraph* crisis, but the sudden death of Hülsen-Haeseler on 14 November, followed by a tense meeting with Bülow, who pressed successfully for a royal promise "to put a guard on his tongue,"[112] finally triggered a nervous breakdown. After a month William recovered sufficiently to return to work, but the man who went through the motions of ruling was even weaker and less confident than before.[113] Now the birds of prey began to circle. "The war party, hurt in its feelings of traditional loyalty to the Supreme Commander, regards war as the only possible means of restoring in the eyes of the masses the monarchy's shaken prestige." Such a conviction, continued the alarmed Russian ambassador, "might tempt this Emperor and give his foreign policy a militant character."[114]

One tempter was Hans von Plessen. At a New Year's Day gathering of the top generals, he cautioned Friedrich von Bernhardi, commander of Seventh Corps (Westphalia), that William had wanted for so long to be "the Prince of Peace" that it was difficult for him to do an about face. Bernhardi was encouraged, nevertheless, that "at least he seems to be considering such a step." During a visit with William the next day, the warmongering General Bernhardi took note of the monarch's approval of an aggressive article written by Schlieffen, adding that now was a propitious moment to dismantle the Triple Entente by attacking France. "Who knows what I might do!" replied the agitated kaiser.[115] Later that month, Einem also urged the kaiser to wage war. He was probably joined by General Staff Chief Helmuth von Moltke and Hülsen's replacement in the Military Cabinet, Moritz von Lyncker.[116]

All of this was not without effect on the malleable monarch. Although Lyncker and Moltke were still worried about the kaiser's resolve, he found the nerve to issue a carte blanche to Austria and then to threaten France with the mobilization of his army if it did not observe strict neutrality in the Balkans.[117] On 19 March, Austria presented an ultimatum to Serbia over Bosnia-Herzegovina, and 3 days later Germany presented its own thinly veiled ultimatum to Russia, warning it to recognize Austria's acquisition of those provinces. Aware that his army had not yet recovered from the Asian debacle of 1904–1905, Nicholas II withdrew support from Serbia the same day.[118] Despite repeated assurances of support from Berlin, Austrian leaders left well enough alone and opted against a pre-emptive strike. The crisis was over—but not the memory of humiliation in Serbia and Russia.

By 1909 the German Army had significantly reduced the kaiser's ability to resist expert military opinion about waging war. It was certain, moreover, that William would not lead his troops into the field. The army would soon get its war, but was the officer corps ready for contemporary warfare?

CHAPTER 7

TOWARD THE GREAT WAR

W

AR IN THE present finds no Napoleonic cluster of generals on a hill, peering through telescopes at a gunsmoke-clouded battlefield. It makes no sense for the commander-in-chief to be near the actual combat, for he sees very little. There is no line of horsemen, massing for a charge. Cavalry units are far away, peforming reconnaisance or preparing to attack enemy flanks with artillery and machine guns or to dismount and fight with carbines. There is no smoke to give away enemy artillery positions. Only barely discernible flashes of light, and small groups of infantrymen, sprinting forward before disappearing again, offer the slightest hint about the source and direction of a rolling barage of artillery shells that are exploding nearby. The killing power of modern weapons necessitates the spread of brigades and divisions to the point where corps and army groups are miles apart. Not even the most powerful binoculars bring the whole battlefield into view, and commanders find themselves far to the rear at high-tech headquarters.

The modern Alexander sits at a large table. He stares angrily. All around him, bespeckled, high-ranking aides sit at staff tables, frantically answering telephones and hectically deciphering the latest telegraphic dispatches from airships and airplanes high above. Outside, motorcycles and automobiles speed away and screech to a halt before this anthill of military activity. Time and again, officers hurry to the big table with the most urgent news, warnings, and pleas for support. Repeatedly the chief fires back explosive words.

"There are no reserves! Advancing army groups must fend for themselves!" In front of him, spread over the top of the big staff table, is a huge map of the campaign area. Modern Alexander furrows his brow, concentrating on the 50 red pins that represent his attacking horde. Now he shakes his fist at an approaching aide. The plan is set! The routes are chosen! All units must keep attacking!

Alfred von Schlieffen's "War in the Present" appeared in January 1909.[1] It was a predictive glance at the next war by the former chief of the Prussian General Staff, now 3 years into retirement. It was a timely piece in many ways. Europe was in the midst of a Balkan crisis that threatened to escalate into a general war. Schlieffen's successor, Helmuth von Moltke, could be sitting at the big table sooner than many realized. The Russo-Japanese War of 1904–1905 had demonstrated beyond any reasonable doubt, the power of modern industrial technology. Schlieffen's vision of the modern Alexander, surrounded by the latest that science had to offer, was definitely influenced by the brutal lessons learned on the killing fields of Manchuria—lessons that the German Army had debated, distilled, and absorbed since the war.

For all its paeans to technology, however, certain contradictory reservations were expressed about its alleged benefits—reservations that were a kind of residual reflection of the controversies that had raged since the 1870s. After 1871 France and Germany struggled to achieve the kind of technical superiority that had enabled Prussia to win at Königgrätz in 1866. The two bitter enemies developed ingenious weapons and occasionally achieved momentary superiority, only to be amazed at how quickly the other side acquired "an even more rapidly firing rifle, cannons that shot even farther, and shells that were even more effective." The Franco-German feud "had spurred on the technologists to the extreme," but nothing was really gained, for "all armies, not just in Europe, but also in the Far East and Far West, possess just about the same weapons."[2] The soldier's job was complicated still more after 1871 by the construction of fortresses to block invasion routes, which led to the development of heavy artillery, which, in turn incited the engineers to produce more impregnable forts. Attempting to gain an advantage, Germany had built its Triple Alliance, but the French eventually brought Europe back into a stalemate by cultivating ties to England and Russia.

Schlieffen's article was very frank—indiscretely so—about German options. Given the overall technological and diplomatic deadlock, the German Army had to place overwhelming numbers of soldiers on the enemy's vulnerable flanks and rear. Every available soldier had to be used in the front lines to achieve numerical superiority at the enemy's weakest spot. Ammunition wagons, not soldiers, would be the only reserves. Moreover, at a certain point, leaders had to face the inevitable and risk frontal charges into modern technology's "rain of bullets."[3] The Russians and Japanese had showed that it was possible. In other words, from the modern Alexander at the top to the common soldier at the bottom, human exertions would decide the next war.

Individual courage would be just as important at home. Germany and its allies could not allow enemy propaganda to generate divisiveness. The enemy would try, as seen by current Russian efforts to fan ethnic hatreds within the Austro-Hungarian Empire. "That the same goal can be achieved in Germany was shown just recently by a short newspaper article filled with cunningly assembled, yet age-old accusations." This oblique reference to Maximilian Harden's allegedly unpatriotic attacks against the kaiser after the monarch's disastrous *Daily Telegraph* "interview" underscored the significance of remaining "brothers one and all," whether the struggle was waged with weapons or by other means. It was also imperative to have "a large, strong, powerful army, absolutely reliable, and guided by a firm hand."[4] This was a tactful allusion to William's anxious nature— and a subtle admission that Harden and other critics of the kaiser were right. Perhaps there was also a sour warning here about Moltke's limitations. Schlieffen's article took stock of Germany's assets, as well as its liabilities.

Modern Alexanders

General Karl von Einem was Prussian war minister from 1903 until 1909. He had come up through the cavalry, serving with the Uhlans during the Wars of Unification, later alternating General Staff assignments with commands in the Dragoons and Currasiers. Einem joined the War Ministry as a department head in 1898, moving up to chief of military operations[5] in 1900. "At that time," wrote the old cavalryman, "the army stood before virgin territory with regard to technological rennovation."[6] The real breakthrough period, according to Einem, occurred during his ministry. Despite the great financial drain of the navy and the stinginess of the Reichstag, a series of "important and to some extent pioneering innovations" were introduced. On his watch, the German Army maintained its "full combat readiness."[7]

We must take such claims with a grain of salt. Although the groundwork was laid, in fact, for Schlieffen's vision of a modern Alexander, the circumstances were more political—and less heroic—than Einem would have it. This was even more the case during the 4-year tenure of Einem's successor, Josias von Heeringen. As Germany and Europe weathered a succession of tension-packed crises—Morocco (1905–1906), Bosnia (1908–1909), Morocco (1911), and the Balkans (1912–1913)—disputes and controversies over the adoption of military technology placed tremendous stress on an army that was struggling to modernize before it was too late.

As chief of military operations, Einem had advised War Minister Heinrich von Gossler against either qualitative or quantitative improvements to the field artillery. The C-96 cannons were "basically equal"[8] to the French semirecoilless 75 mm, and there were already "plenty of them." Given what we know about traditionalism in the mounted corps, it was consistent for Einem to consider cavalry and infantry increases "far more necessary."[9] After 1901, the ministry yielded to General Staff pressure for rapid-firing cannons, but delayed the start of production for experimental batteries until 1904. That the cannons were given such low priority indicates that Einem sympathized with opponents of these guns in his artillery department. The minister accelerated the pace of rearmament somewhat after Japan attacked Port Arthur in 1904 and quickened it again in early 1905, but his repeated insistence that the army was battle-ready—despite the fact that refitting with rapid-firing cannons would last until 1908—is another sign of low esteem for the new weapon. To Einem's disgust, the emperor seized on the issue as a pretext for delaying war during the first Moroccan crisis. One of his many acquired roles was that of "the Peace Kaiser." Rearmament of the field artillery with semirecoilless guns then went forward at breakneck speed.[10]

Einem's insistence that the army was ready, when apparently it was not, unnerved Bernhard von Bülow. Emboldened by Einem, as well as Holstein, the Imperial chancellor had steered a course that could easily have triggered a European conflagration: "With God's help I succeeded in leading Germany out of the Moroccan crisis," he wrote Einem in June 1906. The world was a more dangerous place, however, and Germany's allies were either militarily unrelia-

ble (Italy) or internally weak (Austria-Hungary): "Given these circumstances it is our holy duty to neglect nothing in preparing the
nation to face the storm, which sooner or later will pour down on
us, as well-armed as it is in our power to be." Bülow sought assurances that the German Army was taking the necessary technological
measures to counter recent arms increases in France: "Don't we
need more machine guns? Isn't a quicker rearmament of the field
artillery necessary?" Other questions followed in rapid succession:
"How do things stand with . . . the mobilization of the army's heavy
artillery? With the navigable airships? With [modern] army uniforms?"[11]

Einem must have winced and wriggled, for he did not respect
Bülow and never forgot the perceived slight. But as minister of war
it was his duty to reply to the barrage of embarrassing questions. On
the positive side of the ledger, Einem reported that the army was
discarding its old blue uniforms for field gray colors that afforded
more camouflage. Increased funding was also available for the heavy
artillery and the revolutionary new airships. Assurances were also
quickly given about the field artillery. The last corps would receive
"new-style C-96" (C-96nA) rapid-firing cannons by late 1907, with
the reserve, replacement, and militia formations due to follow in
1908.[12] The new model had shields, shot as rapidly as the French
75, and was more mobile because it weighed less. Because it utilized
old C-96 barrels to save money, however, its range was still 1,000
meters less.

But Einem could not wave off Bülow's first question about machine guns. Not counting the fortresses, Germany had 91 machine
guns, alotted in wartime to 13 cavalry detachments. Based on the
experience of infantry units with machine guns in the Russo-
Japanese War, 4-experimental infantry detachments were being established to determine the device's worth. If test results were positive, 12 more detachments would follow in 1907, and accelerated
rearming for 5 years would mean 1 detachment for each of Germany's 200 infantry regiments: "Before this goes forward, however,
we must await the results of this year's tests."[13]

A host of objections and branch rivalries had stalled machine
gun development before the Russo-Japanese War. The new weapon
was too heavy and cumbersome for the infantry to carry or the cavalry to drag and generally seemed too defensive in nature to aid an
army with proper offensive gusto. But the sight of whole companies
of Japanese soldiers mowed down in seconds by Russian gun crews
strengthened the hand of machine gun enthusiasts. As German in-

Figure 8. The rapid-firing, shielded C-96nA cannon. Source: Köhler, *Der Aufstieg.*

fantry tests proceeded in 1906 and 1907, moreover, a new, light-weight steel prototype became available. Eventually introduced as the MG-08, the improved weapon weighed 17 pounds less than its predecessor.[14] The success achieved by experimental detachments with MG-08s prompted Colonel Franke, director of the Infantry Department (A2), one of seven divisions under the chief of military operations in the War Ministry, to recommend creation of a six-gun battery for every infantry regiment.[15]

His scheme was derailed in 1908 because of the empire's financial problems. The national government had no direct tax base (e.g., income tax) because the federal states—above all, Prussia—feared an increase in Reichstag power and the attendant growth of socialist influence. Given escalating naval expenditures, the army had to prioritize its budget proposals for upcoming years. Forced to cut back to what was "absolutely and urgently necessary," Major Hoffmann, director of A1, the Army Organization Department, rejected the recommendations of his colleague in A2. The world's "numerous technological inventions" in combination with peacetime habits that "blurred clear thinking about what was actually useful in wartime" had created a "danger" for army managers:

"namely, the overestimation of the value of machines and technological means for fighting wars." When forced to choose between
more machines and, say, more officers, the army had to realize
that guns could never compensate for the "deficient discipline"
that would result from a lack of leadership: "The officer leading
his men can never be replaced by a machine gun or a telephone
connection."[16] General Wandel, chief of Military Operations,
agreed. Machine gun detachments should be limited to one for
each of the army's 96 brigades—six Maxims for 6,000 men. Einem
supported Wandel in November 1908.[17] Funding would begin with
the 1911 army bill.

Against his better judgement, Helmuth von Moltke agreed to
this deceleration of machine gun development. Under Schlieffen's
administration, the General Staff had been indifferent to a technology that seemed to offer no advantage to attackers. Impressed
by the Russian and Japanese example—and reports that France was
funding more machine guns—Moltke reversed course and pressed
Einem in 1906 to distribute machine guns to the infantry as soon
as possible.[18] By 1908, however, there were new personalities in the
General Staff. Colonel Erich Ludendorff returned from the War
Academy to head the Mobilization Department in April. The crusty
43-year-old had joined the army as a cadet in 1879, alternating assignments in the infantry, marines, and General Staff as he gradually
ascended through the ranks. Under him, heading a new Technological Section, was Major Hermann von Thomsen, a single-minded
crusader for airships and airplanes. If Thomsen was too preoccupied
with his quest of flight to push for machine guns, he received no
censure from above. Ludendorff proudly admitted that he was no
technological expert, putting more store in his soldierly instinct for
judging what had practical battlefield worth. During weapons tests,
he recalled, "I didn't put up with any humbug."[19] In general, Ludendorff was enthusiastic about the potential of modern field and
heavy artillery—initially, much more the former—to keep pace with
(and provide punching power for) offensive actions.[20] When it came
to the still cumbersome MG-08, Ludendorff wrote it off as "the kiss
of death for every offensive."[21] The weaker of the two personalities,
Moltke suppressed his earlier concerns about "exposing ourselves to
being left behind."[22] Indeed, Germany was falling behind as the Bos-
nian crisis escalated during the winter of 1908–1909. While France,
England, and Russia already had six machine guns per regiment,
Germany planned to deploy six per brigade of two regiments—but
only beginning in 1911.

In absolute numbers, however, this represented an impressive sevenfold expansion of available detachments—from 13 to 96. Extraordinary funding was found, moreover, for the first 4 brigades to receive detachments in 1909, somewhat ahead of the official schedule.[23] This meant that earlier uncertainties over which branch would deploy the guns had to be resolved. Imperial maneuvers in September 1910 were an experiment of sorts. Whereas machine gun detachments usually marched with the cavalry and horse artillery, this year General Alexander von Kluck's Red Army marched with 2 "mixed brigades." One boasted 2 infantry regiments, 1 regiment of horse artillery, 2 machine gun detachments, and a battalion of pioneers. In 1911, regular infantry brigades on both sides had a machine gun detachment, whereas the cavalry rode, as before, with its horse artillery and machine gunners. This arrangement would not change.[24]

As had occurred repeatedly in earlier decades, the adoption of a new technology also triggered a corresponding fight over tactics. The defensive use of machine guns in fortresses, guarding bridges or passes, or with entrenched troops in the field seemed so obvious as to require little elaboration in regulations, especially after the combat experience in Manchuria. The only tactical controversy was how the infantry should attack these kinds of positions. When machine gun enthusiasts returned to the agenda of levering attacks forward with machine gun companies, however, sparks flew as fast as the bullets. With only six Maxims to deploy, brigade commanders were forced to hold their detachments in reserve for use in a trouble-shooting role that brought the guns to the spot where they were most needed: protecting an exposed flank from cavalry, punching through a weak point in enemy lines, or perhaps moving forward with the vanguard to probe for such weaknesses.[25] But skeptics like Ludendorff scoffed at the sight of the machine gun companies with their slow-moving wagons; awkwardly heavy guns; and easily targeted machine gunners wearing shoulder harnesses for gun dragging. On the other side, artillerists were both angry and envious as the machine guns encroached on the mobile field artillery's role of close-range infantry support.[26] Indeed, although they moved with the infantry, cavalry, or independently, machine gun companies seemed to be a kind of artillery auxiliary.

A parallel controversy was raging in the field artillery. Having completed the transition to the C-96nA by 1908, debates soon followed over proper deployment. Most controversial was the concept of placing batteries far behind the lines in concealed positions.[27]

Figure 9. A machine gun detachment waits in ambush. Source: Hoppenstedt, *Das Heer.*

The Boers were the first to fire their guns "from defilade," but the British quickly followed suit and then the Japanese. The Russians were unprepared for this technique in 1904, complaining about the frightening and mysterious "shrapnel from the sky,"[28] but soon they also adopted hidden artillery positions. The French, who had turned the artillery world upside down with their 75 mm, nevertheless preferred half-hidden deployment, regarding defiladed positions as kind of a last resort that was injurious to the spirit of the offense. So did the Germans. To even the most progressive German artillerists, in fact, firing from defilade was a very dubious proposition in most situations. After the pros and cons had been aired at length by others, Heinrich Rohne, the moving force behind the adoption of rapid-firing cannons, came out against concealment in 1907. He predicted that accuracy would be adversely affected by aiming over hills, trees, and other obstacles, especially if the battery had to contend with moving and shifting targets. Worse still, "running for cover" was a "sickness" that sapped the spirit of the attacking force. It was also completely unnecessary with shielded cannons.[29]

New regulations for the field artillery appeared in April 1907. The commission recommended that artillery batteries practice firing from defilade "in order to master this [technique] in an emergency." Hidden positions were necessary, for instance, when superior enemy artillery was within range. But exaggerated reliance on concealment would undermine the artillery's main mission of supporting infantrymen. The artillery still needed to fire on enemy guns, but the old tactic of concentrating fire on opposing cannons and destroying them before helping the infantry was outmoded because of the difficulty of targeting enemy soldiers in their concealed positions. Thus, close cooperation with foot soldiers—eschewed in 1866, achieved in 1870, and glorified thereafter—could not be lost in the next war. If they moved up, the artillery should be close behind "to guard [them] from sudden reverses, bolster [their] reconnaissance with fire, or fall upon an incautious attacker with shelling." Helping the infantry to victory required "sacrificing the advantages of concealed positions."[30]

To be sure, the commissioners made many concessions to changing times. The gloriously long lines of cannons that won at

Figure 10. Half-hidden artillery positions. Source: Hoppenstedt, *Das Heer.*

Sedan—and were reproduced for decades at maneuvers—had to yield to smaller groups of batteries that took advantage of cover while advancing with the infantry. Fire control could still be achieved, concentrating on one target through the adoption of new technology like field telephones—an "indispensable requirement." Better range finders and more attention to forward observation would improve firing from defiladed positions. In general, however,

Figure 11. Hidden artillery positions. Source: Hoppenstedt, *Das Heer.*

the 1907 regulations reflected the difficulty that cannoneers were having in adapting old tactics to new technology.

Maneuvers, exercises, and firing drills bore further witness to this same problem. General Schubert, the newly appointed inspector general of the field artillery, presided over the transition. By autumn 1907, his brigades had worked with the C-96nA for two maneuver seasons and with the new regulations for one. His reports for this early period bemoaned the fact that some units were not practice-firing from defilade—and could not demonstrate the technique during inspections—whereas others "overused it."[31] In 1908, Schubert insisted on a proper balance of firing techniques from all brigades. Although more positive results were achieved,[32] year-end reports still complained about deficient defilade techniques and also criticized units for taking too long to prepare fire from hidden positions.[33] To speed things up, he recommended the installation of telephones and range-finders before the cannons were unlimbered. When deploying in the open field, however, brigades continued to prefer the long lines of the glory years rather than the smaller, dispersed formations prescribed by regulations.[34]

As 1908 yielded to 1909 and 1910, the German field artillery turned a corner of sorts. Schubert's brigades learned the technique of defilade firing, and as they did, earlier fears and objections subsided.[35] The French, who had themselves adopted hidden fire, observed respectfully in 1910 that concealed artillery positions were now preferred by their nemesis. A quiet technological revolution had also occurred. Batteries were equipped with observation towers, telephones, forward observation cars, and a new panoramic range-finder that provided a 360-degree view.[36] Joining the C-96nA in 1910, moreover, was a state-of-the-art, rapid-firing 105-mm howitzer that began to replace the outmoded l.FH-98. The l.FH-98–09 had semirecoilless gun carriages, shields, and a range of 6,300 meters. Delayed fuses enhanced their effectiveness against field fortifications.

Germany added a 3-battery battalion of the new 105s to each of its 23 corps in 1911, creating a nearly equal mix of the older and newer weapons. There was about 1 howitzer for every 5 C-96nA cannon in the field artillery in 1913—664 versus 3,419. Schubert strove unsuccessfully for a 1:1 ratio, but even at 1:5, this was a quantity and versatility the French did not have.[37] Pointing east were 4,088 75s but no 105 mm howitzers.[38] These numbers represented roughly a 100% expansion over the early 1900s, which was all that skeptical radicals in Paris were willing to fund. The overweening pride of the French field artillery for its piece also played a role. Rather than add 105s, the French artillery contented itself with an accessory device, the so-called Plaquette Maladrin, which gave shells curved, howitzer-like trajectories.[39] The German field artillery seemed to have reversed France's lead.

Decades of prideful and willful neglect, however, could not be overcome quickly or easily. Indeed, by 1913, the French probably still had a distinct field artillery advantage. First, French cannons had a 1,000-meter longer range. Secondly, a significant portion of Germany's batteries were commanded by reserve officers, many of whom had no familiarity with Schubert's reforms. The typical reserve commander, recalled one contemporary, "wanted just about nothing to do with modern range finders, telephones, and concealed positions." He belonged to the generation of field artillerists "that wanted to stand on the firing line and give direct orders for hitting targets which were in the open and within an easily calculable range."[40] The level of training among active and reserve officers in France, on the other hand, was more homogeneous.

The attitudes of Germany's large-unit commanders placed further limits on what Schubert could accomplish. Tactical command of the artillery was placed in corps hands in 1899, thereby fulfilling a long-held wish of field artillerists. The typical commanding general of 1913, however, "demanded [that his guns] advance in the open, change positions rapidly, fire directly, and accompany the infantry at close range, almost right behind the skirmish lines." In many army corps firing from more than 5,000 meters "was regarded as a waste of ammunition."[41] With time at corps maneuvers exhausted by close-range support drills, there was little opportunity to coordinate infantry and artillery tactics for those instances when, for one reason or another, guns attempted to fire from defiladed positions farther to the rear.

What was worse, the French artillery had more shells. Accustomed to the rapid-firing 75s since the 1890s, by 1911 France had built up stockpiles of about 1,000 shells per cannon—with plans to increase this number by 1915 to 1,300.[42] Before new production arrived from the homefront, in 1911 Germany had only 800 shells for each field piece and 600 for the light howitzer.[43] Both Ludendorff and Schubert tried to remedy this situation, the latter warning the kaiser personally in December 1910 that "we will have shot up everything after the first victorious battles, and it will take months to replace it." But neither William nor Moltke nor Einem really appreciated how quickly their batteries would "shoot up everything."[44] Whereas the average Prussian cannon shot 53 shells at St. Privat and 37 at Sedan—and only 210 for the entire Franco-Prussian War—Russian cannons fired between 150 and 200 shells per day in the battles of 1904–05.

Years of persistent pressure from field artillery experts and the General Staff finally resulted in an experiment at maneuvers in September 1913. The results surprised even the most determined advocates of munitions expansion. Firing under simulated battle conditions for 27 hours, a regiment exhausted 11,633 shells—an average of 323 per cannon. An alarmed Erich von Falkenhayn, Heeringen's replacement of a few months, now agreed to the goal of 1,200 to 1,500 shells per gun. But by 1914, German field cannons and howitzers still had fewer than 1,000 shells per gun—987 and 973, respectively. Another slugfest like Mukden would place the French in an overwhelmingly superior position after 4 or 5 days, for neither country had plans (or productive potential at war's outbreak) to supplement stockpiles in a grand fashion with new production.[45]

Pulling the pendulum back in the other direction, however, was the undisputed German advantage in heavy artillery. In one of the more remarkable turnarounds in military history, Germany had wrested the lead from its archfoe, expanding batteries of rapid-firing 150-mm howitzers tenfold from 1903 to 1913. Germany could now move 400 150s into the field—4 batteries per corps (i.e., 1 per brigade) to join the 3 batteries of rapid-firing 105s.[46] French numbers went the other way. Suspicious of the army as the Dreyfus affair unfolded, parliamentary radicals fired General Deloye, the man responsible for France's artillery surge in the 1890s. No one of anywhere near equal energy and vision replaced him. As France's 120s and 155s grew older and newer models became necessary, decisive action was hampered by heavy artillery lethargy, field artillery jealousy, and parliamentary opposition to armaments expenditures: "Studies piled upon studies, reports upon reports. Time passed. Nothing happened."[47] In 1903, France could mobilize 280 heavy field guns; but by 1909, the 120s were obsolete and the army could muster only 72 of the 155s. By 1912 there were only 16 heavy howitzers.[48] Prewar panic pushed the numbers of 120s and 155s much higher—210 and 104, respectively—but shells were relatively short. The Germans had stockpiled 800 per 150-mm howitzer, whereas the French 120s and 155s had only 400 to 450 and 540, respectively.[49] All things considered, therefore, the advantages and disadvantages of the French and German artillery establishments probably created a rough parity. It would take the particular circumstances of war to determine which was actually superior.

The debut of rapid-firing artillery and machine guns in the Russo-Japanese War exacerbated long-standing divisions in the German Army over infantry and cavalry tactics. In July 1905, for instance, the General Staff amended field regulations to accommodate the deadly machine gun. Moltke and his colleagues were inspired by Japanese persistence and doggedness, as well as the will to prevail on offensive actions.[50] Nevertheless, attacking infantry and cavalry could expect terrible losses as far away as 1,500 meters. Horses could not charge machine gun detachments unless there was complete surprise or some guns were out of action. Infantry had to form thin skirmish lines, sprint forward in small groups, and take frequent cover. "Any standing up means death."[51] One could find praise in military journals for defensive techniques like foxholes and shielded artillery pieces. "We are no longer Homeric heroes who can bear our breasts to enemy projectiles—besides, even in the murky depths of ancient times there was plenty of armor."[52] But alongside these kinds of articles, drumming them nearly into silence, were paeans to the "overwhelming drive to advance" and the "overpowering will to victory"[53] that was capable of overcoming adverse battlefield odds. Rather than dive for foxholes, infantrymen should fix bayonets. Similarly, true "cavalry spirit" would carry the day, even against enemy machine guns and artillery.[54]

In his characteristically confusing and contradictory way, William II reflected all of these viewpoints. In Berlin on New Year's Day 1906, Paul von Hindenburg, commander of Fourth Corps, listened to a royal monologue on tactics that left him shaking his head. Germany would attack like Boers, mastering the so-called "emptiness of the modern battlefield" technique, but also learn to amass whole army corps "in compact areas." Hindenburg returned to Magdeburg depressed over the mutually exclusive nature of his sovereign's ideas. He was also disturbed by rumors that a commission was drafting new infantry regulations. Such "incompetent doctoring around" would likely "break down the energy of our infantry assault."[55]

The truth was only somewhat reassuring. In the autumn of 1905, William had inspected Second Corps in Pomerania. While there, he became enamored with an alleged variation of the Boer attack developed by the corps commander, General Langenbeck. With one single order, an entire brigade of 6,000 men swung almost automatically into action. "It was the tactic of a single line, without reserves, a throwback to the idea that he who deploys forward the farthest and quickest with the most guns has the greatest firepower." The kaiser was so enthusiastic that he wanted Langenbeck's maneuver to be the basis of new infantry regulations. Einem, who had not been consulted, objected that a mechanical maneuver of this sort undercut the worthy spirit of "delegated tactics." To his credit, William responded that Schlichting's ideas were not uniformly observed in the various corps. "When I'm in East Prussia I find one tactic, when in Metz another—and when I go to Hanover I find something else entirely—which is itself different from Silesia." "If Your Majesty has experienced this," replied Einem cleverly, "then there would be nothing simpler than convening a commission which Your Majesty would charge to produce new infantry regulations." "Yes dear child," said the kaiser, "I've wanted nothing else all along."[56]

There was, of course, a difference. Einem had essentially finessed the monarch into abandoning Langenbeck. When the commission met in January 1906, it consisted of three distinct groupings. On one side were the staunch traditionalists around Hans von Plessen, commander of Imperial Headquarters, who believed victory was inevitable if officers drilled "old Prussian discipline" into a "breed of iron men who overcame all thought of personal danger."[57] The Bavarians assumed that Plessen was appointed "to insure that His Majesty's views prevailed."[58] The center was dominated by Karl von Bülow, commander of Third Corps, who agreed with many of Schlichting's ideas—with the major exception of delegated tactics. Like most corps commanders, Bülow wanted more control over the advancing troops. Modern tactics were essential, but they had to be drummed into recruits and junior officers through endless drills until a few simple commands sufficed. On the opposite extreme were younger, more open-minded types like Major General Fasbender of Bavaria, a tactical modernist who had absorbed the lessons of recent wars. There was no sympathy on the commission, even in Plessen's faction, for Langenbeck's novel views. When the commission stood firm, William caved in, agreeing that Second Corps practices could be "overlooked."[59] The final version of May 1906 was a victory for Bülow and Fasbender.[60] The Schlichtingesque foundations of 1888 regulations were maintained because a majority believed that the Russo-Japanese War had proven their worth. Fasbender even prevailed over Bülow on battlefield decision making by junior officers.

However, that Bülow had sacrificed his notion of drilling "spontaneity" into subordinates was less a victory for Fasbender, than the realization by Bülow that he had the far-reaching independence of command to do as he liked. Uniting all members of the commission, moreover, was their recognition of the power of the all-conquering will. Genuinely impressed by the heroic efforts of Japan, the German infantry rededicated itself to the offensive. Indeed the aggressive spirit of certain passages almost seemed to contradict the commitment in other parts to dispersed formations; prudent use of terrain, foxholes, and field fortifications; waiting for artillery support; and patiently developing the attack. Gone, in fact, were the older version's warnings about the lethality of modern weapons and the power of entrenched defenders, as if mentioning this reality was itself injurious to the spirit of the offensive. "The infantry must cultivate its inherent inner-drive to push forward aggressively, its actions must be ruled by only one thought: forwards against the enemy!" The modern Alexander would attack and succeed, "cost what it may!"[61]

That the rejuvenated spirit of the attack could easily manifest itself in a variety of tactical forms was demonstrated at maneuvers. To return decision-making freedom to the generals—and break with Schlieffen's practice of tolerating constant interference from the kaiser—Moltke adopted a nonprescriptive approach. Left to their own devices in 1906, the commanders of Third (Brandenburg) and Fifth (Posen) Corps gave a textbook demonstration of the new regulations, but Sixth (Silesia) Corps did not, rushing massed infantry and cavalry into open attacks without artillery support, forcing the gunners to play catch-up, and generally ignoring everything that Schlichting had written.[62] Moltke fumed, but 1907 proved even worse. Both Seventh (Westphalia) and Tenth (Hanover) Corps showed the face of the past. It was especially the lack of patience in developing their assaults, the "nervous haste" of the anxious commanders, that bothered him. Everything practiced during the year was "thrown overboard" when it came to imperial maneuvers. In war's real test, these techniques "would decide the matter to our great disadvantage." Not until the autumn of 1908 did Moltke achieve more satisfactory results.[63]

The cavalry, meanwhile, was struggling through a similarly difficult period of transition. In charge of his first September maneuver in 1905, Moltke made sure there were no vainglorious charges.[64] The new chief wanted to begin his tenure on a realistic note, for he knew that horse units had suffered setbacks against the artillery in the Boer War and that the cavalry was rarely deployed in the Asian fighting. Maximilian Edler von der Planitz, the aging inspector general of the cavalry, tried to adjust to the new era. He fought the tendency to live entirely in the past by conducting large-scale reconnaissance exercises in 1905—the first since 1891—and then placing more emphasis on scouting and dismounted fighting at imperial maneuvers in 1906. But the old three-wave tactician could not resist the exciting legacy of bygone centuries. Exploiting the greater freedom Moltke allowed that September, Planitz also unleashed the great masses of horse the kaiser so loved to watch.[65] Moltke noted the foreign criticism and circulated it to all commanders. The inspector general tried to defend what he saw as the balanced performance of his branch but clearly lost his composure. "A slanderous criticism has been made of our use of lances. [Why?] Do [foreigners] fear them? I almost think so." Planitz saved his peroration for those who called for a transformation to mounted infantry: "God and the German Kaiser forbid that this role will ever be expected of the German cavalry."[66] But William made no attempt to save Planitz, who was retired shortly after writing these bitter words.

The new inspector general, Georg Friedrich von Kleist, had been a thorn in Planitz's side for years. Also gaining influence was Friedrich von Bernhardi, another reformer who had harried the outgoing chief. Special exercises and commission deliberations examined the mounted corps' new role. Although Kleist and Bernhardi did not always agree, the course that the cavalry set for itself in 1907 and 1908 was fairly consistently in the direction of the far-reaching reforms that both had advocated since the 1890s. The main mission of the cavalry was now tactical and strategical reconnaissance. The functional and operational unit was the regiment or brigade—occasionally a division or an entire corps—their squadrons moving prudently according to the lay of the land in so-called light formations. Incorporated into the scouting role, obviously, was destruction of the enemy's scouts and advance guards—so old-fashioned combat with thundering hoofs and swinging swords could still be expected. For the most part, however, the cavalry's fighting experience would differ significantly from the day of Mars-la-Tour. Accompanied by detachments of machine guns, horse artillery, and an increasing number of mounted Jäger regiments, cavalry units would either deploy on the wing, hurling themselves into headlong pursuit of routed enemy divisions, or hurry to a trouble spot, dismount, and bolster the infantry. Gone were the three equal or unequal wave tactics practiced at Konitz and Buxtehude in the 1880s. Gone, in fact, was most of the old parade-ground drill. Regulations to this effect were issued in April 1909.[67]

The revamped German cavalry made its debut at imperial maneuvers in September 1909. Kleist commanded an entire corps of cavalry whose task was to fan out in front of Blue Army as it invaded the Red Empire. Reminiscent of the 1900 maneuvers, the two armies began their operations over 100 kilometers apart. The entire 5 days of operations, in fact, accentuated the prebattle stage of a massive campaign. Although the cavalry on both sides saw plenty of action, the reconnaissance and screening mission took precedence.[68] Observing the performance was retired Lieutenant Colonel Gädke, formerly a regimental commander in the field artillery, now the extremely critical military correspondent of the *Berliner Tageblatt*. Accustomed to mocking the outmoded conservatism of the German Army, Gädke heaped praise on his former comrades, especially the willingness of the cavalry to pull away from "the phantom of the shock-troop cavalry" and to dismiss "the wide-roaming phantasy of a future of decisive deeds on horseback." The truth was that cavalry regiments played "a welcome, albeit localized auxiliary role" and would never again rise to the level of "deciding battles."[69]

Observers at exercises, games, and maneuvers from 1909 to 1911 noticed a German Army that was growing increasingly accustomed to the technological dictates of "war in the present."[70] Infantry attacks usually unfolded in a more gradual and patient fashion. The dispersed battle order once condemned by traditionalists as injurious to the offensive spirit became the new orthodoxy. Divisions and corps spread out along broader fronts as commanders more accustomed to telephones sacrificed the close, hands-on control of troops that was considered essential in previous decades. Machine gun detachments once in limbo between the various army branches worked much more closely with the infantry. Cavalry regiments seemed comfortable with the reconnoitering, screening, and auxiliary attack role allotted to them. Reinforcing the modern appearance of the whole scene were the rapid-firing cannons and howitzers of the field and heavy artillery, blasting away from hidden positions.[71] A similar, almost futuristic effect was created in 1909 and 1910, when airships made their first appearance at maneuvers; they were joined by airplanes in 1911. The "unforgettable impression" of the flying machines, defying nature far over the battlefield, "had to convince even the angriest antimodernist that from this point on a new epoch of aerial reconnaissance was dawning."[72]

Of course, such a huge and multilayered organization with such a long history of resisting change could not make a complete transformation in a mere 5 or 6 years. The officer corps was littered, in fact, with men who doubted that the new ways were better than the old or else offered their own versions of the new. No one knew better than Moltke that he had not yet put his stamp on the whole complex organism that was the regular German Army. With the exception of the infamous English Colonel Repington, whose exaggerated critique of German maneuvers in 1911 should be seen as an attempt to undermine the myth of German invincibility,[73] there was no harsher critic of the German Army than its own General Staff chief. As Europe neared the brink of war during the Moroccan crisis of 1911, Moltke's report on autumn maneuvers attacked certain infantry units for advancing too quickly, with skirmish lines packed too tightly. The cavalry divisions attached to the infantry—the so-called division cavalry—were told not to dart off on independent escapades. And the artillery heard the old criticism about moving up too quickly en masse to give support to the infantry.[74]

Clearly the function of German Army maneuvers continued to evolve. The 1890s witnessed a political brawling between factions based in rival corps, escalating efforts by the General Staff to control September exercises and generate valuable tactical and technological lessons, and interference from William II that reduced the potential of maneuvers to accomplish anything positive. Under Moltke, there was now a much more concerted effort to use maneuvers to wean corps commanders from practices and techniques that did not

Figure 12. Infantrymen attack nearly shoulder to shoulder at autumn 1912 maneuvers. Source: Hoppenstedt, *Das Heer.*

conform to the demands of modernity. After the usual heated disagreements over costs and benefits, the army also scurried to introduce new technologies, as well as to learn from maneuver experience how to integrate them most optimally into exisiting military
structures. Moreover although the kaiser was definitely not a
changed man, at least he no longer turned maneuvers into a farce.

Moltke worried, however, that the mobilization of a mere 2 or 3
corps every autumn did not provide him—or anyone else in the
army—with actual experience in conducting a war with millions of
men in scores of corps.[75] In 1914, for example, the three right-wing
western armies alone totaled 640,000 men in 16 corps. Schlieffen's
prescriptions for the modern Alexander may have contained worries
about Moltke's ability to fulfill them, but Moltke saw through Schlieffen's idealistic image to the organizational nightmares that lay ahead.

Another nagging problem was the low quality of reserve officers
whose units were expected to play a major role in wartime. "The
Fatherland expects no combat laurels from you," the kaiser told
assembled reservists in 1913.[76] This was not only tactless but above
all inaccurate because 24 reserve divisions headed west with Germany's 7 armies when the tocsin finally sounded—35 % of the invading tidal wave. That these unseasoned leaders marched with comparatively little artillery and machine gun support was just asking for
trouble.

And then there was the kaiser. Germany's Janus-faced emperor
often played the spokesman for the modernists who were gaining
ascendancy in the army. No one pushed harder for the Zeppelins,
machine guns, and heavy howitzers or seemed prouder than he.
More often than not, however, William's semipublic utterances
about tactics played to traditionalists in his entourage like Hans von
Plessen—men who were almost completely out of touch with recent
army developments and the new reality of war.[77] The continuing pull
of these conservative, Achilles types helps to explain, for example,
the kaiser's strange behavior at a special exercise outside Potsdam
in May 1912. When his position was attacked by a brigade that was
employing the latest tactics, William gave orders for the Guard Corps
to counterattack in tightly packed formation, followed closely by
drummers and the regimental band.[78] He exhibited the same antiquated tactical notions during his critique at imperial maneuvers 4
months later, warning the infantry not to spread out: "Stay right
together, go at the enemy in tight ranks, then charge with banners
unfurled, drums beating, and the band playing!" For the first time,
William recognized the correctness of defilade artillery fire, but then

he quickly undermined the point by stressing the need for "relentless and reckless accompaniment of the infantry right up to the
skirmish line." The emperor also declared that the cavalry would
still win battles: "Woe to him who underestimates the cavalry—for
he can have a rude awakening."[79] These remarks, so backward and
outmoded, caused embarrassed astonishment among many of the
generals in attendance.

William was not alone, however, for there were many supporters
outside of his entourage among older commanders and reserve officers who did not sympathize with, or had not experienced, the
reforms of the Einem-Moltke era. The real reactionaries were older
cavalry officers and their recently retired colleagues. The diehard
horsemen founded a journal, the *Cavalry Monthly* , to trumpet their
cause in 1905. The editors' commitment had flagged not a bit 7
years later when they called it "a holy duty to protect, cultivate, and
rekindle the good old manly equestrian spirit."[80] The journal occasionally opened its pages to more reasonable officers, who argued
for a reduced cavalry role more in keeping with the official line in
Berlin. But the overwhelming emphasis and unmistakable message—
month after month, year in and year out—was the need for cavalrymen to shrink from no battlefield task, however imprudent it
seemed, however many comrades might be killed.[81] The notion that
man on horseback could no longer decide today's mechanized battles sent them into a rage. Thus, General von Unger of the Twentieth Hanoverian Brigade shouted that "any cavalryman who thinks
horses have no use in battle should have his spurs hacked from his
heels and be transferred—if he has any use at all—to the airships
or the flying corps."[82] There was obviously nothing but contempt
here for "the new epoch of aerial reconnaissance."

New Weapons

Shortly after Schlieffen's "War in the Present" article, two events
signaled an intensified race for control of the skies. Baron Ferdinand von Zeppelin, pioneer and inventor of the airship, navigated
his sleek, bullet-shaped craft 600 kilometers across the entire length
of Germany, from Lake Constance to Berlin, where he landed at
Tempelhof before an appropriately impressed Kaiser William II. Although nothing could match the futuristic spectacle of Zeppelin's
140-meter-long silver ship as it descended from the sky, heads also
turned when French aviator Louis Blériot flew his birdlike mono-

plane over the English Channel at a world-record speed of 74 kilometers per hour—almost twice as fast as a Zeppelin. It was the
summer of 1909.

Zeppelin's feat was long in coming. For 20 years the "crazy
South German Baron,"[83] as William dubbed him, tried to convince
everyone that navigable airships were the future of air travel and air
power. Zeppelin finally raised enough funds in 1900 to build a gas-
filled, propeller-driven, aluminum-frame craft powered by internal
combustion engines, but it sustained irreparable wind damage during three flights. A second ship failed on lift-off in 1905, but the
persistent nobleman built a third, which in 1906 flew faster and
higher. Now the German government granted subsidies. A fourth,
improved Zeppelin was even more impressive in 1908, circumnavi-
gating Switzerland in one flight, then flying across southern Germany before it was destroyed during a storm. By this time, however,
Zeppelin had caught the German imagination. An excited public
poured 6 million marks into his coffers in a display of patriotic giving. The army purchased Zeppelin's third and fifth airships in 1909,
redesignated as Z-1 and Z-2. Built that August, Z-2 made a triumphal
entry into Berlin.[84]

However, Zeppelin's rigid aluminum monsters were not alone
among the lighter-than-air ships. The French had grabbed the lead
during the early 1900s, in fact, with a smaller design of the Brothers
Lebaudy. Sixty meters long, the lighter canvas structure carried an
armored basket underneath. Almost as fast as a Zeppelin and flying
just as high—around 1,000 meters—it was less rigid and therefore
less susceptible to wind damage in the air and on the ground. Because the canvas gas container could be deflated and packed up,
the Lebaudy airship was also more transportable. The French had
three of them in 1906, eight in 1908, and planned to double this
number by 1910.[85]

The Prussian Airship Battalion constructed an experimental airship of similar design in 1906. A successor, the M-2, was airborne
all 5 days of maneuvers in the autumn of 1909 whereas the Z-2
braved the winds on only 1 day. Meanwhile, a retired major of the
Bavarian Army, August von Parseval, had built a deflateable blimp
with even fewer rigid parts. Fifty meters long, it could take off and
land almost anywhere and was more easily transported (when deflated) and more versatile in bad weather than the M-2. It was
therefore a promising reconnaissance vehicle for an army that
planned to move quickly. On the other hand, it could carry less
weight than either the M-2 or the Zeppelin. The Airship Battalion

acquired its first Parseval blimp in 1908. An improved version, the PL-3, successfully undertook a 5-day tour over southern Germany in October 1909. The addition that year of the Z-1 and Z-2, with their greater carrying capacity and far greater radius of action—in good weather—gave Prussia a smaller air fleet but a more flexible set of options and thus a solid foundation for future development.[86]

At the same time, the airplane was enjoying its own impressive success story. Americans Wilbur and Orville Wright made the first flight for a few seconds in 1903. In subsequent years, their "flyer," a flimsy wooden and canvas biplane pushed by gasoline-engine-driven propellers, made enough progress to capture the attention of both the French and German armies. Between 1906 and 1908, however, France became the real arena of experimentation and progress, whereas Germany was concentrating its efforts and resources on airships. Joining the Wrights in France were early aviators like Santos Dumont and Henri Farmer, whose innovative flying machines covered distances of 20 kilometers in 20 minutes (i.e., 60 kilometers per hour).[87] In July 1909, Blériot flew 33 kilometers over the English Channel at even faster speeds. A few weeks later at Rheims Air Week, rapidly improving French airplanes reached speeds of 80 kilometers per hour, altitudes of 155 meters, and distances of 190 kilometers.[88] Germans present at Rheims immediately warned Berlin about "the unlimited potential of the airplane as a weapon of war" and "the dangerous gap in the art of flying that exists between us and other nations."[89] And they were right, for after Rheims the French Army acquired airplanes of various designs and trained scores of military pilots in a new flight school. By October 1910, France had 38 army pilots and 30 planes. An additional 46 planes were on order, and there were plans to purchase another 50.[90]

The German Army had watched the airplane develop for 3 years without investing a great deal of confidence—or any money—in its potential. The Prussian War Ministry's flight budget of 2.7 million marks went entirely for airship purchase and development in late 1909.[91] The enthusiastic reports from Rheims tempted Einem's successor, Josias von Heeringen, to support private airplane efforts in Germany, but he wanted to split the minimal 100,000-mark subsidy among five departments. When his colleagues grudgingly agreed, Heeringen put up his 20,000, "chiefly because France now has the lead over Germany."[92] The reaction of the General Staff was similarly lukewarm and mixed. Hermann von Thomsen's Technological Section admitted that Germany had "shamefully little" to match France

in the way of airplanes but that airships seemed to be the most
promising aerial technology. Thomsen warned against exaggerating
the military significance of airplanes that were "purely for sport."[93]
Because France had a lead in 1910, however, Germany began to
train military pilots—10 by the end of the year—and purchased its
first five planes. Airplane expenditures for 1910 totaled 300,000
marks, 12.8% of all outlays for flight.[94]

German attitudes and policies changed quickly in 1911. A series
of Zeppelin crashes in 1910 and the mechanical failure of a Parseval
blimp at maneuvers tempered enthusiasm for airships. Fliers
pointed with soaring pride and arrogance, moreover, to new airplanes that went farther, higher, and faster—exceeding 100 kilometers per hour. The alarming debut of airplanes at French maneuvers in September 1910 reinforced their arguments.
Accordingly, the Prussian War Ministry accelerated the training of
pilots and purchased 24 planes in 1911. Airplane expenditures increased to 2.25 million marks, 51.4% of outlays for flight.[95]

This was not enough for the General Staff. The airplane's meteoric rise and the airship's questionable development led to a radical change of views in Prussia's elite planning agency. The driving
force behind the turnaround was Thomsen. Lambasting the reconnaissance potential of both the cavalry and the airship in early 1911,
he predicted that airplanes would soon represent the main scouting
tool of the army.[96] Thomsen reinforced the point after airplanes
performed a stellar short-range reconnaissance role at maneuvers
that year, the airships' telegraph system broke down, and weather
continued to frequently ground them.[97] After Ludendorff agreed
with Thomsen, and Moltke with Ludendorff, the General Staff insisted that financial support be transfered from M and P-ships to
airplanes that would take over all short-range scouting. Only Zeppelins of the latest design were to receive funding. The combination
of telegraph communications (airplanes still had none) and a 450-
kilometer radius of action—about three times the radius German
military planes could achieve—made the newest Zeppelin Germany's best long-range reconnaissance weapon.[98] The General Staff
also believed that the Zeppelin's rigid structure was ideal for carrying bombs and mounting machine guns for defense against enemy
airplanes. To spare more money for planes, however, the number
of Zeppelins required could be reduced from the earlier plan of 15
to 9—1 for each army group.[99]

The General Staff's demands ignited an intramural struggle over
aerial technology. The inspector general of military transport, Baron

Alfred von Lyncker, bristled with indignation over Moltke's interference in the competency of other departments. Implying that technological matters were better left to the real experts, Lyncker claimed quite logically that Moltke's staff had overlooked the potential of M- and P-ships for strategic reconnaissance. "We should not underestimate the blimp's current advantages over the rigid airship, namely, easy handling on the ground, significantly less size, and transportability when deflated."[100] Lyncker believed that Moltke had also exaggerated the mechanical and communications problems at recent maneuvers. War Minister Heeringen backed Lyncker in March 1912, citing additional reasons for maintaining the M- and P-ships. With half the gas volume, they were far cheaper to operate, and because there was much less gas loss, they were also more efficient. Until Zeppelin's very latest design in the summer of 1911, the smaller ships had also outperformed the larger craft. Although no one could predict future improvements on either side, he found it noteworthy that the French were investing heavily in newly designed P-ships. Moreover, with great discernment, he pointed to the "greater maneuverability" of the canvas ships. This factor could be "of great significance on those days when the Zeppelins are unable to leave their hangars due to cross winds." Heeringen concluded that it made no sense for Germany to abandon the "superior" position of having three different airship systems that "mutually complement one another." The General Staff's proposals were therefore "unacceptable."[101]

Both sides haggled for another 15 months as war clouds gathered and burst in the Balkans. The result was a compromise of sorts.[102] Airplane funding rose more than elevenfold to 25.9 million marks from 1912 to 1914, enabling Germany to acquire over 300 planes and catch up with France. This was more than triple the number that the War Ministry considered necessary but about 150 fewer planes than the General Staff wanted. Meanwhile, airship appropriations climbed twelvefold, from 4.4 million to 26.6 million marks, as the airship regained its percentage priority in the flight budget, averaging 50.9%. This level of spending allowed the fleet of airships to expand to 15—well beyond that which the General Staff wanted. But the War Ministry was forced to abandon its "superior" position of maintaining three airship systems, for the bulk of all new money was poured into new Zeppelins. In 1912, Germany possessed a versatile fleet of 3 Zeppelins, 4 M-ships, and 3 P-ships. In 1914, there were 12 rigid dirigibles, 1 M-ship, and 2 P-ships. Mobilization plans called for 9 Zeppelins to accompany German armies into the field, with one P-ship in reserve near Berlin.

Figure 13. The new epoch of aerial reconnaissance: M-ship (left) and Zeppelin (right) hover above the cavalry at autumn 1912 maneuvers. Source: Hoppenstedt. *Das Heer.*

With war a distinct possibility in 1913, Lyncker and other flight experts were convinced that Germany had squandered its airship superiority over France. They were incredulous and bitter that the army could make such errors with a "matter of national honor"[103] at stake. Time would tell if they were right.

Almost completely overshadowed by the airship controversy were debatable decisions about the best use of airplanes. Although Thomsen realized that Germany's 1911-issue, single-winged Taube had the fuel capacity and speed to return from distances of 150 to 200 kilometers in 4 to 5 hours—and was capable of such flights "in the stronger winds"—his enthusiasm for employing planes over these "longer stretches"[104] was not shared by other experts. During the 1912 maneuvers, army staffs generally ordered fliers to scout for an hour or so and then turn around, giving them action radii of 60 to 100 kilometers. Officers assumed that airplanes were most "purposefully [employed] like the cavalry reconnaissance squadrons."[105] Zealous fliers shook their heads at the "definite disinterest" of army leaders who "frequently reacted to technology with all too great a skepticism."[106] Once again, however, only the particulars of a real

Figure 14. The Taube: Germany's standard reconnaissance airplane after 1911. Source: Hoppenstedt, *Das Heer.*

campaign would prove whether wisdom lay with the Falstaffs or the Hotspurs. For now, the former could point to the fact that most reconnaissance flights at the 1911 maneuvers were less than 2 hours—radii of 50 to 70 kilometers—but still detected the location and outflanking attempts of all enemy corps.[107] As a member of the General Staff, however, Thomsen probably had the "longer stretches" of Belgium in mind.

The heavy artillery underwent a remarkable transformation of roles and functions before 1905. Under Heinrich Edler von der Planitz, inspector general from 1893 to 1902, attempts were made to mobilize the old sluggish siege trains. The foot artillery appeared on the exercise fields with horse-drawn detachments, whose task was to smash France's triple ring of fortresses. By 1900, however, this vision was fading, as engineers on both sides of the Rhine constructed seemingly impregnable structures. Now Schlieffen invested time and resources in the 105-mm howitzer, ignored Planitz's budget requests, and grew increasingly mesmerized with his big push into Belgium.

As dreams yielded to realities, Planitz and his chief of staff, Gustav Adolf Deines, convinced Schlieffen that the heavy artillery, if supplied with enough horse teams, was fully capable of reinforcing

the field artillery mission of destroying the opposing artillery and
then turning on the enemy's infantry.[108] A firing competition between light and heavy howitzers at Münster in 1900 demonstrated
that heavy 150s had superior effect on dug-in artillery batteries. After Planitz stepped down in 1902, Deines, who had moved to the
Fortress Department of the General Staff, continued to cultivate the
heavy artillery's field mission with Planitz's sucessor, General von
Perbandt. The "fortress attack exercises" so characteristic of the
1890s were discontinued in favor of special "battle exercises of all
branches."[109] Prussia's War Ministry sided with Perbandt, Deines,
and the General Staff after completion of these experiments in
1904. Corps commanders received instructions to deploy 150s not
merely "when enemy entrenchments or heavy artillery make it absolutely necessary, rather every time . . . it corresponds to the needs
of battle." The heavy artillery "must be brought in for the decision."[110]

Competition between artillery branches intensified in 1906
when Perbandt yielded to General von Dulitz. A career field artillerist and veteran of the Wars of Unification, he brought along all
of his old corps' pride and prejudice. Regarding shooting range
learning-by-doing as more valuable than scientific gunnery, for instance, Dulitz wanted to eliminate mandatory study at Germany's
Military Technical Academy. In 1908 he redesignated heavy artillery
"companies" as "batteries" to create conformity with the field artillery. The same regulations increased the tempo while hauling guns
from 250 to 300 yards per minute—quicker than the cavalry. Dulitz's fixation with mobility also led to the adoption of lighter, rapid-
firing guns mounted on wheeled carriages, which made wagons and
laboriously constructed shooting platforms unnecessary. Joining the
rapid-firing 150s introduced in 1903 were 210-mm mortars, as well
as new 100- and 130-mm cannons. The hard-driving inspector general also fought successfully for horse teams to make all of this weaponry mobile on the battlefield. Germany had only 10 horse-drawn
heavy artillery detachments in 1904, but 9 years later almost every
army corps marched with at least 1.[111]

With such awesome firepower and mobility, heavy artillerists began to claim that their branch was "trump." Big guns should march
in forward positions, fire first at enemy guns, and secure a path of
advance for trailing infantry and field artillery units.[112] Such boasts
quickly created bad blood throughout the army. Field artillerymen
were especially upset. They scoffed at the arrogance of the heavy
artillery, charging (with perverse logic) that their rivals were aban-

doning siege responsibilities for the easier task of open-field war-fare—an assignment better left, naturally, to the field artillery.[113] Well-informed insiders such as Karl Justrow, a member of the heavy artillery proving commission, pointed to a different kind of moti-vation. The General Staff's demands for a quick overrunning of field fortifications struck a responsive chord among foot artillerymen, tired of their lowly stepsister status. Younger officers were particu-larly eager to go forward in the battle order. They "insisted stormily on more horse-drawn detachments so that every battery had a team—then they wouldn't wear their spurs, the outward symbol of a mounted corps, just for appearance's sake." It was a sort of "jus-tifiable defensive reaction,"[114] designed to earn the respect, once and for all, of the rest of the army.

Results were mixed. Some commanders complained that the "el-ephants" were still too slow.[115] Other leaders, however, began to doubt the allegedly limited potential of the C-96nA. Field artillery champions lashed back, accusing Dulitz's military press of under-mining the army's as well as the popular, faith in the field artillery and thereby serving the enemy's interests.[116] Although this was clearly exaggerated, other criticisms hit closer to the mark. Heinrich Rohne observed how unrealistic it was to drag howitzers and mortars faster than the cavalry's pace, pointing to an alarming 56% rate of after-maneuver lameness of horses.[117] He also sought to exploit di-visions in heavy artillery ranks that had grown increasingly wider since 1900. Rohne knew of "outstanding" foot artillerists who feared that Planitz, Perbandt, and Dulitz had "exaggerated" the field po-tential of their branch while "neglecting fortress warfare, a task that was at least equally important."[118]

One of these artillerists was Max Bauer, a younger officer who cared little about the jangle of spurs. Joining the foot artillery in 1889, he advanced to first lieutenant in 1895 and was assigned to the proving commission in Berlin from 1899 to 1902. During those latter years, the earlier preference of heavy artillery experts for rais-ing calibers above 305 mm began to bow before "the strong current going through the foot artillery of that day," recalled Bauer, "to become a force in the field once again."[119] After commanding a battery in Westphalia, he began a temporary stint in 1905 with the Fortress Department of the Prussian General Staff. Bauer, now a captain, completed a study of the siege of Port Arthur that con-vinced him that heavier guns would have broken Russian resistance much more quickly. But his report was not well received as it cir-culated through General Staff offices because most officers around

Moltke were preoccupied with the lightness and maneuverability of field cannons.[120] Moreover, Quartermaster General Gustav Adolf Deines was "resting somewhat on his laurels" and "hadn't the faintest notion" about complicated technological matters. The heavy artillery's preference for mobility and the prejudice against calibers above 210 mm permeated all departments.[121]

In 1906 Bauer undertook what, by all objective accounts, was a one-man campaign within the General Staff to get approval for larger siege cannons.[122] One by one, he won over the members of his own department, including the chief, Lieutenant Colonel Ilse. Bauer networked in other relevant offices, too, convincing both Ludendorff and General von Stein, Ludendorff's boss in the Mobilization Deparment, of the need for heavier calibers. Even Deines and Moltke swung into line.[123] Moreover, the "spiritus rector"[124] of big guns established contact with heavy artillery technicians at the Krupp Company who proceeded—probably on his advice—to build a colossal 420-mm howitzer. Capable of lobbing a 2,000-pound shell over 14 kilometers, the monstrous 175-ton engine of destruction began its testing in April 1909. "Yesterday my fat cannon exceeded all expectations,"[125] Bauer wrote his wife exuberantly in January

Figure 15. Max Bauer's "fat cannon": the Gamma-Device. Source: Karl Justrow, *Die Dicke Berta und der Krieg* (Berlin, 1935).

1910. Called a gamma-device, the giant howitzer was delivered to artillery proving experts for more tests in early 1911.

Bauer's assignment to the General Staff became permanent during the test firing at Krupps. Ludendorff, now a department head, was so taken with the innovative and persistent artilleryman that he arranged for Bauer to be transferred to his own Mobilization Department. Bauer continued to shine in his new surroundings, developing fortress assault tactics that discarded the older, step-by-step tightening of the ring in favor of one quick rush while defenders scurried for cover to escape the gargantuan projectiles of the "fat cannon."[126]

Once again Ludendorff was impressed—so much so, in fact, that in February 1911 he returned to the idea of breaking through France's eastern fortress wall, a plan that had been idle for 15 years. Because no one on the General Staff wanted to discard Schlieffen's operational spadework, however, Ludendorff recommended attacking the massive fort complexes of Verdun and Toul-Nancy in addition to an assault on Belgium, directly over Liège and Namur, which Schlieffen had always wanted to bypass. Ludendorff reckoned that a great battle of double envelopment over French and Belgian forts required 8 420-mm Gamma Devices, 16 Beta 305-mm mortars; and hundreds of 100, 130, 150, and 210-mm guns—all on top of the artillery battalions and horse-drawn detachments that Dulitz was exacting with difficulty from an ever-stingy War Ministry. After consulting with artillery experts for more than a year, the daring department head drew up estimates for all necessary shells and munitions.[127]

Ludendorff undoubtedly developed these embryonic plans in close cooperation with Moltke. Research on Schlieffen's successor gives us clear insights into Moltke's dark brooding nature; his penchant for the occult; and his pessimism about quick victories, or perhaps about any victory at all.[128] During the Moroccan crisis of 1905, Moltke predicted a "general European war of murder," a "massacre whose horror can only make one shudder to think." An end to the fighting in less than a year was illusory. Rather, "it will be a people's war that cannot be won in one decisive battle but will turn into a long, difficult, painful struggle [*langes mühevolles Ringen*]."[129] The gnawing possibility of a long war loomed larger in his gloomy thoughts after General Staff experts responsible for war scenarios against France concluded in 1910 that a great western victory in one campaign was unlikely.[130] Moltke and his westfront planners joined an impressive list of German soldiers who had braced for a multiyear slugfest: Colmar von der Goltz, Heinrich von Gossler, Friedrich Köpke, and the elder Moltke.

On the other hand, although he refused to follow colleagues who still believed in Schlieffen's prescriptions for victory in 6 to 9 months, Moltke hesitated to abandon operations that offered reasonable chances for an auspicious beginning to a much longer struggle. Thus, in 1908 and again in 1911, the General Staff chief rejected the old idea of advancing along a single route over the French fortresses to Paris. Even if the heavy guns cut through the center, advancing German corps would be vulnerable to flanking attacks launched from surviving forts to the north and south. The Belgian strategy was superior because it catapulted armies far behind the French fortresses, which then became indefensible. Without these bulwarks, France could eventually be defeated. Like Schlieffen before him, however, Moltke had stated repeatedly since assuming office that it would be incorrect to continue the march through Belgium if the French exited their fortresses and attacked into Alsace or Lorraine. Then he wanted Germany's right-wing armies to wheel south and support counterattacking center and left-wing forces.[131] This scenario of double envelopment seemed more likely by 1913 as the French altered previous defensive plans in favor of striking across the border with an "all-conquering will." While keeping the right wing fairly strong, therefore, Moltke and Ludendorff began to commit extra forces to Lorraine, where a French attack was anticipated.[132] In such a battle, both wings of the German Army required massive heavy artillery—hence Ludendorff's studies.

The General Inspection of the Heavy Artillery assumed from all of this attention that it was slated to play a great role in crushing France. Under the leadership, after 1911, of General Lauter, a dyed-in-the-wool heavy artillerist, it returned to siege exercises abandoned a decade earlier. Units were drilled in every conceivable aspect of the great western breakthrough. "After these maneuvers," recalled one artilleryman, "I knew by heart every path and incline on the map of Verdun and Toul, every suitable battery and observation position, all ranges, the most important targets, and the actual firing specifications necessary for direct hits."[133] The assault on Verdun, for example, would be launched from two sides, that is, along both banks of the Meuse.[134] As it had in the 1890s, heavy artillery technology was beginning to alter Germany's western operational thinking.

It remained to be seen, however, whether Bauer and Ludendorff could push through their program. Weapons testers in the War Ministry's Artillery Deparment doubted the technical feasibility of a 420-mm howitzer in 1906, then somewhat more insightfully, its maneuverability. Indeed Bauer's monster could be transported only if it were dismantled into six parts on two separate trains over heavy-duty tracks. Unable to halt the construction of Krupp's Gamma-Device, the proving commission got approval in 1911 for Krupp to build a more mobile 420-mm howitzer. Weighing only 44 tons, the ministry's gun hurled a 1,700-pound projectile 9 kilometers. Although its shells had less crushing effect, the so-called M-Device could be broken down and transported by motorized tractors on roads.[135] Given the War Ministry's initial skepticism about the Gamma-Device—and later investment in an alternative design—it was obviously not inclined to back Ludendorff's artillery requests.

The clash of technical opinions across counterproductive intramural borders resulted in the type of angry compromise that was squelching many sound military ideas in the German Army. Krupp

Figure 16. The Prussian War Ministry's mobile M-Gun. Source: Justrow, *Die Dicke Berta.*

delivered 4 Gamma-Devices and 2 of the more versatile M-Devices during the winter of 1913–1914. The deal left the War Ministry's artillery experts like Karl Justrow scoffing at the General Staff's disregard for mobility considerations, whereas the latter fumed that it was still 2 420s short of estimates. Moltke's men also had to settle for 12 305-mm mortars—instead of 16—and 8 battalions of assorted smaller caliber guns (210s, 150s, etc.) instead of 26.[136] Apparently, Ludendorff and Moltke would not have enough big guns to guarantee a breakthrough on both wings, thus increasing the stakes in a *coup de main* at Liège.[137] Worse still, the War Ministry refused to fund all of the General Staff's munitions demands. Only 75% of the shell supply per gun (which heavy artillery experts had identified as requisite) was actually procured. The less significant 100-mm and 130-mm cannon met their munitions quotas, but the workhorse 210s and 150s did not. The 210s went forward with fewer than 600 shells apiece (far below the General Staff's desired range of 800 to 1,000) and the 150s rushed to the front with around 800 (the target was between 1,750 and 2,000).[138] Like Unger in the cavalry, Lyncker in Military Transport, and Justrow in the heavy artillery's proving comission, Ludendorff believed that unforgivable, near-treasonous mistakes were being made during the dangerous times of escalating crisis in Europe.

Another crucial question concerned the availability of troops for a western assault. As we shall see, the General Staff requested three additional army corps in late 1912 but was frustrated again by Minister of War Josias von Heeringen, the same man who had blunted the General Staff's demands for a rapid buildup of 450 airplanes, hundreds of extra heavy cannons, 24 of the biggest artillery pieces, and huge stockpiles of shells per gun. It was no wonder that Ludendorff tried to convince army leaders to oust Heeringen from office. When he failed, the high-strung colonel was left angry, frustrated, and bitter. "You wouldn't believe how much I hate them,"[139] he confessed to his mother.

Radicals of the Right

Outside of the army, nationalistic radicals were staking out similarly extreme positions. Since its founding in 1894, the Pan-German League had clamored for accelerated colonial expansion and naval development.[140] Its accusation that "showy pomp, festivals, parades, and monument dedications"[141] were no substitute for strong representation of national interests found little resonance with a wider public, still dreaming with William II of a great imperial future. This began to change, not surprisingly, after Germany's hour of embarrassment in the first Moroccan crisis. Now the charge that "the prestige of the imperial crown, the dynasties, and the monarchy has sunk"[142] rang true with an increasing number of German patriots. The *Daily Telegraph* fiasco found Heinrich Class, the militant chairman of the league, leading the charge with other harsh critics of the crown such as Maximilian Harden. Germany "cannot allow itself to be thrown into misfortune through the blunders of a single person" who lacked the "essential qualities of a ruler."[143] Class and his Pan-German troops demanded stricter parliamentary scrutiny of the kaiser and chancellor. Keeping an eye on the Reichstag would be the League itself—the "herald of the German nation."[144]

Included in the pan-Germans' self-proclaimed vigilante duties was a watchdog mission to ensure army readiness. They concluded that the army was not prepared. In 1907, August Keim, an outspoken, retired general who took his place next to Class on the league's executive board, was shocked to observe that army tactics and battlefield practices were "not suited to modern warfare."[145] Keim extended his criticism of alleged army deficiencies in 1909, calling for universal military service—the "people in arms"—to keep pace with French military expansion. Like other right radicals—and some of the generals—he had no illusions about a short war.[146] At the Pan-German convention of September 1910, he went further, berating his former comrades for a shortage of field cannons, insufficient numbers of heavy howitzer horse teams, under-strength infantry regiments, and cavalry neglect. These words echoed in the Reichstag when Ernst Bassermann, leader of the National Liberals, made the same criticisms. Heretofore more likely to balk at more military spending, the people's representatives were beginning to reverse themselves in response to European tensions.[147]

The Prussian Ministry of War did not share this sense of urgency. Although they regretted the "missed" opportunities for overrunning France in 1905 and 1909, both Einem and his successor, Heeringen, felt confident about the strategic situation after the near destruction of Russia's war-making capabilities in 1904–1905.[148] Taking its cue from the experts in February 1910, for example, the German Foreign Office stated confidently that "everyone knows the Russian army will still be incapable of undertaking major military actions abroad for years to come."[149] This reality made the call for "a nation in arms" seem as militarily exaggerated as it was politically and organizationally ill advised. How would the chancellor find a right-center majority for army expansion and avoid making deals with the SPD for unwanted social and political reforms? And even if the army could indoctrinate or reject all socialist radicals from lower ranks—an assumption that noblemen like Herringen doubted—how could it quickly recruit and competently train tens of thousands of politically and socially reliable officers and NCOs?[150] Finally, the ministry knew that many of the problems cited by pan-German army experts, who had retired before 1905, were being eliminated as the army gradually responded to the lessons from Manchuria.

Helmuth von Moltke's views were somewhat closer to those of the pan-Germans. For inexplicable reasons, perhaps because he was lulled by Russia's weakness, Moltke had not pressed as hard as Schlieffen for a rapid troop buildup, lodging only a pro forma protest to the modest increase that Einem had proposed for the upcoming army bill.[151] Worried by the first signs of Russian recovery in August 1910, however, Moltke appears to have quickly and easily shaped the kaiser into a megaphone for voicing the General Staff's concerns. After an in-depth conversation with his friend and long-time adjutant, William wrote Chancellor Bethmann Hollweg about the need to conscript more of the population into military service: "Moltke complained a lot to me about the great mass of unrecruited people we have in the country—people who don't serve, get no discipline and training, and are [not only] a ready catch for the Social Democrats, [but also] at the same time a danger for the nation and the army in tough times because they've never sworn an oath to the colors." Now was the propitious political moment to expand, for "the fearful mood of the people regarding our colossal [army] savings is so very great that they categorically do not want to see money saved on the army—because all have the instinctive feeling that something big is about to happen."[152] But these arguments made no impression on the Prussian ministers. The army bill of April 1911 contained no extra provisions for expanded military service.

That summer a second Moroccan crisis brought Europe to the brink for the third time in 6 years. The deepening and widening anxiety that "something big" was frightfully close was reason enough for German leaders to agree on a quicker military buildup. Heightening their concerns was the rapid recuperation of Russia and the now inevitable prospect of serious combat on two fronts. Adding to the pressure to act was the public furor over Colonel Repington's exaggerated criticism of army backwardness in Germany. Keim's response in December 1911 was the founding of a German Defense League, dedicated to enlightening people "about the urgent necessity of accelerating army expansion in various ways, in order to raise its internal efficiency and bring its war-readiness up to the highest possible level."[153] By spring, the league had claimed tens of thousands of members and had grown very popular in the army itself. Younger officers were mouthing Keim's views, and on some bases all officers joined the German Defense League en masse.[154] Reinforcing Keim's aggressive message was Friedrich Bernhardi's *Germany and the Next War* , a belligerent case for a preemptive struggle. "His arguments," writes historian David Herrmann, "were typical of the [Defense League's] program as a whole and of the right-radical militarist movement that burst into prominence in the wake of the Second Moroccan Crisis."[155]

The convergence of these various causes produced a new army bill in May 1912. The previous year's law had provided for a 5-year phase-in of 113 machine gun detachments, about 1 per brigade, plus additional field and heavy artillery batteries, but only 1 more infantry battalion—hence Moltke's worries. These would now be introduced in 5 months. From 1912 to 1916, moreover, the army received more cavalry squadrons, artillery batteries, and infantry battalions—much of this stretched thinly into 2 new army corps (twenty-fourth and twenty-fifth). Significantly, machine gun detachments were expanded to 1 per regiment. The rapidly expanding navy also got supplementary funding. It was obvious that Germany was girding for war. The predictable result, however, was an intensified arms race as France and Russia hurriedly expanded their own forces. When war erupted in October 1912 between Turkey and an alliance of Balkan states, tensions were ratcheted to an alarming level as the Powers were tempted to intervene. Successive rounds of Balkan fighting kept Europe's diplomats busy—and its soldiers vigilant—until the summer of 1913.[156]

The uneasy armaments consensus in Germany now fell apart. The General Staff came forward at this time with its great airplane-building program, as well as plans for a downsized fleet of expensive, state-of-the-art Zeppelins. Although the War Ministry and General Inspection of Military Transport waged a rather unsuccessful rearguard action against these moves, the resulting compromises nevertheless angered both sides. Simultaneous General Staff designs for a massive expansion of the heavy artillery, especially the big siege guns, met with much less success, prompting bitter charges and countercharges. A parallel struggle waged by Ludendorff to stockpile adequate munitions for the field and heavy artillery generated another alarming measure of intramural bad blood in that quantities of shells were demanded that the War Ministry considered unnecessary and excessive.[157]

The pan-Germans stirred up more emotions by raising "the machine gun question" in the autumn of 1912. The Defense League charged that enemy infantry units were equipped with three to four times as many machine guns as their German counterparts.[158] The accusation was exaggerated, but 5 days later the kaiser pressed Heeringen on the matter, then backed away when his minister argued that current plans to expand the number of machine gun detachments to French and Russian levels by 1916 could not be accelerated. Moreover, a wave of angry incredulity swept through nationalist circles as patriots wondered how the best army in the world could fall behind. General Colmar von der Goltz replied to one worried pastor that the reports might be true, but "to my regret I'm not in a position to do anything about it."[159] Hysteria soon gripped the National Liberal Party, but before its parliamentary interpellation on machine guns came to the Reichstag floor, a General Staff previously indifferent to this allegedly defensive technology requested 80 additional detachments and the greatly accelerated readying of all 200-plus companies by 1913. Thus the Defense League had taken the General Staff in tow.[160] The War Ministry yielded to this pressure in late November.

The league was also campaigning for universal military service.[161] Although the army had grown by two skeletal corps in 1911–1912— a 5% to 10% expansion—this did not represent the 50% increases of hundreds of thousands of troops demanded by August Keim. Moltke did not have these kinds of magnitudes in mind when he intrigued for more infantry in 1910, for he was satisfied with the two recent army bills. Moreover, Ludendorff, Moltke's quartermaster since October 1912, had previously shown no interest in troop increases, concentrating his energies instead on expansion of matériel and technology.[162] His emergence that autumn as a champion of the *levée en masse* —in addition to more planes, siege cannons, and munitions—was therefore something new. Although his turnaround was certainly related to Europe's escalating crisis, there is good reason to believe that Ludendorff was swayed again by Defense League agitation. The pushy colonel, in turn, soon recruited his hesitant chief. In late December, Moltke forwarded a memorandum written by Ludendorff that, requested 300,000 soldiers above the existing 640,000. Included were all infantry, cavalry, and artillery, as well as troops for three new corps.[163]

The General Staff's demands—presented simultaneously, I should reemphasize, with many others—were hugely controversial.[164] Heeringen resisted this latest initiative, arguing logically and consistently that such a radical expansion could not be undertaken while the army was hardpressed to recruit and train the thousands of soldiers and officers already being called up under the army bills of 1911 and 1912. He also worried that a huge influx of workers and bourgeois would further erode the army's upper-class base. After a solid month of acrimonious meetings with the General Staff, the War Ministry proposed a reluctant compromise for a new bill that provided for 136,000 officers, NCOs, and men in 1913. This increase was spread out over scores of infantry, cavalry, artillery, pioneer, and transport units—and one new army corps.

The matter was settled when William agreed with Heeringen, and Moltke acquiesced. Moltke was not willing to go through thick and thin with the bourgeois rebels beneath him.[165] Cooling his radicalism was a deeply ingrained fatalism that spawned an indifference to higher or lower levels of technology. He thought war would come—and "the sooner the better."[166] We also have to assume that Moltke, a nobleman, did not have Ludendorff's indifference to the elite social quality of the army, his "total blindness to the sociopolitical foundations of German militarism."[167] The chief's radical quartermaster was naturally incensed at what he considered to be the blatant incompetence and weakness of superiors who lacked the "robust, iron nature"[168] to do their jobs. Making matters worse for Ludendorff, he was demoted to regimental command in Düsseldorf. The whole experience triggered an expression of "hate" for "our leading cliques."[169] "Feudalization" processes were obviously incapable of coopting recalcitrant bourgeois like Ludendorff. It was equally clear, however, that the pressures of "embourgeoisement" were not yet strong enough to prevail.

That others shared the banished colonel's acidic feelings may have been some consolation. Above him, corps commanders such as Alexander von Kluck, a protégé of the belligerent Goltz, told Bethmann Hollweg that the outcry for a quick army buildup was "completely correct."[170] Many junior officers felt the same way. Thus Hermann Müller-Brandenburg, press chief of the Defense League, recalled that there were many on the General Staff and in the War Ministry who fully sympathized with the efforts of Keim and his compatriot Ludendorff.[171] Corroborating this, Hans von Seeckt, the later army chief, complained about the "cruel comedy" of the new army bill. "A War Minister who turns down the means offered to him! Who really rules? I believe this is the hardest question that we now have to answer."[172] This disgust with the weakness and division of the kaiser's waning personal regime was shared by Müller-Brandenburg and his colleagues outside of the army. "The fatal effects of this monarch are everywhere to be seen." Because William "loves persons who worship him," it was no surprise that a man of "negligible quantity" was chosen as war minister. This abject failure at the top "made the Defense League necessary."[173]

Although the militants had not achieved all of their demands, it was clear that Germany's monarchical establishment was ill equipped to survive repeated rounds of arms increases forced on it from below by impatient patriots blind to upper-class sociopolitical considerations.[174] The bridge between intra- and extra-army radicals who harbored a burning irreverence for the questionable authority of William II was just one sign of the monarchy's widening legitimacy crisis. The parliamentary elections of January 1912 were another, for they gave the Social Democrats 35% of the popular vote, making them the largest Reichstag party. The SPD leaders favored a republic in principle and a democratic parliamentary monarchy in practice; they had called for parliamentary controls in 1908. Almost every bill they proposed was a repudiation from below of the regime's social indifference and class intolerance. The government began to pay attention to the new leftist parliamentary realities by placing most of the tax burden for the 1912 and 1913 army increases on upper-class shoulders.[175]

The "red" election results prompted Heinrich Class to write his scandalous *If I Were the Kaiser*. Published anonymously because of its illegal criticism of a monarch—the title alone was grounds for lèse-majesté—the book lambasted William II for his laxness and weakness at home and abroad. Class's incredibly irreverent egotism was translated into action in August 1913 when the pan-Germans mobilized a loose coalition of rightist associations alarmed by leftist trends in Germany and determined to strengthen the backbone of a state that was seemingly incapable of offering correctives.[176] The solutions proposed by the new Cartel of the Producing Classes included a rollback of labor legislation and a crackdown on trade unions. Also swirling in and around the organizations that assembled in Leipzig that summer were a virulent antisemitism and a war-mongering militarism. Both mind-sets tended to regard combat as the quickest and most effective way to lance Germany's boils. War, in short, was a panacea for all that ailed the nation.

But would "William the Peaceful" be willing to wage it?

Aggressiveness was in the air in 1912 and 1913. After decades of largely defensive plans, the French adopted a new offensive stratagem. Generals no longer content to await the Hun's onslaught devised a bold attack to take back Alsace-Lorraine. Once these provinces were regained, the troops would march to Berlin. The French Army was also swept by a wave of enthusiasm for tactics of attack. Assaults, even frontal assaults, need not be feared in the machine age if the will to overcome everything in one's path—the all-important *èlan vital* —were strong enough.

There had never been a shortage of aggressive strategies in Germany. The emphasis under Moltke and Ludendorff was shifting slightly, however, from a grand, single envelopment through Belgium to a dual-thrust offensive that included crushing France's fortresses. French enthusiasm for frontal assaults was also evident across the Rhine. Chief of the Bavarian General Staff Konrad Krafft von Dellmensingen observed with dismay in November 1912, for instance, that German cavalrymen were regressing to outmoded notions of massed cavalry attacks. In the same memo, contradictorily, Krafft complained that the enfilading tactics of the infantry were not aggressive enough. Berlin had long preached the doctrine of outflanking one's opponent, but Krafft felt that this tactic left the center vulnerable. Germans "laugh at our enemy's fanaticism for the big breakthrough" but overlook the fact that French ideas sprang from "a clear awareness of the weaknesses and exaggerations of our field methods." Taking a stab at Germany's regulation-dispersed formations, Krafft grumbled that "everything flits about and falls apart in endless space."[177] He had overlooked the fact that French infantrymen were also told to spread out.[178]

The army "seemed to have forgotten or consciously abandoned," Krafft continued, "how to set up and execute big concentrated attacks."[179] The Bavarian General Staff chief was probably demonstrating that anti-Prussian bias so typical of his countrymen, for it is doubtful that enthusiasm for frontal assaults had disappeared in the north. Schlieffen had been unable to overcome the prejudice of corps commanders against tactical flanking maneuvers.[180] Moltke hammered away at the same preference for keeping the center strong and pushing up the middle—apparently with more success, as shown by the performance on manuevers. But it is unlikely that

Figures 17 and 18. Autumn 1912 maneuvers: A cavalry division masses (top) and rides forward (bottom). Source: Hoppenstedt, *Das Heer.*

Krafft was alone with his offensive preferences. Karl von Bülow of Third Corps, for instance, believed that troops that drilled endlessly in open-order tactics could move straight forward and prevail. One General Staff officer remembered Bülow as "an intellectual antipode of Count Schlieffen" with "an outspoken preference for massing in front of the enemy."[181] As Dieter Storz has shown, many commanders in Germany and Europe harbored stubborn "we will survive" attitudes that enabled them to scoff at mounting arguments against attacking headlong into a rain of bullets.[182] This Darwinistic mindset grew stronger after the Japanese demonstrated that frontal attacks could succeed. The waning peacetime years, marked by successive and increasingly stressful crises, were even more conducive to the kind of belligerent mentality of denial that favored frontal assaults. Their popularity was clearly growing in Germany by 1913. The big attack, although not as dominant as it was in France, received more rehearsal time during maneuvers that year.[183]

William II was swept up in this dangerous current. Although he had always favored tight formations at maneuvers,[184] during 1912 and 1913 he succumbed completely to the rage for frontal assaults.[185] His most extreme statement came after imperial maneuvers in September 1913, when William scolded his generals for allegedly neglecting "tactical breakthroughs." He knew that they "belonged to the club of 'around the left' or 'around the right,' " but they should now join "the club of 'through the middle' "—in which the French were already ahead. As for Germany's trademark open-order assault, William saw only a "disorderly rabble."[186]

The kaiser's views on tactics were no longer of military significance in 1913, for the generals knew that they, not he, would command in the field. The remarks were more important as a reflection of the persistence of frontal assault mania in many corps. William's words were also important as a sign of the mental gymnastics he was performing to suppress fear. Former War Minister Karl von Einem believed that the kaiser was afraid of the "powerful and pervasive development of contemporary technology which was affecting warfare by creating more and more destructive weapons."[187] Five successive war scares and 6 years of exclusive interaction with hawkish male soldiers who were themselves increasingly in denial wore William down. Thus, he excitedly called a War Council in December 1912 to discuss short- to middle-run measures that would put the nation on a war footing.[188] The kaiser's own frontal assault mania was an attempt to screw up his courage and prepare himself for war.

William would not have long to wait for his final test. Serbian terrorists assassinated Archduke Francis Ferdinand, heir to the throne of Austria-Hungary, at Sarajevo on 28 June 1914. A week later he repeated three times before the industrialist Krupp: "This time I shall not chicken out."[189] That day his government had given Vienna a blank check of military assistance. Over the next weeks, Austria-Hungary prepared for war and presented Serbia with a stiff, and it was hoped, unacceptable ultimatum. Having rebuilt its army, Russia mobilized in a show of support for Serbia. Confident of German backing, Austria bombarded Belgrade on 28 July. The German generals now urged mobilization, for they were worried that Russian military preparations were cutting into the limited time available for the defeat—or at least the crippling—of France. A German ultimatum was presented to the Russians.

Although his instincts struggled on numerous occasions to break free that summer, William, in the end, did not "chicken out."[190] When Russia refused to cancel its mobilization, Germany declared war on Russia and France. On 4 August, units of the German cavalry rode into Belgium. On the same day, England declared war on the violators of Belgian neutrality. Europe's conflagration had begun.

Germany's long debate about war in the machine age had ended. Technological change triggered this controversy in the generation that came after the glorious Wars of Unification. German soldiers struggled over the right strategies and battlefield tactics for an era of magazine repeating rifles, smokeless powder, high explosives, rapid-firing cannons, machine guns, aircraft, and large-caliber guns. For decades, conservatives resisted change in a paean to the superiority of human willpower and soldierly discipline. But change came, slowly and piecemeal at first, then in a flood after the jolting experience of war in Asia and successive crises in Europe. The administrations of Einem and Moltke witnessed a flurry of tactical reforms, operational modifications, new weapons, rapid troop expansion, and all sorts of new controversies and intramural animosities. But now the time for talking and preparing was over. All of the hotly contested arguments would soon be tested in war. Indeed, the battlefield experience of high summer 1914 adjudicated all prewar disputes. It is appropriate to consider this tragic experience in some detail, for it is the climax of our story and a fitting conclusion to this study.

CHAPTER 8

ROLLING THE IRON DICE

T HE FORTRESS OF Maubeuge anchored France's northern line of defense. Whereas other strongpoints along the Belgian border had been allowed to lapse into obsolescence during the expensive era of nitrogen explosives, Paris allocated funds in 1898 for the modernization of structures designed centuries earlier by the great military architect Vauban. The antiquated town walls along the Sambre River became the menacing central citadel for a series of reinforced concrete outposts that commanded all roads and fords likely to attract invaders from the east. During the next 16 years of peace, shrubs and trees and, here and there, civilian buildings sprouted up in front of the ugly martial constructs. Nature and mankind's mercantile pursuits seemed to form a preventive, pacific ring around Maubeuge's 20-mile perimeter of iron and steel and cement.[1]

By mid-August 1914, however, the obstructions—and all of the illusions associated with them—had been demolished and removed. Lines of fire were now clear. Deep trench systems had been dug between every fort, running in some stretches for thousands of meters. Greenery had been torn away from the front of the trench lines, too, and replaced by tons of man-made barbed entanglements. Outside the imposing defensive ring, extending southwest for many kilometers to Le Cateau, were the camps for four divisions of the British Expeditionary Force. England's first 70,000 men had detrained from Boulogne and Le Havre and tramped into the region. No efforts were made in this pre-black-out age to conceal their growing concentration. "There were soldiers everywhere," writes historian Lyn Macdonald. "They were billeted in schoolrooms, in village halls, in barns, in farmyards, in mills, in cottages." Joining the British inside Maubeuge's system of forts, trenches, and heavy wire were 35,000 trigger-happy troops of the French territorial reserve. Anxious to draw first blood, they shot down a British airplane by mistake when the noisy flotilla first approached from the west. On 20 August, the Royal Flying Corps took off to find the Germans.[2]

Several days before the British went into the air over western Belgium, French soldiers prepared a much larger craft for flight. At dusk on 16 August, the rumble of inflating engines was heard from the big airship hangar on the eastern side of Maubeuge's main citadel. Over 80 meters long, the *Montgolfier* was one of five nonrigid P-ships in the French fleet. Thus far it had been a bad month for flying. A late summer heat wave produced turbulent air currents and unleashed frequent thunderstorms, making airships very difficult to control. Yet Maubeuge's craft had gone aloft with the others that August to reconnoiter enemy troop movements. Altogether, the French airfleet flew 28 nighttime reconnaissance missions in 3

Figure 19. French nonrigid airship *Montgolfier.* Source: Charles Christienne et al., *Histoire de l'aviation militaire francaise* (Paris, 1980).

weeks, taking advantage of German campfires to estimate enemy troop strength and location.[3] On that day, Joffre's headquarters had sent the *Montgolfier* on another mission: It would fly along the Meuse River into eastern Belgium to determine if the bridges at Huy were still intact for the rapidly advancing Hun.[4] As the sun set on the odd assortment of British bivouacs in the west, the *Montgolfier* rose high over the trenches. Moments later the captain engaged the twin Clément-Bayard gasoline engines to propel it into the darkening, foreboding east.

A week later, returning from another mission, this ship, too, was shot down by the jittery territorials. Its navigation flares for night landing had been mistaken for enemy fire. After Maubeuge fell in early September, the occupying Germans found photographs of a modern nonrigid airship strewn about a partially destroyed hangar. Proud of their larger, longer Zeppelins, the conquerors quipped that the *Montgolfier* was "just good enough for target practice."[5] They laughed even harder when they learned that this was almost exactly how it had been destroyed.

Last laughs are always cruelest in wartime.

Blind Juggernaut into Belgium

Five German cavalry divisions (with accompanying horse artillery and machine gun detachments) and 10 Jäger battalions invaded Belgium in the first week of the war. From the beginning it was clear that the Belgians would fight back, thus dashing all remaining hope that they would grant the Germans free passage.

The Second and Fourth Cavalry rode over the border on 4 August, crossed the Meuse River north of the citadel of Liège 4 days later, and rode 30 kilometers farther west by 10 August. Their mission was to destroy rail lines into Liège, find the flanks of the small Belgian Army, and reconnoiter for French and British forces 60 kilometers west to the line Antwerp-Brussels-Charleroi. The Ninth Cavalry positioned itself south of Liège on 4 August. Its mission was to destroy rails, guard the flank of German infantry brigades that were assaulting the citadel, and undertake reconnaissance 50 kilometers southwest to Namur and Dinant. The fifth and Guard Cavalry rode across Luxemburg, penetrating into Belgium on 10 August. Their mission was to cut 60 kilometers northwest to Dinant and search for the French along the Meuse as far as the French border northeast of Givet.[6]

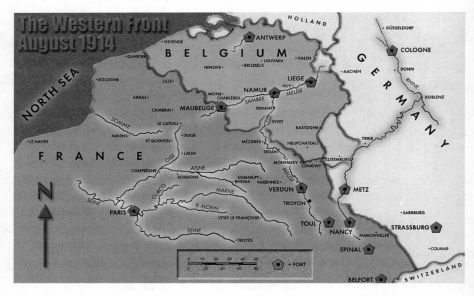

Figure 20.

Although a sizable force in their own right—about 30,000 men—these divisions were just a hint of what was waiting to follow. Indeed, stacked east of Belgium and northern Luxemburg were 3 powerful armies, anxious to flood into the Ardennes and the gently rolling farmland north of the Meuse. Between Aachen and Düsseldorf was Alexander von Kluck's First Army. From Aachen to Bonn stretched Karl von Bülow's Second Army. To his south, extending nearly to Trier, was Max Klemens von Hausen's Third Army. Altogether the right wing boasted 32 infantry divisions—47% of German strength on the western front and nearly 40% of the whole army including reserve divisions. Five hundred trains a day rumbled across Rhine bridges to build up supplies for 640,000 men and 200,000 horses. This force was to sweep around the allied northern flank and exploit opportunities for an early victory.[7] The final important mission of the cavalry was to screen these outflanking armies from early detection by the enemy, thereby preserving an element of shock and surprise.

Shortly before his retirement, Schlieffen had advised disciples "to keep the right as strong as possible."[8] Based on lessons from recent war games, he wanted to expand the army to 81 divisions and crowd 45 of them into Belgium—over 55% of the entire army, leaving virtually nothing in the east. The flurry of army bills on the eve of war made exactly 81 divisions available,[9] but Moltke feared that his center and left were too weak, especially for the kind of double envelopment that the latest giant siege guns made possible. Therefore, he revised Schlieffen's last plan. The right was reduced from 45 to 32 divisions. The 2 center armies in Lorraine and the Saar, opposite Verdun, were increased from 16 to 20 divisions, and the left-wing armies in southern Lorraine and Alsace were expanded from 10 to 16 divisions. The mission of the center and left was to absorb anticipated French assaults,[10] then pierce the French fortress line as the enemy fell back to it. Together with the right, these thrusts would dislodge the French from their forts, inflicting enough casualties to permit transfer of some German corps to the east. Or perhaps the center- and left-wing armies could close a trap with the right as it wheeled around the forts or hurried due south to Lorraine—wherever French armies were to be found—in such ways winning a sudden battle of annihilation. These were best-case scenarios.[10] Thus, Moltke had ignored Schlieffen's advice about the western right; but even without the kind of strength that Schlieffen had intended, this wing was still awesome, having been beefed up since the staff ride of June 1904, which had posited 2 armies of only 20 divisions.[11]

Finally, 2 divisions were deployed in Schleswig-Holstein to guard against a British landing, and 9 divisions were left in East Prussia to deal with the Russians. Moltke's modifications were not permanent: He contemplated shifting forces between wings and from west to east. The 2 divisions in Schleswig-Holstein and an additional 2 reserve divisions—as well as 6.5 "ersatz" divisions—could also be used to reinforce either wing or either front.[12]

To stop the Germans, France would need great strength in the north; and for Kluck, Bülow, and Hausen to follow the cavalry, they first had to capture Liège. No invading force of this immense size could supply itself without utilizing the railroads into the city. The same ironclad logic necessitated taking Brussels, Namur, and Maubeuge. Until Liège fell, the 400 guns of the main citadel and its girdle of 12 outlying forts blocked passage, making it impossible for the massive right wing to advance.[13] Even the comparatively small and quick-moving contingent of Second and Fourth Cavalry lost 2 to 3 days by detouring off the main roads, out of range of the forts' 150-mm guns.[14]

The General Staff planned to seize Liège, therefore, with a bold *coup de main* . Six strong brigades—about 40,000 infantrymen—were assembled for the seemingly easy mission.[15] Their commander, Otto von Emmich of the Tenth Hanoverian Corps, knew there had been no time for the Belgians to dig trenches between forts, clear trees, or lay wire; but he anticipated only a brigade of anxious Belgians, not 35,000 tenacious defenders. The initial attack waves were the first great sacrifices of the war. "They made no attempt at deploying," recalled a Belgian officer, "but came on line after line, almost shoulder to shoulder, until as we shot them down, the fallen were heaped on top of each other in an awful barricade of dead and wounded."[16] It was the first instance of what would be a costly, recurring pattern that month: Infantry regulations were ignored by officers who had either never agreed with the need to disperse or had forgotten the book in the haste of battle.[17] All six assault brigades, supported by 150- and 210-mm guns, were engaged by the night and morning of 5–6 August. The infantry captured the city and citadel of Liège but not the outer forts. Casualties soared to over 4,000, and still the Belgians held.[18] German commanders who arrived in Rhenish staging areas were surprised to learn that the path was still blocked.[19] It was a modern Thermopylae.

Unfortunately for the exuberant—and now themselves overly confident—Belgians, the Germans had a frightening fallback plan. On 8 August, General Bülow agreed with Second Army Quartermaster Erich Ludendorff to bring up the big guns. The former enfant terrible of the General Staff had fought at Liège, leading his brigade into the main citadel, although apparently for nought. Now Germany needed the fat cannons that he and Max Bauer had wanted in all of the front lines. But on reaching Bülow's headquarters, Ludendorff got unsettling news. Of Germany's seven 420-mm howitzers, five Gamma-Devices were assigned to the center and left wings. The best hope for rapid destructive action lay at Krupp's Essen works with two mobile M-Devices, but the crews had not completed training and their guns were still undergoing final tests. Nevertheless, orders from Bülow on 9 August sent the heavy artillerymen on their anxious way to Liège. Six mobile 305s—including four Skodas on loan from the Austrians—were also underway.[20]

After frustrating delays caused by Belgian demolition, the gargantuan engines of death finally took aim late on 12 August. The first giant, 420-mm shell rocketed 12,000 feet into the air and crashed with Armageddon-impact 60 seconds later into Fort Pontisse. "When it hit," recalled the battery chief, "there arose a great pillar of smoke, dust, debris, and fire high up into the heavens."[21] Forty-two shots later, on 13 August, the shell-shocked defenders raised a white flag. The 150s, 210s, and 305s were also firing furiously on other forts that were commanding roads heading west. Kluck's advance corps crossed the Meuse on 14 August, 9 days after the infantry's surprise attack.[22]

The Spartan-like stand of the Belgians at Liège was nevertheless highly significant. They killed or badly wounded thousands of regulars, whose places in the ranks would remain unfilled. Germany entered the western war with fewer soldiers than the Belgians, British, and French. To create numerical superiority and surprise in the north, Germany mobilized all reserves and put them in the front, next to the regulars; 12 of 32 divisions on the right were reserve units. The first hastily trained, poorly equipped ersatz divisions would not be available until the third or fourth week of mobilization.[23] Thus, Kluck warned his officers that "all wastage of manpower must be jealously guarded against, as every possible rifle must be available at the decisive moment of operations."[24] That German commanders had forgotten or ignored the tactics that leaders from Schlichting to Moltke had tried to inculcate was the kind of mistake that could undermine an entire campaign if not quickly corrected.

The panicky haste of the Germans at Liège left other disturbing legacies for the weeks ahead. Like soldiers, artillery shells were a finite and irreplaceable commodity in a short campaign because, like other belligerent countries in 1914, Germany had made no preparations for a war of attrition and matériel. The country whose stockpiles were initially largest or diminished least during the struggle had a decided advantage. When the bombardment began, 136 gun crews went by the book, taking aimed shots at individual turrets and towers, correcting, and then firing again. Within a few hours it became evident that this method saved shells but not time. It was an unenviable tradeoff, but the clock was ticking on Germany's bold outflanking strategy. So orders were issued for massed, rapid fire, "everything you can get out of the barrels."[25] Expenditure of 210-mm ammunition was especially great. And so it went until 16 August, when the last fort fell. Soon, 5,000 horses were hauling 98 heavy field pieces to Namur, where the process would begin again on 21 August.

In the end, Liège bought 4 or 5 days' time for Germany's enemies. The railroadlike timetable of Germany's operational plan had scheduled Kluck's lead corps to pass through Aachen on 10 August, but because Liège held, they could not leave the city until 13 August.[26] If the surprise attack had succeeded, however, elements of his army would surely have marched west on 8 or 9 August. Conscious of being 3 days behind schedule, as opposed to a few days ahead, units were rushed forward, often marching until midnight.[27] The fast pace perpetuated the air of crisis that had spawned costly tactical errors against the forts of Liège.

By 17 August, the great wheeling action of the right wing was well underway. First Army had reached Halen. On Kluck's left, Bülow's troops extended as far as Huy on the Meuse. Below them Hausen's advance guard had moved into the Ardennes. His right flank was 30 kilometers east of Dinant. From there, Third Army's divisions stretched southeast to Bastogne.[28]

It was not the time to look back. But where was the enemy? The cavalry had supplied few valuable clues. On 10–11 August, the Second and Fourth Cavalry encountered advance units of the Belgian Army. Because patrols reported a stronger concentration east of Louvain, the cavalry headed north to find the Belgian left flank. What occurred on the way, however, was difficult to justify on reconnaissance grounds. On 12 August, Fourth Division tried to force its way through the village of Halen, but Belgian infantry with machine guns and artillery were entrenched on high ground west of town. Two German regiments attacked. "Did you charge?" asked one cavalryman of the straggling remnants that returned. "The brigade is destroyed," gasped one dazed survivor. "Rode in against infantry, artillery, and machine guns—hung up in the wire, fell into a sunken road—all shot down."[29] Two more regiments went forward with the same results. Fourth Division was riddled, having lost 477 men and 24 officers—nearly a 16% casualty rate. The real picture was even worse, for 848 horses—more than 28%—had been butchered. Fourth Division had found the enemy's flank, but the Belgians withdrew their five field divisions to Antwerp several days later, after the main body of Kluck's First Army had advanced.

The German Army of 1914, however, was no monolith. It displayed the many faces we would expect of an institution with corps autonomy in the midst of Moltke's determined reforms. "Reconnaissance in force" was executed much more successfully, for instance, to the south. On 15 August, Hausen's cavalry divisions surprised the French at Dinant. Five thousand Jäger, supported by horse artillery and machine guns, overran the fort and town while the Guard Corps and Fifth Cavalry contented themselves with protecting the flanks. After capturing prisoners and determining enemy strength, they withdrew. A day later, northwest of Namur, Ninth Cavalry shocked and routed a Belgian cavalry regiment after machine gun detachments and artillery had thrown the Belgians into a panic. On 18 August, Fourth Cavalry's horse artillery drove back elements of a French cavalry division north of Namur. All three engagements substituted technology for senseless bravado. They also contributed important information on French dispositions. Hausen's men had spotted elements of two corps near Dinant, and the cavalry encounters around Namur indicated that strong enemy forces were pushing north to the Sambre.[30]

By this time, German fliers were able to sharpen the focus on the still-blurry picture. After the lead corps advanced into Belgium, airplanes—eight single-winged Taube per regular corps—began to fan out in a north-south arc ahead of the infantry. Orders prescribed an overcautious 50-kilometer radius of action, even though technology allowed for 150 kilometers. By 18 August, despite these limitations, planes were flying over Louvain and far enough southwest of Namur to spot the right wing of a French army that was forming in the Sambre-Meuse River salient. Two days later, Kluck's army marched through Brussels, Bülow surrounded Namur, and Hausen nearly caught up with his cavalry east of Dinant. Fliers were buzzing past Mons-Charleroi, with cavalry patrols not far behind. Nearly the entire French staging area was surveyed by airplane. Bülow reckoned enemy strength to his south at 14 to 18 divisions.[31] If the German right concentrated the bulk of its 32 divisions, it could crush the French force while Belgium's 5 field divisions were isolated in Antwerp.

But where was the BEF, and how strong was it? And where was Germany's best reconnaissance weapon, the great silver Zeppelin? General Staff headquarters (OHL) in Koblenz had five new airships on the western front. Each had been given specific long-range missions during prewar planning. The two stationed in Düsseldorf and Cologne were to overfly Belgium and northern France, respectively, reporting back by wireless on enemy troop movements.[32] The heat, thunderstorms, and turbulence of August 1914, however, prevented long-range Zeppelin reconnaissance over Belgium and northern France until 1 September. Four times in August, the Z-9 took off from Düsseldorf to find the BEF; it was forced back each time by bad weather. Unlike nonrigid airships, Germany's aluminum-frame giants were too susceptible to wind damage to stay aloft under these conditions. Meanwhile, three brigades of the BEF landed at Boulogne and proceeded across northern France to Maubeuge; nine brigades disembarked at Le Havre. All could have been spotted.[33]

With no Zeppelin braving the bumpy air currents, however, Germany's right wing was extremely near-sighted, forced to rely exclusively on short-range cavalry patrols and underutilized airplanes.

Like other legacies from the prewar period, which were beginning to accumulate, the General Staff's myopia in Belgium had a high price. Kluck, receiving no better intelligence from Koblenz, assumed that the BEF would disembark between Dunkirk and Ostende, moving inland in a southeasterly direction over Lille-Ninove. Therefore, after First Army passed Brussels, he echeloned his corps to face northwest and sent most of his cavalry and airplanes scouting in that direction. Kluck was strengthened in his assumptions by a Belgian newspaper report of 19 August, asserting that the BEF had landed successfully somewhere in France a day earlier. Kluck sent the information to Bülow, who had received overall command of both armies from OHL to coordinate the great wheeling movement through Belgium.

The Second Army's chief agreed that the British would come over Lille, but not soon.[34] Bülow was strengthened in his assumption by a communique from OHL: "A landing of British troops at Boulogne and their advance from Lille must be reckoned with; it is believed that a disembarkation of British troops on a big scale has not yet taken place."[35] Bülow therefore ordered Kluck repeatedly to accelerate his movement in a southwesterly direction, wheeling around Maubeuge to close the trap and destroy the French.[36] This was exactly the type of southern turn that Schlieffen and Moltke had executed in prewar exercises to exploit operational opportunities created by a French offensive into Lorraine. Worried that he might be caught in the rear by the BEF, however, Kluck decided to advance more slowly. Moreover, he complied only halfway with Bülow's orders by bending his left flank south toward Mons but keeping his right 25 kilometers farther north at Ninove. Kluck later justified his semi-insubordination by arguing that "the situation on First Army's right flank was not clarified, neither at that time, nor for the following [days]."[37] It was 21 August.

On 14 August, General Charles Lanrezac, commanding the French Fifth Army, drove to visit his commander-in-chief, General Joseph Joffre. For 10 days, general headquarters (GQG) had received repeated warnings from Lanrezac and General Fournier, military governor of Maubeuge, about an alarming German buildup east of Liège. Piecing together information from Belgian sources and their own long-range aerial reconnaissance, the two were convinced that the French left wing was too weak to withstand what was coming its way. Thus far, Joffre had only fiddled, allowing Lanrezac to move two divisons to Dinant, reinforcing the garrison at Maubeuge, and placing three territorial divisions between Dunkirk and Maubeuge. This would not stop the advance guard of six corps that Lanrezac and Fournier had identified[38]—hence the visit to Joffre.

In the meeting, France's supreme commander continued to dismiss the veracity of these alarming reports, but later that day his own intelligence confirmed the presence of 8 German corps and numerous cavalry divisions north of Luxemburg. A ninth regular corps was spotted on 16 August—making a total of 18 divisions identified. By this time, Joffre had changed his left wing dispositions. On 15 August, he ordered Lanrezac's Fifth Army at Mézières, plus minor reinforcements, into the Sambre-Meuse salient. By 20–21 August, he had 13 divisions in place—far fewer than Bülow's estimate of 14 to 18.[39]

The BEF, meanwhile, had landed at Boulogne and Le Havre between 13 and 16 August, assembling southwest of Maubeuge in the days thereafter. On 20–21 August, its four divisions set out on the road to Mons. There was a 15-kilometer gap, however, between the BEF's right flank at Mons and Lanrezac's nearest forces on the Sambre. There was a 60-kilometer gap between the BEF's left flank and the nearest two divisions of the French territorial reserve far to the west, at Cambrai and Douai, respectively. A third division was even farther away, northwest of Lille.[40]

Making matters even more precarious for these widely scattered 20 divisions of the French left was a deep distrust between Lanrezac and the British commander, Sir John French. They met on 17 August. In response to French's query about why the Germans were crossing the Meuse east of Namur, for instance, Lanrezac answered with acidic sarcasm that they were there "to fish."[41] Not surprisingly, communication, coordination, and the transmission of intelligence was poor. Thus Lanrezac was back on his heels, prepared to withdraw quickly if his intelligence about German strength was correct. He learned from his own staff that day, for instance, that 3 reserve corps trailed Bülow's Second Army, seeming to confirm his worst fears that upward of 700,000 German soldiers were pouring into Belgium; the number, in fact, was 640,000. Sir John French, in contrast, was ready to advance from Mons and chase the Germans out of Belgium.[42]

There were obviously reconnaissance and intelligence failures on both sides of the border. For the French GQG, riveted on the idea of attacking to reclaim Alsace and Lorraine, the problem was more that of utilizing the information available. They were simply unable to believe their own prewar reports, gradually substantiated by reconnaissance, that Germany intended to put all its reserves into line with the regular army.[43] For the OHL and the headquarters of its three advancing armies in Belgium, on the other hand, it was clearly more a problem of having the correct information to analyze. There can be no doubt that a brilliant opportunity was at hand to smash the French and Lanrezac, then envelop France's fortresses. Crippling—if not total—victories near the frontier could free up as many as two armies by early September. Marching back to home railheads, they could be on the eastern front in a week. This had been Schlieffen's best-case scenario.[44]

The Battle of the Frontiers

Joffre's new orders to Lanrezac were a fine-tuning of Plan XVII, the last in a decades-long series of French war strategies but the first to call for a massive offensive. The GQG assumed that the German Army would mass around Metz and then push into France. Joffre intended to outflank this invading force by piercing north and south of Metz. First Army and Second Armies, with 23 divisions, were to seize southern Lorraine around Sarrburg. A smaller Army of Alsace, with 6 divisions, would protect them from southern flank attacks. Joffre ordered the Third and Fourth Armies 20 divisions to swing around the Germans through the Ardennes Forest of southern Belgium into northern Lorraine. Finally, Fifth Army's mission was to stop enemy forces north of the Meuse, or—if the BEF and Belgians were strong enough to cope with the Germans—to join the French incursion into the Ardennes.[45]

With reports mounting of German strength in Belgium, it seemed likely that Lanrezac would have to fight there. Joffre was heartened by this prospect, however, for it seemed to mean that German strength would be diminished at the main points of French incursion farther south. As one of his aides put it, if the Germans tried to swing through Belgium, "why, so much the better." Thus, when French reconnaissance reported 9 corps north of Luxemburg on 16 August, with another 10 corps supposedly in Lorraine and Alsace, the GQG rubbed its hands in eager anticipation of victory.[46] The Germans had contributed to this near-perfect deception by creating reserve corps with the same numerals as their respective regular corps, then placing both together in the line of march. This ruse made it easy for observers to jump to the conclusion that 1 corps was on the move, not 2. The French had identified 19 of the 22 regular corps that were actually on the western front but failed to spot the trailing 12 reserve corps. Germany's reserves were not behind the front—they were already in line. The GQG ignored Lanrezac's bulletin to this effect on 17 August.

The Battle of the Frontiers began in southern Lorraine. The French First and Second Armies crossed into Germany, encountering slight resistance as they approached Saarburg along a broad front. The prospects for success had changed radically since a decade earlier. French soldiers were attacking now, not counterattacking at a propitious moment as envisioned in old Plan XV. The relative infantry strengths were still favorable—23 divisions versus 16—but that was almost twice what the French expected, and the age of machine guns had dawned with all the attendant advantages for defenders. Moreover, France's earlier preponderance of heavy artillery had disappeared. Even though Joffre concentrated 43% of France's heavy field pieces in this sector, 29 batteries of 120- and 155-mm howitzers were outgunned by 42 batteries of 105- and 150-mm howitzers on the German side. This disadvantage was not counterbalanced by the superiority of the French 75-mm field cannon.[47]

The terrain created additional problems. "For the Lorraine gateway," writes historian John Keegan, "is by no means the open plain that a hasty glance at the map suggests."[48] Rather, the country is broken up by rolling hills, numerous rivers and canals, and dense patches of woodland on high ridges ready-made for ambushes. As First and Second Armies proceeded, gaps opened between columns separated by the barriers of nature. The artillery, especially the heavy pieces, lagged far behind. As the French rushed in, Konrad Krafft von Dellmensingen, chief of staff of the German Sixth Army, pressed OHL hard for permission to counterattack. Bavaria's prewar devotee of the frontal assault warned that further retreat was unconscionable. Moltke finally agreed, committing the strong reserve division of the Metz Fortress and five ersatz divisions—the bulk of what little reserve he had—to the bold gamble.[49] Moltke was now committing himself to a double envelopment.

At dawn on 20 August, the German Sixth and Seventh Armies struck back all along the line. The French gave ground initially, then held in most spots, inflicting tremendous losses on German units that once again deployed in dense formations. At two points on the French left, however, the Germans broke through. The extreme left, manned by three reserve divisions, proved too weak for the Third Bavarian Corps, which chased them to the rear. Fifty kilometers away, near the center of the French line, two entire corps were caught by surprise in the open by a furious artillery barrage that sent body parts flying and quickly panicked entire units. The rest of Second Army was now forced to retreat, and its withdrawal toward the French border compelled an overexposed First Army to pull back, too.

Joffre's first offensive had failed, argues Keegan against the conventional wisdom, not because "the French cast themselves to destruction [shoulder to shoulder] in a frenzy of offensive ardour." Rather, defeat resulted from ignoring elementary military principles. "Neither [army] had maintained a proper tactical reserve, reconnoitered their axes of advance or organized continuous fronts [and] as a result their lines had been easily infiltrated and their infantry ambushed in undefended positions." But the Germans had made mistakes, too, particularly tactical mistakes in modern-day battle formations. As a result, the badly mauled German Seventh Army, facing the French First Army, was unable to pursue for two days.[50]

Enemy strength in southern Lorraine surprised Joffre but convinced him that Germany must be weak north of Metz. Therefore, he ordered Third and Fourth Armies' 20 divisions into action. Waiting for them—and for OHL's permission to attack—were 20 divisions of the German Fourth and Fifth Armies. They were backed by 42 batteries of 150- and 105-mm howitzers—twice the heavy artillery of the French. The two determined hordes collided on 22 August along a broad front, bloodying one another amid the hamlets, hilly thickets, and fast-running streams of the Ardennes. On the French left, Fourth Army advanced against the German Fourth Army north of Neufchateau. On this side, the French swung over first to the attack. On the French right, Third Army stopped to defend against the determined onslaught of Crown Prince William's Fifth Army, which was sweeping around the fortress town of Longwy.

All 10 divisions of the German Fifth Army were engaged, 5 suffering terrible losses.[51] Ignoring tactical wisdom, a division of Thirteenth Corps was deployed in thick formations to storm the fortified village of Bleid. One brigade lost half its captains, all its lieutenants, and over 2,000 men—33% casualties—and the other was hit nearly as hard.[52] The neighboring Fifth Corps was caught in the flank by French artillery. "The battlefield afterward was an unbelievable spectacle," remembered a shocked French officer. "Thousands of bodies

were still standing, supported as if by a flying buttress made of bodies lying in rows on top of each other in an ascending arc from the
horizontal to an angle of 60 degrees."[53] Incredibly, the fighting
south of Longwy was even more intense. Some German units kept
attacking into French rifle, machine gun, and artillery fire until the
last trailing battalions had been thrown desperately into the fray.
The French gave ground slowly and grudgingly, probably inflicting
about 20,000 casualties (16% to 17%) on Fifth Army. Moltke now
committed his last ersatz units to pay for this Pyrrhic victory and to
maintain pressure for a double envelopment.[54]

As at Lorraine, however, a disastrous setback near the left-center
of the French line caused the French to make a general retreat. Its
Fourth Army attacked around Neufchateau, its left wing nearly panicking the artillery- and machine-gun–depleted Eighteenth Reserve
Corps, which suffered terrible losses.[55] In a true test of the doctrine
of *élan vital* , the lead division of the elite French Colonial Corps
made successive bayonet charges against well-entrenched German
regulars (Sixth Corps) near Rossignol. They were "trying to beat
down a hail of artillery, machine gun and rifle fire," writes Keegan,
"with bare steel." The division lost 11,000 of its 17,000 men. The
"bloodily unsuccessful attempt"[56] sent the entire corps into reverse—
and with it the rest of Fourth Army, whose retreat in turn forced
Third Army to withdraw as well.

But the ferocity of Fourth Army's attack, particularly its mauling
of Germany's Eighteenth Reserve Corps, may well have prevented a
general disaster for the French. That afternoon, the OHL ordered
Duke Albrecht of Württemberg, commander of the German Fourth
Army, to cross the Meuse with two corps at Givet to cut off Lanrezac,
who was locked in combat on the Sambre (see below). Albrecht
countermanded the order, sending these corps southwest instead to
shore up his hard-pressed reserves corps. Only one of the four divisions saw action that day, however, and by 23–24 August, the
French were falling back to the Meuse.[57]

Karl von Bülow's Second Army bumped into Lanrezac on the afternoon of 21 August, thus initiating the third clash of the Battle of
the Frontiers. Bülow had issued orders for no engagements until 23
August so that he could bring up as many divisions and as much
heavy artillery as possible and then slip around the French flanks.[58]
To Bülow's far left, Hausen had only four of six divisions in place
to cross the Meuse at Dinant. His big guns were a day away. On the
immediate left, Namur, defended by 35,000 soldiers, was besieged

by six divisions. The heavy mortars and howitzers had been shelling intensively for a day, and soon the fortress would have to fall, thus freeing up many units. Along his own front, Second Army was completing a great wheeling maneuver from its previous north-south alignment to east-west positions along the Sambre; but Seventh Corps and Tenth Reserve Corps—the four right-wing divisions of his army—had not reached the river. To the far right, Kluck, worried that the BEF would come over Lille-Ninove, was far to the northeast of Maubeuge. Despite the crucial 3 to 5 days lost at Liège, Bülow believed that there was still time to defeat the French before the British joined them—if only his armies could concentrate.

Generals rarely control the forces they set in motion, however, and so the battle began prematurely. Discovering a few Sambre crossings that the French had left unguarded, perhaps by design, advance elements of Tenth Corps and Guard Corps—the four left-wing divisions of Second Army—established precarious bridgeheads. These were deepened during the morning of 22 August when all of Tenth Corps and Second Guard Division got across. Bülow had only three divisions on the other side when the French sprung their trap.[59] The Guard Division were able to repel three French divisions, largely because the attackers charged without artillery support. Tenth Corps also faced three infantry divisions. Nevertheless, as he had at Liège, Otto von Emmich displayed a costly penchant for old-style tactics, ordering a frontal counterattack in tight formations. The infantry charged before the artillery could offer assistance.[60] Although the 75s tore gaping holes in his ranks, the French retreated. Incredibly, Emmich's gamble had worked. By nightfall, farther west, Tenth Reserve Corps managed to penetrate river defenses around Charleroi, and to their right, Seventh Corps pushed up to the Sambre.

The performance of the artillery sparked controversy all along the frontiers that August. Nowhere, however, were discussions more heated—and decades-old animosities rekindled more quickly—than within Second Army. Charges and countercharges flew back and forth even more furiously after horrific combat on 23 August (discussed below) sent Bülow's casualties to nearly 19%—the second highest among the seven German armies during the Battle of the Frontiers.[61] Infantrymen charged that they were fired on by enemy artillery with an insufficient answer from German guns. Worse, they claimed to be frequent victims of friendly fire. The artillery's indignant response was that it could no longer charge forward in the old fashion without being destroyed. Through years of hard, reforming

work, cannoneers had learned to disperse batteries in numerous
hidden positions connected by wireless. The infantry was not prop-
erly accustomed to these time-consuming artillery procedures from
its own prewar training, nor did Moltke's reforming efforts completely wean corps commanders from their old antiartillery prejudices and the attendant felt need to rush impetuously into combat.
Thus, in August 1914 the infantry went forward while artillery preparations were incomplete, sometimes advancing so far that they were
mistaken for the enemy by German gunners. "Great exertion and
heavy losses were the result," recalled one artilleryman.[62]

Bülow surveyed his rather desperate situation at day's end on 22
August. He had five divisions over the river, confronting more than
twice their number.[63] The coauthor of 1906 infantry regulations was
inclined to press forward with the attack, "cost what it may." But
where were First Army and Third Army? Orders were issued for the
latter to complete its preparations and attack Dinant, the former to
rush four divisions around Maubeuge to outflank the French left.
Second Army would resume its frontal assaults at dawn to prevent
the enemy from slipping away.[64]

Wary as a cat refusing to be cornered, Lanrezac gave orders for
a general defense on 23 August. Bülow sent 8 divisions south against
12.[65] On the right, Karl von Einem's Seventh Corps got 1 division
across the river with great difficulty when his late-arriving artillery
finally offered assistance. As the ex-cavalryman proudly recalled, his
men pressed forward regardless, displaying "a will to attack" that
allegedly "overturned all peacetime theories [about] the need for
taking cover."[66] The Tenth Reserve Corps, very weak in artillery to
begin with,[67] ran headlong into Lanrezac's concentration of heavy
pieces, positioned in the center.[68] The French gave way, but not
before reducing the reservists to almost half their original number.
Emmich's neighboring Tenth Corps suffered badly, too—they had
again rushed ahead of the cannons. The now-united Guard Corps
was the only unit to unleash a well-coordinated attack. It patiently
assembled light and heavy field artillery, sent the machine guns forward with the infantry, and decimated a French corps. In so doing,
however, the Guard Corps advanced so far that their left flank was
exposed to an enfilading stroke from the French right. Just before
counterattacking, however, the commander of the French corps,
Franchet D'Esperey, pulled his divisions back to Dinant to halt Hausen, who was finally crossing the Meuse.

Lanrezac learned of D'Esperey's stopgap action almost simultaneously with the alarming news that Namur was falling and, worse,

that the French Fourth Army was retreating out of the Ardennes. In late afternoon, therefore, he began his withdrawal from the Sambre-Meuse angle. When the German Second and Third Armies attacked again on 24 August, he was gone. In stark contrast to France's other retreating armies, Lanrezac had managed to limit casualties to 10,000 men: "We have been beaten," he said to his staff, "but as long as Fifth Army lives, France is not lost."[69] Contributing to his salvation, however, was Hausen's decision to send his army northwest of Dinant—on Bülow's urgent instructions—rather than southwest over Lanrezac's line of retreat, which Hausen had originally ordered. Let us recall that Duke Albrecht's neighboring Fourth Army had refused to send four divisions to cut off Lanrezac one day earlier. Karl von Clausewitz—the Napoleonic theorist who had written about the "fog of war" that clouds commanders' visions—was no doubt frowning from the grave.

And what of First Army? In fact it had not swung around Maubeuge that day—a move that would have doomed Lanrezac had its execution occurred days earlier, when Bülow ordered it—because its six left-wing divisions collided with the BEF at Mons. For 24 hours before the first morning shots, Kluck's staff struggled to determine the enemy's whereabouts. Cavalry and airplane reconnaissance finally brought many clear indications that there were British around Maubeuge, but was this the main concentration? If earlier reports of northern landings were indeed true, First Army's four right wing divisions needed to remain facing northwest. Reports of troops detraining east of Lille seemed to confirm this necessity.[70] Thus, Kluck petitioned OHL to free his command from Bülow's shackles, which bound First Army to a supposedly disastrous southwesterly course. Moltke rejected the bid, reaffirming Second Army's orders to hurry the southern sweep around Maubeuge—a maneuver consistent with lessons learned and relearned in prewar exercises.[71] Alleging later that it was not the grand northern outflanking movement the master would have preferred, Kluck kept Second Corps and Fourth Reserve Corps plus three cavalry divisions in the north, moving only Fourth, Third, and Ninth Corps south. On 23 August, they were north of the Condé Canal. Entrenched on the other side was the BEF.

The bulk of the heavy fighting took place between Third and Ninth Corps and the British Second Corps. German forces displayed the diversity of tactics we would expect to find in an army undergoing rapid transformation but still allowing great corps autonomy. Modernity's face appeared in the complete absence of cavalry heroics, the aggressive use of machine guns, and the devastating combination of light and heavy field artillery.[72] The infantry of Bülow's old corps (Third) offered a textbook demonstration of the infantry attack as they advanced with short sprints on captains' whistle commands.[73] It was indicative of the problems inherent in "controlled" assaults, however, that Third Corps still experienced steep, 21% casualties.[74] The captains, lieutenants, and sergeants who coordinated the charges were killed and wounded with even greater frequency. Without their leaders, squads and platoons disintegrated into "well-meaning hordes" of brave soldiers "clumped tightly together."[75] The end result, in other words, was similar to that achieved by traditional tactics.

On Third Corps' left, Ninth Corps paid an even higher price for the "medieval" look it presented to "the best riflemen in Europe." British observers saw "nothing of the swiftly weaving lines, the rushes of alternate companies, the twinkle and flicker of a modern attack." The Germans were forced back repeatedly as each British battalion poured upward of 16,000 bullets a minute into the "oncoming grey swarm."[76] "You'd see a lot of them coming in a mass on the other side of the canal and you just let them have it," wrote one soldier.[77] The German casualty rate soared rapidly to 28%.[78] Finally, pounded hard by superior artillery, outnumbered two-to-one, and aware that more Germans were attacking from the northwest, the British withdrew. The BEF had lost 1,600 men, but their sacrifice had snuffed out the last chance for a crushing German victory in Belgium.

Kluck, Bülow, and Hausen then joined the rest of the German Army in the great "pursuit" of late summer 1914. Moving deeper into France toward Paris—and farther away from supply bases, home railheads, and the eastern front—they were forced into Schlieffen's riskiest scenario. But now the German right wing was much weaker than the juggernaut that invaded Belgium 3 weeks earlier. To be sure, Moltke shifted his final 2 reserve divisions from Schleswig-Holstein to Antwerp to strengthen the siege of the fortress city. These reinforcements joined 6 divisions in or around Antwerp, Namur, Maubeuge, and Givet—altogether 8 divisions that were not available for fighting in France. Alarming news of a powerful Russian penetration of East Prussia, moreover, convinced Moltke to transfer 4 divisions from Bülow's Second Army to the eastern front after Namur fell. Of the right's original 32 divisions, therefore, only 22 gave chase. These were the same divisions that bled profusely at Liège, Sambre-Meuse, and Mons. Over 36,000 fell—the equivalent of 3 full-strength divisions. Lanrezac and the BEF lost only 11,600

from their combined 16 divisions, and 18,000 British reinforcements arrived on 24 August. If one counts 3 French reserve divisions, the Lille garrison, and 2 cavalry divisions that were concentrating on the BEF's left, about 21 divisions faced the bloodied
German right wing.

German operations in 1914 had near zero tolerance for error. Because overall numbers favored the allies, victory had to come quickly
in one region before the enemy regained the freedom to maneuver.
Unfortunately for Germany, there was too much truth that year to
the maxim "What can go wrong, will go wrong." The courageous
little kingdom did not grant free passage, as was hoped. Rather,
Belgium defended itself. Liège was not manned by 6,000 troops but
by 35,000, which easily halted Germany's *coup de main* . Brought up
to redeem the infantry, the heavy artillery could not destroy forts
with regulation firing but had to expend a prodigious amount of
shells in short supply. After the sacrifice of men and matériel, 3 to
5 critical days had been lost. Then the cavalry failed to complete its
mission. Men and horses were wasted at Halen, and the right wing's
advance was not screened from the view of enemy airplanes and
airships. Consequently, the Belgians withdrew to Antwerp, drawing
the besiegers with them, and Lanrezac warily entered the Sambre-
Meuse salient. The violation of Belgian neutrality, meanwhile,
brought over 70,000 British troops. Because airplanes were not used
optimally and Zeppelins could not get up into hot, turbulent air,
Kluck, Bülow, and the OHL did not know the BEF's location and
thus could not agree on how to sweep around it. Bülow's guess was
much better than Kluck's, but Kluck disobeyed orders. Further opportunities to trap Lanrezac were missed after first Duke Albrecht
and, then, Hausen, sent units elsewhere.
    So much had gone wrong, but not all by chance. Indeed, the
causes of Germany's failure in Belgium can be traced squarely to
antebellum patterns and predilections. All armies make mistakes in
peacetime, of course, but Germany's prewar failings were far too
numerous for the near perfection that was necessary in 1914. That
three infantry divisions of the right wing lay dead or wounded, for
example, indicated how controversial Schlichting's dispersed-order
tactics had been. Despite the fact that regulations endorsed his
ideas, many commanders still ignored them, adding an extra 10%
or so to the casualties. Multiplying the slaughter was the inadequate
coordination of artillery and infantry, exacerbated by the latter's
long-standing disdain for artillery and its bullheaded penchant for

going it alone. Nor did successive cavalry reforms completely root out decades of die-hardism. The disaster at Halen had been waiting to happen since Konitz. There was also a huge reconnaissance breakdown. Although the cavalry was not capable of finding the BEF in time, aircraft were. But army commanders put more faith in mounted patrols, a sure sign that initial prewar reactions to airplanes as "purely for sport" had not been entirely overcome.[79] This prejudice explains the under-utilization of the new technology: Even the 60 to 100-kilometer radius of action used at the 1912 maneuvers would have spotted the BEF days earlier. That well before this the Zeppelins made no contribution was probably the most disastrous legacy from peacetime, for Military Transport and the War Ministry had argued in 1912–1913 that nonrigid airships gave the army long-range eyes in the kind of windy weather that was unsuited for Zeppelins. But their arguments were rejected. The French were able to get aloft and had the last, cruel laugh.

Attack in Retreat

Kluck's First Army marched confidently to Mons. The air of superiority was felt in every company as soldiers joked about slaying redcoats in outmoded black fur hats or recalled Bismarck's derisive words about sending gendarmes to arrest the harmless British Army if it dared to appear on the continent. On the night of 23 August, feelings were reversed. "Why not just say it: a bad defeat," said one captain who had lost half his men. "Our first battle is a bad defeat, an unheard of bad defeat—and this against the English, the laughable English."[80] But when the search for the BEF continued, thoughts were already turning to revenge.

Joffre had plans too. On 25 August, the GQG transported troops from Alsace to Péronne, 40 to 45 kilometers southwest of Cambrai and Le Cateau. One regular division, 3 reserve divisions, a Moroccan brigade, and 8 mountain battalions were to assemble and join the territorials, the Lille garrison, and other troops on the BEF's left. Together with the French Fifth Army, these forces—a respectable 26 divisions—had orders to counterattack and expel the invaders.[81]

Kluck disrupted these plans in a brilliant 6-day series of engagements.[82] On 24 August he captured a stranded British battalion and outflanked another entire brigade, inflicting 2,000 casualties on the BEF. The next day he collided with the British First Corps at Landrecies, sending it fleeing south, away from the now-isolated Second

Corps, which was struck on 26 August at Le Cateau. Although Kluck's men continued to offer tempting targets to British riflemen and machine-gunners at Le Cateau—the "poor devils" were "falling down like ninepins," wrote one artillery officer—their aggressive use of technology turned the tide. German machine gun detachments attacked "close-massed so that the bullets swarmed across like angry bees." They "pushed forward wherever there was a gap."[83] This was definitely a bright spot that summer, for the machine gunners were improvising, going beyond regulations that prescribed a trouble-shooting role in reserve.[84] German field cannons and heavy howitzers added to the carnage at Le Cateau as Second Corps lost 8,000 men. Now the battered BEF fled so far south, and so rapidly, that the Germans lost contact with them. When the Z-9 finally got airborne on 1 September, its mission was to find the BEF's line of retreat.[85]

Meanwhile, Kluck assaulted the assortment of French divisions that were assembling east of Amiens. In a running battle over Cambrai, Combles, Péronne, and Proyart (26–29 August), Joffre's forces were dispersed before they could unite and attack. Hammered and broken, they fled before the onrushing First Army, whose cavalry approached Compiègne on 30 August.

Kluck's relentless penetration of northern France came at a high price, for First Army suffered another 13,000 casualties. Together with previous losses, marching attrition, and companies peeled off to guard prisoners and lines of supply, his 10 divisions now moved at only 71% strength.[86] Worse had been meted out to the BEF and the new army that Joffre had tried to form, however, and First Army's exertions probably saved Bülow from a devastating defeat.

Joffre, as part of his counteroffensive, insisted that Lanrezac hurl his army westward at the exposed left flank of Bülow's Second Army as it tried to slip around the French. Indeed, a large gap was opening between Bülow and Hausen as the latter's Third Army rushed south over Mézières to render assistance to the hard-pressed armies of Duke Albrecht and Crown Prince William (see below). By 29 August, Hausen's nearest division was 40 kilometers away, and Third Army, for all intents and purposes, had moved from the right wing to the center. On Second Army's right, Kluck had only 1 division within a day's march.[87] Thus Bülow was almost alone with 7½ or 8½ divisions[88] at 80% strength to Lanrezac's 13 divisions at 92% strength. Moreover, separating Bülow's right near St. Quentin (Seventh Corps and Tenth Reserve Corps), from his left, trailing northeast near Guise (Tenth Corps and Guard Corps), was a gap of 20 kilometers. Widening the divide was the Oise River, flowing north-south between the two halves of Bülow's inferior forces.

Two French divisions slipped across the Oise east of St. Quentin in the foggy morning hours of 29 August.[89] By midday three more had followed. Behind them, still marching east of the Oise, were five reinforcing divisions. Fifth Army's reserve of three divisons was a half-day's march farther east. Lanrezac's spearhead took the artillery-poor, machine gun–depleted, and already anemic Tenth Reserve Corps by complete surprise. Only the "cold-blooded"[90] discipline of a few older reserve officers, who formed a defensive line in a hailstorm of bullets and shrapnel, and the rescuing fire of five batteries of 150-mm howitzers from neighboring Seventh Corps prevented a rout. Heavy German shelling gradually blunted the French advance on St. Quentin. The position of Lanrezac's assault divisions grew precarious when the German Tenth and Guard Corps rushed south from Guise to engage his trailing force behind the Oise. As the picture of German strength became clearer, Lanrezac ordered his advance guard to retreat and both corps behind the river to face north. Then he commanded D'Esperey's reserve divisions to hurry west.

German commanders nearly lost control of the battle during the early going. With Tenth Corps artillery still trying to pass through the clogged streets of Guise, elements of Twentieth Division attempted to force a passage along the main road farther south and were cut to pieces by French 75s.[91] To their immediate left, the First Guard Brigade made the same mistake. When fogginess delayed the artillery barrage, the brigadier ordered a hesitant First Regiment forward with the slight consolation that it "will be able to attack a retreating foe this time without artillery preparation."[92] The commander of Third Regiment added to the brigade's technological handicap by ordering his machine gun detachment to deploy in the rear. As the fog lifted, French artillery spotters gazed with martial delight on the thick skirmish lines and dense formations coming their way. The slaughter from above worsened when Guard Corps artillerymen, mistaking the far-off Third Regiment for the enemy, opened fire on their infantry comrades. Finally, displaying the discipline and depth of leadership that only the Guard Corps could muster—over 40 officers fell during the assault—Third Regiment's surviving officers grouped all companies shoulder to shoulder into a single firing line and unleashed a withering rifle fire.[93] The French withdrew. By early afternoon, with the combined artillery of Tenth and Guard Corps finally in position and locked in a duel with French gunners, Lanrezac's divisions fell back.

By late afternoon, Mont d'Origny assumed critical importance. Situated just east of the Oise, the heights there protected the rear flank of French forces still across the river and the left flank of all trailing corps. An entire brigade was entrenched on Mont d'Origny, and the German Tenth Corps sent its Nineteenth Division to push them off.[94] Forming up 2,500 meters away, the attacking battalions demonstrated that tactical lessons had been learned since the previous week's carnage on the Sambre. They moved forward at a trot and immediately fanned out to avoid unnecessary deaths. The wary infantrymen took cover wherever they found it, pausing up to 30 minutes between sprints to return fire. Machine gun detachments protected the exposed left flank from counterattacks, performing their "work of destruction" and hurling the French back in a "frantic jumble of the fleeing and falling."[95] Tenth Corps artillery provided excellent covering fire for hours as the attackers advanced. Schlichting would have been proud. Lacking the machinelike discipline of the Guard Corps, however, Nineteenth Division gradually disintegrated into separate groups, most without live officers, packed tightly together as the rear battalions bumped into forward pockets of men who paused to shoot or take cover. The Nineteenth Divison suffered fewer losses than the First Guard Brigade—22% versus 32%[96]—but failed to take Mont d'Origny. They dug in on the field.

Simultaneously, Franchet D'Esperey's reserve divisions counterattacked, smashing into Germany's Twentieth Division and the Guards Corps. As the French batteries sustained a consistently rapid fire into the evening, France's prewar investment in shells began to earn handsome dividends. In contrast, the Guard Corps artillery was out of ammunition for many hours before finally finding enough supplies to resume firing. The first Division reluctantly yielded some of the ground won earlier at great sacrifice and then entrenched.[97] Emmich was not as fortunate. With his front cracking before the enemy's furious onslaught—"the Germans were running away,"[98] wrote one Frenchman—the corps commander received a galloping field artillerist at headquarters. "Excellency, we are out of ammunition and are under heavy artillery fire. We can't find the French field batteries and heavy guns." "Ride back," said Emmich. "Your unit will know how to die."[99] But German technology of another sort brought a timely reprieve. As the French pushed up the road to

Guise in the dark, their point company was surprised by a detachment of Twentieth Division's machine guns. Seconds later, 150 dead or wounded French soldiers were piled hideously in a "human clump."[100] D'Esperey's infantry decided to pause until morning.

That night, remarkably enough, Bülow formulated an offensive strategy for 30 August. West of the Oise, the Tenth Reserve Corps, reinforced now by Einem's three brigades and the Seventeenth Division from Kluck, would assault Lanrezac's river defenses and cave in his flank. Simultaneously, the Tenth and Guard Corps would attack from the north with everything they had left.[101] Bülow's battle plan was solid testimony to the deep, unalterable, unshakable conviction in the German Army that one should attack under almost any circumstances—even when faced with a difficult cross-river assault, outnumbered two to three, and nearly out of ammunition. We should also not forget that every German general was aware of the need to defeat France quickly before the Russians could threaten Berlin, and the clock was ticking.

A great artillery duel began at dawn. Aware of their own shortages, German commanders on the Oise waited for the French cannonade to let up so their attack could begin. They waited in vain until almost noon and then sent the troops into a steel rain.[102] East of the river, Lanrezac attacked first, sending a few brigades forward behind intense friendly shelling. The weary fighters of Tenth and Guard Corps burrowed into the ground, their spirits lifted only occasionally by answering booms from the 150-mm howitzers. At noon, a crash of cannon fire from the south seemed to signal the main French attack.

The twin battle of Guise–St. Quentin had reached its climax. That the French were gradually winning this slugfest was, once again, not by chance or fluke. Although Bülow's forces fought bravely and demonstrated, at times, "the twinkle and flicker of a modern attack," Second Army was too burdened with prewar baggage to prevail. Artillery ammunition was already in short supply on the first day, and on the second day the 150s nearly fell silent. Prudent officers had predicted these circumstances years earlier. Many infantry commanders showed disdain for the artillery, however, even before the shells grew short. Worse still, the top command believed that somehow German men would prevail even though they were outnumbered and outshelled. By noon on 30 August, however, German men were praying in their foxholes. Then, to the pleasant surprise of every one of them, the French cannonade stopped. It had been covering fire for a well-coordinated withdrawal.[103]

Lanrezac's heart was not in the attack. The previous evening he had warned Joffre that the strategic situation was grave. The BEF was retreating to Compiègne-Soissons, leaving the Fifth Army vulnerable to Kluck's lightning advance. Hausen's push out of Belgium was also worrisome. Lanrezac refused to take responsibility for a victory in battle that could mean loss of the war. "Is Fifth Army to delay in the region of Guise–St. Quentin at the risk of being captured?" he asked Joffre's deputy. The GQG had the notion of capture "absurd"[104] but grudgingly agreed to a retreat. Joffre's orders did not reach Fifth Army, however, until the next morning, and it was early afternoon before Lanrezac could organize the withdrawal.[105]

The Fifth Army fell back in a broad east-west line, with its left flank above Soissons, on 31 August. Lanrezac was trying to bring his divisions into line again with the BEF, which was already below Compiègne. Lanrezac's divisions were bloodied, to be sure, having suffered about 8,000 casualties. Bülow lost almost 9,000, however, and could not give chase until he had let his troops recuperate for an entire day.[106] Bülow the strong-willed devotee of assault "cost what it may," notified Kluck that First Army would have to wheel southeast over Laon "in order to exploit the victory of Second Army."[107]

This is not what Kluck had in mind. Although driven by the idea of swinging around the enemy's flank—the essence of Schlieffen's plans—he believed it would be found farther south-southeast. Therefore, First Army was arcing along a 60-kilometer front around Compiègne by 1 September.[108] Kluck's loyal men had come 200 kilometers since Mons, 9 days earlier. That morning his southernmost unit, the Fourth Cavalry Division, was close to the village of Néry. When word came from patrols that British horse artillery were bivouacked nearby, Lieutenant General von Garnier, the impetuous commander at Halen, instantly decided to charge again.[109] Two brigades went forward, backed by machine guns and artillery. The attack let loose terrible panic and destruction in the British camp, but the men of the BEF rallied, keeping their last cannon firing until an entire reinforcing division arrived. Unaware of British strength, Garnier ordered his third brigade to charge. They rushed forward in three waves, "paying no attention to the heavy rifle, machine gun, and artillery fire"[110] that cut into them. When artillery fire hit their left flank, all three brigades began a mad scramble to save themselves. The division dodged British units all day, eventually finding silent refuge in a forest while the BEF marched past toward the Marne River. Garnier had left behind all of his cannons and nearly

600 dead, wounded, and captured soldiers. The Fourth Cavalry was now at less than 65% strength and could no longer be counted as a division.[111] It was an inauspicious beginning to the final phase of a campaign that was lasting too long.

The Fifth Army of Crown Prince William suffered terrible losses on 22 August, but there was no time for his 10 divisions to rest. In 10 days, William's left wing advanced toward the Meuse against unshaken defenders, who used Verdun as a base for counterattacks. On 2 September, his soldiers reached the limit of the fort's 155-mm guns. By this time, his right wing had moved 50 kilometers around the formidable fortress barrier to positions northeast of Varrenes. At the same time, confronting a shaken but still determined enemy, Duke Albrecht's 10 divisions had slogged even farther. The Fourth Army's left wing advanced 60 kilometers to join William's right, while his swing corps traversed 100 kilometers to Somme Py. Both armies had to struggle for every village and town. Losses mounted with every kilometer—becoming so high, in fact, that Hausen was forced to respond to Duke Albrecht's pleas to wheel due south and outflank the French. Thus, Third Army's 5 divisions hurried over Mézières to new lines northeast of Rheims. Hausen's men covered 125 kilometers in 8 days, executing a maneuver out of Belgium almost identical to prewar staff rides that had exploited field opportunities rather than following preconceived plans.[112]

Not only were the French able to retreat before being trapped, however, but they also forced the Germans to pay with tens of thousands of dead and wounded. The Meuse River contributed significantly to the invaders' difficulties. Duke Albrecht's losses were comparatively light until his army reached the wide waters and steep banks of this natural line of defense. On the far right, Eighth Corps and Eighth Reserve Corps reached Donchery, near historic Sedan, early on 26 August. As their four divisions put across pontoon bridges, French artillery, firing from positions so well hidden that German crews could not locate them, pinned down the advance brigades, almost completely destroying some of these units by day's end.[113] Fourth Army's left wing experienced the same tenacious resistance farther south at Martincourt. Crossing the river there on 27 August, the lead division was counterattacked by strong infantry and artillery after nightfall. "A thick disorderly rabble of [surviving] elements, among them many wounded, streamed back over the pontoon bridge to the opposite bank under continued artillery fire."[114] The approach of Hausen's divisions from the north on 28–29 Au-

gust forced a French withdrawal, enabling the rest of Fourth Army—
and, in its turn, Fifth Army's right wing—to get across. But Third
Army had been forced to abandon Second Army to its nail-biting
fate at Guise–St. Quentin.

The French artillery obviously played an important role at Donchery and Martincourt. That France was able to punish the Germans
terribly all along the central front, in fact, was attributable in large
part to its artillery superiority. And a big part of this advantage was
the 75-mm fieldpiece, which, simply put, outdueled the C-96nA. In
contrast to Kluck's and Bülow's pursuit, which featured pitched battles like Le Cateau and St. Quentin, followed by disengagement or
lost contact, the fighting in the center was more of a running battle.
The French 75 was the ideal gun for this type of hit and run campaign, which emphasized attacking in retreat. It shot 1,000 meters
farther than the C-96nA because Germany had used shorter C-96
barrels. The 75s were also more accurate at long range. Thus,
French generals positioned their hidden batteries left and right of
advancing German columns, then ambushed them with enfilading
fire at maximum range (8,000 meters).

The German gun crews were faced with a series of unenviable
options. The more mobile C-96nA could rush forward to return fire
at close range, or it could march near the front of the column—
techniques that initially appealed to some artillery officers who had
not internalized or never favored firing from defilade, as well as
corps commanders who wanted their batteries forward. Both strategies proved costly because they exposed German artillerymen to
shelling without silencing French guns, which were withdrawn before the C-95nAs came into range. Another option was to stay in
the rear, advancing only slightly to duel with the 75s at longer range.
This technique was also abandoned, however, because German infantrymen, charging wildly forward, were often hit by long-range
friendly fire. In addition, too much ammunition was expended to
hit targets at 7,000 meters, moreover, a normal problem exacerbated by the relative inaccuracy of the C-96nA. With no good option, German guns tended to fire less and less as the campaign proceeded—to the intense dismay of pursuing infantry, who paid dearly
for decades of insistence that mobility trumped firepower.[115]

The German field artillery had good reason to avoid squandering its shells because another factor that silenced German guns as
August drew to a close was a relative shortage of ammunition—a
dilemma that was not limited, as we know, to the central front. Germany entered the war with 4 million field artillery shells—987 per

field cannon and 973 per light howitzer. Woefully short-sighted war-time production quotas, punctually fulfilled in the course of August, increased these figures to 1,029 and 1,044, respectively. France, however, had stockpiled 1,190 shells per field gun—an advantage of more than 200 shells per cannon (i.e., more than 20%), with comparable additions from production in August.[116] Because each side shot great quantities during the first battles, the campaign soon entered a phase that brought Germany closer to the end of its shells than France: "I watched the disappearance of our munitions trains in 1914 with great worry,"[117] remembered Hermann von Stein, quartermaster general of the artillery at OHL. By early September, shell supplies had sunk below 500,000, severely limiting artillery support and realizing the nightmare that General Inspector Schubert had predicted in 1910.[118] As we have observed repeatedly, Germany's prewar chickens were coming home to roost.

In the 10 days after the Battle of the Frontiers, logistical factors lengthened the defender's lead. On the one hand, the German armies advanced far into enemy country without the advantage of rails, which the French had destroyed beyond quick repair. The farther the Germans went, obviously, the more difficult it was to bring up dwindling supplies. On the other hand, the French, had more shells, rails in the interior were still intact, and it was easier to supply units with relatively more abundant ammunition as the armies fell back on rear areas and fortresses where it was kept. France's larger stores were a particular advantage around Paris, Verdun, and the eastern forts.[119]

German howitzers lessened France's artillery superiority. The steep trajectory of the 105s and 150s made them ideal for pummeling French infantry entrenchments and artillery batteries—if the latter could be located. And the 150s shot farther than the 75s. A consensus mounted in the German Army that August, however, that there were simply not enough howitzers.[120] Each regular corps marched with four 150-mm batteries and six 105-mm batteries—three of the newer rapid-firing guns and three of the older—whereas reserve corps had no howitzers and only half as many field guns. The infantry came to curse the C-96nA when all too frequently—most of the time, in fact—their howitzers were helping somebody else. That Germany fielded more heavy guns, each with more shells than France's, was therefore small consolation. And this edge dwindled as each gun's 800 shells[121] were shot up and lengthening supply lines made it hard to bring up what was left.

As the Germans approached Verdun, moreover, the fortress's 73 155-mm guns, each armed at war's outbreak with 500 shells, brought the edge back to France.[122] Indeed, Verdun was becoming a significant factor in the war. Its heavy artillery amounted to three-quarters of the combined capacity of the German Fourth and Fifth Armies. These pieces could not move, of course, but neither could the German armies without taking Verdun into account. Its 20 major and 40 intermediary forts dominated the country for 70 kilometers all around—about half the length of Albrecht's and William's front.[123] Verdun was also a worrisome base of infantry operations against the Fifth Army. Reinforced by the garrison's three divisions, for instance, the French Third Army hit William's flank on 24 August, inflicting damage before retreating.[124] Somehow Verdun had to be neutralized.

The German Sixth and Seventh Armies stopped the French invasion of southern Lorraine on 20–21 August. The victory reactivated a prewar discussion. Bavarian Crown Prince Rupprecht and his chief of staff, Krafft von Dellmensingen, had known for years that Bavarian forces would probably be assigned to this portion of the front. Given their desire to attack, it is understandable that Bavarian exercises had examined the possibility of breaking through France's fortresses.[125] Helmuth von Moltke was tempted by the consistently positive outcome of these war games, for, somewhat like Schlieffen, he was flexible about invasion routes.[126] The development of the 420-mm howitzer, with its terrible destructive power, strengthened Moltke's inclination to attack with both wings. Thus, OHL's mobilization orders envisioned various victory scenarios, including "Case Three": a puncturing of the fortress line in conjunction with the grandiose outflanking movement through Belgium. On 7 August, OHL assigned Sixth Army twenty-four 210s, two 305s, and two 420-mm Gamma-Devices to be ready for this eventuality.[127] It was quite consistent with these prewar plans and mobilization directives, that Krafft insisted on counterattacking in Lorraine and Moltke agreed, adding most of his reserve divisions to the effort. After the victory, Krafft telephoned OHL, receiving a reply from Moltke on 22 August: "Pursue direction Epinal."[128] It was the exhilarating go-ahead order for Case Three.

The center of the German line near Saarburg lay 75 kilometers northeast of Epinal. Within 3 days, the 10 divisions of Sixth and Seventh Armies that spearheaded the offensive were only 20 to 25 kilometers away. Flanking divisions were echeloned farther back as the massive wedge drove into enemy territory.[129] If France's two armies were beaten here, all fortresses to the north would be vulnerable and probably abandoned, especially with 3 German armies slipping around Verdun. To take Epinal and reach for glory, however, the attackers had first to eliminate Fort Manonviller, the forward apex of the Toul-Nancy-Epinal fortress triangle. French fortress engineers had built all of the latest designs into this seemingly impregnable roadblock. More resistant than Liège or Namur, neither 210s nor 305s could destroy its inner works. As Krafft's divisions raced ahead on 25 August, siege troops and heavy artillery encircled Manonviller.

Strong French forces struck back that day as part of Joffre's "attack in retreat" strategy of late August. The brunt of their assault hit the right, echeloned flank of Sixth Army near Lunéville, where Prince Rupprecht had placed weaker reserve and Ersatz divisions. The Germans were overpowered there, forcing both German armies on the defensive for 2 days.[130] When considered with the near routs inflicted on Eighteenth Reserve Corps in the Ardennes (22 August), and on the Tenth Reserve twice, on the Sambre (23 August) and at St. Quentin (29 August), it appears that Germany paid a high price in 1914 for the frontline presence of so many poorly armed reserves and inadequately equipped and trained ersatz units.

However, the besiegers of Manonviller had completed the field railway required for the gargantuan howitzers, rolled them slowly forward, and cemented them into firing positions. Twenty-four hours later an observation balloon reported the awesome results of modern artillery technology. There were thousands of shell craters in the cement inner works, and all armored towers and turrets had been hit and damaged. The entire eastern side of the fort "lay completely out of action in a pile of rubble."[131] On 27 August, the defenders hoisted a white flag. The infantry did not have to assault.

Germany's left wing now received new orders from OHL. Moltke was alarmed by the situation around Verdun. If French counterattacks from the massive fortress area developed into a full-fledged drive on Metz, Germany's center would be pierced and its right unhinged from its left. The possibility unnerved a normally pessimistic Moltke—indeed, he had worried about a counteroffensive use of French fortresses since his prewar discussions with the Bavarians.[132] To prevent such a disaster, OHL reversed its decision to transfer Prince William's fifth Corps to the Russian front—more evidence of the initial intent to head east after quick frontier victories—but he had to keep these two divisions east of the Meuse to shield Metz and the pivot of Germany's seven-army front. Also, to relieve pressure on Fifth Army around Verdun, Rupprect's armies were commanded farther north into the 50-kilometer gap between Epinal and Toul-Nancy.[133]

Max Bauer visited Rupprecht's headquarters on 30 August with yet another modification of plans. The chief of OHL's division of heavy artillery and fortresses had been an eyewitness to the devastation of his fat cannons had caused to Fort Manonviller, and he was aware of previous success in Belgium.[134] Privy to the highest counsels in Koblenz, Bauer also knew of Moltke's worries and evolving operational thoughts about Verdun. The artillerist reported that the German right wing had penetrated far into northern France, where enemy resistance was expected to stiffen along the Marne River. Therefore, said Bauer, Sixth and Seventh Armies would receive heavy artillery reinforcement for an obliterating assault over Nancy—consistent with Ludendorff's proposals of 1911—then proceed toward Vitry-le-Francois to roll up the French flank south of the Marne.[135]

Rupprecht and Krafft unleashed this offensive on 3 September, assembling all of the heavy artillery and ammmunition Bauer had promised. Their spearhead of six divisions met stiff resistance as it slowly approached the artillery's protected position 10 to 12 kilometers east of Nancy—the point where the biggest pieces would be within range but not vulnerable to French guns or counterattacks. Farther south, the rest of Sixth and Seventh Armies tried to push to the Mosel and into the Toul-Epinal gap.[136] The Bavarians who were assaulting Nancy were to receive help because, still concerned about the threat of Verdun, Moltke had ordered Crown Prince William's Fifth Army to begin amassing its heavy artillery, to encircle and "neutralize" the fortress complex of Verdun, and to "take out" the line of five lesser forts on the Meuse between Verdun and Toul.[137]

By 4–5 September, OHL's vision of the final battle of the campaign was in clearer focus. Aerial reconnaissance on 4 September reported that the French were transporting 2 corps from Epinal to Paris. Clearly, Joffre was utilizing the defensive advantages of his eastern fortress line and excellent railroad connections to prepare a counterattack against the German right wing. Moltke's response was logical enough—4 divisions from the left were ordered to cross Belgium by train to bolster Kluck's and Bülow's greatly depleted forces.[138] The 12 divisions remaining under Krafft's command would proceed over Nancy and the Mosel. Fifth Army's assignment remained unchanged: Its 10 divisions were to surround and neutralize Verdun and the forts to its south. Fourth Army's 10 divisions were ordered by OHL to move southeast to Morley, 35 kilometers behind the French defenders at Toul. Third Army's 6 divisions[139] would move toward Troyes, then turn west if needed or, ideally, east to close Moltke's artillery-induced trap of France's 4 armies on the fortress line. The German First and Second Armies, whose 17.5 divisions were passing to the east of Paris, were ordered to face west (i.e., toward Paris) to shield themselves and the other armies from Joffre's impending counteroffensive.[140] When reinforcements arrived from Alsace—and more troops after the fall of Maubeuge—Joffre's counterattack would be deflected or crushed. Thus, by early September, campaign victory was expected of the center and left armies but not the anemic right, which was relegated to flank protection.

The Battle of France

Moltke's final brushstrokes were brilliant, but they were little more than motions in the air. That his last canvas remained empty was due to a complicated mix of factors, among them chance, bad luck, and the unfortunate "fog" of war. But we will not find truly satisfying explanations here. The German defeat of September 1914 was much more than a coincidence. Like missed opportunities in Belgium and mounting difficulties and losses during the great pursuit, the deeper causes of the impending debacle emanated from prewar patterns and predilections. Long-standing artillery shortcomings played a big part. So did Alexander von Kluck, the "last man on the right," and his chief of staff, Hermann von Kuhl, two who claimed to be legatees of Schlieffen's operational thinking.

One wonders what Schlieffen would have said about the options remaining to the weakened, weary, and thinly spread divisions of the once formidable right wing: Sweep around Paris? Or finish off the enemy in the field? Clearly, the former maneuver would have isolated First Army from Second, leaving both vulnerable to flanking attacks from the capital. As Kluck's exhausted units pushed past Compiègne in early September, he contemplated massing heavy artillery for a bombardment of Paris from the northeast. He rejected this option, however, in favor of continuing a relentless southeasterly pursuit that afforded the enemy no opportunity to entrench. This was consistent with arguments of Schlieffen and Waldersee, which held that modern technology in the service of a bold attacker would demoralize defenders, especially in a battle against a "decadent" and "nervous" people like the French.[141] "The jettisoned piles of coats, boots, and ammunition found along the roadside," writes historian Barbara Tuchman, "confirmed Kluck's opinion of a beaten opponent."[142] Thus, Schlieffen may have smiled anxiously from the grave. It was the smile of a late-night gambler, ready to roll the iron dice again but knowing, deep down, that there had been better opportunities to win fortunes earlier in the evening.

Far from Paris, in Luxemburg, OHL worried about the hard-driving commander of First Army. By 1 September, Kluck's divisions were 40 kilometers ahead of Bülow, who was rushing to close the gap. The next day, Moltke ordered Kluck to fall back and echelon his forces on the right rear flank of Second Army. The order was ignored. Two days later, OHL ordered a westward wheel of both armies toward Paris; but it took the appearance on 5 September of a personal emissary from Moltke, Lieutenant Colonel Hentsch, before Kluck finally agreed to comply.[143] At that time his advance divisions were searching for the enemy flank along a broad front 40 to 90 kilometers slightly southeast of Paris. Two reserve divisions and the battered fourth Cavalry trailed behind to guard First Army's right rear flank against sorties from the 50,000 soldiers of the Paris garrison.

Kluck was completely oblivious to what worried Moltke most. As the Germans moved farther and farther into France, the chief of OHL began to doubt the inflated, overoptimistic claims of "routed" opponents that all seven armies sent to general headquarters: "When a million men oppose one another in battle the victor has prisoners," Moltke said to a visiting minister. "Where are our prisoners?"[144] Airplane sightings of troop movements near the eastern fortress wall indicated that the French were also building a new strike force somewhere to the west.

Moltke's reconnaissance-fed instincts were correct. Joining the Paris garrison were the "tatterdemalion collection"[145] of French units that Kluck had dispersed near Amiens, plus troops arriving daily from Lorraine and Algeria—more than 15 divisions when, 4 days hence, all were finally in place under General Michel-Joseph Maunoury.[146] Kluck's rearguard reserves collided with 5 divisions of this coalescing French Sixth Army on 5 September. Neither the fourth Cavalry, still reeling from Néry, nor the air corps had reported anything amiss. Outnumbered nearly three to one, the Germans quickly retreated toward the Ourcq River, a tributary of the Marne, and wired for assistance. Not for the first—or last—time that summer, the French had hammered German reserve units that were weak in artillery and machine guns.

These advance elements of Sixth Army were moving into position to strike Kluck's rear, a possibility that French and British aerial reconnaissance had reported over the previous few days. Joffre planned to incorporate Maunoury's assault into a much grander counteroffensive. The BEF agreed to fall in line on Maunoury's right, strike Kluck's forward left flank, and rush into the gap between the German First and Second Armies. The plan also called for D'Esperey, now commanding the French Fifth Army, to deliver a death stroke to Bülow's depleted legions, while the Ninth—another new army, that was made up of divisions taken from the fortress wall—would bludgeon Hausen's advancing divisions. The French Third and Fourth Armies were also ordered to turn and fight. Their mission was to stop Duke Albrecht and Prince William and relieve pressure on the beleaguered defenders of Nancy. The tide of combat would turn, surprisingly and shockingly, all along a massive front. The Battle of France began precipitously a day before Joffre had planned it, but this was no time to worry about fine points—the nation's survival was at stake.[147]

Kluck turned back two corps to squelch the threat from Maunoury. They attacked into a hornet's nest, however, as more divisions from Paris entered the fray on 6–7 September. Making matters much worse for the Germans was Sixth Army's vastly superior artillery. A constant flow of shells from nearby Paris enabled the 75s, 120s, and 155s to rain hell on infantrymen of First Army, who had not yet experienced the "munitions shortage" rumored among the troops.[148] Indeed, the combination of relatively short prewar stockpiles, heavy fire early in the campaign, lengthening supply lines, and destroyed rails resulted in such desultory German fire that French gunners assumed Kluck must have outrun his guns.[149] The men of First Army suffered the nightmarish consequences:

> The first time in heavy artillery fire without cover [recalled one company commander]: something we will have to learn. It grunts and belches, bellows, peals, smacks, barks, and caterwauls all around and over you in every sound of the animal alphabet. In between, crash after crash in tones which you have heard before only in hours of the most furious uproaring of the elements—the clatter of hail, long rolling thunder, a storm gust, churning surf flying into a rage around a crag, and now, again, a shredding fragmentation as if a bolt of lightning hits. Then a meshing and muddling of everything that just about

cracks your skull and twists your nerves into a spasm, as if waves of
electricity were coursing back and forth pitilessly through your bones.
. . . One wonders whether our artillery even exists at all. What a rotten
dirty trick [for the artillery] to leave us lying up here without even
fighting back.[150]

Kluck lost 11,000 men in a series of senseless attacks on the Ourcq
River. Reduced to "cinders,"[151] what was left of six divisions was soon
pinned down.

First Army desperately needed assistance, but none was forthcoming. To be sure, OHL was shifting two corps from Alsace, and
rail lines were open—on paper at least—from Liège to Chauny, 2
days' forced march (100 kilometers) from Paris. Stopgap rail repairs
made quick and massive troop movements "out of the question,"[152]
however, so that reinforcements from Germany's left wing were
more than a week away. Moreover, despite 10 days' firing at Maubeuge by scores of 150s, 210s, 305s, and 420s, shell-short gun crews
had still not eliminated it. Thus, three brigades around the fortress
would not appear on the Ourcq and the Marne.[153]

Kluck was left to his own devices: "The application of Caesar's
maxim that 'in great and dangerous operations one must act, not
think,' " he wrote later, "necessarily produced in this critical situation rapid alterations in the movements of the First Army."[154] He
decided to disengage Third and Ninth Corps, which were barring
the entire BEF, and D'Esperey's left-wing corps south of the Marne.
The Third and Ninth Corps were force-marched 125 kilometers behind the Ourcq to the left of Maunoury (northeast of Paris). They
arrived in position late on 8 September for an enveloping attack the
next morning.[155]

Now Caesar rolled over in his grave. Maunoury, a thinking man,
shifted his left wing to the west of the onrushing Germans, then
placed an entire cavalry corps on that flank. He had 7.5 infantry
divisions in an arcing front and 2 divisions in reserve.[156] Behind
them were more late-arriving troops, powerful artillery, and the
whole Paris garrison. Indeed, there was no logical reason to believe
that Third and Ninth Corps would be more successful than their
hapless, burnt-out comrades on the Ourcq. Into the gaping 45 to
50-kilometer hole between First and Second Armies, moreover,
Kluck inserted only 1 infantry brigade and 2 cavalry divisions. Bülow
had 2 cavalry divisions on the other side of the gap. Kluck was gambling recklessly on the advice of his general staff chief, Hermann
von Kuhl, that "the repeatedly beaten English"[157] were too demoralized to mount an attack and exploit this brilliant opportunity.

Figure 21. Cavalrymen dismount and fire in exposed positions. Source: Hoppenstedt, *Das Heer.*

Moving against the German screening force—slowly and disbelievingly at first, then more boldly—were 8 allied infantry and 4 cavalry divisions. The German horsemen would be asked to fight on foot, a task that the regulation issue of small quantities of carbine ammunition made next to impossible. To make matters even worse, entrenching tools were unavailable to cavalry units because prewar exercises had emphasized dismounting and firing but not digging in. The British nightmare with slit trenches on Spion Kop comes to mind.[158] Looking aghast to the west, Bülow knew it was "just a matter of time" before the British and French outflanked him. "General von Kuhl is an excellent judge of the enemy," wired a Second Army staffer sardonically to First Army, "but General Bülow is not as optimistic."[159]

He had good reason to worry. On 6–7 September, Second Army's 7.5 divisions collided with 11 divisions of the French Fifth and Ninth Armies. Like Kluck on the Ourcq, Bülow began his third major battle at 71% fighting strength, with no reserves. Artillery shells were short. Along most of the line, both armies attacked into one another. Inevitably, casualties were horendous, but the Germans, with much less support from their guns, bled more.[160] On his right, Bülow retreated, placing 1 brigade and dismounted cavalry units on a tributary of the Marne, the Petit Morin. Because Kluck, had simultaneously withdrawn 2 corps from the same area, Second Army's right flank was now in grave danger. On 8 September, D'Esperey attacked across the Petit Morin with 3 divisions. The French repeatedly bombarded Bülow's entrenched 6 battalions, sending infantry forward after every barrage.[161] But Bülow had one more card to play. On his left flank, the audacious commander

joined Hausen in a predawn assault on the French Fifth and Ninth
Armies. The dark hours were chosen to protect German infantrymen from the artillery pummeling they had suffered for 2 days. The
ploy worked, shoving the shocked defenders back for miles until the
heat of day—and French artillery—halted the attack.[162] As night fell
on 8 September, Bülow's courageous right-wing battalions, pushed
past the point of human endurance, broke and fell back in semi-
disorder. His army had lost nearly 12,500 men and was at a mere
51% of strength.[163]

Naturally, the OHL was alarmed. Moltke had assembled his general staff paladins that morning, lending a sympathetic ear to the
lone pessimist in the circle. Lieutenant Colonel von Hentsch had
served under Kuhl in peacetime but did not look as favorably on
Germany's chances as his former boss.[164] The pragmatic general
staffer had seen the depleted state of First and Second Armies firsthand, shortly before the unfolding battles on the Ourcq and Marne,
concluding that previous losses had seriously undermined their offensive punch. Hentsch's new boss, ever prone to premonitions of
impending catastrophe, believed Kluck had made a serious blunder
by withdrawing Third and Ninth corps and leaving a huge hole in
the line. Moltke selected his junior kindred spirit as the subordinate
officer best able to reach a sober, objective judgment on the scene.
It seems almost certain that he left with verbal orders to order a
retreat of First and Second Armies if he deemed it necessary. From
the beginning of his meeting with Bülow's staff, Hentsch painted a
bleak picture of Kluck's First Army. He left the Petit Morin on 9
September with an even lower assessment of Bülow's prospects: "Second Army is cinders,"[165] he told Kuhl after arriving at First Army
headquarters. Reluctantly, grudgingly—and unforgivingly—Kluck
and Bülow retreated north that afternoon.

Few—not Hentsch, certainly not Kluck or Bülow, perhaps not
even a gloomier Moltke—expected the withdrawal to be far or permanent. It was just a tactical retreat behind the Aisne-Vesle line.
The main point was that two German armies had escaped from a
certain trap. Bolstered by a new army forming at St. Quentin, the
right wing would soon reverse direction and lend support to center
and left-wing forces as they encircled Joffre's four eastern armies.[166]
Indeed, Moltke's attack proceeded steadily on 9–10 September
while the right wing pulled back. Elements of Hausen's army joined
Duke Albrecht and Prince William in an easterly push to the Meuse.
The advance proved very costly, as Fourth and Fifth Armies also
resorted to nighttime attacks to escape the bloody consequences of

France's artillery superiority. Lead units, however, were a mere 11 kilometers from the west bank of the river.[167] Any breakthrough from either bank would make all sacrifices worthwhile if it meant closing a deadly iron ring.

Moltke's bid for total victory faltered on the other side of the Meuse and Mosel. That he failed to dislodge Joffre from his fortresses—or trap him there—was due largely to a complex of heavy artillery–related difficulties. Conceived at OHL in late August, the attacks against Nancy and the five forts south of Verdun were ordered on 2 September. Crown Prince Rupprecht's Bavarians assaulted first. The French had prepared for him a foretaste of the Great War's legendary, stationary slugging matches. Along a 15-kilometer stretch that straddled the Mosel was the so-called Position de Nancy, a heavily fortified area over 2,000 meters deep that was replete with outforts, barbed wire–shielded infantry entrenchments, and hidden artillery batteries near rail lines. "The wide-eyed hopes of the heavy artillerists after their experiences with the evidently antiquated Belgian fortresses," wrote Krafft von Dellmensingen, "were disappointed here," for there was no huge, "isolated fortress" that offered "the 'fat clods' one target to attack." Rather, there were many different targets throughout the fortified area—some of them moving—because French artillery officers tended to fire their guns with terrible effect at charging infantry, then shift them by rail to new concealed positions before German batteries could respond. The Gamma 420s were especially unsuited for this kind of fighting; after being cemented in place, they could only swivel along a 45-degree arc.[168] Adding to the Bavarians' frustration was the withdrawal of two corps to northern France—in the midst of their assault on Nancy and the Toul-Epinal gap. Moreover, the OHL told Krafft to spare heavy artillery shells for Fifth Army's impending efforts around Verdun. A visit by Rupprecht to the OHL in Luxemburg did not revive sagging morale, for Moltke informed the prince that all 210-mm mortars would be withdrawn after a week, evidently for use against Verdun. Dumbfounded, Rupprecht returned to his casualty-ridden army and called off the offensive.

Prince William's attack met with no more success. The heavy artillery battalions of Fifth Army that were expected to demolish forts south of Verdun did not have sufficient shells because the 210s and 305s used at Liège, Namur, and Maubeuge had shot up most of Germany's stockpiles—hence the temptation to take munitions from Rupprecht.[169] Inadequate railroad service also delayed preparations. Although the OHL wanted William to attack the forts from their vulnerable rear west of the Meuse, where there was also higher ground, the French had blown up the tunnel out of Montmédy, blocking rail connections to the west of Verdun. Artillery preparations were painfully slow on the east bank, too, for the retreating French had so thorougly demolished tracks, signals, stations, water towers, and telegraph and telephone lines that hasty repairs restored only extremely limited service. And this situation, in turn, meant that William's heavy artillery would forego the destructive advantages of three Gamma 420s stranded in Berlin-Kummersdorf because they required much sturdier tracks and ties.[170]

Thus the pride of Max Bauer and the General Staff gathered dust in the rear, much to the anguished irritation and frustration of cannoneers who believed that the artillery proving commission and War Ministry had been right to prefer the somewhat less powerful but much more mobile, tractor-pulled M-Devices. One heavy artillerist who was stewing in Kummersdorf, Karl Justrow, placed the blame squarely on the shoulders of backward-looking higher-ups who, years earlier, had defeated proposals for an "engineering general staff" that would never have conceived or tolerated such mistakes.[171] It was not until mid-September—2 weeks after the attack had been ordered—that Germany's two M-guns made their way to the area after the siege of Maubeuge.[172]

Figure 22. Gamma 420-mm mortars moving into place on heavy-duty railroad tracks. Source: Justrow, *Die Dicke Berta.*

By then it was too late. William was forced by the destruction at Montmédy to attack the Meuse forts from the east. The assignment fell to Tenth Division, which moved against Fort Troyon, the second bastion south of Verdun, on 8 September. Bolstering the batteries of mobile 150s and 210s were four Skoda 305s.[173] These guns had helped at Liège and Namur, where they languished until a rail connection between these cities was reopened in early September. From the north they were transported by rail to Montmédy, then by steam-driven tractors to the Meuse. After the German guns belched fire and iron through the first night, tenth Division demanded the fort's surrender. The French refusal was instinctively the correct tactical decision because the Skodas had shot up their entire remaining arsenal of 36 shells—the brave Belgian defense was still paying dividends. The smaller cannons continued to bombard Fort Troyon, but 4 days went by, and still the French answer to the demands for surrender was "never." With Thirty-fourth Division nearing artillery range from the west bank—and GQG actually issuing orders for the complete abandonment of Verdun, orders that were ignored by the feisty commandant—OHL called off the attack. It was as close as the Germans would ever be to "neutralizing" the mighty fortress complex.

Late in the evening of 11 September, Moltke decided on a general retreat. Hentsch had returned to Luxemburg to report on his observations and on-the-spot actions, but the commander of all German armies believed he had to see for himself. Moltke motored to the headquarters of Third Army, the center of the German line, which had to hold firm as the right wing retreated. The chief of OHL was shocked by the bloodied condition of Hausen's battle-depleted divisions. Twelve days of pursuit and 5 days of nonstop fighting on the Marne had brought Third Army below 50% fighting strength. During the night French attacks had inflicted more heavy losses on the Twenty-fourth Reserve Division while it tried to maintain contact with a retreating Second Army on its right.[174] Three weeks of fighting had taught the French that there were high returns to be earned from striking weak German reserve units. Moltke drove next to Bülow's headquarters, finding there even more reason for alarm. "That night General Moltke returned to Imperial Headquarters very ill," recalled his operations chief. "The mental and physical stress of this day was too much for his already slipping health."[175] Orders went out to Hausen, Duke Albrecht, and Prince William on 12 September for a withdrawl north of Verdun.

Germany's new army arrived on the Aisne that same day, halting the allied advance from the Marne—and ending the war of forward movement on the western front. To that date, Germany and France had each lost over 350,000 soldiers.[176]

Germany reaped a bitter harvest in August and September 1914. The bold notion of winning the opening campaign quickly by a powerful outflanking stroke through Belgium had had a desperate quality ever since Schlieffen conceived it. The tradeoff for provoking Belgium and England, however, was a superiority of numbers in one region of the western front. Indeed, it was in Belgium that Moltke probably missed his best chance of "rolling the iron dice" and winning. Like Schlieffen's operational plans of 1898–1904, OHL's wartime chief was tempted to win crippling if not total victories on the frontier when quantities of men and munitions were greatest and with time to spare for the relatively short transport of troops east. All indications are that he strove to outflank France's formidable line of fortresses from the north and penetrate it from the south, thereby neutralizing these forts and destroying numerous enemy corps in the process. That Moltke lost on the promising northern flank was attributable to an overall reconnaissance failure, Kluck's semi-insubordination, and lines of pursuit by Third and Fourth Armies that permitted Lanrezac's escape. Outmoded tactics also lessened the chances of victory. The prewar reforms and innovations of Einem and Moltke were not "too little," but they came "too late" to completely root out the effects of decades of interservice rivalry and conservative, sometimes technophobic thinking. The result at Liège, Halen, the Sambre, and Mons was a costly breakdown of cooperation between infantry and artillery, as well as the frequent adoption of backward cavalry and infantry assault formations. Nearly as great as the cost of a brilliant opportunity missed, however, was the squandering of thousands of troops that would be sorely needed on the Ourcq and the Marne.

The use of reserves and ersatz divisions as frontline troops was another problematic aspect of that summer's campaign. On the one hand, the GQG was caught off guard by this practice, underestimating German strength in the first battles all along the frontier. On the other hand, marching with no heavy artillery, half as many field cannons, and fewer machine guns, these divisons were vulnerable to attacks by French regulars. Time and again Joffre struck these weak spots of the line. The costliest strikes for Germany were those that contributed to failure on the flanks: in the Ardennes on

22 August, for Duke Albrecht had to bolster his panicking reserve corps rather than wreaking havoc on Lanrezac, and at Lunéville on 25 August, for Rupprecht had to fall back rather than continue an assault on Epinal that promised to roll up the southern end of the fortress line.

The inadequacy of prewar technological and economic decision making was also apparent from the beginning to the end of the campaign. The C-96nA was not able to outgun and outduel the French 75, nor were there enough howitzers. Decades of effort by many factions that advocated their adoption had crumbled under the pride and know-it-all arrogance of the field artillery. Tens of thousands of German infantrymen paid a steep price. The General Staff's insistence on its immobile version of the 420-mm howitzer also contributed to the artillery's failure. The Gamma version was ineffective at Nancy, and none could make it overland to finish the campaign at Verdun. Moreover, the inability of Schubert and Ludendorff to convince superiors of the need to stockpile more shells was tragic because German armies were consequently bludgeoned on the Ourcq and Marne, and dreams of double envelopment were dashed on the Meuse and Mosel.

On 8 October 1914, Schubert brought the unpleasant reality of German shell shortages to the kaiser's attention: "And who is to blame for the fact that we have so little ammunition?" queried the indignant head of state. "What were you doing all of those years as my Inspector General of Artillery?"[177] When Schubert replied that in 1910 he had delivered a detailed report on this subject in the presence of the emperor, war minister, and chief of the General Staff, an embarrassed William admitted sheepishly that he now remembered. Always quick to recover his regal posture, however, the kaiser promised Schubert that after the war the artillery would receive a billion marks from war reparations to make everything right again. But neither victory nor reparations—nor, in fact, a reigning kaiser on hand to keep such fatuous promises—were destined to be part of Germany's grim harvest in the Great War.

CHAPTER 9

DENOUEMENT

GENERAL KARL VON EINEM, commander of the German Third Army, left his headquarters northeast of Rheims and drove to the front. The exhilarating, hope-filled days of 1914, when he had led the Seventh Corps under Bülow, were a distant memory in the midst of Europe's Great War. The artillery, especially the bigger guns, was master now, so it was fitting that Einem mounted the battery commander's observation tower and peered south over his troops. The battle-hardened general and former minister of war was not surprised by what he saw, but somehow it saddened him. Empty and desolate, the unplanted fields were criss-crossed by trenchworks whose makeshift tin roofs glistened white in the summer sun. Nothing stirred. No human being could be seen, but hidden away in their cavelike quarters was the "strength of Germany." No one saw this infantry force unless it had to attack or defend. "I, and all of the staffers in the rear, have it good," Einem thought to himself. "We sure have it better than those who have to spend their lives in this desert of trenches out here."[1]

Sixty kilometers northeast of Einem's tower lay Villa Belleaire. Kaiser William II moved to this exquisite residence in 1915, forcing the locals to pay for the ostentatious landscaping and furnishings for this "jewel chest"[2] of a mansion. While Einem's men huddled in their trenches in that summer of 1916, the monarch took 80 soldiers away from the hay harvest to build a riding path. When not trotting around on it, William took excursions to the region's castles, toured nearby Sedan, dined with his chiefs, played cards, talked about art and architecture, and occasionally attended to the conduct of the war.[3] Except for naval affairs, the war took little time from his idle day, for the generals excluded him from most of the decision making. Although he largely accepted this fate, he did complain that he could "go back and live in Germany if I'm of so little use."[4]

William and his aging entourage visited Einem's headquarters 2 weeks later. The awkward appearance of his sovereign, out in the elements and close to battle, gave the general more pensive moments. The kaiser led a luxurious life before the war, playing at soldier but dreaming of peace. This was not a king's role in the divine order of things that necessitated brutal wars. To his credit, William was bearing up fairly well. Still, Einem pitied the man. The future of the monarchy appeared especially bleak after the embarrassing failure of the crown prince at Verdun.[5]

Soon the kaiser departed for the relatively easy life in Charleville, and Einem went back to the grisly business of running the war on his stretch of the western front.

War of Attrition

The failure of the German Army to defeat France in 1914 allowed the nightmarish scenario of prewar games and exercises to come true: a long slugging match on two fronts. The great victory over the Russians at Tannenberg could not prevent this.[6] Faced with an intensifying, widening, and deadlocked war, Germany invested heavily in weapons that had proven themselves since August 1914 or in new technologies that promised victory. The shipyards turned out 52 submarines in 1915, for instance, laying the keels for another 108 that put to sea in 1916. Germany had started the war with only 29 U-boats.[7] On land, machine gun detachments and howitzer batteries received the lion's share of resources. Extremely valuable during many battles of the early campaigns, the "devil's paint brush" became an indispensable addition to infantry firepower with the advent of trench warfare. Thus, Germany's prewar stock of 2,450 machine guns was impressively expanded to 8,000 in 1915. Monthly manufacturing totals rose from 200 to 600 that year, accelerating geometrically to 2,300 by mid-1916 as factories perfected methods of mass production.[8]

The monthly production of field cannons jumped eightfold during the same period, doubling stockpiles to 8,000. There was also an increased emphasis in the armaments works on the 105-mm howitzer. This new workhorse of Germany's field artillery rose from 14% of all field guns in late 1914 to about 30% in 1916.[9] The C-96nA, however, was gradually phased out of existence, refitted in mid-1915 with howitzer gun carriages to increase firing speed at high degrees of barrel elevation. Old C-96 barrels were finally replaced with longer tubes in 1916–1917.[10] The heavy artillery output grew fivefold to sixfold throughout 1915 and early 1916, with 70% of new production devoted to 150-mm howitzers. The biggest German gun in the field had proven its worth for a war of movement, as well as for the static slugfests that characterized fighting in France in 1915. The stock of 150s expanded meteorically from 416 in August 1914 to around 3,000 by early 1916.[11]

It was an important sign of what Germany was planning, however, that armaments factories also turned out over a hundred 210s, 22 Beta 305s, 2 new long-range 380s, 10 mobile M-420s, and 5 Gamma 420s—altogether a doubling of the country's prewar supply of the heaviest siege monsters.[12] Indeed, as he analyzed Germany's wartime prospects in late 1915, Erich von Falkenhayn, OHL chief since Moltke's failure, believed that technology held out great promise for total victory in the new year. He reckoned that an attack on Verdun, supported by an unprecedented buildup of German artillery, would break up French defenses and permit another drive on Paris.[13]

The honor of delivering the coup de grace was given to Crown Prince William, still commanding the German Fifth Army, north of Verdun. Falkenhayn, a royal favorite himself, wanted to bolster monarchical rule in Germany by letting the heir win a great victory, as William I had done in 1866 and 1870.[14] In reality, details of the assault were negotiated among the OHL; the War Ministry; and General Schmidt von Knobelsdorf, the prince's dictatorial chief of staff and overbearing military mentor from prewar days. Through January and early February 1916, the buildup proceeded on the east bank of the Meuse with alacrity and stealth. In camouflaged positions behind ridges and hills were 512 field guns and 631 heavy pieces, including 18 of the 210s and 26 of Germany's giant 305s and 420s. More than 2 million shells were stacked and ready.[15] "In the woods ringing Verdun," writes Alistair Horne, "there was hardly room for a man to walk between the massed cannon and ammunition dumps."[16]

After a day-long bombardment, nine crack divisions went over the top on 21 February. By early March, however, William's hopes of plucking Verdun as a glorious prize of war were dashed.[17] The battle had turned into industrialized, mechanized, high-tech killing on a horrendous scale. By June 1916, 1,777 French artillery pieces were locked in a colossal gunfight with 2,066 German cannons.[18] The crown prince's batteries had fired almost 22 million shells in 4 months—five and a half times the prewar stockpile. Even though the monthly output of shells had risen from 147,000 to 3 million since September 1914, German artillerymen were firing ammunition faster than one of the most productive nations in the world could replace it.

The wear and tear on guns designed to fire no more than a total of 2,000 (larger cannons) to 12,000 shells was also tremendous. Excessive firing warped and expanded tubes, and detonations in barrels destroyed them beyond repair. The Fifth Army's workshops fixed 945 cannon between February and May, and premature detonations ruined another 571. Only 4 of the original 13 420s were still firing, their barrels so worn out that shells keyholed (i.e., turned end over end in flight), greatly lessening their penetrating power.[19] Eventually, the War Ministry issued regulations to identify the slower optimal rate of daily fire required to maximize barrel life and utilize national resources most efficiently.[20] Thus, Germany applied microeconomic principles previously restricted to the mundane world of business to the life-and-death business of war.

Capital replacement would prove much easier than the depressing challenge of replenishing human capital. Falkenhayn's strategy was not working. By early May, Verdun had cost the Germans about 120,000 soldiers and the French, 133,000. The Fifth Army had rotated 26 divisions into the battle, the French 40. "We are all screws in a machine that wallows forward, nobody knows whereto," lamented one disillusioned German soldier. Fighting at Verdun had become a hellish "day's work."[21] The carnage sickened War Minister Wild von Hohenborn, but he admitted he was slowly learning to look at monthy casualty reports "in purely mercantile terms . . . much like a business man looking over his balance books." But because Verdun was exceeding "the limits of human endurance," he concluded that "machines must come to replace men."[22]

Almost as if it had a life of its own, the battle raged to a climax without any substitution of machines for men. The Germans launched a final push on 8 June but failed to break through. A second "final" push on 11 July failed again. With the British attack-

ing along the Somme River, Fifth Army's artillery buildup was gradually reduced to meet this threat. The battle entered its final stage
in August as the French veered to the offensive, regaining much of
the east bank by December. The French boast, "You will not let them
pass," had not been idle. Verdun cost Germany over 222,000 dead,
badly maimed, or missing. An additional 350,000 wounded were
able to return from hospital to the "Meuse killing mill" or the frightening artillery action on the Somme.[23]

There was also a steep political price to pay. Falkenhayn's commitment of resources to Verdun was criticized throughout upper
state and army echelons as an irrational waste of manpower and
matériel. The kaiser withdrew support from his favorite and reluctantly gave supreme command to the ambitious, irreverent, and
haughty duo of Paul von Hindenburg and Erich Ludendorff.[24] In
appointing them, William passed much of his little remaining monarchical authority to his army. Just as harmful to the throne was the
widespread criticism of Verdun by the common soldiers, who regarded the 9-month battle as "a regular hell"[25] that would end in
death or hideous disfigurement. "The Meuse mill ground up the
hearts of the soldiers as much as their bodies,"[26] recalled the crown
prince, but this was charitable phrasing. The real situation on the
front lines was worse, for discipline gradually deteriorated, orders
required policelike enforcement, and incidents of desertion and surrender multiplied. "The great patriotic feelings turn dull, the big
words small," wrote one veteran. "Heroes become victims, volunteers
slaves; life is one hell." Faith in higher authority dissipated as battle-
weary soldiers were transformed into cynics, agnostics, and antimon-
archists.[27]

Indeed, the entire plot to bolster monarchism with a great
"newspaper victory"[28] backfired miserably. It would have been more
"appropriate and important for the monarchical principle," mused
Karl von Einem, had Falkenhayn transfered the crown prince to the
eastern front, where breakthrough victories were being won. As it
was, William was blamed for "the evil events at Verdun."[29] The extent
of this public relations debacle was magnified as more and more
divisions saw action on the Meuse—the total skyrocketed over 10
months from 9 to 48, roughly a third of the army. In letters home,
soldiers lambasted and ridiculed the kaiser's son, who led a good
life with loose women while his men died. Letters from loved ones
at home complained of privations during the brutally cold "turnip
winter" while the crown prince constructed his beautiful Cecilienhof

in Potsdam. William deserved some of this devastating criticism, but it was one of the supreme political ironies of the Great War that he had tried to end the murderous losses, only to be foiled repeatedly by Knobelsdorf and Falkenhayn. Meanwhile, his reputation plummeted so precipitously that Hindenburg had to order unit commanders to halt the malicious rumors spreading in the ranks about the crown prince's guilt for the defeat at Verdun.[30]

The problems of "the future Kaiser"[31] were distressing to all true monarchists. By itself the scandal would not have been so very troubling, for William was years away from inheriting power. Combined with the declining public image of the kaiser himself, however, it gave greater cause for worry. Indeed the monarchy's legitimacy crisis was worsening.

Silent Dictatorship

The kaiser's nerves were already severely overtaxed when war broke out.[32] Nine years of vacillation between "William the Peaceful" and "William the Warlike" had exacted a heavy toll on a monarch who had never learned to cope with the anxieties generated by each role. War itself was too much for him. As the shock brigades assaulted Liège, William took to his bed, overcome by depression. A series of psychological highs and lows moved in unison with Germany's battlefield fortunes until November, when depression finally won out. "If people in Germany think I am the Supreme Warlord, they are grossly mistaken," lamented the kaiser. "The General Staff tells me nothing and never asks my advice."[33]

William's military function declined in importance through 1915 and early 1916. He could not be pulled away from his conspicuously indolent life of leisure unless conflicting state factions were so deadlocked over war policies that they needed his decision. "Once a crisis passed, William returned to the sidelines, was fed misinformation or half-truths, and was treated as a necessary bother rather than as a supreme warlord whose professional military figure had value," observes historian Lamar Cecil. "Only when a new unresolvable difficulty arose did the Kaiser again resume any importance."[34] Very alarming to worried monarchists such as Naval Cabinet Chief Alexander von Müller was the fact that William seemed resigned to this fate. When Müller tried to report on naval matters, he was shocked to find the monarch "dominated by the lone thought: 'Just don't bother me with it.' "[35] Always restless and desirous of distractions, he now seemed to require constant escapes from the painful reality of his marginal political and military importance.

The military's silent dictatorship tightened as a third season of slaughter yielded to a fourth. The appointment of Hindenburg and Ludendorff to head OHL in August 1916 further undercut the kaiser, for both generals were determined to keep William permanently on the sidelines. As Ludendorff's right hand man, Max Bauer, put it, "The Kaiser must be almost completely shut out because his wavering weakness would ruin everything in all the major decisive questions."[36] Hindenburg and Ludendorff manipulated the kaiser or were more brusk if they had to be, but one by one the critical decisions were made by them, not him. In January 1917, the military united around their demand for unrestricted submarine warfare. Next the pushy duo insisted on replacing "defeatist" Chancellor Bethmann Hollweg with a strongman to control the home front while they won a great victory. There were historical precedents for propping up the monarchy in moments of weakness: Frederick William III summoned Baron von Stein in 1806, and William I called the great Bismarck to office in 1862.[37] In July, Hindenburg and Ludendorff threatened to resign if Bethmann were not dismissed. "Now I can just abdicate," William said dejectedly as he caved in and complied. The defeated kaiser was not even consulted on the replacement, Georg Michaelis, a nonentity and lackey of the High Command. "Bethmann's resignation, dictated by the army with little attention to William's feelings and virtually no acknowledgement of his prerogative," concludes Cecil, "was the abdication in principle that would occur in fact in November 1918."[38]

What remained of 3 decades of army anxiety about the potentially disastrous consequences of waging war under William II's command was allayed. The de facto dictators from OHL were now free to pursue a hegemonic victory without the domestic disruptions and controversies that could have resulted from an outright military coup.[39] The army's banishment of the emperor from military and political decision making undermined the monarch by shutting out the head of state, as well as by exacerbating his yearning for idle distractions and psychic peace.[40] That much of this occurred during the year of Verdun proved disastrous for his public image.[41]

The irreverent tough men of the Pan-German League reentered the story at this point. The "hurrah" patriotism of August 1914 had not impressed them. Even before Liège fell, August Keim doubted whether "the present rulers"[42] were tough enough to produce victory. The failure to defeat enemy forces that autumn and winter sent another member, superpatriot Alfred Hugenberg, into a rage against William's incompetent leadership. If Germany's brave people went under, he wrote, the kaiser's name would head "this terrible chapter of world history."[43] Bethmann's refusal to declare unrestricted submarine warfare while land forces were stalemated on all continental fronts was a near-treasonous act to the pan-Germans. They were infuriated that William and his chancellor refused to fight with all technological means, as did the blockading British. Keim saw this weakness as an enervating consequence of decades of pacifism. "And I don't need to remind you," he wrote Heinrich Class, "who the Pacifist-in-Chief was all of these years." The dismissal in March 1916 of Alfred von Tirpitz, a relentless crusader for lifting the last barriers to all-out naval warfare, was a bloody shirt to men like Class and Keim, who believed fervently that Germany's best fighters had been stifled by traditional fuddy-duddies like Kaiser William II.[44]

Tirpitz's martyrdom triggered a concerted pan-German propaganda effort against the crown that spring and summer. They raised funds to reissue *If I Were the Kaiser* and flooded kiosks, cigar stores, barber shops, and corner pubs with thousands of copies of fliers and pamphlets that scurrilously attacked William's motives and behavior. Secret meetings were held all over Germany to mobilize support. The war had broken down the kaiser, they charged, into a crazed religious zealot who prayed for deliverance and spoke with Jesus in the royal bedchamber. The "half-English" monarch refused to unleash the Zeppelins against England, it was said, because he had deposited money in the Bank of England. Worse still, the pan-Germans argued that William ignored his navy's urgings to step up submarine warfare, starve the British into submission, and end the war quickly and victoriously. Instead, hundreds of thousands of German men were dying needlessly at Verdun because of the kaiser's pro-English sympathies.[45]

The pan-German campaign found acceptance among the broad middle strata of the population as a result of other rumors that were beginning to spread. Months of public assurances that the French Army was breaking at Verdun, followed by mounting casualties, repeated attacks, and more promises of victory, had eroded trust in the political establishment. "We have fostered an evil optimism whose prophecies could never be fulfilled," wrote Maximilian Harden in July 1916.[46] Moreover, 2 years of wartime demands and blockade-short supplies, sent food prices soaring. Facing increasing hardships at home, servants in scores of royal palaces across Germany broke faith and told all they knew—or believed they knew—about the kaiser's opulent lifestyle of multicourse meals and eccentric day trips.[47] "Let them eat cake" stories, embellished with every retelling, mixed and merged with rumors about the crown prince's mistresses and mansions—and allegedly murderous disregard for the lives of Fifth Army soldiers. By August, police were searching homes, seizing papers, and making arrests. The damage was irreversible, however, for state officials admitted that rightist venom was weakening the people's will to persevere and "undermining state authority—above all crown authority—in a highly dangerous fashion."[48]

The ascent of Hindenburg and Ludendorff eliminated some of the root causes of Germany's legitimacy crisis. The termination of offensive operations at Verdun and the initiation of unlimited submarine warfare reduced dissent in the ranks and among officers. The redoubled productive efforts of the "Hindenburg Program" raised army morale as greater numbers of machine guns, heavy artillery, airplanes, and munitions arrived in forward lines. Although Falkenhayn's team had made significant contributions to the buildup,[49] soldiers and civilians alike credited the heroes of Tannenberg for all the improvements, not William II or his previous General Staff chief.[50] This stark reality explains the widespread conviction in Germany that Hindenburg and Ludendorff were "untouchable" from above, as Karl von Einem put it rejoicingly. It was a "good feeling" to know, he added, that "no king or emperor can do anything about it."[51] Another officer, Ludwig von Beck, described the indispensability, particularly of Ludendorff, even more forcefully: "Against Ludendorff the 'Dictator'—and he was the eminently competent, clever, and energetic one—there was no protest." If anyone had tried to unseat the man, "even if it were the Kaiser," he would have been "branded by the people as the instigator of defeat, then stoned—so deeply entrenched was the trust of the people and the troops in Ludendorff."[52] There was no improvement after the fall of 1916, therefore, in the plummeting public image of the nation's sovereign.

The collapse of the Russian monarchy in March 1917 brought new public relations challenges to German political leaders worried about their own system's sagging legitimacy. A conference in May, attended by representatives of OHL, Military Cabinet, War Ministry, Reich Chancellery, and various civilian ministries, proposed drastic remedies. The kaiser should be seen more in public, performing charitable functions, visiting the homes of the poor and the bedsides of the wounded, listening to the problems of workers in factories and mines, and conferring in Berlin with party leaders and industrialists. His trips should always have an announced practical purpose. Press releases and official newsreels had to cover these "events," as well as portray the simplicity of the emperor's wartime lifestyle at the front.[53] Although William gradually came to realize the value of these recommendations, it was too late, judging by the kinds of things said about him that summer. Thus, the arrest of a theologian in Königsberg for making slanderous charges against the emperor prompted another right-wing extremist, Hans von Liebig, to lambaste the legal establishment. The minister of justice was no doubt aware, wrote Liebig, "how soldiers at the front and at home, in clinics and on leave, how people on the street talk about His Majesty when anything in the least sets them off." If ministry officials took the pains to document all of these utterances, "then all of the courts in Germany would be overloaded for years with cases of lèse majesté."[54]

As someone caught in the state's investigative net, Liebig could be expected to harbor ill feelings toward William II. But his comments were mirrored by many official reports. The police kept a wary eye, for instance, on rising anti-Hohenzollern sentiment in the nation's big cities.[55] Army reports confirmed the declining respect for royal legitimacy in outlying areas. Major Weiss, General Staff chief of the First Guard Reserve Division, canvassed public opinion in many towns during the summer of 1917. He found that the kaiser had lost all touch with common people—was nowhere to be seen—and the rising resentment of hardships and anger over casualties was increasingly manifested in an ugly rejection of authority. Only the High Command was treated with respect. Somehow, Weiss concluded, Hindenburg and Ludendorff had to use their great prestige to prop up the monarchy.[56]

The testimony of Einem, Beck, and Weiss leaves little doubt about the near-legendary status of the heroes of Tannenberg in the fourth summer of fighting. Their popularity extended from the upper strata of society to many elements of the urban working class itself. Antiwar sentiment among proletarians was on the rise, however, and with its spread came rejection of both the kaiser and his awesome generalissimos. The first hint of trouble came in December 1915, when the left wing of the SPD voted against war loans. The party revolt, eventually culminating in secession, found support on factory floors, and the number of striking workers rose tenfold in 1916. Despite the kaiser's promise of democratic reforms in April 1917, the strike volume expanded another five times that year as laborers protested shop conditions, the state, and the war. Over 1,300,000 would strike in 1918.[57] In July 1917, a Reichstag majority led by the SPD gave vent to some of this popular ill feeling by passing a Peace Resolution that demanded a negotiated peace and return to the status quo ante in Europe.

The OHL had already fired Bethmann and replaced him with Michaelis. The Peace Resolution made it clear, however, that army command needed to expand its own popular base rather than expending scarce political energies on a hopelessly moribund monarchy. The army's propaganda effort began that summer. Special speakers gave "Instruction for the Fatherland," spreading the patriotic word among soldiers at the front and citizens at home. The emphasis in their talks was on sacrifice for *Germany* : to uphold its greatness, to be worthy of its past glories, and to fight to the end to ensure a solid *German* future. References to the Kaiserreich or its beleaguered monarchy were scrupulously avoided. The only exception was Frederick the Great, whose exploits against encircling enemies were part of German legend. Paeans to the nation, not to the monarchy, were the only effective antidotes to the strikers.[58]

This stark reality was obvious to other men of the German Right. While the Reichstag readied its challenge to OHL, a broad coalition of nationalist organizations, with the Leipzig Cartel at its core, prepared to found the so-called Fatherland Party.[59] Led by Wolfgang Kapp, a disgruntled Conservative Party member and superpatriot, the new organization issued its first public appeal on Sedan Day, 2 September 1917. The party's ostensible goal was to rally the nation behind OHL's bid for a smashing victory that would be followed by wide-ranging annexations and undisputed mastery in Europe. Behind the scenes, Kapp's circle wanted to legitimize a military dictatorship or government above the parties, headed preferably by Tirpitz, chairman of the Fatherland Party.[60] If this was not possible— for Hindenburg and Ludendorff preferred their silent dictatorship as long as the war lasted[61] —Kapp was prepared to spearhead opposition to the Left in new elections. Barring this development, the party would exert pressure on the current parliament to rescind its Peace Resolution.

It is significant, however, that the party agenda did not include the bolstering of monarchism. The discussion of a party name made this obvious, as nationalistic and militaristic symbols like Bismarck, Hindenburg, and Unity were considered rather than King, Kaiser, or Crown.[62] The point was made even clearer when *Vorwärts* , the SPD paper, sought to discredit the Fatherland Party by associating it with a "League of the Kaiser-Faithful" that had surfaced from Conservative Party circles in November 1917. Within days, Tirpitz publicly, forcefully—and genuinely—dissociated the Fatherland Party from the league's goal of relegitimizing monarchism.[63]

Indeed, William II seemed irrelevant to the Left-Right political struggle that dominated German politics in the war's final winter. When, for instance, a trade union–backed organization was formed to counterbalance Kapp's party, it was called the People's League for Freedom and Fatherland.[64] Monarchy was no longer a valued and powerful symbol in the populist- and nationalist-charged rhetoric of German politics.

This legitimacy crisis had begun years earlier as an internal army issue. Worried by the kaiser's contradictory and amateurish views on technology, tactics, and strategy, army leaders dashed his dream of leading armies in battle. When William's personal limitations became public after the Daily Telegraph Affair, military men undermined his ability to resist their judgment about when to go to war. After the army got its war, battlefield failures brought Ludendorff and Bauer to the fore. Like right-radicals outside the army, they had little use for the kaiser. William languished embarrassingly in idleness as the public image of monarch and heir declined precipitously. The only question in 1918 seemed to be which system— military dictatorship or democracy—would replace the bankrupt and illegitimate monarchy.

War's End

The forest of Crepy-Fourdrain concealed sinister secrets. Deep inside the primeval woods was a naked concrete command post next to a man-made clearing. Its stark, cold walls, dripping with dew from an early morning fog, contrasted garishly with the greenery and chirping of springtime. Uniformed men entered and walked to a map table, then peered outside at their colossal charge. Clinking and clanking as it cranked to higher degrees of elevation, a monstrous metallic tube seemed to rise out of the misty forest floor. Over 100 feet long and weighing 200 tons, the creature waited for sustenance. Cranes hoisted a brass-tipped projectile! "Toi, toi, toi—do your job, Jeanette!" said one artilleryman affectionately, as the shell disappeared into one end.

Inside the bunker a phone rang. It was the OHL, ordering the giant gun to fire on Paris, 128 kilometers to the southwest. The order to shoot passed down the line. Thirty heavy artillery batteries stood ready to fire their guns simultaneously to provide a camouflage of sorts to prevent immediate counterbattery fire. At 7:09 A.M. on 23 March 1918, the salvo went skyward with a roar. One shell left the others far below, rocketing into the icy stratosphere at 2 kilometers per second. After 2½ minutes it reappeared in the skies high above Paris. Thirty seconds later it plummeted into the City of Light.

The gargantuan "Paris gun" shot 320 shells at the French capital that spring and summer, most exploding in the inner city.[65] Its mission was to break enemy morale as German shock divisions broke through allied lines and drove on Paris. The very existence of this hideous, high-tech cannon was a cruel mockery of the outmoded military world that had practiced its prescriptions for victory on the plains of Konitz 37 years earlier. But it was also a sign and symbol of the German Army's rapid adjustment to the brave new world spawned by Plevna, as well as by the Great War. Would it be enough?

As man faltered, machines had to take his place. Prussian War Minister Wild von Hohenborn reached this conclusion at the climax of Verdun. The duumvirate of Hindenburg and Ludendorff restated the obvious in August 1916,[66] when the famous Hindenburg program sent monthly production of war machinery to new heights. The number of heavy artillery pieces rose from 150 to 300, field cannons from 800 to 1800, and machine guns from 2,300 to 14,500. Rifle figures peaked at nearly 250,000 per month in early 1917—more than the army needed.[67] The monthly output of munitions increased from 6,000 to 12,000 tons—outpacing the production of steel shell casings, which utilized only 83% of available explosives. Indeed, the completion of finished shells was the Achilles heel of the Hindenburg program. Because allied access to world nitrate supplies and international armaments markets gave them vastly greater stockpiles, the OHL responded with a strategic retreat to the brilliantly designed trenchworks of the Siegfried Line in order to maximize explosives per kilometer of the front.[68] Hindenburg and Ludendorff also pushed for unrestricted U-boat warfare to reduce munition supplies to Britain and France.[69] The desperate gamble triggered a U.S. declaration of war in April 1917. A year later, greater numbers of American troops began to arrive in France.

After Russia signed an armistice at Brest-Litovsk in March 1918, Hindenburg and Ludendorff began to move scores of divisions to new positions behind the western front. Ludendorff was in too big a hurry to wait for their completed transfer or forward deployment. Three huge armies, comprising 62 divisions already in the west, unleashed a furious attack on 21 March 1918. The shock troops and supporting artillery units were trained in special tactics designed to pierce enemy trench lines.[70] The elite "attack divisions" were backed by 3,670 airplanes, 14,000 artillery pieces, and 23,000 trucks.[71] Although German casualties were extremely high, the allies fell back. This was the big, final push that the Paris gun in Crepy-Fourdrain was supposed to aid.

It was not to be. German losses surpassed 490,000 in early May, then soared to over 1 million in midsummer as OHL frantically shifted more replacement divisions from eastern army groups. Allied casualties were also high, but the appearance of over 1 million American soldiers in the line tipped the scales. By July, the allies were attacking. Western material advantages made German victory even more remote. As impressive as the OHL's buildup had been, the opponents' was greater: 4,500 aircraft, 18,500 cannons, 100,000 trucks, and 800 tanks that German infantrymen could not stop. The once proud and awesome army fell back and back, its soldiers tired and hungry, tens of thousands deserting or surrendering every day, and discipline barely intact.[72]

The kaiser's forces surrendered on 11 November 1918, but William II was no longer the sovereign. Rather, he was a political victim of near-mutinous conditions in the army and spreading revolution at home. A few weeks earlier, in an attempt at a last-act redemption, he had fired the impertinent and irreverent Ludendorff. Joining Hindenburg at the end was Wilhelm Groener, a General Staff professional since the 1890s. To Groener fell the unpleasant task of notifying William that an officers' poll had determined that German soldiers would not march behind their emperor to suppress the revolution. Instead, the last of the Hohenzollerns motored into Holland and the depressing obscurity of exile.[73]

Afterward, Groener singled out one thing his famous mentor had written: Everything imaginable in military technology had already been achieved, observed Alfred von Schlieffen in 1909. The head of the great chief would have shaken in disbelief, added his disciple, at the sight of warfare by massed machine guns, airplanes,

and mammoth cannons. But what good had it all done? asked Groener.[74] His mocking question reflected a kind of residual technophobia from prewar days, as well as undying respect for Schlieffen's
operational planning. Indeed, Groener, like many devotees of the
former General Staff chief, believed fervently that Germany had
squandered its best chance of winning the war when it altered
Schlieffen's last plan. The trenches, the submarines, the Americans,
and the ignominious defeat could have been avoided. Groener
blamed Moltke for taking too many troops from the right wing and
Bülow for abandoning a great northern sweep in favor of frontal
attacks across the Sambre.[75]

Groener may have been right about the futility of everything
that occurred from 1915 to 1918, but his criticism of the early days'
fighting missed the mark. As we have seen, Moltke's prescriptions
for victory stood as great a chance to succeed as Schlieffen's, probably even greater. That they failed was no fault of the operational
plans, but rather of a plethora of prewar technological decisions and
tactical preferences that impaired the implementation of these operations. In the end, the German soldier and the German monarchy
paid the ultimate price for backward-looking prejudices that had
accumulated over 4 decades of peacetime and could not be re-
formed in time. *Wie die Saat, so die Ernte.*[76]

NOTES

Introduction

1. See Hermann von Kuhl, *Der deutsche Generalstab in Vorbereitung und Durch-führung des Weltkrieges* (Berlin, 1920); Wolfgang Foerster, *Graf Schlieffen und der Weltkrieg* (Berlin, 1921); and Wilhelm Groener, *Das Testament des Grafen Schlieffen* (Berlin, 1929).

2. Eckart Kehr, "Klassenkämpfe und Rüstungspolitik im kaiserlichen Deutschland," reprinted in Hans-Ulrich Wehler (ed.), *Der Primat der Innenpolitik* (Berlin, 1970), 87–110; Bernd F. Schulte, *Die deutsche Armee 1900–1914: Zwischen Beharren und Veränderung* (Düsseldorf, 1977); for the artillery, see Volker Mollin, *Auf dem Wege zur 'Materialschlacht': Vorgeschichte und Funktionieren des Artillerie-Industrie-Komplexes im Deutschen Kaiserreich* (Pfaffenweiler, 1986). Also in this genre is Fritz Fischer, *Krieg der Illusionen: Die deutsche Politik von 1911–1914* (Düsseldorf, 1969).

3. Dieter Storz, *Kriegsbild und Rüstung vor 1914: Europäische Landstreitkräfte vor dem ersten Weltkrieg* (Berlin, 1992); and David G. Herrmann, *The Arming of Europe and the Making of the First World War* (Princeton, N.J., 1996). For an early critique of Schulte, see Dennis E. Showalter, "Army and Society in Imperial Germany: The Pains of Modernization," *Journal of Contemporary History* 18/4 (1983): 583–618. Also see Gerhard Papke and Wolfgang Petter (eds.), *Handbuch der deutschen Militärgeschichte 1648–1939* (Munich, 1979), vol. 3; Hans Linnenkohl, *Vom Einzelschuss zur Feuerwalze: Der Wettlauf zwischen Technik und Taktik im Ersten Weltkrieg* (Koblenz, 1990); and the excellent discussion by Michael Geyer, *Deutsche Rüstungspolitik 1860–1980* (Frankfurt, 1984).

4. Eric Dorn Brose, *The Politics of Technological Change in Prussia: Out of the Shadow of Antiquity 1809–1848* (Princeton, N.J., 1993).

5. See especially Dennis E. Showalter, *Railroads and Rifles: Soldiers, Technology, and the Unification of Germany* (Hamden, Conn., 1975).

6. More reflective of the struggles are Geyer, *Rüstungspolitik*, and—at least

for the infantry—the brief discussion in Martin Samuels, *Command or Control? Command, Training and Tactics in the British and German Armies, 1888–1918* (London, 1995), 73–77.

7. An allegedly more modern navy played no role in 1914 and therefore was no consolation. Doubting navy modernity, however, are Holger H. Herwig, *The German Naval Officer Corps* (Oxford, 1973); and Volker R. Berghahn, "Militär, industrielle Kriegführung und Nationalismus," *Neue Politische Literatur* 26/1 (1981): 20–25.

8. Geoff Eley, *Reshaping the Right: Radical Nationalism and Political Change after Bismarck* (New Haven, Conn., 1980); Roger Chickering, *We Men Who Feel Most German: A Cultural Study of the Pan-German League, 1886–1914* (London, 1984); Stig Förster, *Der Doppelte Militarismus: Die deutsche Heeresrüstungspolitik zwischen Status-Quo Sicherung und Aggression 1890–1913* (Stuttgart, 1985); Marilyn Shevin Coetzee, *The German Army League: Popular Nationalism in Wilhelmine Germany* (New York, 1990); Heinz Hagenlücke, *Deutsche Vaterlandspartei: Die nationale Rechte am Ende des Kaiserreiches* (Düsseldorf, 1997).

Chapter 1

1. This scene is based on Friedrich Karl's report of 31 January 1882, M. Kr. 2957, KAM; Friedrich Karl to King William, 17 June 1881, cited in Wolfgang Foerster, *Prinz Friedrich Karl von Preussen: Denkwürdigkeiten aus seinem Leben* (Stuttgart, 1910), 2:495; *MWB*, 15 January 1881, Sp. 75–78; and SMP to SWM, 25 June 1884, Sächs. Militär. Bevollm. 4497, Bl. 167, HStAD.

2. General von Pelet-Narbonne (ed.), *Das Militärwesen in seiner Entwickelung während der 25 Jahre 1874–1898* (Berlin, 1899), 592–593, 597; Christoper Duffy, *Frederick the Great: A Military Life* (London, 1995), 140–145, 148–154, 163–172; Dennis E. Showalter, *Railroads and Rifles: Soldiers, Technology, and the Unification of Germany* (Hamden, Conn., 1975); Wolfgang von Groote and Ursula von Gersdorff (eds.), *Entscheidung 1866: Der Krieg zwischen Österreich und Preussen* (Stuttgart, 1966); and Geoffrey Wawro, *The Austro-Prussian War: Austria's War with Prussia and Italy in 1866* (Cambridge, 1996).

3. Helmuth von Moltke, *Geschichte des Krieges 1870/71*, 1888, in Stig Förster (ed.), *Moltke: Vom Kabinettskrieg zum Volkskrieg: Eine Werkauswahl* (Bonn, 1992), 271–284; Foerster, *Prinz Friedrich Karl*, 2:187–216; and F. E. Whitton, *Moltke* (Freeport, N.Y. 1972), 222–27.

4. Friedrich Karl's memo of 25 January 1876 is cited in Foerster, *Prinz Friedrich Karl*, 2:493.

5. Maximilian von Poseck, "Die Kavallerie," in General von Eisenhart-Rothe, *Ehrendenkmal der Deutschen Armee und Marine 1871–1918* (Berlin, 1928), 108; Pelet-Narbonne, *Militärwesen*, 594–595.

6. Quotations from Oberstlieutenant Kaehler, *Die Preussische Reiterei von 1806 bis 1876 in ihrer inneren Entwickelung* (Berlin, 1879), 284–286.

7. See Kaehler's article in *MWB*, 16 February 1876, Sp. 262.

8. *MWB*, 19 April 1899, Sp. 919; Poseck, "Kavallerie," 108; Pelet-Narbonne, *Militärwesen*, 597–599; Foerster, *Prinz Friedrich Karl*, 2:491–492; and Kurt von Priesdorff, *Soldatisches Führertum* (Hamburg, n.d.), 8:127–129, 381.

9. Kaehler, *Preussische Reiterei*, 423.

10. SMP to SWM, 16 June 1888, Sächs. Militär. Bevollm. 4499, HStA D; Poseck, "Kavallerie," 107.

11. The tract is cited in *MWB*, 7 September 1881, Sp. 1431.

12. Ibid., 1 March 1882, Sp. 352.

13. SMP to SWM, 25 June 1884, Sächs. Militär. Bevollm. 4497, HStAD.

14. Ibid.

15. See Colmar von der Goltz, *Das Volk in Waffen: Ein Buch über Heerwesen und Kriegführung unserer Zeit* (Berlin, 1883), 47–49; Egon Freiherr von Gayl, *General von Schlichting und sein Lebenswerk* (Berlin, 1913), 53, 161–162; review of Wilhelm von Scherff's *Die Lehre von der Truppenverwendung* (Berlin, 1876) in *MWB*, 8 December 1877, Sp. 1739. For Prussian corps commanders, see Priesdorff, *Soldatisches Führertum*, vols. 7–10. For instance, Wilhelm von Heuduck, leader of the great charges at Konitz, commanded Fifteenth Corps (9:114–119), and Witzendorff headed Seventh Corps (8:127).

16. Waldersee Diary, 1 September 1888, printed in Heinrich Otto Meisner (ed.), *Denkwürdigkeiten des General-Feldmarschalls Alfred Grafen von Waldersee* (Osnabrück, 1922), 2:3. Meisner's purging of the Waldersee Diary of many anti-Semitic and anti-Catholic remarks has encouraged some historians to cross-reference the published version with the original. Because Meisner had no reason to purge comments on army tactics and technology, and obviously did not do so, I have not consulted the original.

17. *MWB*, 17 May 1879, Sp. 706.

18. Kaehler, *Preussische Reiterei*, 286. See also Pelet-Narbonne, *Militärwesen*, 600.

19. See Prince Friedrich Karl's report of 31 January 1882, M. Kr. 2957, KAM.

20. Pelet-Narbonne, *Militärwesen*, 655.

21. See E. R. Huber, *Deutsche Verfassungsgeschichte seit 1789* (Stuttgart, 1969), vol. 4; James J. Sheehan, *German History 1770–1866* (Oxford, 1989); and Eric Dorn Brose, *German History 1789–1871: From the Holy Roman Empire to the Bismarckian Reich* (Providence, R.I. 1997).

22. Manfred Messerschmidt, "Das preussisch-deutsche Offizierkorps 1850–1890," in Hanns Hubert Hofmann (ed.), *Das deutsche Offizierkorps 1860–1960* (Boppard, 1980), 28.

23. Reichstag Proceedings 69 (1882–1883/2), 22 January 1882, 993, 999, 1016–1017.

24. Ibid.

25. See the review in *MWB*, 17 November and 12 December 1877, Sp. 1635–1639, 1845–1852.

26. Cited in General major von Janson, "Die Entwickelung unserer Infanterie-Taktik seit unseren letzten Kriegen," *Beiheft zum Militär-Wochenblatt*, 1895/3, 106.

27. Ibid., 106–109. See also Showalter, *Railroads and Rifles*, 83–116; Wawro, *Austro-Prussian War*, passim; and Martin Samuels, *Command or Control? Command, Training and Tactics in the British and German Armies, 1888–1918* (London, 1995), 64–68.

28. Whitton, *Moltke*, 250–251.

29. Quotations from Moltke's *Geschichte des Kriegs 1870/71*, 293.

30. See Alfred von Schlieffen's recollection, cited in Hans Ritter, *Kritik des Weltkrieges: Das Erbe Moltkes und Schlieffens im grossen Kriege* (Leipzig, 1921), 31.

31. Ibid.

32. Michael Howard, *The Franco-Prussian War: The German Invasion of France, 1870–1871* (New York, 1962), 175. See also Wolfgang von Groote and Ursula von Gersdorff, *Entscheidung 1870: Der Deutsche-Französische Krieg* (Stuttgart, 1970).

33. Moltke, *Geschichte des Krieges 1870/71*, 295; Janson, "Entwickelung unserer Infanterie-Taktik," 110; and Howard, *Franco-Prussian War*, 175–76.

34. Cited in Curt Jany, *Die Königlich Preussische Armee und das Deutsche Reichsheer 1807 bis 1914* (Berlin, 1933), 4:260.

35. Dieter Storz, *Kriegsbild und Rüstung vor 1914: Europäische Landstreitkräfte vor dem Ersten Weltkrieg* (Berlin, 1992), 27–28.

36. Janson, "Entwickelung unserer Infanterie-Taktik," 107–108, 114; August von Boguslawski, *Taktische Darlegungen aus der Zeit von 1859 bis 1892* (Berlin, 1892), 14–15; Walter Görlitz, *The German General Staff: Its History and Structure 1657–1945* (London, 1953), 104.

37. Cited in Janson, "Entwickelung unserer Infanterie-Taktik," 110.

38. Ibid., 110–111.

39. Ibid., 114; *MWB*, 29 December 1877, Sp. 1846.

40. Quotations from Janson, "Entwickelung unserer Infanterie-Taktik," 111–112.

41. Gayl, *Schlichting*, 46.

42. Boguslawski, *Taktische Darlegungen*, 16–17; Janson, "Entwickelung unserer Infanterie-Taktik," 113.

43. *MWB*, 29 December 1877, Sp. 1846.

44. Quotations in Pelet-Narbonne, *Militärwesen*, 551, 559–560. The chapter on infantry tactics was written by August Keim, who had been a company commander from 1878 to 1880. See his description of army conservatism in *Erlebtes und Erstrebtes: Lebenserinnerungen von Generalleutnant Keim* (Hanover, 1925), 34. See also *MWB*, 12 December 1877, Sp. 1755–1756.

45. Waldersee Diary, 8 May 1880, in Meissner, *Denkwürdigkeiten*, 1:203–204; Storz, *Kriegsbild*, 28.

46. Pelet-Narbonne, *Das Militärwesen*, 551.

47. Sigismund von Schlichting, "Über das Infanteriegefecht," *Beiheft zum Militär-Wochenblatt*, 1879, 45.

48. Ibid., 38, 39, 47–48, 52, 53, 56.

49. The German Army had issued entrenchment tools to the infantry after 1871. See *MWB*, 1 July 1882, Sp. 1037.

50. Schlichting, "Infanteriegefecht," 42, 47, 49, 54, 58–62.

51. Ibid., 40.

52. Ibid., 45

53. Gayl, *Schlichting*, 47–48.

54. For a discussion of the polemics, see Joachim Hoffmann, "Die Kriegslehre des General von Schlichting," *Militärgeschichtliche Mitteilungen* 1 (1969): 8, 10–11.

55. See Kessel's "Zur Taktik der Infanterie von 1880," *Beiheft zum Militär-Wochenblatt*, 1880, 331–398. Quotations on 391, 392.

56. Cited in Gayl, *Schlichting*, 85.

57. *MWB*, 10 March 1880, Sp. 347–348.

58. Ibid., 21 February 1883, Sp. 290–292.

59. For the strength of this myth after 1871, see M. Schwarte, *Die Technik*

im Weltkrieg (Berlin, 1920), 2–3, 8; and Ritter, *Kritik des Weltkrieges*, 29–32, 248.

60. Rudolf Wille, *Über die Bewaffnung der Feld-Artillerie*, in KA(P) 1515, Bl. 84, HStAD.

61. *MWB*, 4 August 1880, Sp. 1139; and Hoffmann, "Kriegslehre des Schlichting," 11.

62. Cited in Hoffmann, "Kriegslehre des Schlichting," 10.

63. *MWB*, 25 December 1880, Sp. 1927; 15, 22, 26, 29 January and 2 February 1881, Sp. 79, 133, 149, 171, 187.

64. Ibid., 16 July 1884, Sp. 1177; 1 August 1885, Sp. 1640; and 22 March 1887, Sp. 602; see Priesdorff, *Soldatisches Führertum*, 7:404–405, 8:230. Germany decided for a repeater in early 1884 (SMP to SWM, 5 February 1884, Sächs. Militär. Bevollm. 4497, Bl. 16, HStAD).

65. For this paragraph and the thesis of feudalization, see Eckart Kehr, "Klassenkämpfe und Rüstungspolitik im kaiserlichen Deutschland," reprinted from the 1920s in Hans-Ulrich Wehler (ed.), *Der Primat der Innenpolitik* (Berlin, 1970), 87–110; Franz Carl Endres, "Soziologische Struktur und ihr entsprechende Ideologien des deutschen Offizierkorps vor dem Weltkriege," *Archiv für Sozialwissenschaft und Sozialpolitik* 58/2 (1927): 282–319; Günther Martin, *Die bürgerlichen Exzellenzen: Zur Sozialgeschichte der preussischen Generalität 1812–1918* (Düsseldorf, 1979); Manfred Messerschmidt, "Das preussisch-deutsche Offizierkorps 1850–1890," and Wilhelm Deist, "Zur Geschichte des preussischen Offizierkorps 1888–1918," in Hofmann, *Deutsche Offizierkorps*, 21–57; Hermann Rumschöttel, *Das bayerische Offizierkorps 1866–1914* (Berlin, 1973); and Hartmut John, *Das Reserveoffizierkorps im Deutschen Kaiserreich 1890–1914: Ein sozialgeschichtlicher Beitrag zur Untersuchung der gesellschaftlichen Militarisierung im Wilhelminischen Deutschland* (Frankfurt, 1981).

66. Martin, *Bürgerlichen Exzellenzen*, 106.

Chapter 2

1. Michael Howard, *Franco-Prussian War: The German Invasion of France, 1870–1871* (New York, 1962), 205, 212–213. See also Wolfgang von Groote and Ursula von Gersdorff, *Entscheidung 1870: Der Deutsch-Französische Krieg* (Stuttgart, 1970).

2. Cited in Howard, *Franco-Prussian War*, 207.

3. Cited in Kraft Karl zu Hohenlohe-Ingelfingen, *Aus meinem Leben* (Berlin, 1907), 4:197.

4. Ibid., 4:196.

5. Cited in Howard, *Franco-Prussian War*, 216.

6. Hohenlohe, *Aus meinem Leben*, 4:200.

7. Curt Jany, *Geschichte der Preussischen Armee vom 15. Jahrhundert bis 1914* (Osnabrück, 1967), 4:161.

8. Prince Kraft zu Hohenlohe-Ingelfingen, *Letters on Artillery*, trans. N. L. Wolford, (London, [1887] 1898), 152, 153.

9. Günther Martin, "Technik und preussische Techniker des Krieges im 19. Jahrhundert," *Technikgeschichte* 39 (1972): 188. This sample of 55 commanding officers (major general and higher) from 1840 to 1860 and 54 from 1861 to 1889 found that 82% and 85%, respectively, were born in the bour-

geois class. The sample comprised of 65% artillery officers and 31% pioneers. Another study—Manfred Messerschmidt, "Das preussisch-deutsche Offizier-korps 1850–1890," in Hanns Hubert Hofmann (ed.), *Das deutsche Offizierkorps 1860–1960* (Boppard, 1980), 28—finds that 50% of Prussian regimental artillery commanders were from the bourgeois class between 1875 and 1885, but the newly ennobled (i.e., born bourgeois) were counted as noble.

10. Eric Dorn Brose, *The Politics of Technological Change in Prussia: Out of the Shadow of Antiquity 1809–1848* (Princeton, N.J., 1993), 58, 72–74, 165, 167, 174. For the army and politics in general after midcentury, see Manfred Messerschmidt, "Die politische Geschichte der preussisch-deutsche Armee," in Gerhard Papke and Wolfgang Petter (eds.), *Handbuch der deutschen Militärgeschichte 1648–1939* (Munich, 1975), vol. 2.

11. Hohenlohe, *Letters on Artillery*, 153.

12. Hohenlohe, *Aus meinem Leben*, 3:360.

13. Hohenlohe, *Letters on Artillery*, 155–156. For a detailed account of the artillery at Königgrätz, see Dennis E. Showalter, *Railroads and Rifles: Soldiers, Technology, and the Unification of Germany* (Hamden, Conn., 1975), 191–212. See also Wolfgang von Groote and Ursula von Gersdorff, *Entscheidung 1866: Der Krieg zwischen Österreich und Preussen* (Stuttgart, 1966).

14. Hohenlohe, *Letters on Artillery*, 5–6, 157; and Hohenlohe, *Aus meinem Leben*, 3:376–377.

15. Hohenlohe, *Letters on Artillery*, 157–158.

16. Ibid., 47.

17. *MWB*, 25 June 1900, Sp. 1614.

18. H. Rohne, "Die Entwicklung der modernen Feldartillerie," *VTH* 1/4 (1904): 481–482; Curt Jany, *Die Königlich Preussische Armee und das Deutsche Reichsheer 1807 bis 1914* (Berlin, 1933), 4:273.

19. Dennis E. Showalter, "Prussia, Technology and War: Artillery from 1815 to 1914," in Ronald Haycock and Keith Wilson (eds.), *Men, Machines and War* (Waterloo, Ont., 1988), 130–131.

20. Oberstlt, Marx, "Die Feldartillerie," in General von Eisenhart-Rothe, *Ehrendenkmal der Deutschen Armee und Marine 1871–1918* (Berlin, 1928), 123–125.

21. *MWB*, 6 September 1882, Sp. 1424.

22. See Adolf von Schell's article, ibid., 9 February 1876, Sp. 216.

23. Showalter, "Prussia, Technology and War," 133–134.

24. Marx, "Feldartillerie," 124–125.

25. Max Köhler, *Der Aufstieg der Artillerie bis zum Grossen Krieg* (Munich, 1938), 118.

26. See Schell's article in *MWB*, 9 February 1876, Sp. 213. For Hoffbauer and Schell, see also Volker Mollin, *Auf dem Wege zur 'Materialschlacht': Vorgeschichte und Funktionieren des Artillerie-Industrie-Komplexes im Deutschen Kaiserreich* (Pfaffenweiler, 1986), 177–179.

27. *LJB*, Bd. 5 (1878), 279.

28. Hohenlohe, *Letters on Artillery*, 164.

29. *LJB*, Bd. 5 (1878), 276–279; *MWB*, 16 March 1878, Sp. 369; Mollin, *Auf dem Wege*, 179–180; and Showalter, "Prussia, Technology and War," 129–130, 139–140.

30. SMP to SWM, 31 October 1881, Sächs. Militär. Bevollm. 4493, Bl. 149, HStAD.

31. *MWB*, 27 August 1881, Sp. 1382–1383.

32. SMP to SWM, 31 October 1881, Sächs. Militär. Bevollm. 4493, Bl. 149, HStAD.

33. SMP to SWM, 5 January 1883, Sächs. Militär. Bevollm. 4495, Bl. 5, HStAD.

34. Showalter, "Prussia, Technology and War," 128.

35. Mollin, *Auf dem Wege* . The thesis of embourgeoisment, like that of feudalization (see chap. 1, note 64), stems from the late 1920s; see Karl Demeter's *The German Officer-Corps in Society and State* (London, 1965), esp. 20–46. Building on this theme are Gerhard Ritter, *Staatskunst und Kriegshandwerk: Das Problem des "Militarismus" in Deutschland* (Munich, 1954–1964), 2:128–131; and Wiegand Schmidt-Richberg, "Die Regierungszeit Wilhelms II," in Gerhard Papke and Wolfgang Petter (eds.), *Handbuch zur deutschen Militärgeschichte* (Munich, 1979), 3:85–88.

36. For the siege of Plevna, see F. V. Greene, *The Russian Army and Its Campaigns in Turkey 1877–1878* (New York, 1879), 240, 243–244; and William McElwee, *The Art of War: Waterloo to Mons* (Bloomington, Ind., 1974), 187–206.

37. McElwee, *Art of War,* 194.

38. Heinrich Rohne, "Die Entwicklung der modernen Feldartillerie," *VTH* 1 (1904/4): 491; Mollin, *Auf dem Wege,* 176, 184–185.

39. Showalter, *Railroads and Rifles,* 144–146; Rohne, "Entwicklung," 492; Hermann Schirmer, *Das Gerät der schweren Artillerie vor, in und nach dem Weltkrieg* (Berlin, 1937), 1:40.

40. SMP to SWM, 5 January 1883, Sächs. Militär. Bevollm. 4495, Bl. 5, HStAD.

41. Karl Justrow, *Feldherr und Kriegstechnik* (Oldenburg, 1933), 261–262; General von Lauter, "Unsere Waffe: Die Entwicklung der Schweren Artillerie bis zum Weltkrieg," in Franz Nikolaus Kaiser (ed.), *Das Ehrenbuch der Deutschen Schweren Artillerie* (Berlin, 1931), 1:13.

42. Showalter, "Prussia, Technology and War," 131–132.

43. Helmuth von Moltke, *Die deutschen Aufmarschpläne 1871–1890,* ed. Ferdinand von Schmerfeld (Berlin, 1929), 65–97; Walter Görlitz, *The German General Staff: Its History and Structure 1657–1945* (London, 1953), 99–100; Gordon Craig, *The Politics of the Prussian Army 1640–1945* (New York, 1956), 273–276; Waldersee Diary, 8 March 1880, 8 May 1880, 6 December 1882, and 24 September 1883, in Heinrich Otto Meisner, *Denkwürdigkeiten des General-Feldmarshalls Alfred Grafen von Waldersee* (Osnabrück, 1922), 1:201, 203–204, 222–223, 228. For a qualifying comment on the reliability of the Waldersee Diary, see chap. 1, note 16.

44. Köhler, *Aufstieg der Artillerie,* 122.

45. Ibid., 124.

46. Mollin, *Auf dem Wege,* 208–209.

47. Schirmer, *Gerät,* 1:39–40.

48. Lauter, "Unsere Waffe." See also Köhler, *Aufstieg der Artillerie,* 126.

49. For the following, see ibid., as well as Heinrich Müller, *Die Entwicklung der deutschen Festungs- und Belagerungsartillerie in Bezug auf Material, Organisation, Ausbildung und Taktik von 1875 bis 1895* (Berlin, 1896), 187, 198–199, 230–231.

50. SMP to SWM, 19 April 1885, Sächs. Militär. Bevollm. 4499, Bl. 55, HStAD.

51. Lauter, "Unsere Waffe," 1:14–15.

52. Craig, *Politics of the Prussian Army*, 227.

53. SMP to SWM, 5 January 1883, Sächs. Militär. Bevollm. 4495, Bl. 5, HStAD.

54. Diary of Friedrich von Holstein, 30 January 1883, printed in Norman Rich (ed.), *The Holstein Papers: The Memoirs, Diaries and Correspondence of Friedrich von Holstein 1887–1909* (Cambridge, 1957), 2:31–32.

55. Ibid.

56. Craig, *Politics of the Prussian Army*, 228–229.

57. Ibid., 229.

58. Ibid., 230. For the War Ministry, Military Cabinet, and General Staff in general, see Messerschmidt, "Politische Geschichte," 2:287–327.

59. For the army's aging problem, see Waldersee Diary, 1 January 1878; 15 October 1885; 10, 13, and 14 March 1886; and 9 January 1887, in Meisner, *Denkwürdigkeiten*, 1:174, 263, 277–280, 309. Ranging from 49 to 76, Prussia's 15 corps commanders had an average age of 64 in 1886. Few were retired until the ascension of William II in June 1888. See Kurt von Priesdorff, *Soldatisches Führertum*, (Hamburg, n.d.), vols. 7–9.

60. *MWB*, 26 February 1879, Sp. 310, 312.

61. Goltz's letter is cited in Hermann Teske, *Colmar Freiherr von der Goltz: Ein Kämpfer für den militärischen Fortschritt* (Göttingen, 1957), 33.

62. Cited in *MWB*, 10 November 1886, Sp. 1847–1848.

63. Waldersee Diary, 1 September 1888 and 15 October 1885, in Meisner, *Denkwürdigkeiten*, 2:3 and 1:263.

Chapter 3

1. This scene draws on the detailed description of Bastille Day 1886 in James Harding, *The Astonishing Adventure of General Boulanger* (New York, 1971), 83–86.

2. Ludwig Rüdt von Collenberg, *Die deutsche Armee von 1871 bis 1914* (Berlin, 1922), 122; George F. Kennan, *The Decline of Bismarck's European Order: Franco-Russian Relations, 1875–1890* (Princeton N.J., 1979), 247; Prince William to Waldersee, 1 June 1886, in Heinrich Otto Meisner (ed.), *Aus dem Briefwechsel des Generalfeldmarshalls Alfred Grafen von Waldersee: Die Berliner Jahre 1886–1891* (Stuttgart, 1928), 22–23. See also *MWB*, 1 April 1885, Sp. 539–540; 27 October 1886, Sp. 1782; and 4 May 1892, Sp. 1086–1087. These figures do not include France's colonial forces in Algeria.

3. *MWB*, 24 August 1887, Sp. 1568; SMP to SWM, 23 May 1888, Sächs. Militär. Bevollm. 4502, Bl. 138, HStAD; *LJB* 25² (1898): 564–565, 607–608; and Wilhelm Balck, *Die Französische Infanterie-Taktik in ihrer Entwickelung seit dem Kriege 1870/71* (Berlin, 1902), 3–25.

4. For France's strategy and railway lines, as well as deficiences in mobilization and reserve troops, see Allan Mitchell, *Victors and Vanquished: The German Influence on Army and Church in France after 1870* (Chapel Hill, N.C., 1984), 58, 63–64, 71–82. Using older sources on Germany, Mitchell's comparisons underestimate France's position by overestimating Germany's military capabilities.

5. Harding, *General Boulanger*, 83–86.

6. Ibid., 86; Frederick H. Seager, *The Boulanger Affair: Political Crossroads of*

France 1886–1889 (Ithaca, N.Y., 1969), 47–49; Kennan, *Bismarck's European Order*, 246; and the Waldersee Diary, 10, 13, and 27 October 1886, in Heinrich Otto Meisner (ed.), *Denkwürdigkeiten des General-Feldmarshalls Alfred Grafen von Waldersee* (Osnabrück, 1922), 1:298–299.

7. Waldersee Diary, 2 February 1887, in Meisner, *Denkwürdigkeiten*, 1:312; and Otto Pflanze, *Bismarck and the Development of Germany: The Period of Fortification, 1880–1898* (Princeton, N.J., 1990), 3:218–225.

8. Bismarck to Reuss, 31 December 1885, in Fritz Stern, *Gold and Iron: Bismarck, Bleichröder, and the Building of the German Empire* (New York, 1977), 431.

9. Waldersee Diary, 29 October 1886, in Meisner, *Denkwürdigkeiten*, 1:300. See also the entries for 1 and 16 November 1886, 1:301, 303. On the reliability of the Waldersee Diary, see chap. 1, note 16. For Bismarck and Waldersee, see Konrad Canis, *Bismarck und Waldersee: Die aussenpolitischen Krisenerscheinungen und das Verhalten des Generalstabes 1882–1890* (Berlin, 1980).

10. Ibid., 1 January 1887, 1:309.

11. Ibid., 15 October and 15 November 1885, 27 October and 13 December 1886, and 5 February 1887, 1:263, 267, 299, 308, 313. See also see Gunther E. Rothenberg, "Moltke, Schlieffen and the Doctrine of Strategic Envelopment," in Peter Paret (ed.), *Makers of Modern Strategy from Machiavelli to the Nuclear Age* (Princeton, N.J., 1986), 308–309.

12. For Waldersee's confidence in Germany's repeating rifle, see Waldersee Diary, 1 November 1886, in Meisner, *Denkwürdigkeiten*, 1:301. For its secret adoption, see SMP to SWM, 5 February 1884, Sächs. Militär. Bevollm. 4497, Bl. 16, HStAD. Production of the M-71/84 is described in Captain Gothsche, *Die Königlichen Gewehrfabriken* (Berlin, 1904), 51. For the confidence in high explosives, see Prince William to Bismarck, 10 May 1888, in Meisner, *Denkwürdigkeiten*, 1:398.

13. *MWB*, 11 March and 4 July 1885, Sp. 439, 1089; *LJB* 25/2 (1898): 609–610; J. F. Maurice, *The Balance of Military Power in Europe* (Edinburgh, 1888), 165; Kennan, *Bismarck's European Order*, 247.

14. *MWB*, 16 February and 16 November 1887, Sp. 283–288, 2070; Gothsche, *Königlichen Gewehrfabriken*, 51–53.

15. For the advantages of France's breech and chamber devices, see William H. McNeil, *The Pursuit of Power Technology, Armed Force, and Society since A.D. 1000* (Chicago, 1982), 279. For the lead of the French field artillery at this time, see also *MWB*, 16 February 1889, Sp. 317–318; and Douglas Porch, *The March to the Marne: The French Army 1871–1914* (Cambridge, 1981), 43.

16. Löe to Waldersee, 13 October 1887, in Meisner, *Briefwechsel Waldersee*, 103.

17. Waldersee Diary, 20 November 1886 and 9 January 1887, in Meisner, *Denkwürdigkeiten*, 1:305, 309. For Waldersee's successful negotiations with Albedyll and Bronsart von Schellendorff, see 6 and 12 February 1887, 1:313, 316.

18. Cited in Pflanze, *Bismarck*, 3:251.

19. Ibid., 3:264–271.

20. For the war council, including reference to the kaiser's words to Tsar Alexander, see the Waldersee Diary, 17 December 1887, in Meisner, *Denkwürdigkeiten*, 1:344–345. See also John C. G. Röhl, *Wilhelm II: Die Jugend des Kaisers 1859–1888* (Munich, 1993), 742–752.

21. For Bismarck's struggle with the war party, see Röhl, *Wilhelm II*, 748–755.

22. SMP to SWM, 23 May 1888, Sächs. Militär. Bevollm. 4502, Bl. 138, HStAD; Goltz to Waldersee, 22 November 1887, and Löe to Waldersee, 26 March 1889, in Meisner, *Briefwechsel Waldersee*, 114, 247. See also *MWB*, 15 February 1890, Sp. 415.

23. Diary of Friedrich von Holstein, 13 May 1888, in Norman Rich (ed.), *The Holstein Papers: The Memoirs, Diaries and Correspondence of Friedrich von Holstein 1887–1909* (Cambridge, 1957), 2:421.

24. Waldersee Diary, 27 January, 1 September, and 3 November 1888, in Meisner, *Denkwürdigkeiten*, 1:355–356, 2:2–3, 14. For heavy artillery tests, see the reports in Sächs. Militär. Bevollm. 4502, HStAD. For the production of the M-88, see Gothsche, *Königlichen Gewehrfabriken*, 53–54.

25. Waldersee Diary, 13 and 26 November 1888 and 23 December 1889, 2:19, 23, 83.

26. Ibid., 15 April 1889, 2:48. For reference to army readiness in 1890, see the entry for 21 January 1889, 2:32.

27. *MWB*, 24 April 1889, Sp. 808, 18 June 1890, Sp. 1656; *LJB* 21 (1894): 363; Kennan, *Bismarck's European Order*, 247, 393–395.

28. Waldersee Diary, 10 October 1889, in Meisner, *Denkwürdigkeiten*, 2:69. Moltke's remark of 16 December 1887 is quoted in Röhl, *Wilhelm II*, 746.

29. Friedrich Karl's report of 31 January 1882 is located in M. Kr. 2957, KAM. For subsequent doubts, see SMP to SWM, 25 June 1884, Sächs. Militär. Bevollm. 4497, Bl. 167, HStAD.

30. Friedrich von Bernhardi, *Denkwürdigkeiten aus meinem Leben* (Berlin, 1927), 201–202.

31. For Schlotheim, see General Walther von Löe to Waldersee, 7 November 1886, in Meisner, *Briefwechsel Waldersee*, 44.

32. *MWB*, 19 April 1899, Sp. 919; Kurt von Priesdorff, *Soldatisches Führertum* (Hamburg, n. d.), 8:99; General von Poseck, "Die Kavallerie," in Ernst von Eisenhart-Rothe (ed.), *Ehrendenkmal der Deutschen Armee und Marine 1871–1918* (Berlin, 1928), 109–110; and General von Pelet-Narbonne (ed.), *Das Militärwesen in seiner Entwickelung während der 25 Jahre 1874–1898* (Berlin, 1899), 605–606.

33. In addition to Friedrich Karl and Otto von Kaehler, Karl von Schmidt, the main personality behind three-wave tactics, had died in 1875.

34. Löe to Waldersee, 7 November 1886, in Meisner, *Briefwechsel Waldersee*, 44.

35. Bernhardi, *Denkwürdigkeiten*, 113.

36. Waldersee to Bernhardi, n.d. (June 1894), ibid., 186; Waldersee Diary, 1 September 1888, in Meisner, *Denkwürdigkeiten*, 2:3.

37. Pelet-Narbonne, *Militärwesen*, 606. The cavalry chapter was written by Major Brixen-Hahn, a reformer, in 1898–1899.

38. Waldersee Diary, 12 and 13 May 1887, 1 September 1888, in Meisner, *Denkwürdigkeiten*, 1:324–326, 2:3; Poseck, "Kavallerie," 111.

39. Poseck, "Kavallerie," 110–12.

40. Waldersee Diary, 15 October 1893, 5 January 1894, 6 April 1895, in Meisner, *Denkwürdigkeiten*, 2:295, 301–302, 345. See also Hermann Teske, *Colmar Freiherr von der Goltz: Ein Kämpfer für den militärischen Fortschritt* (Göttingen, 1957), 47.

41. BMP to BWM, 22 September 1894, M. Kr. 37, KAM. For cavalry battles,

see BMP to BWM, 28 September 1893, 20 September 1895, 10 October 1896, and 15 October 1898, in M. Kr. 37 and 38.

42. Karl von Einem, *Erinnerungen eines Soldaten 1853–1933* (Leipzig, 1933), 45; Freiherr von Bissing, *Ausbildung Führung und Verwendung der Reiterei* (Berlin, 1895), 26.

43. For the struggle over regulations, see *LJB* 21 (1894): 327–328, 334; 22 (1895); 333–335.

44. Poseck, "Kavallerie," 111.

45. Teske, *Von der Goltz*, 47; Bernhardi, *Denkwürdigkeiten*, 212, 215–216.

46. The words were Löe's. See his letter to Waldersee, 26 March 1889, in Meisner, *Briefwechsel Waldersee*, 245.

47. For Waldersee's apparent intrigue against Schlichting in 1884 and the latter's revival under Winterfeld, see Priesdorff, *Soldatisches Führertum*, 8:448, and Waldersee Diary, 12 and 13 May 1887, in Meisner, *Denkwürdigkeiten*, 1: 324–326.

48. J. Alden Nichols, *The Year of the Three Kaisers: Bismarck and the German Succession, 1887–88* (Chicago, 1987), 3–18.

49. Egon von Gayl, *General von Schlichting und sein Lebenswerk* (Berlin, 1913), 59. For Pape's deterioration, see Waldersee Diary, 16 June 1888, in Meisner, *Denkwürdigkeiten*, 2:405.

50. Schlichting's *Der Kampf um eine vorbereitete Stellung* (1886) is cited in Gayl, *General von Schlichting*, 77.

51. Ibid., 85–93.

52. Ibid., 90–93; Verdy du Vernois to Waldersee, 26 April 1886, and Löe to Waldersee, 7 November 1886, in Meisner, *Briefwechsel Waldersee*, 14–15, 35; and Wilhelm Groener, *Lebenserinnerungen: Jugend—Generalstab—Weltkrieg* (Göttingen, 1957), 62.

53. Löe to Waldersee, 7 November 1886, in Meisner, *Briefwechsel Waldersee*, 43–44.

54. See Löe to Waldersee, 13 October 1887 and 7 July 1887, ibid., 103 and 92.

55. See the letters cited above, as well as Löe's letters of 9 June 1886, 3 December 1886, 6 April 1887, and 12 May 1887, ibid., 25, 57, 79, and 85.

56. Jacob Meckel, *Ein Sommernachtstraum* (Berlin, 1887); *MWB*, 21 December 1887, Sp. 2317–2330, and 4 February 1888, Sp. 239.

57. Waldersee Diary, 20 November 1886, in Meisner, *Denkwürdigkeiten*, 305. Löe was much closer to Winterfeld and Schlichting than was Waldersee, who suspected the two of intrigues against him. For Löe's opinion, see his letters to Waldersee of 27 November 1887 and 19 October 1888, in Meisner, *Briefwechsel Waldersee*, 120, 199–200.

58. Waldersee to Verdy du Vernois, 9 June 1888, in Meisner, *Briefwechsel Waldersee*, 181; *MWB*, 11 April 1903, Sp. 870–871; Gayl, *General von Schlichting*, 120–123; Dieter Storz, *Kriegsbild und Rüstung vor 1914: Europäische Landstreitkräfte vor dem ersten Weltkrieg* (Berlin, 1992), 28–31; and Martin Samuels, *Command or Control? Command, Training and Tactics in the British and German Armies, 1888–1918* (London, 1995), 71–73.

59. For the relations among Hahnke, Schlichting, Winterfeld, and the others, see Waldersee Diary, 12 May 1887, in Meisner, *Denkwürdigkeiten*, 1:324–325; Priesdorff, *Soldatisches Führertum*, 9: 232, 249, 285–286, 398; Gayl, *General von Schlichting*, 122; and Groener, *Lebenserinnerungen*, 62.

60. Even Schlichting encountered difficulties in getting his message across effectively to subordinates. See Bernhardi, who commanded a division in Fourteenth Corps, *Denkwürdigkeiten*, 183–184.

61. Löe to Waldersee, 26 March 1889, in Meisner, *Briefwechsel Waldersee*, 246.

62. Gayl, *General von Schlichting*, 122. For the reaction to the 1888 regulations, see also Samuels, *Command or Conrol*, 73–75.

63. *MWB*, 14 March 1891, Sp. 585–590.

64. See the reports of the BMP to the BWM, 30 November 1891, 28 September 1893, 20 September 1895, and 10 October 1896, in M. Kr. 37 and 38, KAM; and *LJB* 20 (1893): 300–301, 21 (1894): 312–313, 22 (1895): 321–322, and 24 (1897): 321.

65. Gothsche, *Königlichen Gewehrfabriken*, 53–54.

66. Hans Linnenkohl, *Vom Einzelschuss zur Feuerwalze: Der Wettlauf zwischen Technik und Taktik im Ersten Weltkrieg* (Coblence, 1990), 12.

67. Their number included Wilhelm von Hahnke, chief of the Military Cabinet, and Walther Bronsart von Schellendorff, Prussian minister of war after 1891. See SMP to SWM, 6 June 1894, Sächs. Militär. Bevollm. 4510, Bl. 82, HStAD.

68. BMP to BWM, 20 September 1895, M. Kr. 38, KAM.

69. SMP to SWM, 6 June 1894, Sächs. Militär. Bevollm. 4510, Bl. 82, HStAD.

70. Memo of the BWM, 30 December 1898, M. Kr. 2128. See also BMP to BWM, 17 May 1893, M. Kr. 43, KAM.

71. *MWB*, 8 February 1893, Sp. 298–303; 7 February 1894, Sp. 323; and 21 June 1894, Sp. 1633–1638.

72. Schlichting to Gayl, n.d., cited in Sigfrid Mette, *Vom Geist Deutscher Feldherren: Genie und Technik 1800–1918* (Zurich, 1938), 172. For Schlichting's retirement, as well as a discussion of the subsequent polemic, see Joachim Hoffmann, "Die Kriegslehre des General von Schlichting," *Militärgeschichtliche Mitteilungen* 1 (1969): 16–31. Schlichting's enemies at court in 1896 may have been War Minister Walther Bronsart von Schellendorff and Wilhelm von Hahnke, Schlichting's former ally. See SMP to SWM, 6 June 1894, Sächs. Militär. Bevollm. 4510, Bl. 82, HStAD. See also below, chap. 6.

73. Schlichting to Gayl, n.d., cited in Mette, *Vom Geist*, 172.

74. The only exception is an introductory reference by Bruce I. Gudmundsson, *Stormtroop Tactics: Innovation in the German Army, 1914–1918* (New York, 1989).

75. BMP to BWM, 30 November 1899, M. Kr. 39, KAM.

76. Prince William to Waldersee, 1 June 1886, in Meisner, *Briefwechsel Waldersee*, 22–23.

77. Two of the most influential were Voigts-Rhetz's adjutant, Major Leydhecker, and the inspector of the Second Artillery Inspection in Berlin, Major General Eduard von Lewinski. See Franz Nikolaus Kaiser (ed.), *Das Ehrenbuch der Deutschen Schweren Artillerie* (Berlin, 1931), 469; Priesdorff, *Soldatisches Führertum*, 9:462–463; Major Leydhecker, *Das Wurffeuer im Feld- und Positionskriege* (Berlin, 1887); and SMP to SWM, 19 June 1888, Sächs. Militär. Bevollm. 4502, Bl. 158, HStAD.

78. Prince William to Waldersee, 1 June 1886, in Meisner, *Briefwechsel Waldersee*, 22–23; Heinrich Rohne, "Die Entwicklung der modernen Feldartillerie,"

VTH 1/4 (1904):492; Hermann Schirmer, *Das Gerät der schweren Artillerie vor, in und nach dem Weltkrieg* (Berlin, 1937), 40–41; SMP to SWM, 17 July 1888, Sächs. Militär. Bevollm. 4502, Bl. 171, HStAD.

79. Waldersee to Verdy du Vernois, 26 November 1888, in Meisner, *Briefwechsel Waldersee,* 206–207.

80. Cited in *LJB* 24 (1897); 371.

81. Löe to Waldersee, 26 March 1889, in Meisner, *Briefwechsel Waldersee,* 247; Waldersee Diary, 8 May 1888, in Meisner, *Denkwürdigkeiten,* 1:395; Priesdorff, *Soldatisches Führertum,* 8:420; Kaiser, *Ehrenbuch,* 469. Production of the prototype howitzers at Krupp delayed the first tests until 1888. See Lt. Col. Lautenbach to SWM, 4 January 1888, KA(P) 2223, HStAD.

82. For this paragraph, see Waldersee Diary, 8 May, 8 December, and 25 December 1888, in Meisner, *Denkwürdigkeiten,* 1:395, 2:25–26; Waldersee to Verdy du Vernois, 26 November and 2 December 1888, and Verdy du Vernois to Waldersee, 22 February 1889, in Meisner, *Briefwechsel Waldersee,* 206–1208, 220–221.

83. For the following, see Lt. Col. Lauterbach to SWM, 4 January 1888, KA(P) 2223; SMP to SWM, 19 June 1888, Bl. 158, and 17 July 1888, Bl. 171, Sächs. Militär. Bevollm. 4502, HStAD; Rohne, "Entwicklung der modernen Feldartillerie," 492; and Schirmer, *Gerät,* 44–45.

84. The Saxon MP in Berlin reported that the November 1888 tests of the 120-mm howitzer against dug-in defenders were positive. See his report of 22 December 1888, Sächs. Militär. Bevollm. 4502, Bl. 280, HStAD.

85. The "march-ready" 120-mm howitzer (including cannon, fully loaded caison, and crew) weighed only 92 pounds (2.5%) more than the C-73. See Schirmer, *Gerät,* 44.

86. *LJB* 20 (1893); 341–342, 21 (1894); 361, 23 (1896); 359–360, and especially 25 (1898); Pt. 2, 649–650, 652. For Hoffbauer's schrapnel intrigues, see SMP to SWM, 9 March 1893, KA(P) 1652, Bl. 73, HStAD.

87. SMP to SWM, 19 August 1889, Sächs. Militär. Bevollm. 4503, Bl. 151, and various Saxon reports from August–September 1890, KA(P) 2226, Bl. 1–8, HStAD; Verdy du Vernois to Waldersee, 22 June and 4 August 1890, in Meisner, *Briefwechsel Waldersee,* 383, 398; and Verdy du Vernois to Caprivi, 20 August 1890, RK 1254, Bl. 10–13, BAP.

88. Gossler to Boetticher, 14 December 1896, Reichsmin. des Innern 12042, BAP.

89. For this paragraph, see ibid.

90. See, for instance, the BMP to BWM, 28 September 1893, M. Kr. 37, KAM.

91. See Linnenkohl, *Vom Einzelschuss,* 59–69.

92. SWM to the king, 22 October 1896, KA(P) 2228, Bl. 27–31, HStAD.

93. Cited in Linnenkohl, *Vom Einzelschuss,* 61. The commander was Colonel von Reichenau, head of the Artillery Department of the War Ministry.

94. Mobility and firepower were both important. For an argument that the former was relatively more important, see Colonel von Reichenau's article in *MWB,* 13 March 1895, Sp. 578.

95. For this passage, see Hugo von Freytag-Loringhoven, *Generalfeldmarshall Graf von Schlieffen: Sein Leben und die Verwertung seines geistigen Erbes im Weltkriege* (Leipzig, 1920), 48–53; Priesdorff, *Soldatisches Führertum,* 10:276–279; Max Köh-

NOTES TO PAGES 66–72

ler, *Der Aufstieg der Artillerie bis zum Grossen Kriege* (Munich, 1938), 134–36; Linnenkohl, *Vom Einzelschuss*, 84–86.

96. General von Alten, *Wider die Feldhaubitze* (Berlin, 1903), 10, 80.

97. Köhler, *Aufstieg*, 135. Tests were completed in 1897, and the decision was made to introduce field howitzers in early 1898. See BMP to BWM, 2 January 1898, M. Kr. 45, KAM. Production delayed the distribution of the guns until 1900. For the Schlieffen quote, see Freytag-Loringhoven, *Graf von Schlieffen*, 51.

Chapter 4

1. For the contrast between Moltke's pragmatism and Schlieffen's doctrinaire rigidity, see Jack Snyder, *The Ideology of the Offensive: Military Decision-Making and the Disasters of 1914* (Ithaca, N.Y., 1984), 132–139. For the evolution of the General Staff to a complex professional organization under Schlieffen, see Arden Bucholz, *Moltke, Schlieffen, and Prussian War Planning* (New York, 1991), 134–165.

2. The exchange of October 1902 is quoted in Hermann von Eckardstein, *Lebenserinnerungen und Politische Denkwürdigkeiten* (Leipzig, 1920), 2:399–400.

3. For the debate in Germany over the value of fortresses, see *MWB*, 19 July 1890, Sp. 1910.

4. See Helmuth von Moltke, *Die deutschen Aufmarschpläne 1871–1890*, ed. Ferdinand von Schmerfeld (Berlin, 1929), 77, 86, 89, 94–95, 145, 150–162. For arguments favoring the defense, see *MWB*, 1 July 1882, Sp. 1037, and 4 April 1885, Sp. 557; and for the alleged popularity of these arguments, see 16 July 1884, Sp. 1177, and 21 April 1897, Sp. 1060.

5. *MWB*, 16 July 1884, Sp. 1177.

6. For a sampling of these criticisms, see ibid., 4 August 1880, Sp. 1139; 25 December 1880, Sp. 1927; 28 November 1883, Sp. 1919; 10 December 1884, Sp. 2011; 4 February 1885, Sp. 195; 14 May 1887, Sp. 921; 1 February 1893, Sp. 250.

7. Ibid., 16 July 1884, Sp. 1177, and 22 March 1887, Sp. 602.

8. Ibid., 27 February 1892, Sp. 509.

9. Ibid., 12 February 1890, Sp. 397–398.

10. For this paragraph, see ibid., 1, 5, and 8 March 1890, Sp. 539–544, 560–568, 592–601; 29 November 1890, Sp. 3038; 25 June 1892, Sp. 1519; 1 February 1893, Sp. 250; 14 June 1894, Sp. 1590; 21 June 1894, Sp. 1637–1638; and Major General von Reichenau, "Über die weitere Entwickelung der Kriegsgeschichte," *Beiheft zum Militär-Wochenblatt*, (1898); 395–420. See also the related discussion in George L. Mosse, *The Image of Man: The Creation of Modern Masculinity* (New York, 1996), 77–106.

11. Reichenau, "Weitere Entwickelung," 396.

12. Wilhelm Balck, cited in Antulio Echevarria, "On the Brink of the Abyss: The Warrior Identity and German Military Thought before the Great War," *War & Society* 13 (1995): 24–25.

13. Reichenau, "Weitere Entwickelung," 396.

14. Reinhard Höhn, *Sozialismus und Heer* (Bad Harzburg, 1969), 3: 62.

15. For the SPD's criticism of the army, see Peter Domann, *Sozialdemokratie und Kaisertum unter Wilhelm II* (Wiesbaden, 1974), 168–195.

16. See August von Boguslawski's "Zukunftstaktik" in *MWB*, 21 June 1894, Sp. 1637–1638.

17. Cited in Werner Maser, *Hindenburg: Eine politische Biographie* (Rastatt, 1990), 67.

18. Quotations, respectively, ibid., 21 June 1894, Sp. 1634, and 1 February 1893, Sp. 250.

19. Waldersee Diary, 21 July 1895, in Heinrich Otto Meisner (ed.), *Denkwürdigkeiten des General-Feldmarshalls Alfred Grafen von Waldersee* (Osnabrück, 1922), 2:354–355. For qualifying comments on the reliability of the Waldersee Diary, see Chap. 1, note 16.

20. *MWB*, 21 June 1894, Sp. 1634.

21. Gayl, *General von Schlichting*, 64–67.

22. For this paragraph, see SMP to SWM, 14 January and 17 July 1888, Sächs. Militär. Bevollm. 4502, Bl. 1, 171, HStAD; Xylander to BWM, 13 October 1888, M. Kr. 4663, Bl.1, KAM; an excerpt from Waldersee's unpublished memoirs, n.d. (written between 1891 and 1904), in Otto Meisner, "Aus den Erinnerungen des Generalfeldmarshalls Grafen Waldersees: Über seine Tätigkeit als Generalquartiermeister und Chef des Generalstabs 1882–1891," *Deutsche Revue* 46 (June 1921): 214–215; *MWB*, 12 February 1890, Sp. 397–403; 25 June 1892, Sp. 1519; 12 January 1895, Sp. 106; and Lauter, "Unsere Waffe," in Franz Nikolaus Kaiser, *Das Ehrenbuch der Schweren Artillerie*, 1:14–15. See also Bucholz, *Moltke, Schlieffen*, (ed.), 102, 124.

23. According to Hermann von Kuhl, *Der deutsche Generalstab in Vorbereitung und Durchführung des Weltkrieges* (Berlin, 1920), 33, the alleged "nervousness" of the French factored into German planning for the next 25 years. See also the sources cited above in note 22. Kuhl was General Staff chief of the German First Army of Alexander von Kluck in 1914.

24. For French "decadence" in the 1890s, see Eugen Weber, *France Fin de Siècle* (Cambridge, Mass., 1986), 9–26.

25. SMP to SWM, 19 April 1885 and 19 June 1888, Sächs. Militär. Bevollm. 4499, Bl. 55; and 4502, Bl. 158, HStAD; Kaiser, *Ehrenbuch*, 1:14–15, 2:469.

26. It seems certain that the General Staff was behind the creation of the new General Inspection, for Waldersee was pressuring the War Ministry for a field role for the heavy artillery. See Lauter, "Unsere Waffe," 1:15; and SMP to SWM, 14 January 1888, Sächs. Militär. Bevollm. 4502, Bl. 1, HStAD. Moreover, Major Schweninger of the Bavarian military representation in Berlin asserted that the General Inspection was a General Staff creation (see his report to BWM, 28 November 1891, M. Kr. 3024, KAM). For William's support, see SMP to SWM, 22 December 1888, Sächs. Militär. Bevollm. 4502, Bl. 280, HStAD; and Max Köhler, *Aufstieg der Artillerie bis zum Grossen Krieg* (Munich, 1938), 127–128.

27. For the mobility exercise against Fort Rheinhell, see Xylander to BWM, 13 October 1888, and Waldersee to Prussian WM, 8 December 1888, M. Kr. 4663, KAM.

28. Lauter, "Unsere Waffe," 1:16; and Captain Loé's report of 15 October 1890, M. Kr. 3024, KAM.

29. See the reports of the BWM, 3 October 1890, and Major Renauld of the Prussian Corps of Engineers, 14 October 1890 and 5 October 1891, M. Kr. 3024, KAM.

30. Major Schweninger to BWM, 30 November 1891; for the quotation,

BMP to BWM, 11 December 1891, M. Kr. 37. See also Renauld to BWM, 5 October 1891, M. Kr. 3024, KAM.

31. General Ziethen, "Die Fussartillerie," in General von Eisenhart-Rothe (ed.), *Ehrendenkmal der Deutschen Armee und Marine 1871–1918* (Berlin, 1928), 141–142.

32. Köhler, *Aufstieg*, 128.

33. Allan Mitchell, *Victors and Vanquished: The German Influence on Army and Church in France after 1870* (Chapel Hill, N.C., 1984), 111–112.

34. SMP to SWM, 19 August 1889, Sächs. Militär. Bevollm. 4503, Bl. 151, HStAD; Schirmer, *Das Gerät*, 6, 42–43, 46–47; Lauter, "Unsere Waffe," 1:16, 2: 470; General von Schwierz, "Fussartillerie," in *AM* (1913/1): 447–448.

35. Groener, *Lebenserinnerungen*, 59–60; Einem, *Erinnerungen*, 40; Bernhardi, *Denkwürdigkeiten*, 122–123, 172. See also Hugo von Freytag-Loringhoven, *Menschen und Dinge wie ich sie in meinem Leben sah* (Berlin, 1923), 63–67, 139–142.

36. Gerhard Ritter, *The Schlieffen Plan: Critique of a Myth*, trans. B. H. Liddell Hart (London, 1958); Snyder, *Ideology of the Offensive*, 107–156; Bucholz, *Moltke, Schlieffen*, 158–213; and Stig Förster, "Dreams and Nightmares: German Military Leadership and the Images of Future Warfare, 1871–1914," in Manfred F. Boemeke et al., *Anticipating Total War: The German and American Experiences 1871–1914* (Cambridge, 1999), 356–362.

37. Eberhard Kessel, "Die Tätigkeit des Grafen Waldersee als Generalquartiermeister und Chef des Generalstabs der Armee," *Welt als Geschichte* 14 (1954): 203–204.

38. Waldersee's last plans before dismissal were probably the same as those described in a letter to Friedrich von Bernhardi, n.d. (December 1893), in Bernhardi, *Denkwürdigkeiten*, 159–162.

39. Schlieffen's memorandum of December 1892 is cited in Ritter, *Schlieffen Plan*, 25.

40. See the map of the western front in chap. 8.

41. Schlieffen's 1894 plan is cited in Ritter, *Schlieffen Plan*, 38. For this paragraph, see also Ziethen, "Die Fussartillerie," in Eisenhart-Rothe, *Ehrendenkmal*, 142; Lauter, "Unsere Waffe," in Kaiser, *Ehrenbuch*, 1:16; and Heinz-Ludger Borgert, "Grundzüge der Landkriegführung von Schlieffen bis Guderian," in Gerhard Papke and Wolfgang Petter (eds.), *Deutsche Militärgeschichte* (Munich, 1983), 6:447–448.

42. Prussian Artillery Proving Commission protocols for tests at Cummersdorf on 5–6 July; 30–31 August; 5 and 19 September; 1, 18, and 31 October; and 2 November 1895; and the final test in June 1896, M. Kr. Alter Bestand, A.VI.6f, Bd. 5, KAM.

43. For the order, see Lauter, "Unsere Waffe," 1:31, 2:470. For a General Staff reference to the "failed" tests of 1894–1896, see Moltke to Einem, 6 June and 4 September 1906, M. Kr. 990, KAM.

44. See the unpublished manuscript of Dr. Dieckmann of the Army Research Department, "Der Schlieffen Plan," n.d. (1930s), in W-10/50220, pp. 53–57, BAMAF. The quotations here are from Förster, "Dreams and Nightmares," 355, who first used this source.

45. For requests to raise calibers above 305 mm in the 1890s, see Adolf Vogt, *Oberst Max Bauer: Generalstabsoffizier im Zwielicht* (Osnabrück, 1974), 15. For the "Monstre-Geschütz" quotation, see Heinrich von Müller, *Die Entwicklung*

der deutschenFestungs- und Belagerungsartillerie in Bezug auf Material, Organisation, Ausbildung und Taktik von 1875 bis 1895 (Berlin, 1896), 504–505.

46. Lauter, "Unsere Waffe," 1:18; Schwierz, "Fussartillerie," *AM* (1913/1): 441.

47. For War Ministry opposition, see Schweninger to BWM, 28 November 1891. For Hoffbauer and Reichenau, see Priesdorff, *Soldatisches Führertum*, 8: 439; Köhler, *Aufstieg*, 144–145; Lauter, "Unsere Waffe," in Kaiser, *Ehrenbuch*, 1: 19–20; Freytag-Loringhoven, *Graf von Schlieffen*, 50–51; and Mollin, *Auf dem Wege*, 187, 190–191.

48. The best archival insights to General Staff thinking come from Dieckmann's "Der Schlieffen Plan," n.d. (1930s), W-10/50220, pp. 62ff, BAMAF. This valuable manuscript is analyzed and interpreted in Terence Zuber, "The Schlieffen Plan Reconsidered," *War in History* 6/3 (1999): 262–305.

49. Schlieffen's memo of 2 August 1897 and undated plan are cited in Ritter, *Schlieffen Plan*, 42, 41.

50. Zuber, "Schlieffen Plan Reconsidered," 276–282.

51. See, for example, Colonel Schlieben to Captain Jäckel of the Saxon Foot Artillery, 1 October 1891, KA(P) 1652, Bl. 18, HStAD.

52. Förster, "Dreams and Nightmares," 361.

53. Schlieffen to Gossler, 10 November 1899, in Ludwig Rüdt von Collenberg, "Graf Schlieffen und die Kriegsformation der deutschen Armee," *Wissen und Wehr* 10 (1927): 622.

54. The minisiege train that moved against Fort Rheinhell in the attack exercise of 1888 had a 1:2 ratio of 210s and 150s. By the early 1900s, this ratio in the heavy artillery had sunk to 1:6. See Xylander to BWM, 13 October 1888, M. Kr. 4663; and Moltke to Einem, 4 September 1906, M. Kr. 990, KAM. For General Staff resistance to larger calibers, see Vogt, *Oberst Bauer*, 15.

55. Schlieffen to Gossler, 10 November 1899, in Collenberg, "Graf Schlieffen," 622. In discussing artillery needs, there was no mention of the 305s, whose numbers by 1906 had declined from nine to six; see David Herrmann, *The Arming of Europe and the Making of the First World War* (Princeton, N.J., 1996), 65. See also the memo of Heavy Artillery Inspector General Edler von der Planitz, 10 December 1898, M. Kr. 3025, KAM, which placed hope in the 150s and 210s without mentioning the 305s.

56. See Hoffbauer's memos of 16 and 22 July 1898, M. Kr. 3022; and the kaiser's comments of 15 August 1900, M. Kr. 3025, KAM. See also Köhler, *Aufstieg*, 144–145.

57. See Karl Justrow's remembrance in *Die Schwere Artillerie* 13 (1936): 20–21; and Max Bauer's unpublished memoir, n.d. (1921), NL 22 Bauer, Nr. 7, Bl. 6–13, BAK.

58. SMP to SWM, 17 December 1900, Sächs. Militär. Bevollm. 4517, Bl. 259, HStAD. The words were Karl von Einem's of the War Ministry, but Schlieffen agreed. For Prussian War Minister Gossler's support for the heavy artillery and Schlieffen's opposition, see the Saxon attaché's report of 24 January 1900 (Nr. 4517, HStAD), and Schieffen to Gossler, 27 March 1900, cited in Collenberg, "Graf Schlieffen," 627.

59. Ludwig Rüdt von Collenberg, *Die Deutsche Armee von 1871 bis 1914* (Berlin, 1922), 122.

60. Schlieffen to Gossler, 10 November 1899, in Collenberg, "Graf Schlieffen," 622.

61. Ibid., 627–628; Collenberg, *Deutsche Armee,* 122–123.

62. For the "wartime corps," see Herrmann, *Arming of Europe,* 44.

63. For the argument that Schlieffen did not reckon on the possibility of annihilating the French Army in six weeks, see Zuber, "Schlieffen Plan Reconsidered," 276–282, 304–305. His article does not speculate on the length of war that Schlieffen envisioned, only that he wanted to avoid trench warfare and a struggle of 1 or 2 years (p. 294).

64. Michael Geyer, *Deutsche Rüstungspolitik 1860–1980* (Frankfurt, 1984), 58, 63–64.

65. SMP to SWM, 21 November 1899, 24 January 1900, 17 December 1900, Sächs. Militär.Bevollm. 4516, Bl. 177, 4517 and Bl. 259, HStAD.

66. SMP to SWM, quoting Schlieffen, 16 January 1899, Sächs. Militär. Bevollm. 4516, HStAD.

67. The point is argued at length by Förster, "Dreams and Nightmares," 343–376.

68. Cited in Ritter, *Schlieffen Plan,* 91.

69. Eckardstein, *Lebenserinnerungen,* 2:399–400.

70. For Schlieffen's 1902–1903 deployments, see Zuber, "Schlieffen Plan Reconsidered," 282–283. The interpretation of Zuber's evidence is mine.

71. Endres to BWM, 12 August 1903, M. Kr. 3165, KAM.

72. Zuber, "Schlieffen Plan Reconsidered," 283.

73. See Schlieffen's assessment of 6 July 1902 in G. St. 1234, KAM. That he returned to this assessment in 1904–1905 is discussed in Colmar von der Goltz, *Denkwürdigkeiten* (Berlin, 1929), 211.

74. Zuber, "Schlieffen Plan Reconsidered," 285–297.

75. Snyder, *Ideology of the Offensive,* 123.

76. See Bucholz, *Moltke, Schlieffen,* 145–155.

77. Zuber, "Schlieffen Plan Reconsidered," 295. The interpretation that follows is mine, not Zuber's. For Schlieffen's remarks about the eventuality of war with France and England a year earlier, in November 1904, see Heiner Raulff, *Zwischen Machtpolitik und Imperialismus: Die Deutsche Frankreichpolitik 1904/06* (Düsseldorf, 1976), 76–79.

Chapter 5

1. Cited in Thomas Pakenham, *The Boer War* (New York, 1979), 310. For this scene, see also Emanoel Lee, *To the Bitter End: A Photographic History of the Boer War 1899–1902* (New York, 1985), 99–101.

2. Cited in Pakenham, *Boer War,* 310.

3. Ibid., 283–288.

4. Ibid., 244.

5. *MWB,* 21 February 1900, Sp. 454. Also see Dieter Storz, *Kriegsbild und Rüstung vor 1914: Europäische Landstreitkräfte vor dem Ersten Weltkrieg* (Berlin, 1992), 55.

6. See Joachim Hoffmann, "Die Kriegslehre des General von Schlichting," *Militärgeschichtliche Mitteilungen* 1 (1969): 18–25.

7. See the discussion in *LJB* 26 (1899), 297, and 27 (1900), 278–284, 285.

8. BMP to BWM, 17 November 1900, M. Kr. 39, KAM.

9. See *LJB* 29 (1902), 239–242.

10. SMP to SWM, 22 May 1902, Sächs. Militär-Bevollm. 1424, Bl. 17, HStAD.

11. General Lindenau of the Prussian General Staff spoke to the Military Society in Berlin, *MWB*, 12 March 1902, Sp. 601–602; and General von Caemmerer's articles of 8 March 1902, Sp. 574; see also *Der deutsche Infanterie-Angriff 1902: Nach Praktischen Erfahrungen auf dem Truppen-übungsplatz Döberitz bei Berlin Mai 1902* (Berlin, 1902).

12. For the kaiser's order of 6 May 1902, see M. Kr. 2919, KAM. See also Storz, *Kriegsbild und Rüstung,* 56–57, 73, note 42.

13. See the critical remarks of Colmar von der Goltz, *Das Volk in Waffen; Ein Buch über Heerivesen und Kriegführung unserer zeit* (Berlin, 1899), 282–283.

14. See *Deutsche Infanterie-Angriff,* passim. The kaiser's order of 6 May 1902 (M. Kr. 2919, KAM) followed the innovators' argumentation almost verbatim.

15. SMP to SWM, 22 May 1902, Sächs. Militär-Bevollm. 1424, Bl. 31, HStAD.

16. *MWB*, 16 April 1903, Sp. 905.

17. Ibid., 28 February 1903, Sp. 495. See also the defense of advancing by short sprints, but in tight formations, by the Bavarian Major Hurt, ibid., 13 September 1902, Sp. 2124.

18. Wilhelm von Scherff, *Gewehr und Gelände im heutigen Angriffskampf* (Berlin, 1904). See also conflicting reactions to Scherff's book in *MWB*, 3, 6, and 8 December 1904, Sp. 3509, 3539, and 3560, and 12 January 1905, Sp. 93.

19. Grosser Generalstab, *Kriegsgeschichtliche Einzelschriften,* Heft 32 (Berlin, 1903) and Heft 33 (Berlin, 1904); and *Studien zur Kriegsgeschichte und Taktik, Bd. 3: Der Schlachterfolg* (Berlin, 1903). The first two booklets are also discussed in Storz, *Kriegsbild und Rüstung,* 58–59.

20. See Grosser Genevalstab, *Kriegsgeschichtliche Eingelschriften,* Heft 33, p. 84.

21. SMP to SWM, 22 May 1902, Sächs. Militär-Bevollm. 1424, Bl. 31, HStAD. See also *Deutsche Infanterie-Angriff,* 53.

22. Quotations are from Bülow's memorandum of 16 April 1904, M. Kr. 2922, KAM.

23. Hugo von Freytag-Loringhoven, *Menschen und Dinge wie ich sie in meinem Leben sah* (Berlin, 1923), 99, referring to a conversation with Schlieffen circa 1905. For army resistance to outflanking maneuvers, see also Friedrich von Bernhardi, *Denkwürdigkeiten aus meinem Leben,* (Berlin, 1927), 214–215, citing a letter from a General Staff contact in 1899; and especially, Endres to BWM, 18 September 1903, M. Kr. 3165, KAM. Schlieffen devoted the 1903 maneuvers to overcoming this resistance.

24. The exception is an introductory reference by Bruce I. Gudmundsson, *Stormtroop Tactics: Innovation in the German Army, 1914–1918* (New York, 1989).

25. BMP to BWM, 20 December 1905, M. Kr. 2149, KAM.

26. Storz, *Kriegsbild und Rüstung,* 59–60. There is no discussion here, however, of corps commander autonomy.

27. All quotations are from BMP to BWM, 4 June 1903, M. Kr. 43, KAM.

28. Robert Zedlitz-Trützschler, *Zwölf Jahre am deutschen Kaiserhof* (Berlin, 1925), 42.

260 NOTES TO PAGES 91-95

29. The reaction of later war minister and General Staff chief, Erich von Falkenhayn, is cited in Holger Afflerbach, *Falkenhayn: Politisches Denken und Handeln im Kaiserreich* (Munich, 1994), 60.

30. Cited in Zedlitz-Trützschler, *Zwölf Jahre*, 83.

31. Brother of the inspector general of the heavy artillery.

32. Maximilian von Poseck, "Die Kavallerie," in General von Eisenhart-Rothe (ed.), *Ehrendenkmal der Deutschen Armee und Marine 1871–1918* (Berlin, 1928), 114–115; Bernhardi, *Denkwürdigkeiten*, 212, 285.

33. BMP to BWM, 18 February 1898, M. Kr. 45, KAM; SMP to SWM, 19 September 1899, Sächs. Militär-Bevollm. 4516, Bl. 129, HStAD.

34. Friedrich von Bernhardi, *Unsere Kavallerie im nächsten Krieg* (Berlin, 1899).

35. Major Brixen-Hahn, *Die Taktik der Kavallerie 1874–1898* (Berlin, 1899).

36. Poseck, "Kavallerie," 111.

37. For the connection between the cavalry lessons of the Boer War and the 1900 maneuvers, see *LJB* 27 (1900); 303. See also *MWB*, 24 February 1900, Sp. 481; and Grosser Generalstab, *Kriegsgeschichtliche Einzelschriften*, Heft 32, 52, 77.

38. BMP to BWM, 17 November 1900, M. Kr. 39, KAM.

39. All quotations are from Bernhardi, *Denkwürdigkeiten*, 218.

40. Waldersee to Bernhardi, n.d. (early 1903), cited ibid., 251–252.

41. Ritter von Endres to BWM, 12 August 1903, M. Kr. 3165, KAM.

42. *MWB*, 6 December 1902, Sp. 2829–2836. For the reviving idea of mass cavalry attacks, see also *LJB* 29 (1902), 269–270, and 30 (1903), 324–325.

43. Poseck, "Kavallerie," 118.

44. *MWB*, 14 March 1905, Sp. 730–731. For another defense of the kaiser's attacks, see *LJB* 29 (1902), 269.

45. John Ellis, *The Social History of the Machine Gun* (Baltimore, 1975), 89–98.

46. Hiram S. Maxim, *My Life* (New York, 1915), 209–210.

47. For Loewe's license and the first guns, see Hans Linnenkohl, *Vom Einzelschuss zur Feuerwalze: Der Wettlauf zwischen Technik und Taktik im Ersten Weltkrieg* (Koblenz, 1990), 15; Manfred Lachmann, "Zur Entwicklung und zum Einsatz des Maschinengewehrs," *Zeitschrift für Militärgeschichte* 12 (1973): 723; and Dolf L. Goldsmith, *The Devil's Paintbrush: Sir Hiram Maxim's Gun* (Toronto, 1989), 131–133.

48. See Hutten-Czapski to Holstein, 15 November 1895, in Norman Rich and M. H. Fisher (eds.), *The Holstein Papers: The Memoirs, Diaries and Correspondence of Friedrich von Holstein 1887–1909* (Cambridge, 1961), 3:561.

49. *KTZ*, Heft 1 (1898), 60. This article, written by Major General C. von Herget, notes that Germany was alone among the Great Powers to introduce machine guns to the artillery.

50. Prussian Allgemeines Kriegs-Departement to BWM, 9 December 1898, M. Kr. 1183; and the documents from 1899 in M. Kr. Alter Bestand, A.X.8, Bd. 1, KAM.

51. Prussian Allgemeines Kriegs-Departement to BWM, 9 December 1898; BWM to Prince Luitpold, 18 September 1901, M. Kr. 1183, KAM; and *LJB* 27 (1900): 292, 310; 28 (1901): 297; and 29 (1902): 269–270. In 1898 the Prussian War Ministry was still considering integrating the detachments into the

Jäger battalions, and this form was employed in 1900 maneuvers. By 1901, however, the looser affiliation with the Jäger and the cavalry was in effect.

52. BMP to BWM, 30 November 1899 and 17 November 1900, M. Kr. 39, KAM. For weight data, see Storz, *Kriegsbild und Rüstung*, 355.

53. The draft of March 1901 (see M. Kr. 1183, KAM) went into effect in May 1902. For artillery sensitivity to machine guns, see *MWB*, 12 March 1902, Sp. 595–598; *KTZ*, Heft 7 (1904); 532; and *AM*, 1, Nr. 3 (March 1907): 255–256.

54. See BMP to BWM, 17 November 1900, M. Kr. 39, KAM; and especially the review of objections to machine guns in *KTZ*, Heft 7 (1904); 530–537.

55. Cited in G. Däniker, *Die Maschinenwaffe im Rahmen der Taktik* (Berlin, 1942), 13.

56. SMP to SWM, 19 September 1899, Sächs. Militär-Bevollm. 4516, Bl. 129, HStAD; *MWB*, 23 June 1900, Sp. 1383; BMP to BWM, 17 November 1900, M. Kr. 39, KAM.

57. Lt. Col. Marx, "Die Feldartillerie," in Ernst von Eisenhart-Rothe, *Ehrendenkmal der Deutschen Armee und Marine 1871–1918* . (Berlin, 1928), 128.

58. SMP to SWM, 19 September 1899, Sächs. Militär-Bevollm. 4516, Bl. 129, HStAD.

59. Ibid.; *MWB*, 10 August 1899, Sp. 1809; *KTZ*, Heft 7 (1904); 531.

60. For the 1903 maneuvers, see the General Staff's official report, *Kaiser-Manöver 1903*, 65, 68, AE100, KAM; and *LJB* 30 (1903), 322–324.

61. Wandel to Einem, 31 October 1908, cited in W-10/50199, Bl. 109–112, BAMAF.

62. Einem to Bülow, 19 June 1906, in Karl von Einem, *Erinnerungen eines Soldaten 1853–1933* (Leipzig, 1933), 101. Eighty machine guns guarded imperial ramparts in 1906.

63. *AM*, 1, Nr. 3 (March 1907): 255–256.

64. BMP to BWM, 26 December 1901 and 26 March 1902, M. Kr. Alter Bestand, A.X.2, Bd. 12d, Bd. 1, KAM. See also his articles in *KTZ* : "Das moderne Feldgeschütz," Heft 1 (1898): 9ff.; and "Studie über Schnellfeuer-Feldgeschütze in Rohrrücklauflafette," Heft 4 (1901): 394ff.

65. The arguments are summarized in *KTZ*, Heft 6 (1903): 569.

66. Ibid. For the quotation, see SMP to SWM, 13 December 1900, Sächs. Militär. Bevollm. 4517, Bl. 258, HStAD.

67. Quotations are from BMP to BWM, 30 November 1901, M. Kr. Alter Bestand, A.X.2, Bd. 12d, Bd. 1, KAM. See also the BMP's report of 26 December 1901 and BWM to Prince Luitpold, 21 December 1905 (Bd. 12d/Bd. 2). For the inclination of the Artillery Department of the Prussian War Ministry to adopt shields, see SMP to SWM, 5 September 1901, Sächs. Militär. Bevollm. 4518, Bl. 73, HStAD.

68. SMP to SWM, 5 September 1901, Sächs, Militär Bevollm, 4518, Bl. 73, HSTAD.

69. BMP to BWM, 26 December 1901, M. Kr. Alter Bestand, A.X.2, Bd. 12d, Bd. 1, KAM.

70. Einem, *Erinnerungen,* 86. Einem spoke with William in 1903, but a year earlier the kaiser wanted shields to prevent the French from inflicting heavy casualties. See SMP to SWM, 3 February 1902, Sächs. Militär. Bevollm. 1424, Bl. 13, HStAD.

71. Brother of the inspector general of cavalry in Prussia.

72. For this paragraph, see General Schwierz, "Fussartillerie," in *AM*, 1, Nr. 78 (June 19): 442; and General von Lauter, "Unsere Waffe," in Franz Niklaus Kaiser (ed.), *Das Ehrenbuch der Deutschen Schweren Artillerie* (Berlin, 1931), 1: 21–23.

73. Cited in Max Köhler, *Der Aufstieg der Artillerie bis zum Grossen Krieg* (Munich, 1938), 146. Köhler describes this kind of "prejudice" against the heavy artillery as "rather common" among commanding generals after 1900.

74. Planitz to all corps commanders, 25 February 1902, M. Kr. 39, KAM. For the denigration of the foot artillery at this time, see also Ziethen, "Fussartillerie," 146; and Lauter, "Unsere Waffe," 1:19–20.

75. Einem to all corps commanders, 2 July 1904, M. Kr. 3022, KAM; also cited in David G. Herrmann, *The Arming of Europe and the Making of the First World War* (Princeton, N.J., 1966), 91.

76. BMP to BWM, 2 January 1903, M. Kr. Alter Bestand, A.X.2, Bd. 12d, Bd. 1; Einem, *Erinnerungen*, 86.

77. *KTZ*, Heft 6 (1903): 91–94, 426–436, 569–586; *VTH* 1, 4, (1904): 486–491.

78. Einem to BWM, 19 June 1904, M. Kr. Alter Bestand, A.X.2, Bd. 12d, Bd. 1, KAM.

79. Unknown author to Bernhardi, n.d. (late 1901), cited in Bernhardi, *Denkwürdigkeiten*, 306.

80. The opportunities were there even before the advent of semi-recoilless cannons. Captain Hoehn of the Bavarian field artillery observed as early as 1900 that resistance to firing from hidden positions was disappearing in his regiment as familiarity with the new techniques spread. See *KTZ*, Bd. 3 (1900): 65.

81. Helmut Schnitter, *Militärwesen und Militärpublizistik: Die militärische Zeitschriftenpublizistik in der Geschichte des Bürgerlichen Militärwesens in Deutschland* (Berlin, 1967), 78–81, 197–213.

82. *Archiv für die Artillerie- und Ingenieur-Offiziere des deutschen Reichsheeres*, Bd. 130 (1896): 25–30.

83. *KTZ*, Heft 1 (1898): 1.

84. See ibid., 213–223; Heft 5 (1902): 1–6, Heft 6 (1903): 76–77; and Heft 7 (1904), 225–235, 292–297, 354–359.

85. For Rohne, see ibid., Heft 4 (1901): 394ff. Four articles on the machine gun appeared in the first year (1898), with two or three annually in subsequent years.

86. Ibid., Heft 1 (1898): 1.

87. Ibid., Hefte 1–7 (1898–1904): passim.

88. General Rothe, "Über Bedingungen des Wertes heutiger Heere," *Deutsche Revue* 27/11 (November 1902): 207.

89. All quotations in this paragraph are from Woelki, "Werth und Organisation der Kriegstechnik," in *KTZ*, Heft 6 (1903): 72, 77.

90. Goltz, *Das Volk in Waffen*, 286–290. The 1883 edition (see pp. 340–341) had less appreciation for the power of defenders.

91. See chapter 4.

92. Generalfeldmarshall Goltz published an article, in December 1903, praising the Boers. See Colmar von der Goltz, *Denkwürdigkeiten* (Berlin, 1929), 253.

93. Goltz's proposals are analyzed at length, ibid., 177–188.

94. For both Planitz and Schliefen, see ibid., 210–212, 215–216. See also Schlieffen's exercise critique of 6 July 1902 in G. St. 1234, KAM.

95. Waldersee Diary, 19 March 1902, in Heinrich Otto Meisner (ed.), *Denkwürdigkeiten des General-Yeldmarshalls Alfred Grafen von Walderee*, (Osnabrück, 1922), 3:181.

96. Goltz, *Denkwürdigkeiten*, 216.

97. Ibid., 187.

98. SMP to SWM, 17 December 1900, Sächs. Militär-Bevollm. 4517, Bl. 259, HStAD. See also the reports of 5 January and 22 March 1901, Sächs. Militär-Bevollm. 4518, Bl. 3, 39.

99. Goltz to Mudra, 29 January 1904, in Goltz, *Denkwürdigkeiten*, 227.

100. Goltz to Gossler, n.d. (Spring 1901), ibid., 1901.

101. Goltz to Mudra, 29 May 1902, ibid., 225.

102. Goltz to Alexander, 18 February 1903, ibid., 226.

103. Kersting to Jüstrow, March 1921, in Karl Jüstrow, *Feldheer und Kriegstechnik* (Oldenburg, 1933), 327.

104. Ibid.

105. *KTZ*, Heft 5 (1902): 3, and Heft 7 (1904): 8–9.

106. Jüstrow, *Feldheer und Kriegstechnik*, 127.

107. See the map of the western front in chap. 8.

108. See Gerhard Ritter, *The Schlieffen Plan: Critique of a Myth*, trans. B. H. Liddell Hart (London, 1958), 42, 44–45; and Terence Zuber, "The Schlieffen Plan Reconsidered," *War in History* 6/3 (1999): 285–287. For German deployments I use the *percentage* of divisions allocated to right, center, and left during the June 1904 staff ride. The absolute number of divisions is based on what was actually available for the western front—23 active corps (46 divisions) and 15 reserve divisions—as opposed to the total of 84 divisions used in the exercise. Three active corps and 4 reserve divisions went east.

109. All French deployments and division strengths from the French Plan XV were in effect since March 1903. See Ministère de la Guerre, *Les Armées françaises dans la Grande Guerre* (Paris, 1936), 1:29–30. See also Samuel R. Williamson, Jr., *The Politics of Grand Strategy: Britain and France Prepare for War, 1904–1914* (Cambridge, Mass., 1969), 24, 52–55, 117–118, 123, 125; and Herrmann, *Arming of Europe*, 47–48.

110. Ritter, *Schlieffen Plan*, 44–45.

111. Herrmann, *Arming of Europe*, 49.

112. Williamson, *Politics of Grand Strategy*, 46–47, 92–94; and Herrmann, *Arming of Europe*, 42–44, 47–50. The figure of 50,000 is based on the British war game of early 1905.

113. Ritter, *Schlieffen Plan*, 44.

114. The German corps had 144 cannons, the French only 92; but the 75 mm shot 20 shells per minute, the C-96 only 8. For maximum rates of fire, see Heinrich Rohne, "Die Entwicklung der modernen Feldartillerie," *VTH* 1/4 (1904): 488.

115. The usual assumption in the literature (e.g. Herrmann, *Arming of Europe*, 47) that German heavy artillery was superior is incorrect. The French army had 24 batteries of 120-mm and 30 batteries of 155-mm howitzers that were mobile and moved with the field army, not in the siege train [see the German Army's detailed study, *Fussartillerie fremder Heere* (Berlin, 1902), 39, in M. Kr. 4075, KAM]. The French committed 15 batteries of 120s and 30 bat-

teries of 155s to the 14 corps that were leading the Saar counteroffensive (see Ministère de la Suerre, *Armées francaises*, 27, note 3 and 29, note 4). For German howitzer figures in the early 1900s, see *KTZ*, Heft 2 (1899); 241–247; and Lauter, "Unsere Waffe," 1:21. The German Army had a total of 69 105-mm batteries (3 per corps). In 1903 Germany had 10 batteries of the new 150-mm howitzers, which Schlieffen wanted on the right wing for use against fortresses in Belgium and France. Most of Germany's 10 horse-drawn detachments (with 150-mm and 210 mm howitzers and mortars) would also have been in Belgium. Most of these had the older (1893) 150s.

116. For France's more prudent artillery tactics, see *LJB* 4 (1897): 376–378, and 28 (1901): 328–337.

117. For French infantry and cavalry trends in the 1890s and early 1900s, see *LJB* 25/2 (1898): 618–621; and 29 (1902): 256; and 31 (1904): 250–253; Julius von Pflugk-Harttung, *Die Heere und Flotte der Gegenwart, Bd. 5: Frankreich: Das Heer am Ende des neunzehten Jahrhunderts* (Berlin, 1900), 434–439; and Wilhelm Balck, *Die Französische Infanterie-Taktik in ihrer Entwickelung seit dem Kriege 1870/71* (Berlin, 1902), passim.

118. During the modifications of Plan XV in 1906, the Fifth Army was redeployed from Vesoul-Lure to north of Verdun—a likely move in any crisis. See Wolfgang Foerster, *Aus der Gedankenwerkstatt des Deutschen Generalstabs* (Berlin, 1931), 115.

119. For the coastal troops, see Williamson, *Politics of Grand Strategy*, 118. Coastal defense plans were eliminated in 1908 during the writing of Plan XVI.

120. Ministère de la Guerre *Armées francaises*, 1: 29, note 5.

121. Ritter, *Schlieffen Plan*, 45; Zuber, "Schlieffen Plan Reconsidered," 289–291.

Chapter 6

1. The exchange, as well as the dramatic entry on board, is related in Richard von Kühlmann, *Erinnerungen* (Heidelberg, 1948), 228–230. See also Wilhelm von Schoen, *Erlebtes: Beiträge zur politschen Geschichte der neuesten Zeit* (Stuttgart, 1921), 19–20.

2. Cited in Eugene N. Anderson, *The First Moroccan Crisis 1904–1906* (Hamden, 1966), 189.

3. Kühlmann, *Errinerungen*, 230.

4. Thomas A. Kohut, *Wilhelm II and the Germans: A Study in Leadership* (Oxford, 1991). See also his "Kaiser Wilhelm II and His Parents: An Inquiry into the Psychological Roots of German Policy toward England before the First World War," in John C. G. Röhl and Nicolaus Sombart (eds.), *Kaiser Wilhelm II: New Interpretations: The Corfu Papers* (Cambridge, 1982), 63–89.

5. All quotations are from Kohut, "Kaiser Wilhelm II," 66, 83.

6. Cited in Kohut, *Wilhelm II*, 106.

7. Ibid., 106.

8. For the quotations, and a discussion of Plessen, Senden, and Hahnke, see Isabel V. Hull, *The Entourage of Kaiser Wilhelm II 1888–1918* (Cambridge, 1982), 177–179, 185–186.

9. Courtier Philipp zu Eulenburg's comments are cited in John C. G. Röhl,

Philipp Eulenburgs Politische Korrespondenz (Boppard, 1979), 2:1283; and Michael Balfour, *The Kaiser and His Times* (New York, 1972), 151.

10. BMP to BWM, 22 September 1894, M. Kr. 37, KAM.

11. Lamar Cecil, *Wilhelm II: Prince and Emperor, 1859–1900* (Chapel Hill, N.C., 1989), 1: 126–127; Hull, *Entourage*, 183; and Waldersee Diary, 9 October 1888, in Heinrich Otto Meisner (ed.), *Denkwürdigkeiten des General-Feldmarshalls Alfred Graf von Waldersee* (Osnabrück, 1922), 2: 4.

12. Waldersee Diary, 5 January 1894, in Meisner, *Denkwürdigkeiten*, 2:301–302.

13. Ibid., 6 April 1895, 2:345.

14. Cited in BMP to BWM, 7 October 1912, M. Kr. 39, KAM.

15. BMP to BWM, 28 September 1893, M. Kr. 37, KAM.

16. SMP to SWM, 6 June 1894, Sächs. Militärbevollm. 4510, Bl. 82, HStAD.

17. For this episode, see Cecil, *Wilhelm II*, 240–250.

18. Marshall to Eulenburg, 30 April 1896, and Holstein to Eulenburg, 1 May 1896, in Röhl, *Eulenburgs Korrespondenz*, 3:1667–1668, 1670–1672.

19. Lerchenfeld to Crailsheim, 31 March 1901, cited in Hull, *Entourage*, 178.

20. For these quotations, see, respectively, Eulenburg's notes, 5 April 1894, and Eulenburg to Holstein, 20 October 1894, in Röhl, *Eulenburg's Korrespondenz*, 2:1283, 1390.

21. BMP to BWM, 19 May 1893, M. Kr. 43, KAM. See also Bernd F. Schulte, *Die deutsche Armee 1900–1914: Zwischen Beharren und Verändern* (Düsseldorf, 1977), 261–262. His thesis that Germany adhered to antiquated tactics for internal (i.e., anti-Socialist) reasons is exaggerated but does have limited applicability to Plessen and his circle in the army.

22. BMP to BWM, 20 September 1895, M. Kr. 38; and 17 November 1900, M. Kr. 39. See also the article of retired Colonel Gädke, *Berliner Tageblatt*, 1 October 1907 (clipping in M. Kr. 43), KAM; and Waldersee Diary, 17 December 1899, in Meisner, *Denkwürdigkeiten*, 2:440.

23. Waldersee Diary, 6 April 1895, in Meisner, *Denkwürdigkeiten*, 2:345; and Friedrich von Bernhardi, *Denkwürdigkeiten aus meinem Leben* (Berlin, 1927), 215.

24. Fof Waldersee's influence, see Cecil, *Wilhelm II*, 182.

25. Waldersee Diary, 6 December 1882, in Meisner, *Denkwürdigkeiten*, 1: 222–223.

26. William to Waldersee, 1 June 1886, and Waldersee to Verdy, 26 November 1888, in H. O. Meisner (ed.), *Aus dem Briefwechsel des Generalfeldmarschalls Alfred Grafen von Waldersee: Die Berliner Jahre 1886–1891* (Stuttgart, 1928), 22–23, 206–207; Waldersee Diary, 8 December and 25 December 1888, in Meisner, *Denkwürdigkeiten*, 2:25–26; Max Köhler, *Der Aufstieg der Artillerie bis zum Grossen Kriege* (Munich, 1938),127.

27. Cited in Hull, *Entourage*, 168. The statement probably referred to the three ministers mentioned above, not Verdy, Kaltenborn, and the younger Bronsart.

28. Köhler, *Aufstieg der Artillerie*, 145. See also the report of the Bavarian representative at heavy artillery maneuvers in Metz, May 1900, M. Kr. 3191, KAM.

29. For the following, see Cecil, *Wilhelm II*, 291–306, and Kohut, *Wilhelm*

II, 209–220. For the navy in general, readers should consult the classic study by Volker R. Berghahn, *Der Tirpitz-Plan: Genesis und Verfall einer innenpolitischen Krisenstrategie unter Wilhelm II* (Düsseldorf, 1971).

30. Kohut, *Wilhelm II,* 218.

31. Hohenlohe Diary, 12 December 1896, cited in Hull, *Entourage,* 179.

32. Ibid., 2 July 1896, 3:241.

33. Alfred von Tirpitz, *My Memoirs* (New York, 1919), 1:121.

34. Ibid., 1:128.

35. Hutten-Czapski to Holstein, 15 November 1895, in Norman Rich and M. H. Fisher (eds.), *The Holstein Papers: The Memoirs, Diaries and Correspondence of Friedrick von Holstein 1887–1909,* (Cambridge, 1957). 3:561.

36. Hans Linnenkohl, *Vom Einzelschuss zur Feuerwalze: Der Wettlauf zwischen Technik und Taktik im Ersten Weltkrieg* (Koblenz, 1990), 15.

37. Hull, *Entourage,* 159–160. Krupp deluged the young prince with technical literature in the 1880s. Their relationship became stronger between 1885 and 1888. For the kaiser's commitment to fortresses from about 1888, see Karl von Einem, *Erinnerungen eines Soldsten 1853–1933* (Leipzig, 1933), 95.

38. Waldersee Diary, 4 July 1897, in Meisner, *Denkwürdigkeiten,* 2:401–402.

39. Hull, *Entourage,* 167.

40. Colmar von der Goltz, *Denkwürdigkeiten* (Berlin, 1929), 215–218, 222.

41. Ibid., 216.

42. For both Planitz and Schliefen, see ibid., 210–212, 215–216.

43. Waldersee Diary, 19 March 1902, in Meisner, *Denkwürdigkeiten,* 3:181.

44. BMP to BWM, 16 March 1903, M. Kr. 43, and 18 September 1903, M. Kr. 3165, KAM.

45. Observations of Karl von Einem, Gossler's successor as war minister in 1903. See BMP to BWM, 13 December 1908, M. Kr. 42, KAM.

46. Waldersee Diary, 17 September 1891, in Meisner, *Denkwürdigkeiten,* 2: 216.

47. Holstein to Eulenburg, 4 July 1890, in Röhl, *Eulenburgs Korrespondenz,* 1: 559.

48. Quotations in Arden Buchholz, *Moltke, Schlieffen and Prussian War Planning* (New York, 1991), 129; Cecil, *Wilhelm II,* 1: 127.

49. Waldersee Diary, 21 September and 24 September 1890, 7 February 1891, in Meisner, *Denkwürdigkeiten,* 2:145, 148, 188.

50. Ibid., 15 January 1895 and 21 August 1895, 2:335, 356.

51. Wilhelm Groener, *Lebenserinnerungen: Jugend—Generalstab—Weltkrieg* (Göttingen, 1957), 59–60; Einem, *Erinnerungen,* 40; Bernhardi, *Denkwürdigkeiten,* 122–123, 172–175, 178–182. See also Hugo von Freytag-Loringhoven, *Menschen und Dinge wie ich sie in meinem Leben sah* (Berlin, 1923), 63–67, 139–142. Although Freytag-Loringhoven was more tactful in his criticisms than Einem and Bernhardi, his recollections show clearly how heavily "burdened" Schlieffen's men were by incompetence at the top after 1890, when the army faced "the worst conceivable" strategic position, "worse than any army had ever faced" (p. 139).

52. Cited in Hermann Teske, *Colmar Freiherr von der Goltz: Ein Kämpfer für den militärischen Fortschritt* (Göttingen, 1957), 47.

53. Bernhardi, *Denkwürdigkeiten,* 215–216, kaiser quotation, 212. Waldersee Diary, 17 December 1899, in Meisner, *Denkwürdigkeiten,* 2:440.

54. Waldersee Diary, late September 1902, 19 October 1902, and 26 October 1903, in Meisner, *Denkwürdigkeiten*, 3:188, 192, 219.

55. BMP to BWM, 4 June 1903, M. Kr. 43, KAM. For SPD criticism of the army, see Peter Domann, *Sozialdemokratie und Kaisertum unter Wilhelm II* (Wiesbaden, 1974), 168–195.

56. Endres to BWM, 18 September 1903, M. Kr. 3165, KAM.

57. Robert von Zedlitz-Trützschler, *Zwölf Jahre am deutschen Kaiserhof* (Stuttgart, 1925), 37–38, 42. The two undated diary entries are from the late summer and autumn of 1903.

58. Hull, *Entourage*, 103.

59. Diary of Baroness Hildegard von Spitzemberg, 25 November 1903, in Rudolf Vierhaus (ed.), *Das Tagebuch der Baronin Spitzemberg* (Göttingen, 1960), 436.

60. Wiiliam proposed the change to Schlieffen in a letter of 29 December 1903, in Eberhard Kessel (ed.), *Generalfeldmarschall Graf Alfred von Schieffen : Briefe* (Göttingen, 1958), 303–304.

61. Einem, *Erinnerungen*, 148. Einem cites a conversation in early 1904 with Plessen.

62. Bernhardi to Hülsen, 11 April 1904, in Bernhardi, *Denkwürdigkeiten*, 255. The Austrian military plenipotentiary reported in October 1904 that these criticisms of Moltke were very widespread in leading army circles. Hull, *Entourage*, 232.

63. Holger H. Herwig, *'Luxury' Fleet: The Imperial German Navy 1888–1918* (London, 1991), 49; Heiner Raulff, *Zwischen Machtpolitik und Imperialismus: Die Deutsche Frankreichpolitik 1904/06* (Düsseldorf, 1976), 71–74.

64. Einem to Bernhardi, n.d. (mid-February 1904), cited in Bernhardi, *Denkwürdigkeiten*, 309.

65. Goltz to Mudra, 25 June 1904, in Goltz, *Denkwürdigkeiten*, 269.

66. For Plessen's remarks during the Boer War, see Hermann von Eckardstein, *Lebenserinnerungen und Politische Denkwürdigkeiten* (Leipzig, 1920), 2: 45. For a war party in the entourage in 1904–1905, see 2:435–436; Holstein memorandum, 22 October 1904, in Rich, *Holstein Papers*, 4:312; and Raulff, *Machtpolitik*, 104, who cites French sources from April 1905.

67. Albrecht Moritz, *Das Problem des Präventivkrieges in der deutschen Politik während der ersten Marokkokrise* (Frankfurt, 1974), 95–96; Raulff, *Machtpolitik*, 76–79.

68. Moritz, *Präventivkrieg*, 91, 219. See also Gerhard Ritter, *The Schlieffen Plan: Critique of a Myth*, trans. B. H. Liddell Hart (London, 1958), 44–45, 55–56.

69. Holstein said this in April 1904 (Spitzemberg Diary, 23 April 1904, in Vierhaus, *Tagebuch*, 440). The counselor's close relationship with Schlieffen [see Oscar von der Lancken-Wakenitz, *Meine Dreissig Dienstjahre 1888–1918* (Berlin, 1931), 58–59] suggests that the opinion stemmed from the military. For similar sentiments about avoiding international crises because of incompetence at the top, see the Zedlitz-Trützschler Diary, 30 January 1905, in Zedlitz-Trützschler, *Zwölf Jahre*, 107.

70. Printed in Kessel, *Schlieffen: Briefe*, 303.

71. Moltke related the conversation with the kaiser in a letter to his wife, 29 January 1905, in Generaloberst Helmuth von Moltke, *Erinnerungen Briefe*

Dokumente 1877–1916 (Stuttgart, 1922), 305–312. Unless otherwise noted, the quotations that follow are from Moltke's letter.

72. Although it is not inconsistent with Moltke's letter, this portion of the conversation is from Franz Karl Endres, chief of the Bavarian General Staff and military plenipotentiary in Berlin until 1904, *Die Tragödie Deutschlands* (Stuttgart, 1923), 97. He probably heard the story from his replacement, Ludwig von Gebsattel, who was also well connected in leading army circles in Berlin.

73. Quotations in Einem, *Erinnerungen*, 96, 97, and Bernhardi, *Denkwürdigkeiten*, 262–263.

74. Moritz, *Präventivkrieg*, 154–188; Raulff, *Machtpolitik*, 71–73, 95–96, 99.

75. Einem, *Erinnerungen*, 111.

76. Raulff, *Machtpolitik*, 95–96; Robert K. Massie, *Dreadnought: Britain, Germany, and the Coming of the Great War* (New York, 1991), 355–358.

77. Kohut, *Wilhelm II*, 209–214.

78. William to Bülow, 23 November 1904, cited in Raulff, *Machtpolitik*, 126. For fears of an English attack, see also Bülow to Holstein, 25 December 1904, in Rich and Fisher, *Holstein Papers*, 4:322; and Moltke to his wife, 29 January 1905, in Moltke, *Erinnerungen*, 305.

79. Cecil, *Wilhelm II*, 2:108.

80. Cited in the Spitzemberg Diary, 24 March 1905, in Vierhaus, *Tagebuch*, 446n18.

81. That Schlieffen was suppressing doubts is the implication of Moritz's analysis, *Präventivkrieg*, 90–91, 219–224.

82. BMP to BWM, 18 September 1903 and 20 December 1906, M. Kr. 3165, KAM. According to Endres, it was "the top commanders," indeed, "the very best generals," who resented William's dilettantism and lack of training. Endres's replacement, Ludwig von Gebsattel, reported on 8 January 1906 (M. Kr. 43) that the army wanted the chief of the General Staff to function as a kind of generalissimo next to the kaiser.

83. Spitzemberg Diary, 10 November 1905, in Vierhaus, *Tagebuch*, 450. It is clear from this entry that Varnbüler was referring to something more than the earlier agreement not to lead armies during exercises and maneuvers.

84. See a recollection of the aftermath of the meeting by a colleague of Schlieffen's nephew, cited in Raulff, *Machtpolitik*, 131–132. That it was the kaiser, not Schlieffen or Einem, who drew this conclusion from the inferior status of the field artillery seems very clear. Schlieffen reacted angrily to the outcome of the meeting, no doubt because he put far more emphasis on the contribution to victory of the light and heavy howitzers than on the C-96 field cannons. For his part, Einem had always believed that the C-96 had certain advantages over the French 75 [see Einem to Schlieffen, 14 November 1899, in Ludwig Rüdt von Collenberg, "Graf Schlieffen und die Kriegsformation der deutschen armee," *Wissen und Wehr* 10 (1927): 625]. This helps to explain the very gradual transition in Germany to a recoilless model after 1901–1902 (SMP to SWM, 5 September 1901, Sächs. Militärbevollm. 4518, Bl. 73; 3 March 1902, Sächs. Militärbevollm. 1424, Bl. 13, HStAD; and Einem, *Erinnerungen*, 85–87). There is no reason to conclude that Einem's opinion had changed so much by early 1905 that he believed that the German Army was unready for war. He maintained consistently throughout 1905, on the contrary, that the army was ready (*Erinnerungen*, 111, 112). It was only the accelerated adoption of a recoilless cannon in the latter half of 1905, and especially the outbreak of revo-

lution in Russia, that made him somewhat more prudent (see Einem to Cammerer, 7 January 1906, in Raulff, *Machtpolitik*, 132; and BMP to BWM, 30 March 1906, M. Kr. 42, KAM).

85. Observations of Hull, *Entourage*, 184.

86. Cited in Lancken Wakenitz, *Dreissig Dienstjahre*, 63.

87. Radolin to Bülow, 11 June 1905, cited in Raulff, *Machtpolitik*, 133.

88. The quotations are in Einem, *Erinnerungen*, 112, 115–116.

89. Bülow to Holstein, 22 February 1906, printed in Rich, *Holstein Papers*, 4:396–397.

90. Einem, *Erinnerungen*, 112–114.

91. Groener, *Lebenserinnerungen*, 85; Raulff, *Machtpolitik*, 130–131; Moritz, *Präventivkrieg*, 223.

92. For the mood, see BMP to BWM, 23 September 1905, M. Kr. 45, and 2 November 1905 and 3 January 1906, M. Kr. 43, KAM; Spitzemberg Diary, 1 January 1906, in Vierhaus, *Tagebuch*, 454; Einem, *Erinnerungen*, 112–114; Bernhardi, *Denkwürdigkeiten*, 272–273. For Schlieffen's feelings about the 1905 maneuvers, see Moltke's letters of 29 January and 7 March 1905, in Moltke, *Erinnerungen*, 313, 319–320. Moltke had asked the kaiser for control of maneuvers in early 1905, noticing Schlieffen's adverse reaction when William agreed. In August, Schlieffen broke his leg and could not attend the maneuvers.

93. See Harden to Holstein, 31 December 1907, printed in Rich, *Holstein Papers*, 4:512; and Eulenburg's notes to a letter from Hahnke, 26 May 1908, printed in Röhl, *Eulenburgs Korrespondenz*, 3:2183, note 3.

94. Findlay to Grey, 27 June 1908, cited in Hull, *Entourage*, 129.

95. Ibid., 130.

96. *Zukunft*, 13 April 1907, cited in Harry F. Young, *Maximilian Harden: Censor Germaniae* (The Hague, 1959), 96.

97. *Zukunft*, 15 June 1907, cited ibid., 101.

98. *Zukunft*, 9 November 1907, cited in Hull, *Entourage*, 134.

99. *Zukunft*, 15 June 1907, cited in Young, *Maximilian Harden*, 101.

100. For the role of the military entourage, see Hull, *Entourage*, 142–144; quotations on 144–145.

101. Harden to Holstein, 31 December 1907, in Rich *Holstein Papers*, 4:512.

102. Zedlitz-Trützschler, *Zwölf Jahre*, 160, entry for 7 June 1907.

103. Bernhard von Bülow, *Memoirs of Prince von Bülow*, trans. Geoffrey Dunlop (Boston, 1931), 2:396. See 390–392 for a full account of the kaiser's remarks.

104. Naumann's article in *Hilfe* (November 1908) is cited in Helmuth Rogge, *Holstein und Harden: Politisch-publizistisches Zusammenspiel zweier Aussenseiter des Wilhelminischen Reichs* (Munich, 1959), 376.

105. Cited ibid., 375.

106. Harden to Holstein, 15 November 1908, in John C. G. Röhl, *The Kaiser and His Court: Wilhelm II and the Government of Germany* (Cambridge, 1996), 63.

107. Rogge, *Holstein und Harden*, 374; Diary of the Baroness Spitzemberg, 8 and 26 November 1908, in Vierhaus, *Das Tagebuch*, 491, 494; Goltz to his son Fritz, 4 November 1908, in Goltz, *Denkwürdigkeiten*, 330–331; Bülow, *Memoirs*, 2:403.

108. Zedlitz-Trützschler, *Zwölf Jahre*, 226, entry for 26 March 1909.

109. Einem's speech to the ministers is cited in Bülow, *Memoirs*, 2:403, and his remarks to the Bavarian representative Ludwig von Gebsattel are cited in Gebsattel's report of 13 December 1908, M. Kr. 42, KAM. Einem claimed later (*Erinnerungen*, 121) that he did not make the speech, but Bülow's version is very consistent not only with previous statements by Einem but also with his comments to Gebsattel a few weeks later.

110. Harden to Holstein, 4 January 1909, in Rogge, *Holstein und Harden*, 436.

111. The phrase is Martin Kitchen's in *The Silent Dictatorship: The Politics of the German High Command under Hindenburg and Ludendorff, 1916–1918* (New York, 1976).

112. Bülow, *Memoirs*, 2:420.

113. See Einem, *Erinnerungen*, 122.

114. Osten-Sacken to Isvolsky, n.d. (March 1909), in Fritz Fischer, *War of Illusions: German Policies from 1911 to 1914*, trans. Marian Jackson (New York, 1975), 62.

115. Bernhardi, *Denkwürdigkeiten*, 292–293.

116. Ibid., 332; Zedlitz-Trützschler, *Zwölf Jahre*, 226, entry for 26 March 1909.

117. Cecil, *Wilhelm II*, 175; David Herrmann, *The Arming of Europe and the Making of the First World War* (Princeton, N.J., 1996), 126.

118. Fischer, *War of Illusions*, 60–61.

Chapter 7

1. Alfred von Schlieffen, "Der Krieg in der Gegenwart," *Deutsche Revue* 34/1 (January 1909): 13–24. For "Modern Alexander," see 18.

2. Quotations ibid., 13–14.

3. Ibid., 15.

4. Ibid., 24.

5. Chief of the Allgemeines Kriegsdepartment.

6. Karl von Einem, *Erinnerungen eines Soldaten 1853–1933* (Leipzig, 1922), 48.

7. Ibid., 82.

8. Gossler (Einem) to the General Staff, 19 October 1899, in Ludwig Rüdt von Collenberg, "Graf Schlieffen und die Kriegsformation der deutschen Armee," *Wissen und Wehr* 10 (1927): 618.

9. This quotation and reference to "plenty of them" are reported in SMP to SWM, 17 December 1900, Sächs. Militär-Bevollm. 4517, Bl. 259, HStAD.

10. Initial plans called for the rearming of about two corps per year. The intended pace increased to five per year in mid-1904. The decision was taken at the end of the year to accelerate "as quickly as possible." Ten corps were rearmed between late 1904 and mid-1906—fewer than one per month. Twelve were rearmed between mid-1906 and mid-1907—two per month. See the documents from 1903–1905 in M. Kr. Alter Bestand, A.X.2, Bd. 12d/Bd. 1 and 2, KAM; and Einem to Bülow, 18 June 1906, in Einem, *Erinnerungen*, 102.

11. Bülow to Einem, 1 June 1906, W-10/50199 ("Rüstung bis 1914"), Bl. 297, BAMAF. Also printed in Einem, *Erinnerungen*, 99.

12. The militia and part of the replacement batteries still used the antiquated C-73 cannons. See the BWM's memo of May 1907, M. Kr. 2989, KAM.

13. Einem to Bülow, 18 June 1906, in Einem, *Erinnerungen*, 102.

14. Dolf L. Goldsmith, *The Devil's Paintbrush: Sir Hiran Maxim's Gun* (Toronto, 1989), 141, 142.

15. Hoffmann to Wandel, n.d. (mid-1908), W-10/50199 ("Rüstung bis 1914"), Bl. 105, BAMAF.

16. Hoffmann to Wandel, n.d. (mid-1908), ibid., Bl. 101–104.

17. Wandel to Einem, 31 October 1908, and Moltke to Einem, 1 December 1908, ibid., Bl. 106–114.

18. Dieter Storz, *Kriegsbild und Rüstung vor 1914. Europäische Landstreitkräfte vor dem ersten Weltkrieg* (Berlin, 1914), 341; David G. Herrmann, *The Arming of Europe and the Making of the First World War* (Princeton, N.J., 1996), 69.

19. Erich Ludendorff, *Mein militärischer Werdegang: Blätter der Erinnerung an unser stolzes Heer* (Munich, 1937), 121; see also 86–90.

20. Moltke (Ludendorff) to Einem, 13 October 1909, W-10/50199 (Rüstung vor 1914"), Bl. 194–197, BAMAF.

21. Cited in Manfred Lachmann, "Probleme der Bewaffnung des kaiserlichen deutschen Heeres," *Zeitschrift für Militärgeschichte* 6/1 (1967): 24.

22. Moltke's comments of October 1906 are cited in Herrmann, *Arming of Europe*, 69. For his agreement with Einem, see Moltke to Einem, 1 December 1908, W-10/50199 ("Rüstung vor 1914"), Bl. 113–114, BAMAF.

23. *LJB* 36 (1909); and BWM to commanders of the Second and Third Bavarian Corps, 24 November 1908, M. Kr. Alter Bestand, A.X.8, Bd.1/Pt. 2, KAM. Four brigades would establish machine gun detachments by October 1909.

24. See the General Staff's materials for the 1910 maneuvers and its official report for 1911, *Bericht über das Kaisermanöver 1911*, in AE100, KAM.

25. For machine gun tactics and experiments at maneuvers, see the excellent discussions in Herrmann, *Arming of Europe*, 68–70, and Storz, *Kriegsbild und Rüstung*, 341–342.

26. See *AM*, 1, Nr. 1 (January 1907): 255–256.

27. For the following, see Herrmann, *Arming of Europe*, 91–96.

28. *MWB*, 29 December 1906, Sp. 3709.

29. Ibid., 2 March 1907, Sp. 671–672. Part 2 of Rohne's article appeared on 5 March 1907, Sp. 694–700. See also Storz, *Kriegsbild und Rüstung*, 180–181.

30. *Exerzier-Reglement für die Feldartillerie*, April 1907, especially 163–216 ("Das Gefecht"), M. Kr. 2989, KAM. Excerpts from the 1907 regulations are also printed in *VTH* 4/4 (1907): 774, 776. See also Storz, *Kriegsbild und Rüstung*, 182.

31. Schubert to Kaiser William, 6 January 1908, FZM 2240, KAM.

32. See Captain Reck's report of 15 May 1908, M. Kr. 2139, KAM. See also Rohne, "Manöverrückblicke," *AM* 2, Nr. 22 (October 1908): 262–272.

33. Schubert to the kaiser, 23 December 1908, FZM 2241, KAM.

34. Storz, *Kriegsbild und Rüstung*, 182–183.

35. Schubert to the kaiser, 23 December 1909 and 18 January 1911, FZM 2241, KAM.

36. Storz, *Kriegsbild und Rüstung*, 183–185.

37. For the specifications of the l.FH-98/09, see Alfred Muther, *Das Gerät*

der leichten Artillerie vor, in und nach dem Weltkrieg (Berlin, 1925), 22–25. For the expansion of field artillery battalions in 1911–1912, see Ludwig Rüdt von Collenberg, *Die deutsche Armee von 1871 bis 1914* (Berlin, 1922), 122–123. For the numbers of howitzers and field cannons, and Schubert's efforts, see, respectively; the appendix to the report of the Allgemeine Kriegsdepartment, 18 December 1914, PH2/Nr. 87, and W-10/50777 ("Die Vorbereitungen für die ersorgung des deutschen Heeres mit Munition vor Ausbruch des Krieges"), in BAMAF.

38. Hermann Müller-Brandenburg, *Von Schlieffen bis Ludendorff* (Leipzig, 1925),144; and Ministère de la Guerre, *Les armées francaises dans la grande Guerre* (Paris, 1936), Tome I, 1:521.

39. *LJB* 39 (1912): 298; Douglas Porch, *The March to the Marne: The French Army 1871–1914* (Cambridge, 1981), 235, 238–239, 243.

40. William Balck's wartime memoirs are cited in Storz, *Kriegsbild und Rüstung*, 205, note 199.

41. Max Köhler, *Der Aufstieg der Artillerie bis zum Grossen Krieg* (Munich, 1938), 138. See also Ernst von Eisenhart-Rothe, *So war die alte Armee* (Berlin, 1935), 75–76; Walter Elze, *Tannenberg: Das deutsche Heer von 1914* (Breslau, 1928), 49. Confirming these recollections are a Bavarian report about field artillery practice in Karl von Bülow's Third Corps (see Gebsattel to BWM, 6 September 1910, M. Kr. 39, KAM), and the remarks of Ninth Corps commander, General von Bock und Polach, chair of a commission that rewrote infantry regulations (see the commssion's protocols for 12 January 1906 in M. Kr. 2922, KAM).

42. See the postwar study "Die Vorbereitungen für die Versorgung des deutschen Heeres mit Munition vor Ausbruch des Krieges," in W-1050777, Bl. 25, BAMAF. According to one French artilleryman (General Herr), there were 1,300 shells per cannon in August 1914 (Bl. 64n1). According to Ministère de la Guerre, *Armées francaises*, 1:521, there were 1,190.

43. For the remainder of this paragraph, see mainly "Vorbereitungen," Bl. 11, 13, 15, 25, 45–46, 66–67; BAMAF. See also the Allgemeine Kriegsdepartment memo of 18 December 1914, as well as General Muther's study, n.d. (1919), both in PH2/87, BAMAF.

44. Schubert's oral report of December 1910 is cited in "Vorbereitungen," Bl. 25, BAMAF.

45. The standard work is Lothar Burchardt, *Friedenswirtschaft und Kriegsvorsorge: Deutschlands wirtschaftliche Rüstungsbestrebungen vor 1914* (Boppard, 1968).

46. Herrmann, *Arming of Europe*, 204.

47. Porch, *March to the Marne*, 242; see also 240–241.

48. *Fussartillerie fremder Heere* (Berlin, 1902), 39, in M. Kr. 4075, KAM; Ministère de la Guerre, *Armées francaises*, 1:35, note 3; and Porch, *March to the Marne*, 244.

49. Ministère de la Guerre, *Armées francaises*, 1:522; and General Muther's study, n.d. (1919), PH2/87, BAMAF.

50. General Staff, "Erfahrungen der letzten Kriege über Infanterie-taktik," 28 December 1905, M. Kr. 2922, KAM.

51. *MWB*, 2 September 1905, Sp. 2475.

52. Ibid., 1 June 1905, Sp. 1579–1580; see also 16 November 1905, Sp. 3235–3236.

53. Ibid., 28 December 1905, Sp. 3658; see also 26 October 1905 and 6 January 1906, Sp. 41; 9 January 1906, Sp. 70; and 17 March 1906, Sp. 778.

54. Ibid., 14 March 1905, Sp. 730–731; 25 December 1906, Sp. 3683–3694. See also the offensive-mindedness of *LJB* 32 (1905): 262, and 33 (1906): 283.

55. Hindenburg described these impressions to one of his division commanders, Friedrich von Bernhardi. See Bernhardi, *Denkwürdigkeiten aus meinem Leben* (Berlin, 1927), 272–273.

56. All quotations above are in Einem, *Erinnerungen*, 91, 93. See also ibid., 273.

57. Noted by Ludwig von Gebsattel, *Generalfeldmarschall Karl von Bülow* (Munich, 1929), 33.

58. BMP to BWM, 20 December 1905, M. Kr. 2149, KAM.

59. Fasbender to BWM, 29 January 1906, M. Kr. 2919, KAM. See also the commission protocols for 8 January 1906, M. Kr. 2922, when Langenbeck's ideas were discussed and rejected. Speaking against him were Bülow, Kessel (Guard Corps), and commssion Chairman Bock und Polach.

60. For the infantry regulations of 1906, see Heinz-Ludger Borgert, "Grundzüge der Landkriegführung von Schlieffen bis Guderian," in Gerhard Papke and Wolfgang Petter, *Handbuch zur deutschen Militärgeschichte* (Munich, 1983), 6:431–432; and Storz, *Kriegsbild und Rüstung*, 167–170.

61. Cited in Borgert, "Grundzüge der Landkriegführung," 6:432. See also Martin Samuels, *Command or Conrol? Command, Training and Tactics in the British and German Armies, 1888–1918* (London, 1995), 76–77.

62. For the 1906 maneuvers, see BMP to BWM, 20 December 1906, M. Kr. 3165, and various reports from autumn of 1906 in M. Kr. 3192, KAM. See also Storz, *Kriegsbild und Rüstung*, 170–173.

63. See the General Staff's official reports, *Kaisermanöver 1907* and *Kaiser-Manöver 1908*, AE100, KAM. See also Storz, *Kriegsbild und Rüstung*, 190–193.

64. Diary of the Baroness Spitzemberg, 10 November 1905, in Rudolf Vierhaus (ed.), *Das Tagebuch der Baronin Spitzemberg* (Göttingen, 1960), 450.

65. General von Poseck, "Die Kavallerie," in Ernst von Eisenhart-Rothe (ed.), *Ehrendenkmal der Deutschen Armee und Marine 1871–1918* (Berlin, 1928), 114–115; Storz, *Kriegsbild und Rüstung*, 271–273.

66. Planitz to the corps commanders, 12 January 1907, M. Kr. 3191, KAM.

67. BWM to corps commanders, 18 March 1908, M. Kr. 2959, KAM; Poseck, "Die Kavallerie," 115–117; Eisenhart-Rothe, *So war die alte Armee*, 60; Bernhardi, *Denkwürdigkeiten*, 280–287; and Colmar von der Goltz, *Denkwürdigkeiten* (Berlin, 1929), 287.

68. See Colonel von Unger, *Die Kavalleriedivisionen im deutschen Kaisermanöver 1909* (Munich, n.d.), in G. St. 1156, KAM; and *LJB* 36 (1909): 306.

69. *Berliner Tageblatt*, Nr. 618, 6 December 1909 (clipping in G. St. 1156, KAM).

70. For this paragraph, see BMP to BWM, 15 September 1911, M. Kr. 39, KAM; Goltz, *Denkwürdigkeiten*, 305–306; and Storz, *Kriegsbild und Rüstung*, 193–196, 342.

71. For the heavy artillery, see below.

72. See Rohne's editorial in *AM*, 1912/1, Nr. 61 (January); 21.

73. Storz, *Kriegsbild und Rüstung*, 195–196.

74. General Staff, *Bericht über das Kaisermanöver 1911,* AE100, KAM.
75. Terence Zuber, "The Schlieffen Plan Reconsidered," *War in History* 6/3 (1999): 303.
76. See Hartmut John, *Das Reserveoffizierkorps im Deutschen Kaiserreich 1890–1914: Ein sozialgeschichtlicher Beitrag zur Untersuchung der gesellschaftlichen Militarisierung im Wilhelminischen Deutschland* (Frankfurt, 1981), 141–150, quotation on 471.
77. Einem, *Erinnerungen,* 148–151.
78. BMP to BWM, 28 June 1912, M. Kr. 39, KAM.
79. Ibid., 7 October 1912, KAM.
80. *KM,* 1912/5 (May): 348.
81. For some of the best examples, see ibid., 1909/12 (December): 998–1001, 1910/3 (March): 185–190, 1911/7–8 (July–August): 552–553, 1911/10 (October): 739–742, 1912/11 (November): 908.
82. Ibid., 1912/1 (January), 171.
83. Cited in Karl Franz Endres, *Die Tragödie Deutschlands* (Stuttgart, 1923), 100.
84. *Die Militärluftfahrt bis zum Beginn des Weltkrieges 1914* (Frankfurt, 1965), 1:27–75.
85. Ibid., 47, 57–58; 2:33–34.
86. Ibid., 1:44–47, 69, 76; *Danzer's Armee-Zeitung,* 16 December 1909 (clipping in AE100, KAM); and report of the Prussian General Staff's Technological Section, October 1909, PH3/215, BAMAF.
87. *Militärluftfahrt,* 1:111–115, 118; 2:107–108.
88. For Rheims Air Week, see Pustau to Heeringen, 31 August 1909, RK 1335, Bl. 197–205, BAP.
89. Pustau to Heeringen, 31 August 1909, ibid.
90. Report of the Prussian Army Commission on the Military Potential of Airplanes, January 1911, printed in *Militärluftfahrt,* 2:126.
91. For early responses to airplanes, see ibid., 111–117. For the flight budget, see Wermuth to Bülow, 28 September 1909, RK 1335, Bl. 228, BAP.
92. Heeringen to Bülow, 30 September 1909, and for the quotation, Heeringen to the Ministry of Public Works, 17 March 1910, RK 1335, Bl. 223, 296, BAP.
93. See the report of his section, October 1909, PH3/215, BAMAF.
94. For the figures, see *Militärluftfahrt,* 2:Nr. 106; and John Howard Morrow, Jr., *Building German Airpower, 1909–1914* (Knoxville, Tenn., 1976), 52.
95. *Militärluftfahrt,* 1:82–85, 2: 79, plus Chart Nr. 106; Morrow, *Building German Airpower,* 52.
96. See Thomsen's "Die Bedeutung der technischen Hilfsmittel für die Fernaufklärung im Felde," *VTH,* 7/2 (1911): 325–326, 336–342.
97. See Thomsen's marginalia to a pro-airplane report by Lt. Wilberg, n.d. (Fall 1911), as well as his comments on detailed situational reports from maneuvers, 26 October 1911, PH3/219, BAMAF. See also Moltke to Heeringen, 30 September 1911, in *Militärluftfahrt,* 2: 72–73; and the General Staff's *Bericht über das Kaisermanöver 1911,* p. 88, in AE100, KAM.
98. In June 1911, the Swabia (LZ-10) was completed. For the capabilities of Germany's single-winged Taube in 1911, see Karl Köhler, "Organisationsgeschichte der Luftwaffe von den Anfängen bis 1918," in Gerhard Papke and

Wolfgang Petter (eds.), *Handbuch zur deutschen Militärgeschichte* (Munich, 1979), 3:285, 289.

99. Moltke to Heeringen, 30 September 1911 and 2 January 1912, printed in *Militärluftfahrt*, 2:72–73, 76–77; and Moltke to Heeringen, 2 March 1911, 29 March 1912, and 23 May 1912, excerpts in PH3/221, Bl. 17, 21, 23, BA-MAF.

100. Lyncker to Moltke, 18 December 1911, in *Militärluftfahrt*, 2:74.

101. Heeringen to Moltke, 5 March 1912, ibid., 2:80–81.

102. See the excerpts from the War Ministry–General Staff correspondence of 1912–1913 in PH3/221, Bl. 22–28, 251–262, BAMAF; *Militärluftfahrt*, 1:90, 107, 149–150 and 2:Chart Nr. 106 and Luftschiff-Tabelle (Anfang 1914); and Morrow, *Building German Airpower*, 52.

103. Lyncker to Heeringen, 13 January 1913, PH24/40, Bl. 181–182, BA-MAF.

104. See Thomsen's article in *VTH*, 7/2 (1911): 340–341. See also Köhler, "Organisationsgeschichte," 3:285, 289.

105. See the army's guidelines for 1912, "Luftfahrzeuge im Kaisermanöver 1912," in PH3/136, p. 9, BAMAF.

106. Hans Ritter, *Der Luftkrieg* (Berlin, 1926), 25–26.

107. See Lt. Wilberg's report, n.d. (Fall 1911), PH3/219, pp. 26–30, BA-MAF.

108. For their influence on Schlieffen, see Kurt von Priessdorff (ed.), *Soldatisches Führertum* (Hamburg, n.d.), 10:49; and BMP to BWM, 12 August 1903, M. Kr. 3165, KAM.

109. See Karl Justrow's article in *Die Schwere Artillerie* 13 (1936): 20–21; for the quotation, Einem to the BWM, 2 July 1904, M. Kr. 3022, KAM. Justrow's claims are confirmed by information in Einem's letter, as well as by the absence of documents on fortress exercises after 1902 in M. Kr. 3025 and 3191. Justrow was active on the heavy artillery's proving commission before the war.

110. Einem to the BWM, 2 July 1904, M. Kr. 3022, KAM.

111. Major General Schwierz, "Fussartillerie," *AM*, (1913)/1, Nr. 78 (June): 442, 451–453; Lt. Gen. Ziethen, "Die Fussartillerie," in Eisenhart-Rothe, *Ehrendenkmal*, 148–149; and Gen. von Lauter, "Unsere Waffe," in Franz Nikolaus Kaiser (ed.), *Das Ehrenbuch der Deutschen Schweren Artillerie* (Berlin, 1931), 1: 24–28.

112. See Hans Friederich, *Die taktische Verwendung der schweren Artillerie* (Berlin, 1910): for the 'trump' quotation, Köhler, *Aufstieg*, 148. Köhler had served in the heavy artillery.

113. *AM* 1, Nr. 39 (March 1910): 176–186, 1914/1, Nr. 90 (June): 416–417.

114. See Justrow's memoir in *Die Schwere Artillerie* 13 (1936): 20.

115. See Köhler, *Aufstieg*, 146.

116. *AM* 1, Nr. 88 (April 1914): 302–305.

117. Ibid., 1909/2, Nr. 34 (October): 280.

118. Ibid., 1910/1, Nr. 39 (March): 185.

119. See Bauer's memoir of 1921, NL 22 Bauer, Nr. 7, Bl. 7, BAK.

120. Ibid., Bl. 13.

121. Ibid., Bl. 7; for the Deines quotation, Bl. 8.

122. See the excellent summary of the evidence and the literature in Adolf

Vogt, *Oberst Max Bauer: Generalstabsoffizier im Zwielicht* (Osnabrück, 1974), 16–23, 585–586. Also see Rausenberger (of Krupp) to Bauer, 11 April 1923, and Guse to Ernst Bauer, 24 July 1929, NL 22 Bauer, Nr. 7, Bl. 255, 127–129, BAK.

123. Vogt, *Oberst Max Bauer*, 18, 26; and Moltke to Einem, 4 September 1906, M. Kr. 990, KAM.

124. According to Rausenberger of Krupp in his letter to Bauer, 11 April 1923, NL 22 Bauer, Bl. 255, BAK.

125. Bauer to his wife, 4 January 1910, NL 22 Bauer, Nr. 56, Bl. 1, BAK.

126. Max Bauer, *Der grosse Krieg in Feld und Heimat: Erinnerungen und Betrachtungen* (Tübingen, 1921), 49–50; Vogt, *Oberst Max Bauer*, 29.

127. See Ludendorff's memo of 8 February 1911, in Ludendorff, *Mein militärischer Werdegang*, 139–40; and O. Reg. Rat Dieckmann's unpublished postwar manuscript "Die Vorbereitungen für die Versorgung des deutschen Heeres mit Munition vor Ausbruch des Krieges," W-10/50777, p. 32, BAMAF. Both sources make it clear that Verdun and Toul-Nancy were the priority assignments for available heavy artillery. Liège, an older fortress, was apparently a lower priority for the biggest guns—hence plans for a *coup de main* dating from 1911–1912. For the dating, see Herrmann, *Arming of Europe*, 158, 275, note 47.

128. Isabel V. Hull, *The Entourage of Kaiser Wilhelm II 1888–1918* (Cambridge, 1982), 239–242.

129. Moltke to his wife, 29 January, 26 July, and 30 July 1905, in Helmuth von Moltke, *Erinnerungen Briefe Dokumente 1877–1916* (Stuttgart, 1922), 307–308, 329, 331.

130. See Stig Förster's arguments in "Dreams and Nightmares: German Military Leadership and the Images of Future Warfare, 1871–1914," in Manfred F. Boemeke et al. (eds.), *Anticipating Total War: The German and American Experiences 1871–1914* (Cambridge, 1999), 362–367. Also see, however, Zuber, "Schlieffen Plan Reconsidered," 262–305, who demonstrates that Schlieffen envisioned a longer war than is usually assumed.

131. Moltke to Endres, 15 August 1906, G. St. 1238, and Moltke to Fasbender, 12 June 1908, G. St. 1291, KAM; see also Moltke's comments on the Schlieffen Plan, n.d. (1911), in Gerhard Ritter, *The Schlieffen Plan: Critique of a Myth*, trans. B. H. Liddell Hart (London, 1958), 165–167. The 1908 letter was in response to Bavarian war games in 1906–1907, which claimed to demonstrate the feasibility of a western breakthrough with heavy artillery. The 1906 letter advocated a southern wheeling of the right wing if the French attacked Germany. The move through Belgium was not "an end in itself" but rather "a means to an end." That Schlieffen would not necessarily have disagreed, see Ritter, *Schlieffen Plan*, 55–56, and Zuber, "Schlieffen Plan Reconsidered," 277–305.

132. Ritter, *Schlieffen Plan*, 54–65; and Gunther E. Rothenberg, "Moltke, Schlieffen, and the Doctrine of Strategic Envelopment," in Peter Paret (ed.), *Makers of Modern Strategy from Machiavelli to the Nuclear Age* (Princeton, N.J., 1986), 320–323. See also Jehuda L. Wallach, *Das Dogma der Vernichtungsschlacht* (Munich, 1970), 132–150.

133. Karl Justrow, *Die Dicke Berta und der Krieg* (Berlin, 1935), 63. Justrow belonged to the heavy artillery's proving commission.

134. See Alistair Horne, *The Price of Glory: Verdun 1916* (New York, 1962), 153.

135. Vogt, *Oberst Max Bauer*, 22, 27.

136. Justrow, *Dicke Berta*, 62; Lauter, "Unsere Waffe," 1:31. Ludendorff claimed later (*Mein miltärischer Werdegang*, 140) that his requests represented only a "slight increase," but Germany had only 40 heavy artillery battalions in 1911, 48 in 1913, and 55 in 1914, whereas he was demanding an additional 33, that is, a total of 73.

137. See note 127.

138. "Die Vorbereitung," W-10/50777, Bl. 72, and General Muther's memo, n.d. (1919), PH2/87, BAMAF.

139. Ludendorff to his mother, 9 April 1913, N77 Ludendorff, Nr. 18, Bl. 56, BAMAF.

140. Geoff Eley, *Reshaping the German Right: Radical Nationalism and Political Change after Bismarck* (New Haven, Conn., 1980), 48–58; and Roger Chickering, *We Men Who Feel Most German: A Cultural Study of the Pan-German League, 1886–1914* (London, 1984), 44–73.

141. See the printed version of Heinrich Class's speech at the Pan-German Congress of September 1903, in ADV 506, BAP.

142. Ibid.

143. Cited in Chickering, *We Men*, 222–223.

144. Cited in Stig Förster, *Der Doppelte Militarismus: Die deutsche Heeresrüstungspolitik zwischen Status-Quo Sicherung und Aggression 1890–1913* (Stuttgart, 1985), 183–184.

145. Keim's accusations in *Der Tag* were picked up by Gädke in the *Berliner Tageblatt*, 1 October 1907 (clipping in M. Kr. 43, KAM).

146. See Stig Förster, "Alter und neuer Militarismus im Kaiserreich," in Jost Dülffer and Karl Holl (eds.), *Bereit zum Krieg: Kriegsmentalität im wilhelminischen Deutschland 1890–1914* (Göttingen, 1986), 138, 145, note 56.

147. August Keim, *Erlebtes und Erstrebtes: Lebenserinnerungen von Generalleutnant Keim* (Hannover, 1925), 161–162; Chickering, *We Men*, 268; Förster, *Doppelte Militarismus*, 203–204.

148. Herrmann, *Arming of Europe*, 122–146.

149. Cited ibid., 135.

150. Ibid., 180–191; Storz, *Kriegsbild und Rüstung*, 322–330.

151. See Moltke to Einem, 13 October 1909, and Einem to Moltke, 23 July 1909, in "Rüstung bis 1914," W-10/50199, Bl. 194–197, 240–242, BAMAF.

152. William to Bethmann Hollweg, 7 August 1910, ibid., Bl. 118–121.

153. Keim's article in the *Tägliche Rundschau*, 12 December 1911, is printed in Erich Schwinn, *Die Arbeit des deutschen Wehrvereins und die Wehrlage Deutschlands vor dem Weltkriege* (Würzburg, 1940), 35–36 For the league's founding, see also Fischer, *War of Illusions*, 105–109; Eley, *Reshaping the Right*, 328–329; Roger Chickering, "Der Deutsche Wehrverein und die Reform der deutschen Armee 1912–1914," *Militärgeschichtliche Mitteilungen* 25 (1979): 7–11; and Marilyn Shevin Coetzee, *The German Army League: Popular Nationalism in Wilhelmine Germany* (New York, 1990), 14–29.

154. Heeringen to Bethmann Hollweg, 24 February 1912, RK 2273, Bl. 4, BAP; Wandel to Heeringen, 26 February 1913, PH2/16, Bl. 109–110, BAMAF.

155. For the situation in and out of the army in 1911–1912, see Herrmann, *Arming of Europe*, 161–172, 165 for quotation.

156. Ibid., 173–180; Collenberg, *Deutsche Armee*, 122–123.

157. "Die Vorbereitungen für die Versorgung des Heeres mit Munition vor Ausbruch des Krieges," W-10/50777, Bl. 32–34, BAMAF.

158. Hans Herzfeld, *Die deutsche Rüstungspolitik vor dem Weltkriege* (Leipzig, 1923), 49–50; and especially "Die Entstehung der Wehrvorlage 1913," W-10/50281, Bl. 54–96, BAMAF.

159. Goltz to Stürmer, 26 October 1912, RK 1275, Bl. 122, BAP.

160. I favor this conclusion over Chickering's interpretation ("Deutsche Wehrverein," 23–24, 32) that is, that Ludendorff and the General Staff used the Defense League.

161. In its first public declarations, the league bemoaned the fact that Germany could no longer claim to be "a people in arms," pointing to a German-Austrian peacetime deficit of 700,000 soldiers vis-à-vis France and Russia. The statements of December and January 1911–1912 are printed in Schwinn, *Arbeit des deutschen Wehrvereins*, 36, and Keim, *Erlebtes und Erstrebtes*, 172–173.

162. "Die Entstehung der Wehrvorlage 1913," W-10/50281, Bl. 59, BA-MAF.

163. See ibid., Bl. 61, 79, 93–94; and Schwinn, *Arbeit des deutschen Wehrvereins*, 51, 56. Chickering, "Der Deutsche Wehrverein," 32, and Förster, *Doppelte Militarismus*, 250–51, doubt the veracity of Schwinn's claim that Keim's son, who worked under Ludendorff, furthered his father's cause with Ludendorff. But the claim appears to be true, for in August 1916 Keim referred to a prewar letter written by Ludendorff to Keim's son in which Ludendorff praised the Defense League's troop demands and predicted that they would be sorely missed in the next war. See Keim to Ludendorff, 4 September 1916, ADV 406, Bl. 240–241, BAP.

164. For this paragraph, see Collenberg, *Deutsche Armee*, 122–123; Herrmann, *Arming of Europe*, 180–191; and especially "Die Entstehung der Wehrvorlage 1913," W-10/50281, Bl. 133–156, 166–179, BAMAF.

165. "Die Entstehung der Wehrvorlage 1913," W-10/50281, BAMAF.

166. Moltke's comments of 8 December 1912 are cited in Hull, *Entourage*, 263. His underlying indifference to levels of technology can be gleaned from William to Bethmann, 7 August 1910, in "Rüstung bis 1914," W-10/50199, Bl. 118–121, BAMAF.

167. Gerald D. Feldman, "Les fondements politiques et sociaux de la mobilisation économique en Allemagne (1914–1916)," *Annales Economies, Sociétés, Civilisations* 24 (1969): 107.

168. Ludendorff to his mother, 6 April 1913, N77 Ludendorff, Nr. 18, Bl. 55, BAMAF.

169. Ludendorff to his mother 9 April 1913, ibid., Bl. 56.

170. Alexander von Kluck, *Wanderjahre-Kriege-Gestalten* (Berlin, 1929), 169.

171. Müller-Brandenburg, *Von Schlieffen bis Ludendorff*, 29.

172. Seeckt to his mother, 28 January 1913, N247 Seeckt, Nr. 210, BA-MAF.

173. Müller-Brandenburg, *Von Schlieffen bis Ludendorff*, 12.

174. See the apt conclusions of Chickering, "Deutsche Wehrverein," 25–26. See also Michael Geyer, *Deutsche Rüstungspolitik 1860–1980* (Frankfurt, 1984), 89–90.

175. See Peter Domann, *Sozialdemokratie und Kaisertum unter Wilhelm II* (Wiesbaden, 1974); and Vernon L. Lidtke, *The Alternative Culture: Socialist Labor in Imperial Germany* (New York, 1985).

176. For the following, see Fischer, *War of Illusions*, 272–290; Eley, *Reshaping the Right*, 317–321, 330–336; Chickering, *We Men*, 282–286; and Heinz Hag-

enlücke, *Deutsche Vaterlandspartei: Die nationale Rechte am Ende des Kaiserreiches* (Düsseldorf, 1997), 40–48. Hagenlücke downplays the unity of the Leipzig Cartel, except its antisocialism.

177. See Krafft's memo of 2 November 1912, G. St. 1192, KAM.

178. For French infantry practices, see *Die französische Armee* (Berlin, 1913), 84–85, 167, 170; and *MWB*, 26 June 1913, Sp. 1926.

179. Kraft memo of 2 November 1912, G. St. 1192, KAM.

180. See the report of the BMP to BWM over imperial maneuvers, 18 September 1903, M. Kr. 3165, KAM.

181. Wilhelm Groener, *Das Testament des Grafen Schlieffen, Wissen und Wehr* (1925/4), 202.

182. Storz, *Kriegsbild und Rüstung,* 369–373, passim.

183. See the official *Bericht über das Kaiser-Manöver 1913*, pp. 29, 48, 50, in AE100, KAM.

184. For remarks made in 1905, see Bavarian MP to Bavarian WM, 26 October 1905, M. Kr. 3191, KAM.

185. For two incidents, see BMP to BWM, 28 June 1912 and 7 October 1912, M. Kr. 39, KAM.

186. BMP to BWM, 29 September 1913, M. Kr. 39, KAM.

187. Einem, *Erinnerungen,* 112, 115–116.

188. The best discussion of the War Council and the historiography of preventative war is Hull, *Entourage,* 238–265. Also see Wolfgang J. Mommsen, "The Topos of Inevitable War in Germany in the Decade before 1914," in Volker R. Berghahn and Martin Kitchen (eds.), *Germany in the Age of Total War* (London, 1981), 23–45. Erich von Falkenhayn also noticed a change of heart in William, who was convinced now that war would come, even though he still fought against it. See Falkenhayn to Hanneken, 30 September 1912, in Holger Afflerbach, *Politisches Denken und Handeln im Kaiserreich* (Munich, 1994), 100–101.

189. Cited in Hull, *Entourage,* 238.

190. The best description of William's struggle with himself that summer is Afflerbach, *Falkenhayn,* 153–160.

Chapter 8

1. Allan Mitchell, *Victors and Vanquished: The German Influence on Army and Church in France after 1870* (Chapel Hill, N.C., 1984), 115; Lyn Macdonald, *1914* (New York, 1988), 126.

2. Macdonald, *1914,* 74–75, 126; quotation on 73.

3. For missions, see GQG to the commandants of Mézierès, Verdun, and Toul, 6 August 1914, and Commandant of Maubeuge to GQG, 7 August 1914, cited in Ministère de la Guerre, *Les Armées francaises dans la grande Guerre* (Paris, 1936), Tome 1, 1: 131, note 2, 134, note 1; and Charles Christienne et al., *Histoire de l'aviation militaire francaise* (Paris, 1980), 65, 68–70. For *Montgolfier's* technical specifications, see Bernard Fitzsimons (ed.), *The Illustrated Encyclopedia of 20th Century Weapons and Warfare* (New York, 1978), 1935–1936.

4. GQG to Commandant of Maubeuge, 16 August 1914, cited in Ministère de la Guerre, *Armées francaises,* 1:181, note 2.

5. The shooting down of the *Montgolfier* probably occurred shortly before

the Battle of Mons (23 August). First, after Mons, with German positions known, the *Montgolfier* would not have been ordered up. Second, the damage of a French airship by friendly fire over Rheims on 24 August prompted GQG to ground the fleet until April 1915 (see Christienne et al., *Histoire de l'aviation*, 69). For the Germans in Maubeuge, see the firsthand account of Ernst A. Lehmann and Howard Mingos, *The Zeppelins* (New York, 1927), 32–33 quotation on 32.

6. Maximilian von Poseck, *Die Deutsche Kavallerie 1914 in Belgien und Frankreich* (Berlin, 1922), 5, 9–10.

7. For the disposition of all units of all seven western armies circa 10 August 1914, see Reichsarchiv, *Der Weltkrieg 1914–1918: Die militärischen Operationen zu Lande* (Berlin, 1925), 1, Karte 2; Peter Graf Kielmansegg, *Deutschland und der Erste Weltkrieg* (Frankfurt am Main, 1968), 33 (also for numbers of daily transports); and John Keegan, *The First World War* (New York, 1999), 77 (for horses). Moltke's belief that the Belgian operation was not an end in itself, and that the right wing should seek out the French where they were in the field, see Moltke to Endres, 15 August 1906, G. St. 1238, KAM.

8. See Schlieffen's "great memorandum" of December 1905, in Gerhard Ritter, *The Schlieffen Plan: Critique of a Myth* (London, 1958), 134–148, quotation on 138.

9. Hermann von Kuhl, *Der Weltkrieg 1914–1918* (Cologne, 1929), 1:11.

10. For Moltke's assumptions about a French assault in Lorraine, see ibid., 12. Kuhl was a General Staff officer before the war and chief of staff of First Army in August 1914. For the Germans envisioning a scenario of driving attacking French armies back to the fortress line, then breaking through it, see the documents on the 1902 staff ride in G. St. 1234, as well as Moltke to Fasbender, 12 June 1908, G. St. 1291, KAM. For pre-war plans of Schlieffen and Moltke to adapt the right wing to unfolding opportunities, see Moltke to Endres, 15 August 1906, G. St. 1238, KAM, and Terence Zuber, "The Schlieffen Plan Reconsidered," *War in History* 6/3 (1999), 262–305.

11. Ritter, *Schlieffen Plan*, 42. See also, chapters 4–5.

12. Reichsarchiv, *Weltkrieg*, 1:23; Kuhl, *Weltkrieg*, 1:11.

13. For a good description of the fortress, see Keegan, *First World War*, 77.

14. Poseck, *Deutsche Kavallerie*, 9–13.

15. For the attack on Liège, see Reichsarchiv, *Weltkrieg*, 1:108–120; and Erich von Ludendorff, *Ludendorff's Own Story* (New York, 1919), 28, 37–45.

16. Cited in Barbara Tuchman, *The Guns of August* (New York, 1962), 200.

17. For the widespread use of dense columns and thick skirmish lines in 1914, see Wilhelm Balck, *Entwickelung der Taktik im Weltkrieg* (Berlin, 1922), 50, 230, 239–240. That these were often the tactics of preference, see Ernst von Eisenhart-Rothe, *Ehrendenkmal der Deutschen Armee und Marine 1871–1918* (Berlin, 1928), 90, 92. See also Bruce I. Gudmundsson, *Stormtroop Tactics: Innovation in the German Army, 1914–1918* (New York, 1989), 21–24.

18. Reichsarchiv, *Weltkrieg*, 1:113, lists casualties for one of the six brigades as 1,180. However, some were hit harder, and the lead battalions that were attacking Fort Barchon were decimated.

19. Karl von Einem, *Erinnerungen eines Soldaten 1853–1933* (Leipzig, 1933), 170–171.

20. D. R. Schindler, *Eine 42 cm. Mörser-Batterie im Weltkrieg* (Breslau, 1934), 83–84; *Die K. B. Schwere Artillerie im Grossen Kriege 1914–1918* (Munich, 1928), 708, 710; Einem, *Erinnerungen*, 170–171. Always a lesser priority, plans for using

the big guns at Liège were apparently dropped after War Ministry cutbacks of the General Staff's heavy artillery requests. See also chap. 7, note 127.

21. Schindler, *42 cm. Mörser-Batterie*, 84.

22. Alexander von Kluck, *The March on Paris and the Battle of the Marne* (New York, 1920), 16.

23. For the low quality of these units, see Wilhelm Balck, *Kriegserfahrungen* (Berlin, 1922), 3–10.

24. Kluck's order of 10 August 1914 is printed in Kluck, *March on Paris*, 9.

25. For the heavy artillery around Liège and the quotation, see the recollections of Paul Buhle, "Der schnelle Fall von Festungen 1914," *Die Schwere Artillerie* 13 (1937): 67.

26. Kluck, *March on Paris*, 12.

27. Walter Bloem, *Vormarsch — Sturmsignal — Das Ganze halt!* (Leipzig, 1939), 37–55.

28. For dispositions on 17 August, see Reichsarchiv, *Weltkrieg*, 1, Karte 2.

29. Cited in Maximilian von Poseck (ed.), *Das 1. Brandenburgische Dragoner-Regiment Nr. 2 im Weltkriege 1914 bis 1918* (Berlin, 1933), 12. See also Poseck, *Deutsche Kavallerie*, 20–26.

30. Poseck, *Deutsche Kavallerie*, 28–29, 32–33, 43–45; Kluck, *March on Paris*, 22–23.

31. Poseck, *Deutsche Kavallerie*, 31, 35; Kluck, *March on Paris*, 30; Ludwig von Gebsattel, *Karl von Bülow* (Munich, 1929), 53.

32. For prewar planning, see Reichsarchiv, *Weltkrieg*, 1:126. The airship based at Cologne participated in the attack on Liège and was destroyed on 6 August. It was replaced immediately by an airship from Saxony. See Lehmann and Mingos, *Zeppelins*, 12, 21.

33. Reichsarchiv, *Weltkrieg*, 1:95, 127; Georg Paul Neumann, *Die deutschen Luftstreitkräfte im Weltkriege* (Berlin, 1920), 348; Ernst von Hoeppner, *Deutschlands Krieg in der Luft* (Leipzig, 1921), 14–15. One of Z-9's aborted missions occurred on 14–15 August, the exact time that British brigades disembarked at Boulogne and moved inland. The "silver ghost" was spotted by troops of Kluck's Third Corps at sunset on 14 August northwest of Liège. See Bloem, *Vormarsch*, 41.

34. Kluck, *March on Paris*, 18, 33–37; Reichsarchiv, *Weltkrieg*, 1:219–20.

35. OHL to Second Army, 20 August 1914, cited in Kluck, *March on Paris*, 38.

36. Reichsarchiv, *Weltkrieg*, 1:221, 353; Gebsattel, *Karl von Bülow*, 54.

37. Alexander von Kluck, *Wanderjahre — Kriege — Gestalten* (Berlin, 1929), 172. Kluck's marching orders for 22 August, issued on the previous evening, are printed in Kluck, *March on Paris*, 39. For the prewar exercises, see chapter 4, and Terence Zuber, "The Schlieffen Plan Reconsidered," *War in History* 6/3 (1999): 262–305.

38. Ministére de la Guerere, *Armées Francaises*, 1:131–134, 167–171. See also John Keegan, *Opening Moves: August 1914* (New York, 1971), 92.

39. Reichsarchiv, *Weltkrieg*, 1, Karte 7; Keegan, *Opening Moves*, 98–99.

40. Reichsarchiv, *Weltkrieg*, 1:95; Macdonald, *1914*, 75.

41. Cited in Keegan, *Opening Moves*, 114.

42. Ministére de la Guerre, *Armées francaises*, 1:185; Macdonald, *1914*, 88–91.

43. Keegan, *Opening Moves*, 98.
44. Zuber, "Schlieffen Plan Reconsidered," 262–305.
45. Keegan, *Opening Moves*, 58–59, 64, 73, 99.
46. Ministére de la Guerre, *Armées francaises*, 1:175. The quotation is in Tuchman, *Guns of August*, 237.
47. For French artillery in this sector, see Ministére de la Guerre, *Armées francaises*, 1:540, 547. For German artillery strength per regular corps, see "Rüstung bis 1914," W-10/50199, Bl. 34, BAMAF.
48. Keegan, *Opening Moves*, 62.
49. Ibid., 66–67.
50. Reichsarchiv, *Weltkrieg*, 1:263–279, and Karte 4; Keegan, *Opening Moves*, 67–73, quotation on 73. For evidence that the French infantry tended to spread out according to regulations in 1914, see Reichsarchiv, *Schlachten des Weltkrieges in Einzeldarstellungen* (Berlin, 1928), 7b:224.
51. For Longwy, see Reichsarchiv, *Weltkrieg* 1:318–326, and Karte 3.
52. Otto von Moser, *Feldzugsaufzeichnungen als Brigade-Divisionskommandeur und als kommandierender General 1914–1918* (Stuttgart, 1920), 8–9, 27; Reichsarchiv, *Weltkrieg*, 1:319.
53. Cited in Tuchman, *Guns of August*, 272.
54. Moser, *Feldzugsaufzeichnungen*, 25; Balck, *Kriegserfahrungen*, 3.
55. For Neufchateau, see Reichsarchiv, *Weltkrieg*, 1:326–332, and Karte 3. German reserve corps marched with half the field artillery of a regular corps, no heavy artillery, and few or in some cases no machine gun detachments.
56. Keegan, *Opening Moves*, 81.
57. Reichsarchiv, *Weltkrieg*, 1:328, 332–335.
58. For Bülow's orders and the position of First, Second, and Third Armies on 21 August, see ibid., 1:347, 352, and Karte 2.
59. Ibid., 1:386. Later the Germans discovered on the battlefield an order from Lanrezac that instructed his troops to permit the lead German divisions to cross before counterattacking and destroying these isolated units.
60. Ibid., 1:358, 362; Keegan, *Opening Moves*, 108.
61. Casualties were probably around 18,000 out of 96,000 infantrymen of the four corps. See Reichsarchiv, *Schlachten des Weltkrieges*, 7a:24, 7b:244–245, for the strength of the Tenth Corps, the Tenth Reserve Corps, and the Guard Corps before Second Army's next battle at St. Quentin. Allowance is made for march attrition and previous losses of the Twenty-seventh and Thirty-eight Brigades at Liège. For the fighting of the Seventh Corps, see Reichsarchiv, *Weltkrieg*, 1:356, 391–392. Bülow claimed in December 1914 [Karl von Bülow, *Mein Bericht zur Marneschhlacht* (Berlin, 1919), 26] that total casualties were only 11,000. This was most certainly inaccurate.
62. Hermann von Stein, *Erlebnisse und Betrachtungen aus der Zeit des Weltkrieges* (Leipzig, 1919), 156; and the report of a western front general, n.d. (Autumn 1914), solicited by the Prussian War Ministry to improve the training of replacements, M. Kr. 2923, KAM. The quotation is from Stein.
63. Lanrezac now had 12 divisions south of the Sambre, with his lone reserve division (fifty-first) moved up to guard the Meuse at Dinant.
64. Reichsarchiv, *Weltkrieg*, 1:364–370.
65. For action on 23 August, see ibid., 1:378–392, and Keegan, *Opening Moves*, 109.

66. Einem, *Erinnerungen*, 171.

67. See note 55.

68. Fifth Army had only 17 batteries of 155- and 120-mm guns (Ministère de la Guerre, *Armées francaises*, 1:567), whereas the five regular corps of Second and Third armies had 35 batteries of 150- and 105-mm field howitzers.

69. Cited in Tuchman, *Guns of August*, 286. According to Tuchman (292, 384), France lost 135,000 men in Lorraine and the Ardennes and 5,000 at Sambre-Meuse. According to Bülow (*Mein Bericht*, 26), the French Fifth Army lost twice as many soldiers as the German Second Army. Although this is most certainly an exaggeration, Tuchman's figure does seem too low. Keegan, *First World War*, 97, reports that the French Third and Tenth Corps lost 5,150 soldiers on August 22nd alone.

70. A cavalry patrol later determined, but not until the Battle of Mons had begun, that the troops were a brigade of French reservists. Reichsarchiv, *Weltkrieg*, 1:420.

71. Ibid., 1:364–366, 417–418.

72. Reichsarchiv, *Weltkrieg*, 1:418–422; Macdonald, *1914*, 98–105.

73. Bloem, *Vormarsch*, 56–70.

74. For Third Corps casualties at Mons, see Reichsarchiv, *Schlachten des Weltkrieges*, 26:347–48. Volume 26 lists regimental strengths in the First Army before the Marne, the Third Corps's next major battle after Mons. Subtracting for companies left in rear areas (listed here), a marching attrition of 2.5% (half the rate of the Fourth Reserve Corps before the Marne; see 7a: 24), casualties of the Eleventh Brigade at Liège (about 750), and limited action on 28–29 August (about 500), one arrives at casualties of 5,000 (20.8%) at Mons.

75. For losses of officers and NCOs, see Reichsarchiv, *Schlachten des Weltkrieges*, 7a:23–24; Bloem, *Vormarsch*, 70–71; and the report of a western front general, n.d.(Autumn 1914), solicited by the Prussian War Ministry in order to improve training techniques of replacement units, M. Kr. 2923, KAM. The quotations are from the Kriegsarchiv document.

76. Arthur Conan Doyle, *A History of the Great War* (New York, 1916), 1:67, is based on eyewitness accounts. For the firepower of British battalions, see Keegan, *Opening Moves*, 114. See also Keegan, *First World War*, 97–100.

77. A British soldier's account of the oncoming Ninth Corps, cited in Macdonald, *1914*, 99.

78. Casualties were almost 6,800. Kluck admitted that he "suffered heavy losses" at Mons (*March on Paris*, 48). Otherwise, see the sources and methods described in note 74. The Thirty-fourth Brigade had lost 1,150 men at Liège.

79. For the low opinion of airplane reconnaissance, see Hoeppner, *Deutschlands Krieg*, 1–15. He was chief of staff of Hausen's Third Army in 1914.

80. Bloem, *Vormarsch*, 72; for prebattle gaiety, see 55.

81. Reichsarchiv, *Weltkrieg*, 3: 342; Kluck, *March on Paris*, 74–75.

82. For the action of 24–29 August, see Reichsarchiv, *Weltkrieg*, 1:425–430, 517–532, 3:119–133, and Karte 2 and 6.

83. For the above quotations, see Macdonald, *1914*, 165, 176. Also for Le Cateau, see Keegan, *First World War*, 102.

84. For machine-gunner improvisations that summer, see Balck, *Entwickelung der Taktik*, 201.

85. Neumann, *Deutsche Luftstreitkräfte*, 348. John Morrow, *The Great War in*

the Air (Washington, 1993), 68, confuses the Z-9's 1 September flight with the flights of Z-7 and Z-8 over Alsace on 22 August. No Zeppelins were in the air over northern France until 10 days later.

86. For casualties between 24–29 August, see Reichsarchiv, *Schlachten des Weltkrieges*, 26:347–348. See also notes 75 and 79.

87. For the positions of the three armies on 29 August, see Reichsarchiv, *Weltkrieg*, 3:129, and Karte 2 and 4.

88. One brigade of Einem's Seventh Corps was besieging Maubeuge.

89. For the ensuing 2-day battle of St. Quentin–Guise, see Reichsarchiv, *Weltkrieg*, 3: 159–179, 358–367, and Karte 4; Reichsarchiv, *Schlachten des Weltkriegs*, 7a and 7b, passim.

90. Reichsarchiv, *Weltkrieg*, 3:152.

91. Reichsarchiv, *Schlachten des Weltkrieges*, 7b:101–111.

92. Ibid., 129.

93. Ibid., 132, 134, 136.

94. For the attack, see ibid., 194–202.

95. Ibid., 201.

96. Ibid., 244–245.

97. Ibid., 179, 190–192.

98. Cited in Tuchman, *Guns of August*, 423.

99. Cited in Reichsarchiv, *Schlachten des Weltkrieges*, 7b: 211.

100. Ibid., 207.

101. Reichsarchiv, *Weltkrieg*, 3: 164–168.

102. Gebsattel, *Karl von Bülow*, 80–81.

103. Reichsarchiv, *Schlachten des Weltkrieges*, 7b:216–228.

104. Quotations in Tuchman, *Guns of August*, 424.

105. Reichsarchiv, *Weltkrieg*, 3:366–367.

106. For Second Army, see Reichsarchiv, *Schlachten des Weltkrieges*, 7a:106, 204, 7b:244–245. These figures, totaling 8,100, do not include the losses of five brigades (of seven) that assaulted across the Oise on 30 August. Fifth Army's losses were probably somewhat lower, given the tendency of French infantry units to attack in a very loose formation (see 7b:224). Bülow's claim (*Mein Bericht*, 42) that only 6,000 men were lost is once again an exaggeration.

107. Cited in Reichsarchiv, *Schlachten des Weltkrieges*, 7b:234. See also Gebsattel, *Karl von Bülow*, 82.

108. Kluck, *March on Paris*, 86–87.

109. For the battle, see Poseck, *Deutsche Kavallerie*, 77–79. See also Macdonald, *1914*, 250–57, 260.

110. The war diary of one German cavalry officer is cited in Poseck, *Deutsche Kavallerie*, 78.

111. The fighting strength after Néry is given in Reichsarchiv, *Schlachten des Weltkrieges*, 26:350.

112. For the progress of the German Third, Fourth, and Fifth Armies, see Max von Hausen, *Erinnerungen an den Marnefeldzug 1914* (Leipzig, 1922), 145–164; Reichsarchiv, *Weltkrieg*, 3:14–118.

113. The "fighting strength" of the Sixteenth Division of Eighth Corps was "so strongly shaken" that it could not fight for days. Reichsarchiv, *Weltkrieg*, 3: 23.

114. Ibid., 3:31.

115. Moser, *Feldzugsaufzeichnungen,* 14–17, 19–20, 26; Balck, *Entwickelung der Taktik,* 56, 59–60, 314–317; Einem, *Erinnerungen,* 171. See also the detailed discussion in the excerpt from the unpublished memoirs of Lieutenant General von Schubert, n.d., W-10/50792, Bl. 7–8, 18–19, BAMAF.

116. For French numbers, see Ministère de la Guerre, *Armées francaises,* 1: 521. For German stockpiles and August production, see the Allgemeine Kriegsdepartment memo of 18 December 1914 and General Muther's study, n.d. (1919), both in PH2/87, BAMAF.

117. Stein, *Erlebnisse,* 92–93.

118. Excerpt from the unpublished memoirs of Lieutenant General von Schubert, n.d., W-10/50792, Bl. 8–9, 15–20, BAMAF. Schubert asserted that there was an average of only six shots a day for field cannons in early September (i.e., about 25,000 shells a day), meaning that overall stockpiles must have been around 500,000—enough for very limited fire for 3 weeks. In September 1914, Germany produced another 225,000 shells for the C-96nA and 106,000 for the light howitzers (see Allg. Kriegsdept. memo of 18 December 1914, PH2/87, BAMAF).

119. Ibid. (Schubert); Moser, *Feldzugsaufzeichnungen,* 19–22, 26. See also Wolfgang Paul, *Entscheidung im September: Das Wunder an der Marne* (Esslingen, 1974), 143–144.

120. Balck, *Entwickelung der Taktik,* 315–316; Moser, *Feldzugsaufzeichnungen,* 21–22, 26; Paul Buhle, "Festungen 1914," *Die Schwere Artillerie* 14 (1937): 68.

121. For 150-mm stockpiles, see the memo of General Muther, n.d. (1919), PH2/87, BAMAF.

122. Ministère de la Guerre, *Armées francaises,* 1:538–539.

123. See Reichsarchiv, *Weltkrieg,* 3, Karte 2.

124. Ibid., 1:553–54.

125. Over Fort Manonviller in 1898, Nancy in 1905, and between Verdun and Toul in 1906–1907. See the documents, respectively, in G. St. 1288/1–2, and 1291–96, KAM.

126. Moltke to Endres, 15 August 1906, G. St. 1238, and Moltke to Fasbender, 12 June 1908, G. St. 1291, KAM; see also Moltke's comments on the Schlieffen Plan, n.d. (1911), in Ritter, *Schlieffen Plan,* 165–167. The 1908 letter rejected the idea of a simple attack against the fortresses. The 1906 letter advocated a southward wheeling out of Belgium if the French attacked Germany. The move through Belgium was not "an end in itself," but rather "a means to an end."

127. K. B. *Schwere Artillerie im Grossen Kriege* (Munich, 1928), 708.

128. Cited in Reichsarchiv, *Weltkrieg,* 1:569.

129. See ibid., 1, Karte 4.

130. Ibid., 1:584–603.

131. K. B. *Schwere Artillerie,* 715. For all facets of the Manonviller campaign, see 708–718.

132. Moltke to Fasbender, 12 June 1908, G. St. 1291, KAM.

133. For Moltke's concerns, see Reichsarchiv, *Weltkrieg,* 1:592–593; 3: 95–96, 221, 226.

134. K. B. *Schwere Artillerie,* 715.

135. Reichsarchiv, *Weltkrieg,* 3:223, 284–285.

136. Ibid., 3:294–301.

137. Ibid., 3:232–233.

138. General von Tappen, *Bis zur Marne 1914* (Berlin, 1920), 15–16. Tappen was a colonel at OHL in 1914.

139. The Twenty-fourth Reserve Division, which had besieged Givet, was rapidly catching up with the other five divisions of Third Army.

140. Hausen, *Erinnerungen*, 190–192; Reichsarchiv, *Weltkrieg*, 3:231, 302–313.

141. Kluck, *March on Paris*, 110–112; Kuhl, *Weltkrieg 1914–1918*, 1:36–39. For French "nerves," see also Kuhl's *Der deutsche Generalstab in Vorbereitung und Durchführung des Weltkrieges* (Berlin, 1920), 33.

142. Tuchman, *Guns of August*, 440.

143. For the best discussion, see ibid., 440–447, 462, 468.

144. Cited ibid., 467. Moltke claimed that there were only 30,000–40,000 prisoners.

145. Ibid., 443.

146. Kluck, *March on Paris*, 118.

147. Tuchman, *Guns of August*, 447–483; Kluck, *March on Paris*, 116–117; Reichsarchiv, *Weltkrieg*, 4:53–54.

148. Reichsarchiv, *Weltkrieg* 4:45, 53, 56, 59–61, 64, 66, 70, 198; Bloem, *Vormarsch*, 116–124; Kluck, *March on Paris*, 126. See also Paul, *Entscheidung*, 143–144.

149. General F. Herr, *L'Artillerie* (Paris, 1923), 28. Herr was the chief advocate of expanding France's heavy artillery before the war. Martin van Creveld's observation [*Supplying War: Logistics from Wallenstein to Patton* (Cambridge, 1977), 128] that ammunitiion shortages were not a problem until after the Battle of the Marne is incorrect.

150. Bloem, *Vormarsch*, 120, 124.

151. This expression was used by the officers of Second Army to describe the condition of First Army. Reichsarchiv, *Weltkrieg*, 4:235–236.

152. Ibid., 3:338.

153. Although the guns opened fire on 29 August, Maubeuge did not surrender until 7 September. Ibid., 3:320, 324.

154. Kluck, *March on Paris*, 121.

155. Ibid., 122–124; Reichsarchiv, *Weltkrieg*, 4:195.

156. See Reichsarchiv, 4, *Weltkrieg*, Skizze 4.

157. For the forces arrayed in the area, see ibid., Karte 4. For Kuhl's communique to Bülow on 6 September, see ibid., 4:75.

158. See General Köberle's analysis of the inherent problems that limited the dismounted cavalry's effectiveness in the 1914 campaign, 30 November 1914, M. Kr. 2923, KAM.

159. Quotations in Reichsarchiv, *Weltkrieg*, 4:75, 182.

160. Ibid., 4:65, 71–73, 88–89.

161. Ibid., 4:173.

162. Ibid., 4:183; Hausen, *Erinnerungen*, 199, 202.

163. Reichsarchiv *Weltkrieg*, 4:179–180. For exact casualties of the Second Army, see Reichsarchiv, *Schlachten des Weltkrieges*, 25:233–236.

164. For the following, see the definitive discussion in Reichsarchiv, *Weltkrieg*, 4:221–245.

165. Cited in Kuhl, *Weltkrieg 1914–1918*, 1:44.

166. Tappen, *Bis zur Marne,* 26; Hausen, *Erinnerungen,* 206–212; Reichsarchiv, *Weltkrieg,* 4:224, 243.

167. Reichsarchiv, Weltkrieg, 4:297–305, and Karte 10.

168. Karl Justrow, *Die Dicke Berta und der Krieg* (Berlin, 1935), 66.

169. See the remembrances of heavy artillerists Karl Justrow and Paul Buhle, respectively, in *Die Schwere Artillerie* 13 (1936): 20–21, and 14 (1937): 67, as well as the discussion of 210-mm shell shortages at Maubeuge in Reichsarchiv, *Weltkrieg,* 3:320–321, 324.

170. Reichsarchiv, *Weltkrieg,* 3:233, 335–336; Justrow, *Dicke Berta,* 56, 66.

171. Remembrances of Justrow, *Dicke Berta,* 55–56, and especially *Die Schwere Artillerie* 13 (1936); 21.

172. See ibid. as well as Buhle's "Schnelle fall von festungen," 67–68. The two 420s used to shell Antwerp in late September and early October were Gammas from Kummersdorf. The two 420 positions that Justrow prepared northwest and northeast of Verdun in September–October must have come from Maubeuge, for they were the only 420s mobile enough to move into this devastated area.

173. For the following, see Buhle, "Schnelle fall von festungen," 67; Reichsarchiv, *Weltkrieg,* 3:335, 4:163, 309–11; and Karte 10; and Martin Gilbert, *The First World War: A Complete History* (New York, 1994), 77.

174. Hausen, *Erinnerungen,* 204, 214–215, 220–225; Tappen, *Bis zur Marne,* 26–28.

175. Tappen, *Bis zur Marne,* 28.

176. For fighting on the Aisne, see Keegan, *First World War,* 122–126. French casualties by mid-September were 385,000 [Michael Howard, "Men against Fire: The Doctrine of the Offensive in 1914," in Peter Paret (ed.), *Makers of Modern Strategy from Machiavelli to the Nuclear Age* (Princeton, N.J. 1986), 523]. The American ambassador in Berlin reported German casualties from August to November at 467,500, but losses had been mounting quickly on both fronts since September [Robert B. Asprey, *The German High Command at War: Hindenburg and Ludendorff Conduct World War I* (New York, 1991), 136].

177. Schubert described the conversation in his unpublished memoirs, n.d., W-10/50792, Bl. 8–9, BAMAF.

Chapter 9

1. Einem described his thoughts in a letter to his wife, 29 July 1916, N324 Einem Papers, Nr. 53, Bl. 123, BAMAF.

2. The disapproving words are from Admiral Georg Alexander von Müller, chief of the Naval Cabinet, in Walter Görlitz (ed.), *Regierte der Kaiser? Kriegstagebücher, Aufzeichnungen und Briefe des Chefs des Marine-Kabinetts Admiral Georg Alexander von Müller 1914–1918* (Göttingen, 1959), 136.

3. Ibid., 196, 203–204, 208–209.

4. Cited in Lamar Cecil, *Wilhelm II. Prince and Emperor, 1859–1900* (Chapel Hill, n.c., 1996), 2:233.

5. See Einem's notations (*Aufzeichnungen*) of 15 August and 28 November 1916, N324 Einem Papers, Nr. 53, Bl. 133–134, 182, BAMAF.

6. For the Battle of Tannenberg, see Dennis E. Showalter, *Tannenberg:*

Clash of Empires (Hamden, 1991). Showalter offers his excellent study as a contribution to the history of armies in transition from peacetime to war. For fighting in 1915, see Holger H. Herwig, *The First World War: Germany and Austria-Hungary 1914–1918* (London, 1997), 126–172; Robert B. Asprey, *The German High Command at War: Hindenburg and Ludendorff Conduct World War I* (New York, 1991), 177–210; Norman Stone, *The Eastern Front 1914–1917* (New York, 1975), 144–191; and Lyn Macdonald, *1915: The Death of Innocence* (New York, 1993).

7. Holger Herwig, *'Luxury' Fleet: The Imperial German Navy 1888–1918* (London, 1991), 222, 291 (Table 29).

8. Manfred Lachmann, "Zur Entwicklung und zum Einsatz des Maschinengewehrs," *Zeitschrift für Militärgeschichte* 12 (1973): 724–725; and "Erfahrungen des Weltkrieges in der Massenbeschaffung von Gerät, insbesondere von Maschinengewehren," Msg. 2/775, Bl.8–20, BAMAF.

9. Hans Linnen Kohl, *Vom Einzelschuss zur Feuerwalze: Der Wettlauf zwischen Technik und Taktik im Ersten Weltkrieg* (Koblenz, 1990), 276; Hermann Schirmer, *Das Gerät der schweren Artillerie vor, in und nach dem Weltkrieg* (Berlin, 1937), 286; Allgemeine Kriegsdepartment memorandum of 18 December 1914, PH2/Nr. 87, Bl. 7, BAMAF. Kohl lists the number of specific cannon types on the eastern front in 1916, Schirmer lists those used at Verdun, and the 1914 memo gives the *overal*l cannon and light howitzer figures. The howitzer figure for the eastern front in 1916 (41%) is higher than that for Verdun (24.5%)—hence the 30% estimate.

10. Alfred Muther, *Das Gerät der leichten Artillerie vor, in und nach dem Weltkrieg* (Berlin, 1925), 34–36.

11. Schirmer, *Gerät*, 315–316, 326–327.

12. Ibid., 315–316.

13. See Holger Afflerbach, *Falkenhayn: Politisches Denken und Handeln im Kaiserreich* (Munich, 1994), 360–365, 376–403, 543–545, who doubts the genuineness of Falkenhayn's oft-cited "Christmas Memorandum" of 1915 with its advocacy of a "bleed them white" strategy at Verdun. Going further than Afflerbach, Hew Strachan argues convincingly that the real goal was breakthrough ("German Strategies during the War," unpublished paper delivered at the May 2000 Seminar of the Great War Society).

14. Hans von Seeckt to his wife, 26 February 1916, N247 Seeckt Papers, Nr. 220, Bl. 99, BAMAF. Seeckt was one of Falkenhayn's favorites. This letter seems to strengthen Strachan's thesis about breakthrough as the real goal.

15. Schirmer, *Gerät*, 286; Aufzeichnungen (notations) of OHL's Gerhard Tappen, W-10/50661, Bl. 87, and Oberstleutnant Muths, "Die schwere Artillerie von Ende 1915 bis Ende August 1916," W-10/50774, B. 17, BAMAF.

16. Alistair Horne, *Verdun 1916: The Price of Glory* (New York, 1962), 43.

17. Ibid., 70–124, 151–172, 242–266.

18. Statistics in this paragraph are from Schirmer, *Gerät*, 284, 337; Horne, *Verdun*, 215, 228, 246, 300; General Muths, "Deutsche Schwere Artillerie," W-10/50774, Bl. 75–76, 83, and Truppenamt to Wrisberg, April 1919, PH2/86, BAMAF.

19. Five 420s were destroyed by barrel detonations, four by counter-battery fire from French 155s. See Schirmer, *Gerät*, 286, and Horne, *Verdun*, 248 (also for "key-holing").

20. See the reports in Fussartillerie-Regiment, Nr. 19, Nr. 36269–36270, HStAD.

21. Ernst Toller's eloquent description is cited in Herwig, *First World War*, 198.

22. For the quotations, see, first, Hohenborn to his wife, 5 August 1916, cited in Helmut Reichold and Gerhard Granier (eds.), *Wild von Hohenborn: Briefe und Tagebuchaufzeichnungen des preussischen Generals als Kriegsminister und Truppenführer im ersten Weltkrieg 1914 bis 1918* (Boppard, 1986), 79; second, Hohenborn's notation of 3 August 1916, W-10/50662, Bl. 202, BAMAF.

23. Horne, *Verdun*, 267–300. For German casualties, see Herwig, *First World War*, 222–223.

24. Cecil, *Wilhelm II*, 2:236–238; Asprey, *German High Command*, 246–252.

25. Hindenburg's description, cited in Horne, *Verdun*, 304.

26. William's memoirs are cited in Herwig, *First World War*, 198.

27. For the citation and discipline problems, see ibid., 198, and Asprey, *German High Command*, 225; for agnosticism, see Horne, *Verdun*, 186–187.

28. Seeckt to his wife, 30 March 1916, N247 Seeckt Papers, Nr. 220, Bl. 115–116, BAMAF.

29. Einem notation of 28 November 1916, N324 Einem Papers, Nr. 53, Bl. 182, BAMAF.

30. Horne, *Verdun*, 164, 188; report by Major Weiss of the first Guard Reserve Division, 24 July 1917, NL Bauer 22, Nr. 11, Bl. 136–137, BAK; Karl-Ludwig Ay, *Die Entstehung einer Revolution: Die Volksstimmung in Bayern während des Ersten Weltkrieges* (Berlin, 1968), 97–133; and Hindenburg's Order, Nr. 2125, 2 April 1917, RMI 12475, Bl. 325, BAP. See also Roger Chickering, *Imperial Germany and the Great War, 1914–1918* (Cambridge, 1998), 101–103.

31. Seeckt to his wife, 26 February 1916, N247 Seeckt Papers, Nr. 220, Bl. 99, BAMAF.

32. The classic works are Martin Kitchen, *The Silent Dictatorship: The Politics of the German High Command under Hindenburg and Ludendorff, 1916–1918* (New York, 1976); and Wilhelm Deist, *Militär und Innenpolitik im Weltkrieg, 1914–1918* (Düsseldorf, 1970), 2 vols.

33. Müller Diary, 6 November 1914, in Görlitz, *Regierte der Kaiser*, 68. See also Deist, *Militär und Innenpolitik*, 2: 216–217; and Isabel V. Hull, *The Entourage of Kaiser Wilhelm II 1888–1918* (Cambridge, 1982), 266.

34. Cecil, *Wilhelm II*, 2:230.

35. Müller Diary, 8 August 1916, in Görlitz, *Regierte der Kaiser*, 209.

36. Bauer's remarks of December 1916 are cited in Hull, *Entourage*, 269.

37. See Bauer's memorandum of Autumn 1917 in NL22 Bauer, Nr. 1E, Bl. 371, BAK.

38. Cecil, *Wilhelm II*, 2:251. For William's abdication remark, see 250.

39. When the pan-Germans urged Ludendorff to support a military government in September 1916, he refused because he wanted "no domestic strife." Keim to Ludendorff, 4 September and 20 September 1916, ADV 406, Bl. 240–245, 258–261, BAP. For a full discussion of the army and the dilemma of alternatives to monarchical rule, see Bruno Thoss, "Nationale Rechte, militärische Führung und Diktaturfrage in Deutschland 1913–1923," *Militärgeschichtliche Mitteilungen* 42/2 (1987): 47–62.

40. William was basically "entirely at peace" with his total exclusion from

decisions. See the Müller Diary, 8 February 1917, in Görlitz, *Regierte der Kaiser*, 259.

41. Agents of the Reichs Chancellery, attending over 100 public meetings from January to June 1916, reported that the kaiser's image remained solid until mid-1916, when it began to deteriorate rapidly. See the Chancellery's investigative memorandum of 15 September 1916, RK 1418, Bl. 110, BAP.

42. Keim to Class, 8 August 1914, ADV 406, Bl. 150, BAP.

43. Hugenberg to Class, 24 December 1914, ADV 395, Bl. 83, BAP. For other letters that blame the kaiser, see Hugenberg's letters to Class, 19 January and 18 April 1915, Bl. 86–87, 98.

44. For the quotation, see Keim to Class, 6 February 1916, ADV 406, Bl. 175, BAP. See also Keim to Hopfen, 20 March 1916, Bl. 189. War Minister Wild von Hohenborn also detected pan-German rage against the kaiser (Hohenborn notation of 10 March 1916, W-10/50662, BAMAF).

45. See Wahnscafffe to Bethmann Hollweg, 30 August 1916, RK 1418, Bl. 8–9; and especially the Reichs Chancellery investigative memorandum of 15 September 1916, RK 1418, Bl. 108–128. See also Hobohm to Rohrbach, 24 May 1916, RK 1417, Bl. 184; Stegerwald to Reichs Chancellery, 10 August 1916, RK 1417/2; Ruge to Bethmann Hollweg, 21 October 1916, RK 1418/1, Bl. 78–84; and Liebig to the Justice Ministry, 24 June 1917, RK 1418/2, Bl. 83— all documents in BAP.

46. Harden to Kessel, 20 July 1916, RK 2437/9, Bl. 75, BAP.

47. See minutes of a War Ministry conference on antimonarchical trends in Germany, 25 May 1917, RMI 12475/1, Bl. 309, BAP. Low-level clerks in the Reichs Chancellery and Foreign Office were also criticizing the luxurious life of the kaiser. See Müller Diary, 31 August 1916, in Görlitz, *Regierte der Kaiser*, 217–218. For the food crisis, see the classic study of Gerald D. Feldman, *Army, Industry, and Labor in Germany 1914–1918* (Princeton, N.J., 1966), 97–116.

48. Wahnschaffe to Justice Ministry, 18 August 1916, RK 1417/2, BAP. For William's sinking image with common people, see Müller to Plessen, 2 September 1916, in Görlitz, *Regierte der Kaiser*, 218–219.

49. See Herwig, *First World War*, 263–266.

50. See Hohenborn to Zorn, 1 January 1917, N44 Hohenborn Papers, Nr. 6, Bl. 5; and Einem notation of 2 October 1916, N324 Einem Papers, Nr. 53, Bl. 152, both in BAMAF.

51. Einem notation of 30 September 1916, N324 Einem Papers, Nr. 53, Bl. 151, BAMAF.

52. Beck to his fiancée, 28 November 1918, N28 Beck Papers, Bl. 2, BA-MAF.

53. Minutes of War Ministry conference on antimonarchical trends in Germany, 25 May 1917, RMI 12475/1, Bl. 308–309, BAP.

54. Liebig to the Justice Ministry, 24 June 1917, RK 1419, Bl. 83, BAP.

55. See Ingo Materna et al. (eds.), *Dokumente aus geheimen Archiven 4: Berichte des Berliner Polizeipräsidenten zur Stimmung und Lage der Bevölkerung Berlins 1914–1918* (Weimar, 1987), 170 ff.; and Volker Ullrich, *Kriegsalltag: Hamburg im ersten Weltkrieg* (Cologne, 1982), 51–56.

56. Report of Major von Weiss, 24 July 1917, NL Bauer 22, Nr. 11, Bl. 136–137, BAK. For the spreading antiauthority mood, see also two reports from

the Second Corps, Stettin, 3 July and 2 October 1917, RMI 12475/1, Bl. 330–333, RMI 12476, Bl. 88–90, BAP.

57. William A. Pelz, *The Spartakusbund and the German Working Class Movement 1914–1919* (Lewiston, Me., 1987), 96–110. See also Feldman, *Army, Industry, and Labor*, 334, 349–373; and Ay, *Entstehung einer Revolution*, 123–133.

58. Reinhard Höhn, *Sozialismus und Heer* (Bad Harzburg, 1969), 3:768–777.

59. For this paragraph, unless otherwise noted, see Heinz Hagenlücke, *Deutsche Vaterlandspartei: Die nationale Rechte am Ende des Kaiserreiches* (Düsseldorf, 1997), 216–228, 276–281; and Raffael Scheck, *Alfred von Tirpitz and Geman Right-Wing Politics, 1914–1930* (Atlantic Highlands, n.2., 1998), 65–77.

60. Tirpitz wrote that the Fatherland Party did not intend to be a party in the usual sense but rather a "bulwark for a future Reichs Chancellorship (*eine künftige Reichsleitung*)." See his letter to Krupp, 2 October 1917, NL 231 Hugenberg, Nr. 29, Bl. 197, BAK.

61. Pan-German contacts were told at OHL in July 1917 that Hindenburg and Ludendorff "think that it will still come to a military dictatorship," but "they don't want to use up the generals before that." See Senator Neumann's remarks in the Pan German Executive Committee, 7 July 1917, ADV 115, Bl. 8, BAP. Ludendorff had rejected Pan German urgings for a military government in September 1916 because he wanted to avoid "domestic strife." See Keim to Ludendorff, 4 September and 20 September 1916, ADV 406, Bl. 240–245, 258–261, BAP.

62. See the successive drafts of party statutes in Rep. 92, NL Kapp, Nr. 447, Bl. 2–3, 8, 18, 33, GStAPKB.

63. For the "Bund der Kaisertreuen," see the programmatic statements and correspondence of November 1917 in NL Cuno von Westarp, Nr. 20, Bl. 184, 186–187, 190, BAP. For the official statement of the Fatherland Party, declaring that it was "completely opposed" to the bund's goals, see NL Kapp, Nr. 571, Bl. 3, GStAPKB.

64. See Eric Dorn Brose, *Christian Labor and the Politics of Frustration in Imperial Germany* (Washington, D.C., 1985), 357.

65. For this scene, see Heinz Eisgruber, *So Schossen Wir nach Paris* (Berlin, 1934), 50, 65–77, 156.

66. Hindenburg to Bethmann Hollweg, 2 November 1916, N46 Groener Papers, Nr. 117, Bl. 22, BAMAF.

67. Schirmer, *Gerät*, 316. See also "Erfahrungen des Weltkrieges in der Massenbeschaffung von Gerät, insbesondere von Maschinengewehren," Msg. 2/775; and Truppenamt to Wrisberg, April 1919, PH2/86, Bl. 1–10, BAMAF.

68. For the Siegfried Line, see Herwig, *First World War*, 246–252.

69. Feldman, *Army Industry and Labor*, 266–268, 272–273, 494–495.

70. For details, see Bruce I. Gudmundsson, *Stormtroop Tactics: Innovation in the German Army, 1914–1918* (New York, 1989, passim; Martin Samuels, *Doctrine and Dogma: German and British Infantry Tactics in the First World War* (New York, 1992), passim; David T. Zabecki, *Steel Wind: Colonel Georg Bruchmüller and the Birth of Modern Artillery* (Westport, Conn., 1994), passim.

71. Herwig, *First World War*, 400–403.

72. Ibid., 403–428.

73. For William's last days as kaiser, see Cecil, *Wilhelm II*, 2:282–295.

74. See Groener's "Die Liquidation des Weltkrieges," Pt. 9: "Millionen-heere und Technik," n.d. (1920s), clipping in N46 Groener Papers, Nr. 54, Bl. 297, BAMAF.

75. See Wilhelm Groener, *Das Testament des Grafen Schlieffen* (Berlin, 1929), 225–227; Ludwig von Gebsattel, *Generalfeldmarshall Karl von Bülow* (Munich, 1929), 51–65.

76. The equivalent English saying is "You reap what you sow."

BIBLIOGRAPHY AND ABBREVIATIONS

Primary Sources from Archives and Special Repositories

The following sources are alphabetized by city. The abbreviations used in the notes are in brackets.

Geheimes Staatsarchiv preussischer Kulturbesitz, *Berlin-Dahlem [GStAPKB]*

1. Personal Papers [Rep. 92]
   A. Wolfgang Kapp

Sächsisches Hauptstaatsarchiv, *Dresden [HStAD]*

1. Records of the Saxon Armaments Department [KA(P)]
2. Reports of the Saxon military plenipotentiary in Berlin [SMP] to the Saxon war minister [SWM] [Sächs. Militär. Bevollm.]
3. Records of Saxon Foot Artillery Regiments No. 12 and No. 19

Bundesarchiv-Militärarchiv, *Freiburg/Breisgau [BAMAF]*

1. Personal Papers
   A. Ludwig Beck
   B. Karl von Einem
   C. Karl Hoffmann
   D. Adolf Wild von Hohenborn
   E. Wilhelm Groener
   F. Erich Ludendorff (partial collection)
   G. Hans von Seeckt
   H. Hermann von Stein

I. Gerhard Tappen
J. Alfred Tirpitz
2. former *Militärarchiv der DDR*
   A. Military History Research Office (pre-1945) [W-10]
3. Records of the Great General Staff [PH3]
4. Records of the Prussian War Ministry [PH2]
5. Records of the Prussian Military Transport Proving Commission [PH9-V, PH24]

Bundesarchiv, *Koblenz [BAK]*

1. Personal Papers
   A. Max Bauer
   B. Alfred Hugenberg

Bayerisches Hauptstaatsarchiv, Abteilung IV: Kriegsarchiv, *Munich [KAM]*

1. Records of the Bavarian War Ministry [M. Kr.]
2. Reports of the Bavarian military plenipotentiary in Berlin [BMP] to the Bavarian war minister [BWM] [in M. Kr.]
3. Records of the Bavarian General Staff [G. St.]
4. Records of the Bavarian Feldzeugmeisterei [FZM]
5. Records (copies) of the Prussian Artillery Proving Commission [M. Kr., Alter Bestand, A VI 6f]

Deutsches Museum, *Munich*

1. Library Holdings (Rare Books)
2. Journals
   A. *Löbells Jahresberichte über die Veränderungen und Fortschritte im Militärwesen [LJB]*
   B. *Die Schwere Artillerie*

New York Public Library

1. Journals
   A. *Militär-Wochenblatt [MWB]*
   B. *Beiheft zum Militär-Wochenblatt Bundesarchiv*, Potsdam [BAP]
2. Personal Papers
   A. Conrad von Wangenheim
   B. Cuno von Westarp
3. Records and Personal Papers of the Pan-German League [ADV]
4. Records of the Imperial Chancellery [RK]
5. Records of the Imperial Ministry of the Interior [RMdI]

Militärgeschichtliches Forschungsamt, *Potsdam*

1. Journals
   A. *Archiv für die Artillerie und Ingenieur-Offiziere des deutschen Reichsheeres*
   B. *Artilleristische Monatshefte [AM]*

C. *Kavalleristische Monatshefte* [*KM*]
D. *Kriegstechnische Zeitschrift* [*KTZ*]
E. *Militär-Wochenblatt*[*MWB*]
F. *Vierteljahrshefte für Truppenführung und Heereskunde* [*VTH*]

Published Primary Sources

Alten, General von. *Wider die Feldhaubitze.* Berlin, 1903.

Balck, Wilhelm. *Entwickelung der Taktik im Weltkrieg.* Berlin, 1922.

————. *Die Französische Infanterie-Taktik in ihrer Entwickelung seit dem Kriege 1870/ 71.* Berlin, 1902.

————. *Kriegserfahrungen.* Berlin, 1922.

Bauer, Max. *Der grosse Krieg in Feld und Heimat: Erinnerungen und Betrachtungen.* Tübingen, 1921.

Bernhardi, Friedrich von. *Denkwürdigkeiten aus meinem Leben.* Berlin, 1927.

————. *Unsere Kavallerie im nächsten Krieg.* Berlin, 1899.

Bissing, Freiherr von. *Ausbildung Führung und Verwendung der Reiterei.* Berlin, 1895.

Bloem, Walter. *Vormarsch—Sturmsignal—Das Ganze halt!* Leipzig, 1939.

Boguslawski, August von. *Taktische Darlegungen aus der Zeit von 1859 bis 1892.* Berlin, 1892.

Brixen-Hahn, Major. *Die Taktik der Kavallerie 1874–1898.* Berlin, 1899.

Bülow, Bernhard von. *Memoirs of Prince von Bülow* , trans. Geoffrey Dunlop. Boston, 1931.

Bülow, Karl von. *Mein Bericht zur Marneschhlacht.* Berlin, 1919.

Caemmerer, Lt. Gen. von. *Die Entwicklung der strategischen Wissenschaft im 19. Jahrhundert.* Berlin, 1904.

Deist, Wilhelm. *Militär und Innenpolitik im Weltkrieg, 1914–1918* , 2 vols Düsseldorff, 1970.

Der deutsche Infanterie-Angriff 1902: Nach Praktischen Erfahrungen auf dem Truppenübungsplatz Döberitz bei Berlin Mai 1902. Berlin, 1902.

Eckardstein, Hermann von. *Lebenserinnerungen und Politische Denkwürdigkeiten.* Leipzig, 1920.

Einem, Karl von. *Erinnerungen eines Soldaten 1853–1933.* Leipzig, 1933.

Eisenhart-Rothe, Ernst von. *Ehrendenkmal der Deutschen Armee und Marine 1871– 1918.* Berlin, 1928.

————. *So war die alte Armee.* Berlin, 1935.

Eisgruber, Heinz. *So Schossen Wir nach Paris.* Berlin, 1934.

Elze, Walter. *Tannenberg: Das deutsche Heer von 1914.* Breslau, 1928.

Endres, Franz Carl. *Die Tragödie Deutschlands.* Stuttgart, 1923.

Falkenhayn, Erich von. *General Headquarters and Its Critical Decisions 1914–1916.* London, 1921.

Foerster, Wolfgang. *Aus der Gedankenwerkstatt des Deutschen Generalstabs.* Berlin, 1931.

————. *Graf Schlieffen und der Weltkrieg.* Berlin, 1921.

————. *Prinz Friedrich Karl von Preussen: Denkwürdigkeiten aus seinem Leben.* Stuttgart, 1910.

Förster, Stig, ed. *Moltke: Vom Kabinettskrieg zum Volkskrieg: Eine Werkauswahl.* Bonn, 1992.

Die französische Armee. Berlin, 1913.

Freytag-Loringhoven, Hugo von. *Generalfeldmarshall Graf von Schlieffen: Sein Leben und die Verwertung seines geistigen Erbes im Weltkriege.* Leipzig, 1920.

————. *Menschen und Dinge wie ich sie in meinem Leben sah.* Berlin, 1923.

Friederich, Hans. *Die taktische Verwendung der schweren Artillerie.* Berlin, 1910.

Fussartillerie fremder Heere. (Study by German Army), Berlin, 1902.

Gayl, Egon Freiherr von. *General von Schlichting und sein Lebenswerk.* Berlin, 1913.

Gleich, Gerold von. *Die Alte Armee und ihre Verwirrungen.* Leipzig, 1919.

Goltz, Colmar von der. *Denkwürdigkeiten.* Berlin, 1929.

————. *Das Volk in Waffen: Ein Buch über Heerwesen und Kriegführung unserer Zeit.* Berlin, 1883.

Görlitz, Walter (ed.). *Regierte der Kaiser? Kriegstagebücher, Aufzeichnungen und Briefe des Chefs des Marine-Kabinetts Admiral Georg Alexander von Müller 1914–1918.* Göttingen, 1959.

Groener, Wilhelm. *Lebenserinnerungen: Jugend—Generalstab—Weltkrieg.* Göttingen, 1957.

————. *Das Testament des Grafen Schlieffen.* Berlin, 1929.

Grosser Generalstab. *Kriegsgeschichtliche Einzelschriften ,* Heft 32. Berlin, 1903.

————. *Kriegsgeschichtliche Einzelschriften ,* Heft 33. Berlin, 1904.

————.*Studien zur Kriegsgeschichte und Taktik 3: Der Schlachterfolg.* Berlin, 1903.

Hausen, Max von. *Erinnerungen an den Marnefeldzug 1914.* Leipzig, 1922.

Herr, F. *L'Artillerie.* Paris, 1923.

Hindenburg, Paul von. *Aus meinem Leben.* Leipzig, 1920.

Hoeppner, Ernst von. *Deutschlands Krieg in der Luft.* Leipzig, 1921.

Hohenlohe-Ingelfingen, Kraft Karl zu. *Aus meinem Leben ,* 4 vols. Berlin, 1907.

————. *Letters on Artillery ,* trans. N. L. Wolford. London, [1887] 1898.

Hoppenstedt, Julius. *Das Volk in Waffen,* Vol. 1: *Das Heer.* Dachau, 1913.

Justrow, Karl. *Die Dicke Berta und der Krieg.* Berlin, 1935.

————. *Feldherr und Kriegstechnik.* Oldenburg, 1933.

Kaehler, Oberstlieutenant. *Die Preussische Reiterei von 1806 bis 1876 in ihrer inneren Entwickelung.* Berlin, 1879.

Kaiser, Franz Nikolaus (ed.). *Das Ehrenbuch der Deutschen Schweren Artillerie.* Berlin, 1931.

Die K. B. Schwere Artillerie im Grossen Kriege 1914–1918. Munich, 1928.

Keim, August. *Erlebtes und Erstrebtes: Lebenserinnerungen von Generalleutnant Keim.* Hanover, 1925.

Kessel, Eberhard (ed.). *Generalfeldmarschall Graf Alfred von Schlieffen: Briefe.* Göttingen, 1958.

Kluck, Alexander von. *The March on Paris and the Battle of the Marne.* New York, 1920.

————. *Wanderjahre-Kriege-Gestalten.* Berlin, 1929.

Köhler, Max. *Der Aufstieg der Artillerie bis zum Grossen Krieg.* Munich, 1938.

Kuhl, Hermann von. *Der deutsche Generalstab in Vorbereitung und Durchführung des Weltkrieges.* Berlin, 1920.

————. *Der Weltkrieg 1914–1918.* Cologne, 1929.

Kühlmann, Richard von. *Erinnerungen.* Heidelberg, 1948.

Lancken-Wakenitz, Oscar von der. *Meine dreissig Dienstjahre 1888–1918.* Berlin, 1931.

Lehmann, Ernst A., and Howard Mingos. *The Zeppelins.* New York, 1927.

Leydhecker, Major. *Das Wurffeuer in Feld-und Positions Kriege.* Berlin, 1887.

Ludendorff, Erich von. *Ludendorff's Own Story*. New York, 1919.

———. *Mein militärischer Werdegang: Blätter der Erinnerung an unsèr stolzes Heer.* Munich, 1937.

Materna, Ingo. *Dokumente aus geheimen Archiven 4: Berichte des Berliner Polizeipräsidenten zur Stimmung und Lage der Bevölkerung Berlins 1914–1918.* Weimar, 1987.

Maxim, Hiram S. *My Life*. New York, 1915.

Meckel, Jacob. *Ein Sommernachtstraum.* Berlin, 1887.

Meisner, Heinrich Otto (ed.). *Aus dem Briefwechsel des Generalfeldmarshalls Alfred Grafen von Waldersee: Die Berliner Jahre 1886–1891.* Stuttgart, 1928.

———. "Aus den Erinnerungen des Generalfeldmarshalls Grafen Waldersees: Über seine Tätigkeit als Generalquartiermeister und Chef des Generalstabs 1882–1891." *Deutsche Revue* 46 (June 1921): 208–224.

———. *Denkwürdigkeiten des General-Feldmarshalls Alfred Grafen von Waldersee* , 3 vols. Osnabrück, 1922.

Ministère de la Guerre. *Les Armées francaises dans la Grande Guerre* , Tome 1, Vol. 1. Paris, 1936.

Moltke, Helmuth von. *Die deutschen Aufmarschpläne 1871–1890* , ed. Ferdinand von Schmerfeld. Berlin, 1929.

———. *Erinnerungen Briefe Dokumente 1877–1916.* Stuttgart, 1922.

Moser, Otto von. *Feldzugsaufzeichnungen als Brigade-Divisionskommandeur und als kommandierender General 1914–1918.* Stuttgart, 1920.

Müller, Heinrich. *Die Entwicklung der deutschen Festungs-und Belagerungsartillerie in Bezug auf Material, Organisation, Ausbildung und Taktik von 1875 bis 1895.* Berlin, 1896.

Müller-Brandenburg, Hermann. *Von Schlieffen bis Ludendorff.* Leipzig, 1925.

Pelet-Narbonne, General von (ed.). *Das Militärwesen in seiner Entwickelung während der 25 Jahre 1874–1898.* Berlin, 1899.

Pflugk-Harttung, Julius von. *Die Heere und Flotte der Gegenwart, Bd. 5: Frankreich: Das Heer am Ende des neunzehten Jahrhunderts.* Berlin, 1900.

———. *Die Heere und Flotte der Gegenwart, Bd. 3: Russland.* Berlin, 1898.

———. *Die Deutsche Kavallerie 1914 in Belgien und Frankreich.* Berlin, 1922.

Poseck, Maximilian von. *Das 1. Brandenburgische Dragoner-Regiment Nr. 2 im Weltkriege 1914 bis 1918.* Berlin, 1933.

Reichold, Helmut, and Gerhard Granier (eds.). *Wild von Hohenborn: Briefe und Tagebuchaufzeichnungen des preussischen Generals als Kriegsminister und Truppenführer im ersten Weltkrieg 1914 bis 1918.* Boppard, 1986.

Reichsarchiv. *Schlachten des Weltkrieges in Einzeldarstellungen* , 37 vols. Berlin, 1921–1930.

———. *Der Weltkrieg 1914 bis 1918: Kriegsrüstung und Kriegswirtschaft* , 2 vols. Berlin, 1930.

———. *Der Weltkrieg 1914–1918: Die militärischen Operationen zu Lande* , 14 vols. Berlin, 1925–1944.

Rich, Norman and M. H. Fisher (eds.). *The Holstein Papers: The Memoirs, Diaries and Correspondence of Friedrich von Holstein 1887–1909.* Cambridge, 1957.

Ritter, Hans. *Kritik des Weltkrieges: Das Erbe Moltkes und Schlieffens im grossen Kriege.* Leipzig, 1921.

———. *Der Luftkrieg.* Berlin, 1926.

Rogge, Helmuth. *Holstein und Harden: Politisch-publizistisches Zusammenspiel zweier Aussenseiter des Wilhelminischen Reichs.* Munich, 1959.

Röhl, John C. G. *Philipp Eulenburgs Politische Korrespondenz* , 3 vols. Boppard, 1979.
Rothe, General. "Über Bedingungen des Wertes heutiger Heere." *Deutsche Revue* 27/11 (November 1902): 198–210.
Scherff, Wilhelm von. *Gewehr und Gelände im heutigen Angriffskampf.* Berlin, 1904.
Schindler, D. R. *Eine 42 cm. Mörser-Batterie im Weltkrieg.* Breslau, 1934.
Schlieffen, Alfred von. "Der Krieg in der Gegenwart." *Deutsche Revue* 34/1 (January 1909): 13–24.
Schoen, Wilhelm von. *Erlebtes: Beiträge zur politschen Geschichte der neuesten Zeit.* Stuttgart, 1921.
Schwarte, M. *Die Technik im Weltkrieg.* Berlin, 1920.
Stein, Hermann von. *Erlebnisse und Betrachtungen aus der Zeit des Weltkrieges.* Leipzig, 1919.
Tappen, General von. *Bis zur Marne 1914.* Berlin, 1920.
Tirpitz, Alfred von. *My Memoirs* , 2 vols. New York, 1919.
Ullrich, Volker. *Kriegsalltag: Hamburg im ersten Weltkrieg.* Cologne, 1982.
Vierhaus, Rudolf (ed.). *Das Tagebuch der Baronin Spitzemberg.* Göttingen, 1960.
Zedlitz-Trützschler, Robert. *Zwölf Jahre am deutschen Kaiserhof.* Berlin, 1925.

Select Secondary Sources

Afflerbach, Holger. *Falkenhayn: Politisches Denken und Handeln im Kaiserreich.* Munich, 1994.
Anderson, Eugene N. *The First Moroccan Crisis 1904–1906.* Hamden, 1966.
Asprey, Robert B. *The German High Command at War: Hindenburg and Ludendorff Conduct World War I.* New York, 1991.
Ay, Karl-Ludwig. *Die Entstehung einer Revolution: Die Volksstimmung in Bayern während des Ersten Weltkrieges.* Berlin, 1968.
Balfour, Michael. *The Kaiser and His Times.* New York, 1972.
Berghahn, Volker R. "Militär, industrielle Kriegführung und Nationalismus." *Neue Politische Literatur* 26/1 (1981): 20–41.
———. *Der Tirpitz-Plan: Genesis und Verfall einer innenpolitischen Krisenstrategie unter Wilhelm II.* Düsseldorf, 1971.
Berghahn, Volker R., and Martin Kitchen (eds.). *Germany in the Age of Total War.* London, 1981.
Boemeke, Manfred F., *Anticipating Total War: The German and American Experiences 1871–1914.* Cambridge, 1999.
Brose, Eric Dorn. *Christian Labor and the Politics of Frustration in Imperial Germany.* Washington, D.C., 1985.
———. *German History 1789–1871: From the Holy Roman Empire to the Bismarckian Reich.* Providence, R.I., 1997.
———. *The Politics of Technological Change in Prussia: Out of the Shadow of Antiquity 1809–1848.* Princeton, N.J., 1993.
Bucholz, Arden. *Moltke, Schlieffen, and Prussian War Planning.* New York, 1991.
Burchardt, Lothar. *Friedenswirtschaft und Kriegsvorsorge: Deutschlands wirtschaftliche Rüstungsbestrebungen vor 1914.* Boppard, 1968.
Canis, Konrad. *Bismarck und Waldersee: Die aussenpolitischen Krisenerscheinungen und das Verhalten des Generalstabes 1882–1890.* Berlin, 1980.

Cecil, Lamar. *Wilhelm II. Prince and Emperor, 1859–1900* , 2 vols. Chapel Hill, N.C., 1989, 1996.

Chickering, Roger. "Der Deutsche Wehrverein und die Reform der deutschen Armee 1912–1914." *Militärgeschichtliche Mitteilungen* 25 (1979): 7–33.

———. *Imperial Germany and the Great War, 1914–1918.* Cambridge, 1998.

———. *We Men Who Feel Most German: A Cultural Study of the Pan-German League, 1886–1914.* London, 1984.

Christienne, Charles, *Histoire de l'aviation militaire francaise.* Paris, 1980.

Coetzee, Marilyn Shevin. *The German Army League: Popular Nationalism in Wilhelmine Germany.* New York, 1990.

Collenberg, Ludwig Rüdt von. *Die deutsche Armee von 1871 bis 1914.* Berlin, 1922.

———. "Graf Schlieffen und die Kriegsformation der deutschen Armee." *Wissen und Wehr* 10 (1927): 605–634.

Craig, Gordon. *The Politics of the Prussian Army 1640–1945.* New York, 1956.

Däniker, G. Die Maschinenwaffe im Rahmen der Taktik. Berlin, 1942.

Deist, Wilhelm. *Militär, Staat und Gesellschaft: Studien zur preussisch-deutschen Militärgeschichte.* Munich, 1991.

Demeter, Karl. *The German Officer-Corps in Society and State.* London, 1965.

Domann, Peter. *Sozialdemokratie und Kaisertum unter Wilhelm II.* Wiesbaden, 1974.

Doyle, Arthur Conan. *A History of the Great War.* New York, 1916.

Duffy, Christopher. *Frederick the Great: A Military Life.* London, 1995.

Dülffer, Jost, and Karl Holl (eds.). *Bereit zum Krieg: Kriegsmentalität im wilhelminischen Deutschland 1890–1914.* Göttingen, 1986.

Echevarria, Antulio. "On the Brink of the Abyss: The Warrior Identity and German Military Thought before the Great War." *War & Society* 13 (1995): 23–40.

Eley, Geoff. *Reshaping the German Right: Radical Nationalism and Political Change after Bismarck.* New Haven, Conn., 1980.

Ellis, John. *The Social History of the Machine Gun.* Baltimore, 1975.

Endres, Franz Carl. "Soziologische Struktur und ihr entsprechende Ideologien des deutschen Offizierkorps vor dem Weltkriege." *Archiv für Sozialwissenschaft und Sozialpolitik* 58/2 (1927): 282–319.

Farrar, L. L. *Arrogance and Anxiety.* Iowa City, 1981.

Feldman, Gerald D. *Army, Industry and Labor in Germany 1914–1918.* Princeton, N.J., 1966.

Fischer, Fritz. *Krieg der Illusionen: Die deutsche Politik von 1911–1914.* Düsseldorf, 1969.

——— *War of Illusions: German Policies from 1911 to 1914,* trans. Marian Jacls pm. New York, 1975.

Förster, Stig. "Der deutsche Generalstab und die Illusion des kurzen Krieges, 1871–1914: Metakritik eines Mythos." *Militärgeschichtliche Mitteilungen* 54 (1995): 61–95.

———. *Der Doppelte Militarismus: Die deutsche Heeresrüstungspolitik zwischen Status-Quo Sicherung und Aggression 1890–1913.* Stuttgart, 1985.

Gebsattel, Ludwig von. *Generalfeldmarschall Karl von Bülow.* Munich, 1929.

Geyer, Michael. *Deutsche Rüstungspolitik 1860–1980.* Frankfurt, 1984.

Gilbert, Martin. *The First World War: A Complete History.* New York, 1994.

Goldsmith, Dolf L. *The Devil's Paintbrush: Sir Hiram Maxim's Gun.* Toronto, 1989.

Görlitz, Walter. *The German General Staff: Its History and Structure 1657–1945.* London, 1953.

Gothsche, Captain. *Die Königlichen Gewehrfabriken.* Berlin, 1904.

Groote, Wolfgang von, and Ursula von Gersdorff (eds.). *Entscheidung 1866: Der Krieg zwischen Österreich und Preussen.* Stuttgart, 1966.

———. *Entscheidung 1870: Der Deutsche-Französische Krieg.* Stuttgart, 1970.

Gudmundsson, Bruce I. *Stormtroop Tactics: Innovation in the German Army, 1914–1918.* New York, 1989.

Hagenlücke, Heinz. *Deutsche Vaterlandspartei: Die nationale Rechte am Ende des Kaiserreiches.* Düsseldorf, 1997.

Hauessler, Helmut. *General William Groener and the Imperial German Army.* Madison, 1962.

Haycock, Ronald, and Keith Wilson (eds.). *Men, Machines and War.* Waterloo, Ont., 1988.

Herrmann, David G. *The Arming of Europe and the Making of the First World War.* Princeton, N.J., 1996.

Herwig, Holger H. *The First World War: Germany and Austria-Hungary 1914–1918.* London, 1997.

———. *The German Naval Officer Corps.* Oxford, 1973.

———. *'Luxury' Fleet: The Imperial German Navy 1888–1918.* London, 1991.

Herzfeld, Hans. *Die deutsche Rüstungspolitik vor dem Weltkriege.* Leipzig, 1923.

Hoffmann, Joachim. "Die Kriegslehre des General von Schlichting." *Militärgeschichtliche Mitteilungen* 1 (1969): 5–35.

Hofmann, Hanns Hubert (ed.). *Das deutsche Offizierkorps 1860–1960.* Boppard, 1980.

Höhn, Reinhard. *Sozialismus und Heer*, 3 vols. Bad Harzburg, 1969.

Horne, Alistair. *The Price of Glory: Verdun 1916.* New York, 1962.

Howard, Michael. *The Franco-Prussian War: The German Invasion of France, 1870–1871.* New York, 1962.

Huber, E. R. *Deutsche Verfassungsgeschichte Seit 1789*, 4 vols. Stuttgart, 1969.

Hull, Isabel V. *The Entourage of Kaiser Wilhelm II 1888–1918.* Cambridge, 1982.

Jany, Curt. *Geschichte der Preussischen Armee vom 15. Jahrhundert bis 1914.* Osnabrück, 1967.

———. *Die Königlich Preussische Armee und das Deutsche Reichsheer 1807 bis 1914.* 4 vols. Berlin, 1933.

John, Hartmut. *Das Reserveoffizierkorps im Deutschen Kaiserreich 1890–1914: Ein sozialgeschichtlicher Beitrag zur Untersuchung der gesellschaftlichen Militarisierung im Wilhelminischen Deutschland.* Frankfurt, 1981.

Keegan, John. *The First World War.* New York, 1999.

———. *Opening Moves: August 1914.* New York, 1971.

Kennan, George F. *The Decline of Bismarck's European Order: Franco-Russian Relations, 1875–1890.* Princeton, N.J., 1979.

Kessel, Eberhard. "Die Tätigkeit des Grafen Waldersee als Generalquartiermeister und Chef des Generalstabes der Armee." *Welt als Geschichte* 14 (1954): 181–211.

Kielmansegg, Peter Graf. *Deutschland und der Erste Weltkrieg.* Frankfurt am Main, 1968.

Kitchen, Martin. *The Silent Dictatorship: The Politics of the German High Command under Hindenburg and Ludendorff, 1916–1918.* New York, 1976.

Kohut, Thomas A. *Wilhelm II and the Germans: A Study in Leadership.* Oxford, 1991.

Lachmann, Manfred. "Zur Entwicklung und zum Einsatz des Maschinengewehrs." *Zeitschrift für Militärgeschichte* 12 (1973): 720–730.

————. "Probleme der Bewaffnung des kaiserlichen deutschen Heeres." *Zeitschrift für Militärgeschichte* 6 (1967): 23–37.

Lee, Emanoel. *To the Bitter End: A Photographic History of the Boer War 1899–1902.* New York, 1985.

Lidtke, Vernon L. *The Alternative Culture: Socialist Labor in Imperial Germany.* New York, 1985.

Linnenkohl, Hans. *Vom Einzelschuss zur Feuerwalze: Der Wettlauf zwischen Technik und Taktik im Ersten Weltkrieg.* Koblenz, 1990.

Macdonald, Lyn. *1914.* New York, 1988.

————. *1915: The Death of Innocence.* New York, 1993.

McElwee, William. *The Art of War: Waterloo to Mons.* Bloomington, Ind., 1974.

McNeil, William H. *The Pursuit of Power: Technology, Armed Force, and Society since A.D. 1000.* Chicago, 1982.

Martin, Günther.*Die bürgerlichen Exzellenzen: Zur Sozialgeschichte der preussischen Generalität 1812–1918.* Düsseldorf, 1979.

————. "Technik und preussische Techniker des Krieges im 19. Jahrhundert." *Technikgeschichte* 39 (1972): 186–202.

Maser, Werner. *Hindenburg: Eine politische Biographie.* Rastatt, 1990.

Mette, Sigfrid. *Vom Geist Deutscher Feldherren: Genie und Technik 1800–1918.* Zurich, 1938.

Die Militärluftfahrt bis zum Beginn des Weltkrieges 1914. Frankfurt, 1965.

Mitchell, Allan. *Victors and Vanquished: The German Influence on Army and Church in France after 1870.* Chapel Hill, N.C., 1984.

Mollin, Volker. *Auf dem Wege zur 'Materialschlacht': Vorgeschichte und Funktionieren des Artillerie-Industrie-Komplexes im Deutschen Kaiserreich.* Pfaffenweiler, 1986.

Moritz, Albrecht. *Das Problem des Präventivkrieges in der deutschen Politik während der ersten Marokkokrise.* Frankfurt, 1974.

Morrow, John Howard Jr. *Building German Airpower, 1909–1914.* Knoxville, Tenn., 1976.

————. *The Great War in the Air.* Washington, D.C., 1993.

Mosse, George L. *The Image of Man: The Creation of Modern Masculinity.* New York, 1996.

Muther, Alfred. *Das Gerät der leichten Artillerie vor, in und nach dem Weltkrieg.* Berlin, 1925.

Neumann, Georg Paul. *Die deutschen Luftstreitkräfte im Weltkriege.* Berlin, 1920.

Otto, Helmuth. *Schlieffen und der Generalstab: Der preussisch-deutsche Generalstab unter Leitung des Generals von Schlieffen 1891–1905.* Berlin, 1966.

Pakenham, Thomas. *The Boer War.* New York, 1979.

Papke, Gerhard, and Wolfgang Petter (eds.). *Handbuch der deutschen Militärgeschichte 1648–1939* , 6 vols. Munich, 1979.

Paret, Peter (ed.). *Makers of Modern Strategy from Machiavelli to the Nuclear Age.* Princeton, N.J., 1986.

Paul, Wolfgang. *Entscheidung im September: Das Wunder an der Marne.* Esslingen, 1974.

Pelz, William A. *The Spartakusbund and the German Working Class Movement 1914–1919.* Lewiston, Me., 1987.

Pflanze, Otto. *Bismarck and the Development of Germany: The Period of Fortification, 1880–1898.* Princeton, N.J., 1990.

Porch, Douglas. *The March to the Marne: The French Army 1871–1914.* Cambridge, 1981.

302   BIBLIOGRAPHY AND ABBREVIATIONS

Priesdorff, Kurt von. *Soldatisches Führertum* , 7 vols. Hamburg, n.d.

Raulff, Heiner. *Zwischen Machtpolitik und Imperialismus: Die Deutsche Frankreichpolitik 1904/06.* Düsseldorf, 1976.

Ritter, Gerhard. *The Schlieffen Plan: Critique of a Myth* , trans. B. H. Liddell Hart. London, 1958.

———. *Staatskunst und Kriegshandwerk: Das Problem des "Militarismus" in Deutschland* , 3 vols. Munich, 1954–1964.

Röhl, John C. G. *The Kaiser and His Court: Wilhelm II and the Government of Germany.* Cambridge, 1996.

———. *Wilhelm II: Die Jugend des Kaisers 1859–1888.* Munich, 1993.

Rumschöttel, Hermann. *Das bayerische Offizierkorps 1866–1914.* Berlin, 1973.

Samuels, Martin. *Command or Control? Command, Training and Tactics in the British and German Armies, 1888–1918.* London, 1995.

———. *Doctrine and Dogma: German and British Infantry Tactics in the First World War.* New York, 1992.

Scheck, Raffael. *Alfred von Tirpitz and Geman Right-Wing Politics, 1914–1930.* Atlantic Highlands, N.J., 1998.

Schirmer, Hermann. *Das Gerät der schweren Artillerie vor, in und nach dem Weltkrieg.* Berlin, 1937.

Schnitter, Helmut. *Militärwesen und Militärpublizistik: Die militärische Zeitschriftenpublizistik in der Geschichte des Bürgerlichen Militärwesens in Deutschland.* Berlin, 1967.

Schulte, Bernd F. *Die deutsche Armee 1900–1914: Zwischen Beharren und Veränderung.* Düsseldorf, 1977.

Schwinn, Erich. *Die Arbeit des deutschen Wehrvereins und die Wehrlage Deutschlands vor dem Weltkriege.* Würzburg, 1940.

Sheehan, James J. *German History 1770–1866.* Oxford, 1989.

Showalter, Dennis E. "Army and Society in Imperial Germany: The Pains of Modernization," *Journal of Contemporary History* 18/4 (1983): 583–618.

———. *Railroads and Rifles: Soldiers, Technology, and the Unification of Germany.* Hamden, 1975.

———. *Tannenberg: Clash of Empires.* Hamden, 1991.

Snyder, Jack. *The Ideology of the Offensive: Military Decision-Making and the Disasters of 1914.* Ithaca, N.Y., 1984.

Stone, Norman. *The Eastern Front 1914–1917.* New York, 1975.

Stern, Fritz. *Gold and Iron: Bismarck, Bleichröder, and the Building of the German Empire.* New York, 1977.

Stevenson, David. *Armaments and the Coming of War: Europe, 1904–1914.* Oxford, 1996.

Storz, Dieter. *Kriegsbild und Rüstung vor 1914: Europäische Landstreitkräfte vor dem ersten Weltkrieg.* Berlin, 1992.

Teske, Hermann. *Colmar Freiherr von der Goltz: Ein Kämpfer für den militärischen Fortschritt.* Göttingen, 1957.

Thoss, Bruno. "Nationale Rechte, militärische Führung und Diktaturfrage in Deutschland 1913–1923." *Militärgeschichtliche Mitteilungen* 42/2 (1987): 47–62.

Tuchman, Barbara. *The Guns of August.* New York, 1962.

Tyng, Sewell. *The Campaign of the Marne.* New York, 1935.

Vogt, Adolf. *Oberst Max Bauer: Generalstabsoffizier im Zwielicht.* Osnabrück, 1974.

Wallach, Jehuda L. *Das Dogma der Vernichtungsschlacht.* Munich, 1970.

Wawro, Geoffrey. *The Austro-Prussian War: Austria's War with Prussia and Italy in 1866*. Cambridge, Mass., 1996.

Weber, Eugen. *France Fin de Siècle*. Cambridge, 1986.

Wehler, Hans-Ulrich, ed. *Der Primat der Innenpolitik*. Berlin, 1970.

Whitton, F. E. *Moltke*. Freeport, N.Y., 1972.

Williamson, Samuel R., Jr. *The Politics of Grand Strategy: Britain and France Prepare for War, 1904–1914*. Cambridge, Mass., 1969.

Young, Harry F. *Maximilian Harden: Censor Germaniae*. The Hague, 1959.

Zabecki, David T. *Steel Wind: Colonel Georg Bruchmüller and the Birth of Modern Artillery*. Westport, Conn., 1994.

Zuber, Terence. "The Schlieffen Plan Reconsidered," *War in History* 6/3 (1999): 262–305.

INDEX

232, 234, 235, 236, 237, 238,
239
Hodenberg, General von, 60
Hoffbauer, Ernst, 33–34, 64, 67, 79,
80, 98, 99
Hoffmann, Major, 143–144
Hohenlohe-Ingelfingen, Karl Kraft
zu, 27, 28, 33–34, 38
Hollmann, Friedrich, 121
Holstein, Friedrich von, 76, 82, 83,
129, 130
Horne, Alistair, 228
horse artillery, 13, 14, 32, 91, 96,
155; in the Great War, 185, 208.
See also heavy artillery, horse-drawn
howitzers, 40, 62, 63–64, 66, 67, 68,
70, 74, 75, 76, 80, 81, 99–100,
102, 110, 124, 149, 151, 156, 165,
253n84/n85, 254n97, 264n115;
in the Great War, 188, 189, 195,
196, 205, 207, 211, 225, 228,
288n9; resistance to, 37, 62–68,
70, 71, 80, 94, 98, 100, 225. See
also field artillery, conservative
tactics and weapons preference of;
heavy artillery, field artillery
opposition to; and specific howitzer
models : l.FH-98, l.FH-98–09,
s.FH-02
Hülsen-Häseler, Dietrich von, 106,
107, 122, 123, 125, 126, 133
Hugenberg, Alfred, 233
Hull, Isabel, 121, 122
Hussars, 8, 9, 10, 11, 116, 119

Ilse, Colonel, 168
Imperial Headquarters, 6, 55, 115
infantry, 6; conservative tactics
(company columns, half/full
battalions) of, 4, 13, 16–25, 41–42,
47, 56–62, 68, 70, 87–91, 102,
110, 117–118, 157; Great War
tactics of, 188, 189, 195, 196, 197,
198, 199, 200–201, 202, 205–206,
207, 220, 224, 239; innovative

tactics of, 19–22, 56–62, 63, 68,
70, 87–90, 152–153, 156, 259n17;
maneuvers of, 21, 24, 59. See also
ammunition; Boer Attack;
controlled attack; delegated tactics;
frontal charges; infantry
regulations of 1888; infantry
regulations of 1906; M-71 Mauser;
M-88 Mauser; M-98; needle gun;
Schlichting, Sigismund von
infantry regulations of 1888, 58, 60,
68, 73, 88–89, 125, 153
infantry regulations of 1906, 152–
154

Jäger battalions, 94–95, 96, 97, 155,
260–261n51; in the Great War,
185, 190. See also mounted infantry
Joffre, Joseph, 192, 193, 194, 196,
203, 204, 215, 217, 220, 224
Journal of Technological Warfare, 103
Justrow, Karl, 167, 172, 275n109; in
the Great War, 222, 287n172

Kaehler, Otto von, 10, 12, 52, 54
Kaltenborn, Hans von, 119
Kameke, Arnold von, 13, 15, 16, 34,
40–41
Kapp, Wolfgang, 236, 237
Katkov, Mikhail, 45
Keegan, John, 195, 197
Keim, August, 173, 174–175, 176,
177, 244n44, 278n163; in the
Great War, 232, 233
Kersting, General, 108
Kessel, Bernard von, 23
Kessel, General von, 90, 91
Kleist, Georg Friedrich von, 54, 68,
92, 155, 156
Kluck, Alexander von, 145, 177; in
the Great War, 186, 189, 190–192,
198, 200, 201, 202, 203–204, 207,
208, 214, 215–218, 219, 220, 224,
255n23
Königgrätz, Battle of, 19, 29, 69, 139